PRAISE AND BRACHA FOR THE NAVI ILLUSTRATE
(LISTED IN ALPHABE

"I LIKE THE IDEA AND IT IS ACCEPTABLE TO DRAW R HOLY PATRIARCHS... HOWEVER WHEN YOU ILLUSTRATE AVRAHAM AVINU AND MOSHE RABBEINU MAKE THEM NOT DISCERNIBLE."
– ***RABBI YISRAEL BELSKY*** ZT"L

"BRINGS THE STORIES OF NAVI TO LIFE FOR A NEW GENERATION OF CHILDREN."
– ***RABBI YAAKOV BENDER***, ROSH YESHIVA, YESHIVA DARCHEI TORAH

"MY CHILDREN THOROUGHLY ENJOYED THE GRAPHIC NOVEL (AND SO DID I)"
– ***DR. ALYSSA BERLIN***, PSYD, CLINICAL PSYCHOLOGIST

"THIS IS A REALLY WONDERFUL PROJECT AND I WISH YOU MUCH BRACHA AND HATZLACHA."
– ***RABBI YITZCHAK BREITOWITZ***, RAV, OHR SOMAYACH

"AN EXCELLENT RESOURCE TO OPEN UP THE STORIES AND LESSONS OF NACH TO BOTH YOUNG AND OLD"
– ***RABBI AVRAHAM CZAPNIK***, DIRECTOR, JEWISH LEARNING EXCHANGE

"A NEW AND INNOVATIVE WAY TO TEACH NAVI."
– ***RABBI SHLOMO EINHORN***, DEAN, YESHIVAT YAVNEH

"AFTER SHOWING FACIAL ILLUSTRATIONS OF THE HOLY AVOS (FOREFATHERS) TO KVOD HARAV ELIYASHIV, ZT'L, HE STATED TO ME, THERE IS NO PROHIBITION TO ILLUSTRATE LIKE THAT."
– ***RAV YONI GERSTEIN***, AUTHOR, ILLUSTRATOR, CARTOONIST

"A POSUK BY POSUK NARRATIVE... WONDERFUL INTRODUCTION TO NAVI FOR BOTH YOUNG AND OLD."
– ***RABBI PINCHOS GRUMAN*** ZT"L, MUSMACH OF RAV AHARON KOTLER ZT"L, AND RAV MOSHE FEINSTEIN ZT"L

"IT BRINGS TANACH TO LIFE AND MAKES IT UNFORGETTABLE."
– ***RABBI YAACOV HABER***, MORA D'ASRA KEHILLAS SHIVTEI YESHURUN

"SINCE THIS PROJECT IS SUPPORTED BY OUR GREAT TORAH EDUCATORS WORLDWIDE, I WISH THIS PROJECT MUCH HATZLACHA."
– ***RABBI SHMUEL KAMENETSKY,*** ROSH YESHIVA, TALMUDICAL YESHIVA OF PHILADELPHIA

"I COMMEND THE DEVELOPERS OF THIS PROGRAM FOR A QUALITY PRESENTATION AND ENCOURAGE THEM TO CONTINUE TO SEE IT TO COMPLETION."
- ***RABBI ZEFF LEFF***, ROSH YESHIVA, YESHIVA GEDOLA MATITIYAHU

"I WISH TO BLESS RAV SHLOMO MERMELSTEIN ON HIS UNIQUE AND WONDERFUL INITIATIVE OF ENDEARING THE STUDY OF NAVI TO BNEI YISRAEL. YOUR PRECISE ILLUSTRATIONS BASED ON MIDRASHIM AND CHAZAL REFLECT HOW EXTREMELY DEEP AND UNIQUE YOU HAVE LABORED..."
- ***RABBI SHLOMO LEVI***, ROSH YESHIVA, MEMBER OF RABBINICAL CHAMBER, RISHON L'TZION, ISRAEL

"IT IS MY HOPE THAT THE OUTSTANDING STRENGTH AND POWER INFUSED INTO THIS PROJECT WILL DRASTICALLY INCREASE PEOPLE LEARNING THE HOLY NAVI."
- ***RABBI YITZCHOK MENACHEM***, TOLNA REBBE

"THIS NAVI ILLUSTRATED TEAM HAS DONE A GREAT SERVICE TO KLAL YISRAEL WITH THIS INNOVATIVE AND GLORIOUS CONCEPT OF THE GRAPHIC DEPICTION OF NAVI - BASED ON CHAZAL."
- ***RABBI SHMUEL MOELLER***

"THIS IS A BEAUTIFUL PROJECT. THIS WILL ENCOURAGE THE LEARNING OF NAVI AND THAT IS SO VERY IMPORTANT."
- ***RABBI AVIGDOR NEBENZAHL***, ROSH YESHIVA, NETIV ARYEH

"EXCELLENT PRESENTATION... MAKES THE STORY COME ALIVE... I WOULD RECOMMEND THIS FOR MY GRANDCHILDREN."
- ***RABBI DOVID THALER***, MENAHEL, YESHIVA OHR ELCHONON CHABAD

IT IS EVIDENT FROM THE DETAILS INCLUDED IN THIS WORK THAT THE AUTHOR RESEARCHED THE CLASSIC MEFORSHIM IN ORDER TO ILLUMINATE THE DRAWINGS AND TO ENSURE THEY ARE CONSISTENT WITH OUR MESORAH.
- ***RABBI BENZION TWERSKI***, RAV, CONGREGATION BETH JEHUDAH

"THIS IS A VERY NEEDED AND IMPORTANT PROJECT AND I WISH YOU ALL THE HATZLACHA IN THE WORLD."
- ***RABBI BEREL WEIN***, HISTORIAN, AUTHOR, RABBI

"STORIES PACKED WITH MIDRASHIM... IT EVEN HAS SOURCES IN THE BACK..."
- ***RABBI BARUCH ZHEUTLIN***, REBBE, ASHAR HEBREW DAY SCHOOL

Yitzchok M. Weinberg
RABBI OF TOLNA
Rechov David Chazan 10
JERUSALEM ISRAEL

יצחק מנחם וינברג
נכד אדמו"ר זצללה"ה
מטאלנא
רחוב דוד חזן 10
עיה"ק ירושלים תובב"א

Tel. 02-582-5543 .טל

בעזהשי"ת, יום שישי עש"ק חיי שרה
תשע"ו

כבוד ידידי היקר מאד כמהר"ר יעקב פינסקי נ"י
שלו' וברכה

הנני בזה בדבר היותך בגשתך להו"ל
ביאור ספרי הנביאים הקדושים כמהר"ר שלמה ממלשטיין נ"י
הנה אין ספק שיש בביאור המקראות עזרה רבה
בלימוד הנביאים בבחינת והיו עיניך רואות אלא
שנדרש לזה בהירות מופלגה ועל אחת כמה
אישיות רבנית נכבדה ומוכרת [illegible] הרב
[illegible] שליט"א אשר הפליג על זה בבהירות
המפורסם הנני בזה בברכה נאמנה ותקוה
בפועלו שעי' החיבור הזה יתרבו לומדי הנביאים
הקדושים ביתר שאת ויזכה עוד ימים רבים [illegible]
ספרי [illegible] ותחזינה עינינו במהרה בטוב ירושלים
בב"א וראה

הכו"ח בהערכה ובהוקרה
יצחק מנחם
נכד אדמו"ר מטאלנא
זצלה"ה זי"ע

בס"ד

Rabbi Zev Leff | **הרב זאב לף**

Rabbi of Moshav Matityahu
Rosh HaYeshiva—Yeshiva Gedola Matityahu

מרא דאתרא מושב מתתיהו
ראש הישיבה—ישיבה גדולה מתתיהו

D.N. Modiin 71917 **Tel: 08-976-1138 'טל** **Fax: 08-976-5326 'פקס** **ד.נ. מודיעין 71917**

Dear Friends,

I have seen samples of the "Nach Illustrated" manuscript. Although the format resembles "comics" and could be misconstrued to trivialize the Kisvei HaKodesh, I feel that this project is acceptable and praiseworthy.

It would seem that learning and mastering the Tanach, the very basis of all Torah, would be an understood neccessity for every Jew. Surely a ben Torah or Talmid Chacham could not be considered such if he was ignorant of the very foundation of all learning. However, as a reaction to the Haskalah who used the learning of Tanach to the exclusion of Torah She Ba'al Peh, and distorted how it should be learned to further their agenda to obliterate Torah and Yiras Shomayim from Klal Yisrael, the learning of Tanach was de-emphasized in the yeshiva world. This echoed the dictate of Chazal when the early minim (heretics) declared that the only relevant part of Torah was the Aseres Hadibros (Ten Commandments). Chazal took the Ten Commandments out of the daily service in order to de-emphasize its centrality, lest one be misled by the minim.

Boruch Hashem, this aspect of Haskalah for the most part has passed from the world, substituted by other "ism's" and false philosophies which seek to obliterate true Yiddishkeit in other ways but surely not by emphasizing or distorting Tanach. Hence, the basic learning and knowledge of Tanach is something every Jew should acquire. Since this learning has been neglected for so long by the masses, any program that encourages making Tanach a part of one's learning and facilitates one's mastery of it is a welcome and important development.

Since illustrations raise one's interest and awareness, and this project does not only express the works of Tanach in pictures but, enhances it with Midrashim that help elucidate the text, I feel it can be used as a companion and tool to engender an interest in learning Tanach not only for children but even for adults.

I strongly feel however that this work not be presented as a substitute for learning the text of Nach itself, but rather a companion to learning the actual text..I also suggest that it not be referred to as "comics" but rather as "Nach illustrated" so as not to trivialize Kisvei Hakodesh and reduce it to the genre of comics.

I commend the developers of this program for a quality presentation and encourage them to continue to see it to completion.

Sincerely,
With Torah blessings
Zev Leff
Rabbi Zev Leff

הרבנות הראשית המועצה הדתית ראשון לציון

רחוב דרור 7 ראשון לציון

בס"ד

י' בכסלו תשפ"ב

הרב שלמה לוי

ראש הישיבה חבר לשכת הרבנות

ראשון לציון

המלצה מכתב ברכה

בשבח והודיה לד' יתברך ברצוני לברך את מכובדי היקר והחשוב איש רב פעלים לתורה ולתעודה הרב שלמה מרמלשטיין הי"ו על היוזמה המיוחדת ונפלאה לקרב את לימודי הנביא לצעירי הצאן אשריך.

התמונות המדויקות לפי מדרשי חז"ל מלמדות על העבודה המעמיקה והמיוחדת, הפירושים המובאים בתוך הדברים, מעידים על לימוד מעמיק בספר יהושע שעליו נאמר בדברי חז"ל (נדרים כב) : "אמר רב אדא ברבי חנינא אלמלא לא חטאו ישראל לא ניתן להם אלא חמשה חומשי תורה וספר יהושע בלבד, שערכה של ארץ ישראל הוא".

המברכו מעומק ליבי ומברכו להפיץ את אור התורה

שלמה לוי.

שלמה הלוי

הרבנות הראשית
הרב שלמה לוי
חבר לשכה ורב שכונה
ראשון-לציון

Navi Illustrated

YEHOSHUA

יהושע

SCRIPT	ARI GUIDRY
DIALOGUE	SHLOMO MERMELSTEIN
ARTWORK	VICTOR VALDEZ
	MICHEL FORTIN
EDITOR	YAAKOV PINSKY
	DINA WILSHINSKY
DESIGN EDITOR	MARIANA MERMELSTEIN

ISBN 978-0-9966335-9-8

PLEASE ADDRESS ANY COMMENTS OR QUESTIONS TO THE AUTHORS AT:
NAVIILLUSTRATED@GMAIL.COM

YESTERDAY'S HISTORY IS TODAY'S REALITY

CAN YOU IMAGINE A MODERN-DAY "MESSAGE IN A BOTTLE" THAT CAN HELP ANSWER SOME OF THE MOST COMPLEX CHALLENGES OF THE 21ST CENTURY; CHALLENGES THAT ARE NOT ONLY LIMITED TO AN INSULAR SECLUDED SITUATION BUT ALSO CAN BE RELEVANT NATIONALLY, POLITICALLY, AND OF COURSE, TO OUR OWN UNIQUE, MULTIFACETED LIVES?

THE TANACH – TORAH – NEVIIM – KETUVIM, THESE HOLY BOOKS ARE OUR "MESSAGE IN A BOTTLE." THEY ARE THE SOURCE OF OUR ABSOLUTE KNOWLEDGE AND OUR NAVIGATOR OF LIVING LIFE TO ITS FULLEST.

PROPHETS (A LOOSE TRANSLATION FOR NEVIIM) LIVED IN BIBLICAL TIMES AND COMMUNICATED DIRECTLY THROUGH DIVINE INSPIRATION WITH HASHEM. OUR SAGES TAUGHT US THAT THERE WERE MANY, LITERALLY, MILLIONS OF PROPHETS, YET THE ONES THAT WE HAVE VERIFIED TODAY TOTAL FORTY-EIGHT MALE PROPHETS AND SEVEN FEMALE PROPHETESSES. THEY ALSO EXPLAINED THAT THOSE MILLIONS OF PROPHETS WERE ONLY SIGNIFICANT TO THE CONFINED POPULATION OF THAT TIME, WHEREAS THE FIFTY-FIVE RECORDED PROPHETS ARE RELEVANT FOR ALL ETERNITY (MEGILLA 14A).

THE BOOK OF YEHOSHUA IS ABOUT PROMISES MADE, PROMISES KEPT. HASHEM GUARANTEES THAT AVRAHAM'S CHILDREN, YISRAEL, WILL INHERIT THE LAND. THIS BOOK TESTIFIES HASHEM DELIVERED ON THAT PLEDGE. AS IT STATES: בַּיּוֹם הַהוּא כָּרַת ה׳ אֶת־אַבְרָם בְּרִית לֵאמֹר לְזַרְעֲךָ נָתַתִּי אֶת־הָאָרֶץ הַזֹּאת ("ON THAT DAY, HASHEM FORMED A COVENANT WITH AVRAM, SAYING, TO YOUR OFFSPRING, I HAVE GIVEN THIS LAND") (BERESHEET 15:18).

PERHAPS, HOWEVER, THIS RELATIONSHIP OF HASHEM – LAND AND YISRAEL (ERETZ YISRAEL) BEGAN MUCH EARLIER. בְּרֵאשִׁית בָּרָא אֱלֹקִים אֵת הַשָּׁמַיִם וְאֵת הָאָרֶץ ("IN THE BEGINNING, HASHEM CREATED THE HEAVENS AND THE EARTH.") THE HOLY ONE, BLESSED BE HE, CREATED THE WORLD AND CAN GRANT THE LAND TO WHOMEVER HE WISHES (RASHI, BERESHEET 1:1), RESERVING THE RIGHT TO DESIGNATE (AND TAKE AWAY) ONE SPECIFIC PIECE OF LAND EXCLUSIVELY APPROPRIATED FOR HIS CHOSEN PEOPLE.

THE TORAH STATES THAT PISHON FLOWS OUT OF THE GARDEN OF EDEN AND "SURROUNDS HAVILAH WHERE THERE IS GOLD, AND THE GOLD IS GOOD..." (BERESHEET 2:11-12) "HAVILAH" MEANS THE LAND OF YISRAEL, "WHERE THERE IS GOLD" REFERS TO TORAH AND "THE GOLD OF THAT LAND IS GOOD" TEACHES THAT THERE IS NO TORAH LEARNING LIKE THE TORAH OF ERETZ YISRAEL WITH NO WISDOM LIKE THE WISDOM OF ERETZ YISRAEL. (BERESHEET RABBA 16:4).

ALL OTHER NATIONS CONQUER LAND FOR POWER. YISRAEL CONQUERS THE LAND TO DEEPEN THEIR SPIRITUAL CONNECTION TO HASHEM. LOVE OF THE LAND IS NOT EXPRESSED MERELY BY MOUTHING PATRIOTIC SLOGANS, BUT BY MAINTAINING A STANDARD OF LOYALTY TO HASHEM AND LIVING ACCORDING TO THE MORAL IDEALS SET BY THE TORAH. THIS WILL GRANT US THE PRIVILEGE OF REMAINING IN OUR BELOVED LAND, WITH SANCTITY AND SERENITY.

THIS BOOK ALSO DESCRIBES THE TRANSFER OF LEADERSHIP FROM MOSHE TO YEHOSHUA. THE SAGES CHARACTERIZE MOSHE AS THE SUN AND YEHOSHUA AS THE MOON (BABA BASRA 75A), ILLUSTRATING A CHANGE FROM THE LUSTER MOSHE ILLUMINATED UPON YISRAEL TO THE REFLECTION OF MOSHE UPON YEHOSHUA. THIS DESCRIPTION IS APROPOS OF THE NATION'S TRANSITION; THEY NO LONGER HAVE MOSHE AS THEIR LEADER AND SUBSEQUENTLY LACK THAT DIRECT LINK TO HASHEM. YISRAEL MUST NOW RELY ON THE מִלְחָמָה שֶׁל תּוֹרָה (INTENSE ENGAGEMENT OF LEARNING TORAH) TO ENSURE THAT THERE IS A DEEP UNDERSTANDING OF THE FUTURE APPLICATION OF OUR TORAH IN A MODERN NEW WORLD AND THAT IT NEVER BE FORGOTTEN. (TEMURA 16A).

ON PESACH, WE READ IN THE HAGGADA A FEW VERSES FROM YEHOSHUA, TRANSMITTING A POWERFUL MESSAGE. HAVING A SINCERE AND DEVOTED RELATIONSHIP WITH THE ONE ABOVE, ONE BECOMES ENVELOPED IN HIS BLESSINGS AND MERIT TO BE IN THE HOLY LAND OF YISRAEL. EVERY JEW, EVERY YEAR ACROSS THE GLOBE, REITERATES THIS PERPETUAL MESSAGE OF OUR EXISTENCE AND CONNECTION TO THE LAND OF YISRAEL. AS IT STATES IN THE HAGGADA: "YEHOSHUA SAID TO ALL THE PEOPLE THUS SAYS HASHEM, THE G-D OF YISRAEL, IN OLDEN TIMES, YOUR FATHERS TERACH, FATHER OF AVRAHAM AND NACHOR LIVED BEYOND THE EUPHRATES RIVER, AND THEY SERVED OTHER GODS. AND I TOOK YOUR FATHER AVRAHAM FROM BEYOND THE EUPHRATES RIVER, AND LED HIM THROUGHOUT ALL THE LAND OF CANAAN, AND MULTIPLIED HIS OFFSPRING, AND GAVE HIM YITZCHAK. AND I GAVE TO YITZCHAK, YAAKOV AND EISAV. I GAVE TO EISAV, MOUNT SEIR, TO POSSESS IT, AND YAAKOV AND HIS CHILDREN WENT DOWN INTO EGYPT..." (YEHOSHUA 24:2-4). THE HAGGADA THEN CONTINUES TO PARAPHRASE THE REMAINING WORDS WRITTEN IN THIS CHAPTER OF YEHOSHUA, TELLING US HOW HASHEM TOOK US OUT OF EGYPT FROM BONDAGE AND SAVED US TIME AND TIME AGAIN, ONLY ASKING THAT WE FEAR HIM AND SERVE HIM WITH SINCERITY AND TRUTH. (YEHOSHUA 24:14).

THE ONE TO LEAD THE BUDDING NATION OF YISRAEL MUST BE A YEHOSHUA, A LEADER WHO UNDERSTANDS THE MOST PROFOUND EMOTIONS, INNER WORLDS, REQUIREMENTS, AND WANTS OF EVERY SINGLE JEWISH PERSON IN HIS GENERATION. אִישׁ אֲשֶׁר־רוּחַ בּוֹ ("AN INSPIRED MAN") (BAMIDBAR 27-18).

THE (SIFRI, PINCHAS 23) TELLS US THAT YEHOSHUA HAD THE RUACH, THE SPIRIT OF EVERY JEWISH PERSON WITHIN HIM. HIS רַחֲמִים (COMPASSION) WAS THE KEY TO HIS LEADERSHIP. YES, THE PROPHETS ARE THE INSPIRATION FOR EVERY GENERATION, AND IF ONE LISTENS CLOSELY TO THE INSIGHTS THAT YEHOSHUA FORMULATED, EVERYONE WILL BE FORTUNATE TO EMBRACE HIS HANDCRAFTED GUIDE FOR HIS OWN LIFE'S JOURNEY.

NAVI ILLUSTRATED, WHAT WE ARE ABOUT

AS NOTED ABOVE, WE HAVE ALWAYS FELT IT WAS ESSENTIAL TO ILLUSTRATE THE NAVI'S RELEVANCE IN OUR DAILY LIVES. YOU WILL FIND THROUGHOUT THE GRAPHIC NOVEL THE HINT OF CONTEMPORARY ISSUES. THESE OVERTONES ADD A COMPLETELY DIFFERENT DIMENSION TO THE STORY AND IMPACT THE READER WITH MUCH FOOD FOR THOUGHT.

ALTHOUGH WE RECOMMEND THESE PAGES FOR CHILDREN AGES TEN AND ABOVE, WE WOULD LIKE TO SUGGEST THAT PARENTS SPEND QUALITY TIME READING THESE STORIES TO YOUNGER CHILDREN, A FANTASTIC BONUS OPPORTUNITY OF FULFILLING THE MITZVAH OF וְשִׁנַּנְתָּם לְבָנֶיךָ ("AND YOU SHALL TEACH YOUR CHILDREN") (DEVARIM 6:7).

TO HELP THE STORYLINE FLOW, WE HAVE TAKEN A FEW LIBERTIES. ONE IS THE DIALOGUE. WHEN A CHARACTER SPEAKS, WE ARE NOT חָס וְשָׁלוֹם (G-D FORBID) ADDING TO THE WORDS OF YEHOSHUA OR ANY OTHER PROPHET. ON THE CONTRARY, WE HAVE INVESTED THOUSANDS OF HOURS OF RESEARCH INTO THESE CHAPTERS TO ENHANCE THE READING EXPERIENCE AND BRING YOU A FULLY SOURCED, RICHLY ILLUSTRATED EXPLANATION.

THE SECOND IS REGARDING THE CHARACTERS' FACIAL EXPRESSIONS. OBVIOUSLY, NO ONE KNOWS WHAT YEHOSHUA LOOKED LIKE; THEREFORE, WITH THE HELP AND ADVICE OF RABBANIM, WE ILLUSTRATED HIM WITH SLIGHTLY VARIED FACES. THEREFORE, YOU WILL NOTICE YEHOSHUA'S LOOKS CHANGE THROUGHOUT THE GRAPHIC NOVEL.

COME AND JOIN US FOR A JOURNEY THROUGH YEHOSHUA THAT WILL BE EDUCATIONAL, INSPIRING, ENGAGING, AND MOST OF ALL, A GIFT FROM HASHEM, ILLUMINATING YOUR WORLD WITH THE RICHES OF INSPIRATION FOR ETERNITY.

PLEASE FEEL FREE TO LET US KNOW IF YOU FIND ANY MISTAKES OR HAVE ANY CONCERNS OR COMMENTS. OUR EMAIL ADDRESS IS NAVIILLUSTRATED@GMAIL.COM. YOU CAN ALSO ORDER COPIES ONLINE AT OUR WEBSITE AT NAVIILLUSTRATED.COM.

North

Yam Hagadol

(Mediterranean Sea)

Tzidon

Chelba

Tzur

Achziv

Akko

ZEVULEN זבולון

HarTabor

Givat Hamoreh

Megiddo   Beit Hashita

Dor   Yezreel

Ein Harod   Beit Shean

MENASHE מנשה   Avel Mechulah

Tzreiratah

Shechem   Har   Succot

Ophra   Gilead   Penuel

אפרים

DAN דן   EPHRAYIM   Shilo   GAD גד   Yogbeha

Beit El

Ashdod   Ai

Akron   Yerushalayim   Yericho

Ashkelon   Bezek

REUVEN ראובן

Azza   Chevron

YEHUDAH יהודה

Dvir (Kiryat Sefer)

Tzfat Chorma

שמעון

Beer Sheva

SHIMON

Dead Sea

Beit Anat

Beit Shemesh
(North)

Kinneret

מנש
MENASHE

YEHOSHUA
יהושע

YEHOSHUA CHAPTER 1
יהושע פרק א

AND MOSHE WENT UP FROM THE PLAINS OF MOAV TO MOUNT NEVO, TO THE TOP OF THE SUMMIT FACING YERICHO. AND HASHEM SHOWED HIM ALL THE LAND... (DEVARIM 34:1)

1 AND IT WAS AFTER THE DEATH OF MOSHE, THE SERVANT OF HASHEM,

א. וַיְהִי אַחֲרֵי מוֹת מֹשֶׁה עֶבֶד ה' - -

YEHOSHUA, IT'S BEEN THIRTY DAYS SINCE MOSHE RABBEINU'S DEATH. YISRAEL IS GETTING RESTLESS AND FEELING LOST...
I UNDERSTAND AND REALIZE HOW DIFFICULT IT IS FOR THE ENTIRE NATION
BUT IT IS PAINFUL FOR ME AS WELL, FOR OVER 40 YEARS, I WAS SO CLOSE TO MOSHE, OUR TEACHER.
WHEN I WAS YOUNGER, I WOULD FOLLOW HIM WHEREVER HE WENT.
I WOULD SOAK UP EVERY WORD OF TORAH. I COULD NEVER GET ENOUGH.

I MADE IT MY RESPONSIBILITY TO DO EVERYTHING FOR HIM, EVEN IF HE DIDN'T ASK.
IT WAS A HONOR AND A PRIVILEGE FOR ME..
WHEN HE WAS ABOUT TO DIE HE ASKED ME...
DO YOU HAVE ANY FINAL QUESTIONS...
I ANSWERED...
MY MASTER, HAVE I EVER LEFT YOUR SIDE FOR EVEN A SHORT TIME AND GONE SOMEWHERE ELSE?
DID YOU NOT WRITE IN THE TORAH, ABOUT ME, "BUT HIS SERVANT YEHOSHUA, SON OF NUN, A YOUTH, DID NOT DEPART FROM THE TENT?" (SHMOT 33:11)
BEFORE, I EVEN SAID THOSE WORDS, I KNEW I HAD HURT HIM...
IMMEDIATELY, I COULD SEE THAT HE LOST ALL OF HIS STRENGTH...
HERE MOSHE RABBEINU SHARED WITH ME A VISION OF LIFE AND I REDUCED OUR RELATIONSHIP TO NOTHING MORE THAN AN OLD MAN GIVING ME A LIST OF INTERESTING FACTS.

THAT'S THE REASON I FORGOT ALMOST 300 LAWS...
IT'S A WONDER NONE OF YOU ACTUALLY HAD ME KILLED...
THANK HASHEM FOR OTHNIEL BEN KENAZ... HE WAS ABLE TO RETRIEVE ALL THOSE LAWS WITH HIS TRUST IN HASHEM AND USING HIS OWN INTELLECT..
WHAT ABOUT ASKING HASHEM FOR HELP? YOU ARE THE LEADER NOW, YOU ARE THE ONE CHOSEN BY HASHEM...
DO YOU THINK IT WORKS LIKE THAT NOW? MOSHE IS DEAD. THERE WILL NEVER BE A PROPHET LIKE MOSHE EVER AGAIN...
HE HAD A DIRECT LINK, SO TO SPEAK, WITH HASHEM. IF HE HAD A QUESTION, HE COULD ASK HASHEM DIRECTLY.
I AM NOT MOSHE!
THINK ABOUT IT... SO MANY OF US STANDING HERE TODAY, ACTUALLY HEARD HASHEM SPEAK AT HAR SINAI. IF YOU WERE OLDER THAN 60 OR YOUNGER THEN 20 YOU DID NOT DIE IN THE DESERT BECAUSE OF THE SIN OF THE SPIES.
AND THOSE OF YOU WHO WERE BORN AFTER HASHEM GAVE THE TORAH AT HAR SINAI, HEARD THE WORD OF HASHEM THROUGH MOSHE.
THAT IS ALL OVER! FROM NOW ON, IF WE HAVE ANY NEW QUESTIONS REGARDING THE LAW, WE HAVE TO USE THE TORAH TO FIGURE IT OUT FOR OURSELVES.
IT IS TRUE, I CAN USE THE URIM V'TUMIM, BUT AS FAR AS GAINING EVEN A LOWER LEVEL OF PROPHESY, THERE ARE NO GUARANTEES THAT HASHEM WILL GRANT ME THAT HONOR ...

- - THAT HASHEM SPOKE TO YEHOSHUA, THE SON OF NUN, MOSHE'S ATTENDANT, SAYING:
2 'MOSHE, MY SERVANT, IS DEAD; PREPARE TO CROSS THE YARDEN, TOGETHER WITH ALL THE PEOPLE, INTO THE LAND THAT I AM GIVING TO THE CHILDREN OF YISRAEL.
דברים
HASHEM IS TELLING YEHOSHUA TO **ENGAGE** YISRAEL IN WAR SINCE THEY ARE BEGINNING TO ACT REBELLIOUS.
3 EVERY PLACE THAT THE SOLE OF YOUR FEET WILL TREAD I HAVE GIVEN TO YOU, AS I HAVE PROMISED MOSHE.
4 YOUR TERRITORY WILL EXTEND FROM THE DESERT AND THE LEVANON TO THE GREAT RIVER, THE EUPHRATES RIVER, THE ENTIRE LAND OF THE CHITIM, AND UP TO THE GREAT SEA (MEDITERRANEAN) ON THE WEST.
WHATEVER LAND YOU **CONQUER**, SHALL ALWAYS BE HOLY FROM THAT DAY FORWARD...
- - וַיֹּאמֶר ה' אֶל יְהוֹשֻׁעַ בִּן נוּן מְשָׁרֵת מֹשֶׁה לֵאמֹר. **ב.** מֹשֶׁה עַבְדִּי מֵת וְעַתָּה קוּם עֲבֹר אֶת הַיַּרְדֵּן הַזֶּה
אַתָּה וְכָל הָעָם הַזֶּה אֶל הָאָרֶץ אֲשֶׁר אָנֹכִי נֹתֵן לָהֶם לִבְנֵי יִשְׂרָאֵל. **ג.** כָּל מָקוֹם אֲשֶׁר תִּדְרֹךְ כַּף רַגְלְכֶם בּוֹ
לָכֶם נְתַתִּיו כַּאֲשֶׁר דִּבַּרְתִּי אֶל מֹשֶׁה. **ד.** מֵהַמִּדְבָּר וְהַלְּבָנוֹן הַזֶּה וְעַד הַנָּהָר הַגָּדוֹל נְהַר פְּרָת כֹּל אֶרֶץ הַחִתִּים
וְעַד הַיָּם הַגָּדוֹל מְבוֹא הַשָּׁמֶשׁ יִהְיֶה גְּבוּלְכֶם.

5 NO MAN WILL STAND UP TO YOU AS LONG AS YOU LIVE.
YOU WILL NOT HAVE ANY INTERNAL OPPOSITIONS SUCH AS KORACH AND HIS ASSEMBLY...
AS I WAS WITH MOSHE,
WHO DID NOT HAVE ANY EXTERNAL OPPOSITION WHEN HE APPEARED BEFORE PARO...
SO I WILL BE WITH YOU
WHEN YOU FIGHT THE CANAANIM...
I WILL NOT FAIL YOU
BY BEING EXPOSED TO EVIL SOURCES...
OR FORSAKE YOU
PERSONALLY. FOR IN THE FUTURE WHEN YOU DIE, I WILL NOT ALLOW YOUR BODY TO DECAY.
6 BE STRONG AND STEADFAST, FOR YOU WILL CAUSE THIS PEOPLE TO INHERIT THE LAND WHICH I SWORE TO THEIR FATHERS TO GIVE THEM.
BE STRONG AND STEADFAST IN דרך ארץ AND IN ALL AREAS OF TORAH AND MITZVOT DURING PEACE AND WAR...

ה. לֹא יִתְיַצֵּב אִישׁ לְפָנֶיךָ כֹּל יְמֵי חַיֶּיךָ כַּאֲשֶׁר הָיִיתִי עִם מֹשֶׁה אֶהְיֶה עִמָּךְ לֹא אַרְפְּךָ וְלֹא אֶעֶזְבֶךָּ. ו. חֲזַק וֶאֱמָץ
כִּי אַתָּה תַּנְחִיל אֶת הָעָם הַזֶּה אֶת הָאָרֶץ אֲשֶׁר נִשְׁבַּעְתִּי לַאֲבוֹתָם לָתֵת לָהֶם.

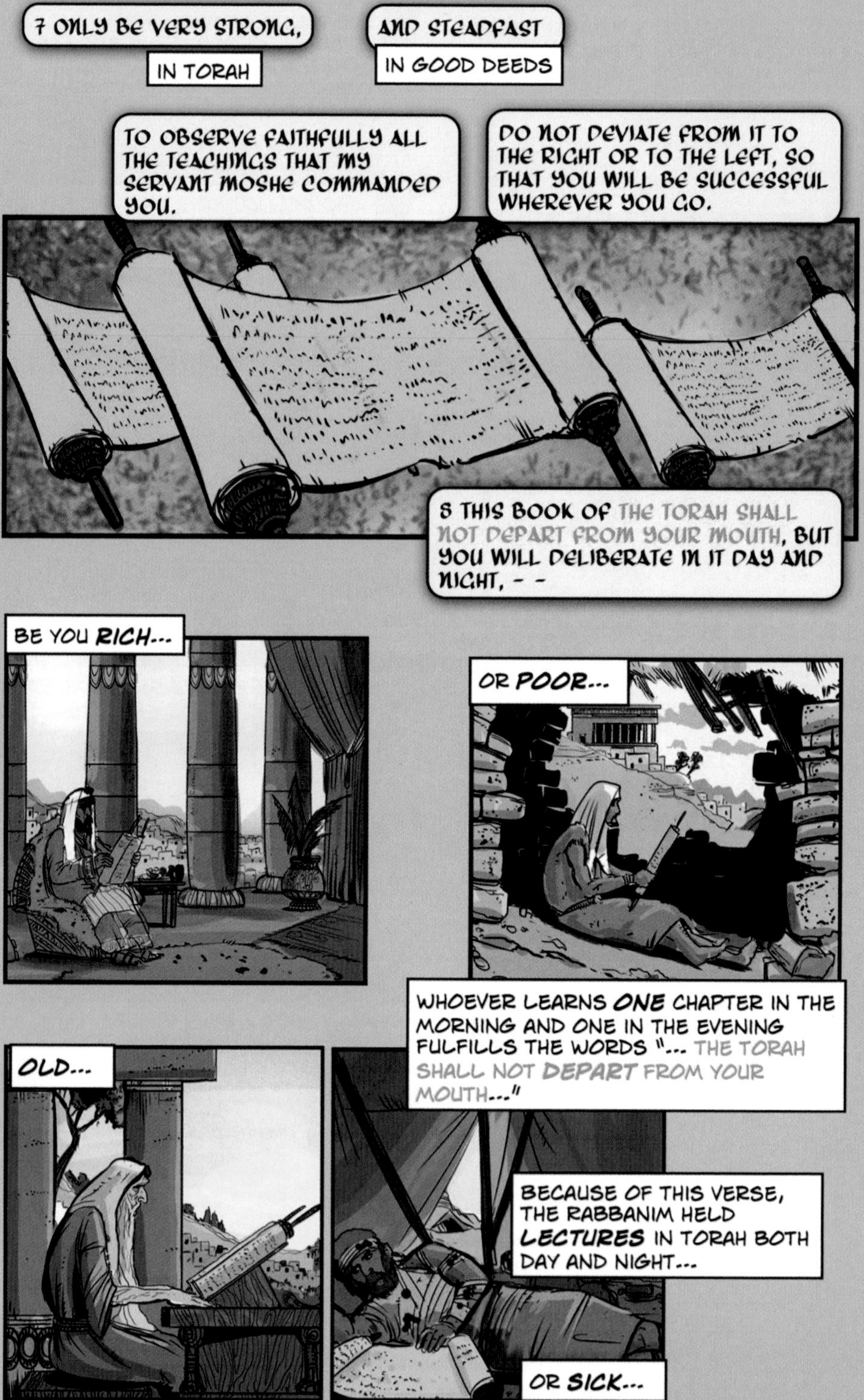
7 ONLY BE VERY STRONG,
IN TORAH
AND STEADFAST
IN GOOD DEEDS
TO OBSERVE FAITHFULLY ALL THE TEACHINGS THAT MY SERVANT MOSHE COMMANDED YOU.
DO NOT DEVIATE FROM IT TO THE RIGHT OR TO THE LEFT, SO THAT YOU WILL BE SUCCESSFUL WHEREVER YOU GO.
8 THIS BOOK OF THE TORAH SHALL NOT DEPART FROM YOUR MOUTH, BUT YOU WILL DELIBERATE IN IT DAY AND NIGHT, - -
BE YOU RICH...
OR POOR...
WHOEVER LEARNS ONE CHAPTER IN THE MORNING AND ONE IN THE EVENING FULFILLS THE WORDS "... THE TORAH SHALL NOT DEPART FROM YOUR MOUTH..."
OLD...
BECAUSE OF THIS VERSE, THE RABBANIM HELD LECTURES IN TORAH BOTH DAY AND NIGHT...
OR SICK...

ז. רַק חֲזַק וֶאֱמַץ מְאֹד לִשְׁמֹר לַעֲשׂוֹת כְּכָל הַתּוֹרָה אֲשֶׁר צִוְּךָ מֹשֶׁה עַבְדִּי אַל תָּסוּר מִמֶּנּוּ יָמִין וּשְׂמֹאול לְמַעַן
תַּשְׂכִּיל בְּכֹל אֲשֶׁר תֵּלֵךְ. ח. לֹא יָמוּשׁ סֵפֶר הַתּוֹרָה הַזֶּה מִפִּיךָ וְהָגִיתָ בּוֹ יוֹמָם וָלַיְלָה - -

- - THAT YOU MAY OBSERVE FAITHFULLY ALL THAT IS WRITTEN IN IT, ONLY THEN YOU WILL PROSPER IN ALL THAT YOU WILL DO, AND ONLY THEN YOU WILL BE SUCCESSFUL.
THEREFORE WHOEVER OCCUPIES THEMSELVES WITH *TORAH* WILL PROSPER.
9 HAVE I NOT COMMANDED YOU, BE STRONG AND STEADFAST, DO NOT FEAR, AND DO NOT BE DISMAYED, FOR HASHEM YOUR G-D IS WITH YOU WHEREVER YOU GO.'
HASHEM *COMMANDED* YEHOSHUA THROUGH MOSHE AS IT STATES:
... GIVE YEHOSHUA INSTRUCTIONS, STRENGTHEN HIM AND ENCOURAGE HIM, FOR HE WILL CROSS AT THE HEAD OF THIS PEOPLE, AND HE WILL CAUSE THEM TO *INHERIT* THE LAND THAT YOU MAY ONLY SEE. (DEVARIM 3:28)

- - לְמַעַן תִּשְׁמֹר לַעֲשׂוֹת כְּכָל הַכָּתוּב בּוֹ כִּי אָז תַּצְלִיחַ אֶת דְּרָכֶךָ וְאָז תַּשְׂכִּיל. ט. הֲלוֹא צִוִּיתִיךָ חֲזַק וֶאֱמָץ אַל
תַּעֲרֹץ וְאַל תֵּחָת כִּי עִמְּךָ ה' אֱלֹקֶיךָ בְּכֹל אֲשֶׁר תֵּלֵךְ.

י. וַיְצַו יְהוֹשֻׁעַ אֶת שֹׁטְרֵי הָעָם לֵאמֹר. **יא.** עִבְרוּ בְּקֶרֶב הַמַּחֲנֶה וְצַוּוּ אֶת הָעָם לֵאמֹר הָכִינוּ לָכֶם צֵידָה כִּי
בְּעוֹד שְׁלֹשֶׁת יָמִים אַתֶּם עֹבְרִים אֶת הַיַּרְדֵּן הַזֶּה לָבוֹא לָרֶשֶׁת אֶת הָאָרֶץ אֲשֶׁר ה' אֱלֹקֵיכֶם נֹתֵן לָכֶם לְרִשְׁתָּהּ.
יב. וְלָראוּבֵנִי וְלַגָּדִי וְלַחֲצִי שֵׁבֶט הַמְנַשֶּׁה אָמַר יְהוֹשֻׁעַ לֵאמֹר.

13 REMEMBER THE WORD THAT MOSHE, THE SERVANT OF HASHEM, COMMANDED YOU, SAYING: 'HASHEM YOUR G-D, IS GIVING YOU A SAFE HAVEN, AND HAS GIVEN YOU THIS LAND.
14 LET YOUR WIVES, CHILDREN, AND CATTLE, REMAIN IN THE LAND WHICH MOSHE GAVE YOU ON THE OTHER SIDE OF THE YARDEN
REUVEN, GAD AND THE HALF-TRIBE OF MENASHE WERE GIVEN LAND ON THE EAST SIDE OF THE YARDEN ON THE CONDITION THAT THEY WILL LEAD THE OTHER TRIBES IN ***CONQUERING*** THE REST OF THE LAND ON THE WEST SIDE.
BUT EVERYONE OF YOUR WARRIORS WILL GO ACROSS ARMED, AHEAD OF YOUR BROTHERS AND HELP THEM.
15 UNTIL HASHEM HAS GIVEN YOUR BROTHERS A SAFE HAVEN, SUCH AS YOU HAVE, AND THEY TOO TAKE POSSESSION OF THE LAND THAT HASHEM YOUR G-D, GAVE THEM.
THEN YOU WILL RETURN TO THE LAND ON THE EAST SIDE OF THE YARDEN WHICH MOSHE, THE SERVANT OF HASHEM, GAVE TO YOU AS YOUR INHERITANCE AND YOU MAY POSSESS IT'.
יג. זָכוֹר אֶת הַדָּבָר אֲשֶׁר צִוָּה אֶתְכֶם מֹשֶׁה עֶבֶד ה' לֵאמֹר ה' אֱלֹקֵיכֶם מֵנִיחַ לָכֶם וְנָתַן לָכֶם אֶת הָאָרֶץ הַזֹּאת.
יד. נְשֵׁיכֶם טַפְּכֶם וּמִקְנֵיכֶם יֵשְׁבוּ בָּאָרֶץ אֲשֶׁר נָתַן לָכֶם מֹשֶׁה בְּעֵבֶר הַיַּרְדֵּן וְאַתֶּם תַּעַבְרוּ חֲמֻשִׁים לִפְנֵי אֲחֵיכֶם כֹּל
גִּבּוֹרֵי הַחַיִל וַעֲזַרְתֶּם אוֹתָם. **טו.** עַד אֲשֶׁר יָנִיחַ ה' לַאֲחֵיכֶם כָּכֶם וְיָרְשׁוּ גַם הֵמָּה אֶת הָאָרֶץ אֲשֶׁר ה' אֱלֹקֵיכֶם
נֹתֵן לָהֶם וְשַׁבְתֶּם לְאֶרֶץ יְרֻשַּׁתְכֶם וִירִשְׁתֶּם אוֹתָהּ אֲשֶׁר נָתַן לָכֶם מֹשֶׁה עֶבֶד ה' בְּעֵבֶר הַיַּרְדֵּן מִזְרַח הַשָּׁמֶשׁ.

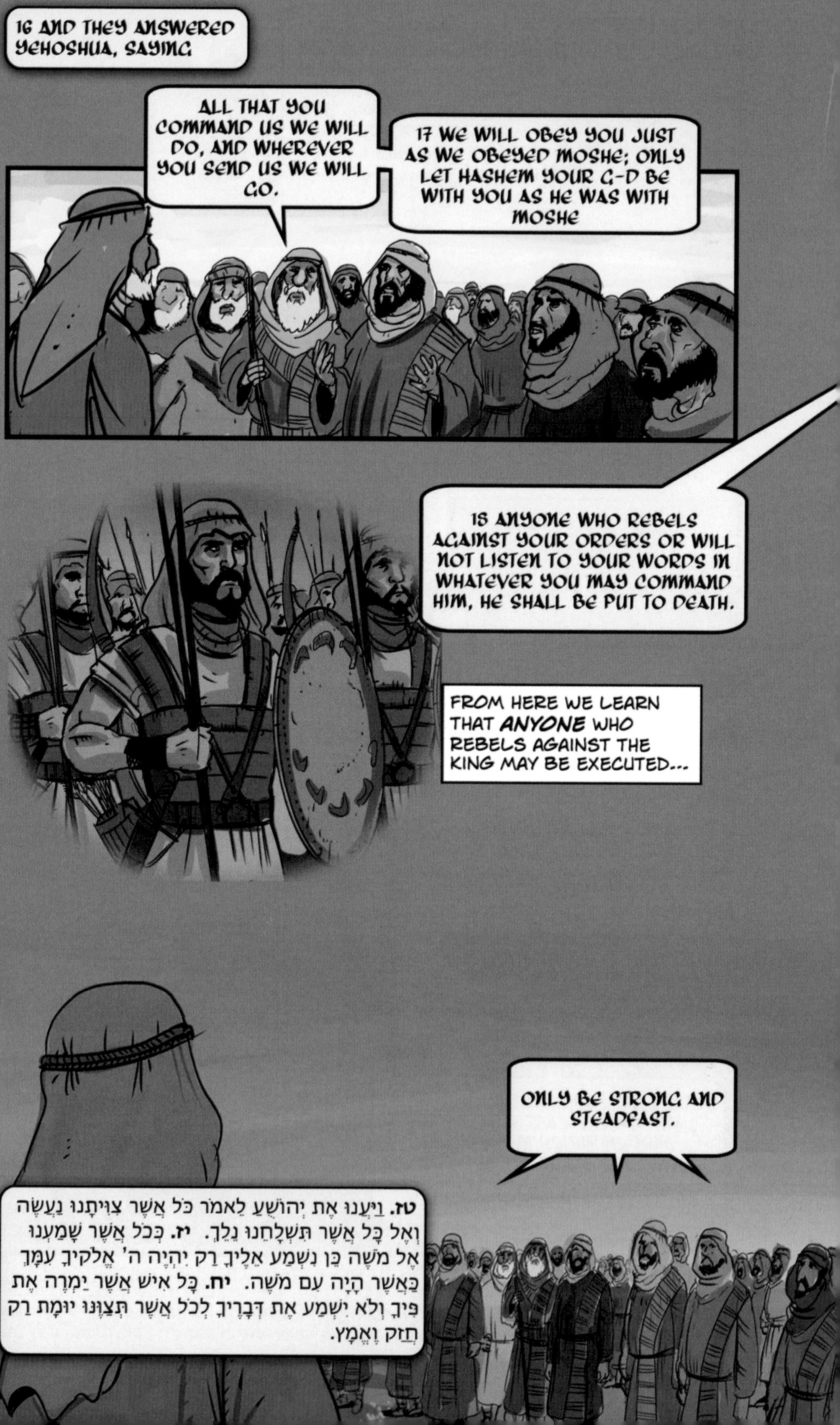
16 AND THEY ANSWERED YEHOSHUA, SAYING
ALL THAT YOU COMMAND US WE WILL DO, AND WHEREVER YOU SEND US WE WILL GO.
17 WE WILL OBEY YOU JUST AS WE OBEYED MOSHE; ONLY LET HASHEM YOUR G-D BE WITH YOU AS HE WAS WITH MOSHE
18 ANYONE WHO REBELS AGAINST YOUR ORDERS OR WILL NOT LISTEN TO YOUR WORDS IN WHATEVER YOU MAY COMMAND HIM, HE SHALL BE PUT TO DEATH.
FROM HERE WE LEARN THAT ***ANYONE*** WHO REBELS AGAINST THE KING MAY BE EXECUTED...
ONLY BE STRONG AND STEADFAST.
טז. וַיַּעֲנוּ אֶת יְהוֹשֻׁעַ לֵאמֹר כֹּל אֲשֶׁר צִוִּיתָנוּ נַעֲשֶׂה
וְאֶל כָּל אֲשֶׁר תִּשְׁלָחֵנוּ נֵלֵךְ. **יז.** כְּכֹל אֲשֶׁר שָׁמַעְנוּ
אֶל מֹשֶׁה כֵּן נִשְׁמַע אֵלֶיךָ רַק יִהְיֶה ה' אֱלֹקֶיךָ עִמָּךְ
כַּאֲשֶׁר הָיָה עִם מֹשֶׁה. **יח.** כָּל אִישׁ אֲשֶׁר יַמְרֶה אֶת
פִּיךָ וְלֹא יִשְׁמַע אֶת דְּבָרֶיךָ לְכֹל אֲשֶׁר תְּצַוֶּנּוּ יוּמָת רַק
חֲזַק וֶאֱמָץ.

YEHOSHUA CHAPTER 2
יהושע פרק ב
I NEED TO SEND OUT SPIES...
WE DID THIS ONCE BEFORE, REMEMBER? THE OUTCOME WAS NOT A GOOD ONE. THE ENTIRE NATION WAS PUNISHED. WE SPENT 40 YEARS IN THE DESERT AND COULD NOT ENTER THE PROMISED LAND.
KALEV, HOW COULD I POSSIBLY FORGET. YOU AND I WERE THERE AND WE WERE THE ONLY 2 SPIES THAT SURVIVED, THE OTHERS WERE KILLED...
BUT THIS TIME WILL BE DIFFERENT. IT IS PERFECTLY APPROPRIATE AND NECESSARY TO SEND OUT SPIES.
HOW CAN YOU BE SURE? THE STAKES ARE WAY TOO HIGH! THE PEOPLE CAN EASILY FALL INTO THE SAME TRAP.
THAT'S WHY WE ARE SENDING OUT THE SPIES IN SECRECY, SO NO ONE WILL KNOW. NO ANNOUCMENTS AND NO FANFARE.
TRUTH TO BE TOLD, THE PEOPLE DO NOT NEED TO KNOW. THIS WILL BE OUR SECRET, BETWEEN YOU, PINCHAS AND ME...
1 AND YEHOSHUA THE SON OF NUN, SENT TWO SPIES FROM SHITTIM, SECRETLY, SAYING: 'GO VIEW THE LAND, AND YERICHO.' - -
HERE WE GO AGAIN... MAY HASHEM BE ON OUR SIDE.
א. וַיִּשְׁלַח יְהוֹשֻׁעַ בִּן נוּן מִן הַשִּׁטִּים שְׁנַיִם אֲנָשִׁים מְרַגְּלִים חֶרֶשׁ לֵאמֹר לְכוּ רְאוּ אֶת הָאָרֶץ וְאֶת-יְרִיחוֹ - -

THERE IT IS... YERICHO, THE MOST FORTIFIED CITY IN THE LAND!
THEY SAY THE WIDTH OF ITS WALLS ARE THE SAME AS ITS HEIGHT...
WHAT AN EXCITING TIME WE LIVE IN. WITH THE HELP OF HASHEM WE WILL BE ABLE TO CONQUER ALL OF THIS LAND REGARDLESS OF HOW STRONG THEY ARE...
WHY ARE WE ATTACKING YERICHO FIRST?
BECAUSE IT IS ON THE BORDER OF THE YARDEN AND IT IS THE STRONGEST CITY IN CANAAN. ONCE WE CONQUER IT, OUR VICTORY WILL INJECT FEAR INTO THE HEARTS OF ALL THROUGHOUT THE LAND..

ALSO, IT IS A VERY CULTURED CITY. LEADERS AND DIGNITARIES VISIT THERE ALL THE TIME...
WHAT IS OUR OBJECTIVE WHEN WE ENTER THE CITY?
WE ARE GOING IN PRETENDING TO BE POTTERY MERCHANTS TO AVOID SUSPICION ...
THEN WE WILL MEET THE FAMOUS INNKEEPER, RACHAV, SHE KNOWS EVERYTHING ABOUT EVERYONE. ACCORDING TO WHAT INFORMATION SHE GIVES US WE WILL DETERMINE THE MORALE OF THE CIVILIANS.
WE WILL GATHER INTELLIGENCE TO KNOW IF THE PEOPLE OF CANAAN HAVE THE DETERMINATION TO FIGHT YISRAEL WHO ARE SITTING AT THEIR DOORSTEPS ON THE OTHER SIDE OF THE YARDEN...
DO YOU SEE THOSE WALLS... THEY'RE MASSIVE!!!
THIS PLACE IS HEAVILY FORTIFIED WITH GUARDS AT EVERY CORNER...
EXCUSE ME; WE ARE POTTERY MERCHANTS WHO HAVE JUST ARRIVED IN YOUR CITY. WE NEED A PLACE TO SLEEP. WHERE IS RACHAV'S INN?
UP AHEAD TO THE RIGHT...

- - AND THEY WENT, AND ARRIVED AT THE HOUSE OF AN INNKEEPER NAMED RACHAV.
WELL, WE HAVE BEEN TRAVELING ALL DAY AND WE WOULD LIKE A ROOM FOR THE EVENING...
BUSINESS HAS BEEN SLOW AROUND HERE, EVER SINCE YISRAEL HAS BEEN CAMPING AT OUR BORDERS...
I CAN GIVE YOU A GREAT ROOM RIGHT UP THE STAIRS...
THANK YOU, WE WILL TAKE IT...
DO YOU THINK SHE RECOGNIZES WHICH NATION WE ARE FROM?
MAYBE, BUT WE WILL KNOW SOON ENOUGH IF THE GUARDS START BREAKING DOWN OUR DOOR...
AND SLEPT THERE.
- - וַיֵּלְכוּ וַיָּבֹאוּ בֵּית אִשָּׁה זוֹנָה וּשְׁמָהּ רָחָב וַיִּשְׁכְּבוּ שָׁמָּה.

ב. וַיֵּאָמַר לְמֶלֶךְ יְרִיחוֹ לֵאמֹר הִנֵּה אֲנָשִׁים בָּאוּ הֵנָּה הַלַּיְלָה מִבְּנֵי
יִשְׂרָאֵל לַחְפֹּר אֶת הָאָרֶץ.

ג. וַיִּשְׁלַח מֶלֶךְ יְרִיחוֹ אֶל רָחָב לֵאמֹר הוֹצִיאִי הָאֲנָשִׁים הַבָּאִים אֵלַיִךְ אֲשֶׁר בָּאוּ לְבֵיתֵךְ
כִּי לַחְפֹּר אֶת כָּל הָאָרֶץ בָּאוּ. **ד.** וַתִּקַּח הָאִשָּׁה אֶת שְׁנֵי הָאֲנָשִׁים וַתִּצְפְּנוֹ וַתֹּאמֶר כֵּן
בָּאוּ אֵלַי הָאֲנָשִׁים וְלֹא יָדַעְתִּי מֵאַיִן הֵמָּה.

5 AND AT DARK, WHEN THE CITY GATE WAS ABOUT TO BE CLOSED, THE MEN LEFT. I DO NOT KNOW WHERE THEY WENT.
CHASE AFTER THEM QUICKLY, SO YOU WILL BE ABLE TO OVERTAKE THEM (OUTSIDE THE GATE)...
I EXPECT THE GATEKEEPERS TO BE PUNISHED BECAUSE THEY EVIDENTLY DIDN'T CLOSE THE GATES ON TIME...
YES MA'AM...
HURRY UP, THE GATES ARE CLOSING...
AND THEY WON'T REOPEN UNTIL TOMORROW MORNING...
ה. וַיְהִי הַשַּׁעַר לִסְגּוֹר בַּחֹשֶׁךְ וְהָאֲנָשִׁים יָצָאוּ לֹא יָדַעְתִּי אָנָה הָלְכוּ הָאֲנָשִׁים רִדְפוּ מַהֵר אַחֲרֵיהֶם כִּי תַשִּׂיגוּם.

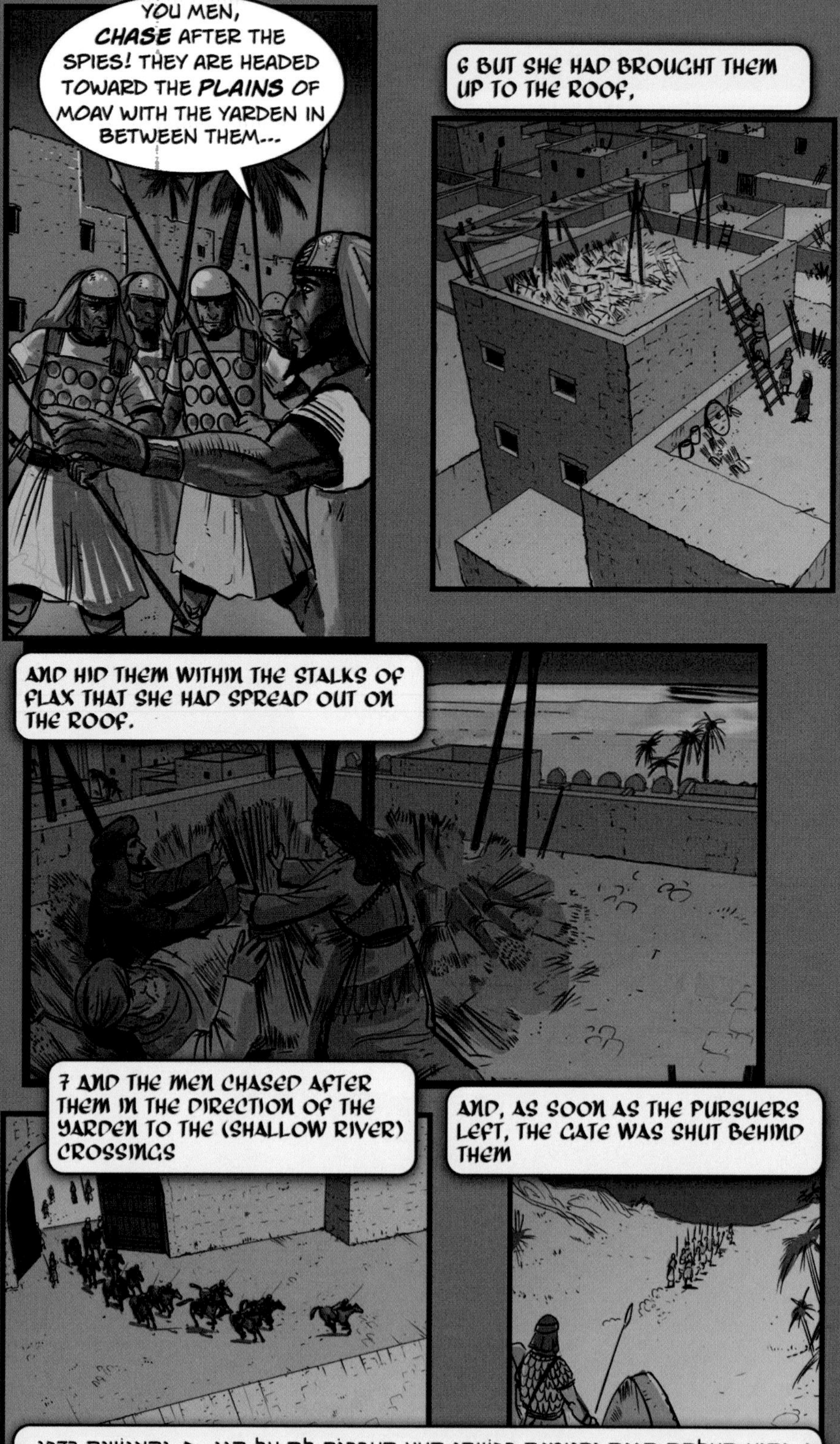

YOU MEN, CHASE AFTER THE SPIES! THEY ARE HEADED TOWARD THE PLAINS OF MOAV WITH THE YARDEN IN BETWEEN THEM...
6 BUT SHE HAD BROUGHT THEM UP TO THE ROOF,
AND HID THEM WITHIN THE STALKS OF FLAX THAT SHE HAD SPREAD OUT ON THE ROOF.
7 AND THE MEN CHASED AFTER THEM IN THE DIRECTION OF THE YARDEN TO THE (SHALLOW RIVER) CROSSINGS
AND, AS SOON AS THE PURSUERS LEFT, THE GATE WAS SHUT BEHIND THEM

ו. וְהִיא הֶעֱלָתַם הַגָּגָה וַתִּטְמְנֵם בְּפִשְׁתֵּי הָעֵץ הָעֲרֻכוֹת לָהּ עַל הַגָּג. ז. וְהָאֲנָשִׁים רָדְפוּ
אַחֲרֵיהֶם דֶּרֶךְ הַיַּרְדֵּן עַל הַמַּעְבְּרוֹת וְהַשַּׁעַר סָגָרוּ אַחֲרֵי כַּאֲשֶׁר יָצְאוּ הָרֹדְפִים אַחֲרֵיהֶם.

8 AND BEFORE THEY WENT TO SLEEP, SHE CAME UP TO THEM ON THE ROOF,
9 AND SHE SAID TO THE MEN
I KNOW THAT HASHEM HAS GIVEN YOU THE LAND, AND THAT THE FEAR OF YOU HAS FALLEN UPON US,
AND THAT ALL THE INHABITANTS OF THE LAND MELT AWAY BECAUSE OF YOU.

ח. וְהֵמָּה טֶרֶם יִשְׁכָּבוּן וְהִיא עָלְתָה עֲלֵיהֶם עַל הַגָּג. **ט.** וַתֹּאמֶר אֶל הָאֲנָשִׁים יָדַעְתִּי כִּי
נָתַן ה' לָכֶם אֶת הָאָרֶץ וְכִי נָפְלָה אֵימַתְכֶם עָלֵינוּ וְכִי נָמֹגוּ כָּל יֹשְׁבֵי הָאָרֶץ מִפְּנֵיכֶם.

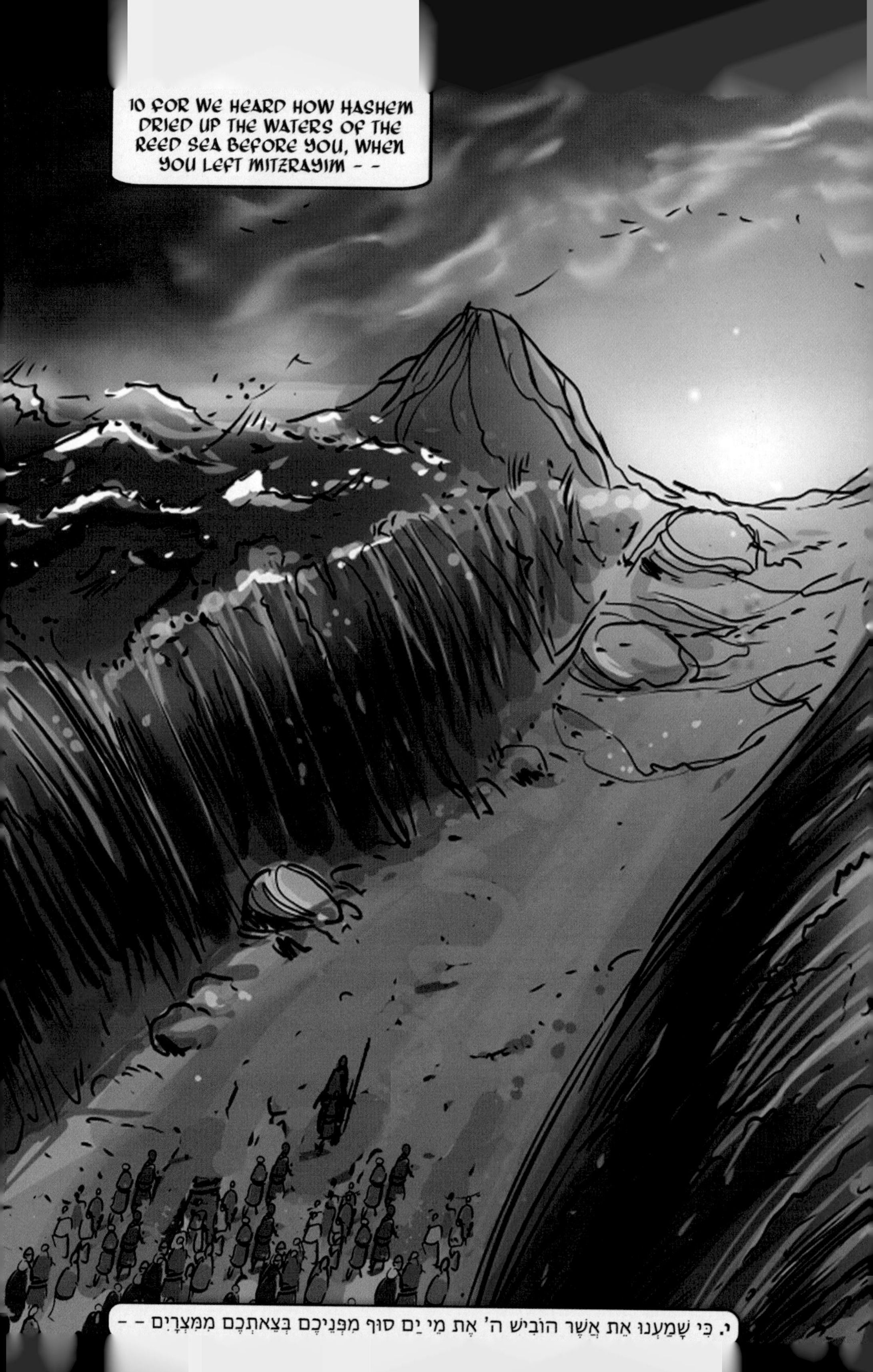
10 FOR WE HEARD HOW HASHEM DRIED UP THE WATERS OF THE REED SEA BEFORE YOU, WHEN YOU LEFT MITZRAYIM – –
י. כִּי שָׁמַעְנוּ אֵת אֲשֶׁר הוֹבִישׁ ה' אֶת מֵי יַם סוּף מִפְּנֵיכֶם בְּצֵאתְכֶם מִמִּצְרָיִם – –

- - AND WHAT YOU DID TO THE TWO KINGS OF THE AMORI, WHO WERE ON THE OTHER SIDE OF THE YARDEN, SICHON AND OG, WHO YOU UTTERLY DESTROYED.
YOUR ATTACK AGAINST THE AMORI WAS DEVASTATING WHEN HASHEM SENT HORNETS TO STING THEM IN THEIR EYES...
THE POISON CAUSED THE SOLDIERS TO COLLAPSE AND DIE.
EVERYONE KNEW THAT THE TWO KINGDOMS OF SICHON AND OG AND THEIR ARMIES WERE INVINCIBLE. THE NEIGHBORING NATIONS LIVING ON THE BORDERS OF SICHON AND OG FELT COMPLETELY PROTECTED FROM ANYONE THAT WOULD ATTACK THEM.
- - וַאֲשֶׁר עֲשִׂיתֶם לִשְׁנֵי מַלְכֵי הָאֱמֹרִי אֲשֶׁר בְּעֵבֶר הַיַּרְדֵּן לְסִיחֹן וּלְעוֹג אֲשֶׁר הֶחֱרַמְתֶּם אוֹתָם.

11 AND AS SOON AS WE HEARD IT, OUR HEARTS MELTED,
THE SOLDIERS WOULD SAY...
IT'S HOPELESS, EVERYTHING IS HOPELESS...!
I KNOW, BUT WE MUST REMAIN STRONG!
BUT WHAT CHANCE DO WE HAVE AGAINST YISRAEL'S MIGHTY G-D?
NO SPIRIT REMAINED IN ANY MAN, BECAUSE OF YOU
FOR HASHEM YOUR G-D, HE IS G-D IN THE HEAVENS ABOVE, AND ON THE EARTH BELOW.
AT THIS POINT, RACHAV DENOUNCED ALL FORMS OF IDOL WORSHIP AND ACCEPTED HASHEM.
12 AND NOW. PLEASE, SWEAR TO ME BY HASHEM, SINCE I HAVE DEALT KINDLY WITH YOU, THAT YOU WILL ALSO DEAL KINDLY WITH MY FATHER'S HOUSEHOLD AND GIVE ME A TRUE SIGN
TO DIFFERENTIATE IN BATTLE BETWEEN MY FATHER'S HOME AND OTHER HOUSES...
13. KEEP MY FATHER, MOTHER, BROTHERS AND SISTERS, AND ALL THAT THEY HAVE ALIVE, AND SAVE OUR SOULS FROM DEATH.
BECAUSE I HAVE NO HUSBAND OR CHILDREN, THIS IS MY FAMILY...

יא. וַנִּשְׁמַע וַיִּמַּס לְבָבֵנוּ וְלֹא-קָמָה עוֹד רוּחַ בְּאִישׁ מִפְּנֵיכֶם כִּי ה' אֱלֹקיכֶם
הוּא אֱלֹהִים בַּשָּׁמַיִם מִמַּעַל וְעַל הָאָרֶץ מִתָּחַת. **יב**. וְעַתָּה הִשָּׁבְעוּ נָא לִי בַּה'
כִּי עָשִׂיתִי עִמָּכֶם חָסֶד וַעֲשִׂיתֶם גַּם אַתֶּם עִם בֵּית אָבִי חֶסֶד וּנְתַתֶּם לִי אוֹת
אֱמֶת. **יג**. וְהַחֲיִתֶם אֶת אָבִי וְאֶת אִמִּי וְאֶת אַחַי וְאֶת אחותי (אַחְיוֹתַי), וְאֵת כָּל
אֲשֶׁר לָהֶם וְהִצַּלְתֶּם אֶת נַפְשֹׁתֵינוּ מִמָּוֶת.

14 AND THE MEN SAID TO HER
OUR LIFE FOR YOURS EVEN UNTIL DEATH. IF YOU DO NOT DISCLOSE THIS MISSION OF OURS, WE WILL DEAL KINDLY AND FAITHFULLY WITH YOU WHEN HASHEM GIVES US THE LAND.
15 THEN SHE LET THEM DOWN BY A CORD THROUGH THE WINDOW FOR HER HOUSE WAS BUILT INTO THE SIDE OF THE WALL, AND SHE LIVED WITHIN THE WALL.
16 AND SHE SAID TO THEM,
GO TO THE MOUNTAIN, TO PREVENT THE PURSUERS FROM CATCHING YOU
AND HIDE YOURSELVES THERE FOR THREE DAYS, UNTIL THE PURSUERS RETURN. THEN YOU MAY CONTINUE ON YOUR WAY.
17 AND THE MEN SAID TO HER
WE WILL BE CLEARED OF YOUR OATH WHICH YOU MADE US SWEAR (UNLESS YOU DO THE FOLLOWING).
18 WHEN WE COME INTO THE LAND, YOU WILL TIE THIS CORD OF SCARLET THREAD IN THE WINDOW THROUGH WHICH YOU LOWERED US.
AND YOU WILL GATHER INTO YOUR HOUSE, YOUR FATHER, YOUR MOTHER, YOUR BROTHERS, AND ALL YOUR FATHER'S ENTIRE HOUSEHOLD.
19 AND IT WILL BE THAT WHOEVER GOES OUT OF THE DOORS OF YOUR HOUSE INTO THE STREET, HIS BLOOD WILL BE ON HIS HEAD, AND WE WILL BE GUILTLESS. AND WHOEVER WILL BE WITH YOU IN THE HOUSE, HIS BLOOD WILL BE ON OUR HEAD, IF ANY HAND IS (LAID) UPON HIM.
20 BUT IF YOU TELL ANYONE OF OUR AGREEMENT, WE WILL BE ABSOLVED OF THIS OATH WHICH YOU HAVE MADE US SWEAR.
21 AND SHE SAID
SO SHALL IT BE ACCORDING TO YOUR WORDS, - -

יד. וַיֹּאמְרוּ לָהּ הָאֲנָשִׁים נַפְשֵׁנוּ תַחְתֵּיכֶם לָמוּת אִם לֹא תַגִּידוּ אֶת דְּבָרֵנוּ זֶה וְהָיָה בְּתֵת ה' לָנוּ אֶת
הָאָרֶץ וְעָשִׂינוּ עִמָּךְ חֶסֶד וֶאֱמֶת. **טו.** וַתּוֹרִדֵם בַּחֶבֶל בְּעַד הַחַלּוֹן כִּי בֵיתָהּ בְּקִיר הַחוֹמָה וּבַחוֹמָה הִיא
יוֹשָׁבֶת. **טז.** וַתֹּאמֶר לָהֶם הָהָרָה לֵּכוּ פֶּן יִפְגְּעוּ בָכֶם הָרֹדְפִים וְנַחְבֵּתֶם שָׁמָּה שְׁלֹשֶׁת יָמִים עַד שׁוֹב
הָרֹדְפִים וְאַחַר תֵּלְכוּ לְדַרְכְּכֶם. **יז.** וַיֹּאמְרוּ אֵלֶיהָ הָאֲנָשִׁים נְקִיִּם אֲנַחְנוּ מִשְּׁבֻעָתֵךְ הַזֶּה אֲשֶׁר הִשְׁבַּעְתָּנוּ.
יח. הִנֵּה אֲנַחְנוּ בָאִים בָּאָרֶץ אֶת תִּקְוַת חוּט הַשָּׁנִי הַזֶּה תִּקְשְׁרִי בַּחַלּוֹן אֲשֶׁר הוֹרַדְתֵּנוּ בוֹ וְאֶת אָבִיךְ וְאֶת
אִמֵּךְ וְאֶת אַחַיִךְ וְאֵת כָּל בֵּית אָבִיךְ תַּאַסְפִי אֵלַיִךְ הַבָּיְתָה. **יט.** וְהָיָה כֹּל אֲשֶׁר יֵצֵא מִדַּלְתֵי בֵיתֵךְ הַחוּצָה
דָּמוֹ בְרֹאשׁוֹ וַאֲנַחְנוּ נְקִיִּם וְכֹל אֲשֶׁר יִהְיֶה אִתָּךְ בַּבַּיִת דָּמוֹ בְרֹאשֵׁנוּ אִם יָד תִּהְיֶה בּוֹ. **כ.** וְאִם תַּגִּידִי אֶת
דְּבָרֵנוּ זֶה וְהָיִינוּ נְקִיִּם מִשְּׁבֻעָתֵךְ אֲשֶׁר הִשְׁבַּעְתָּנוּ. **כא.** וַתֹּאמֶר כְּדִבְרֵיכֶם כֶּן הוּא - -

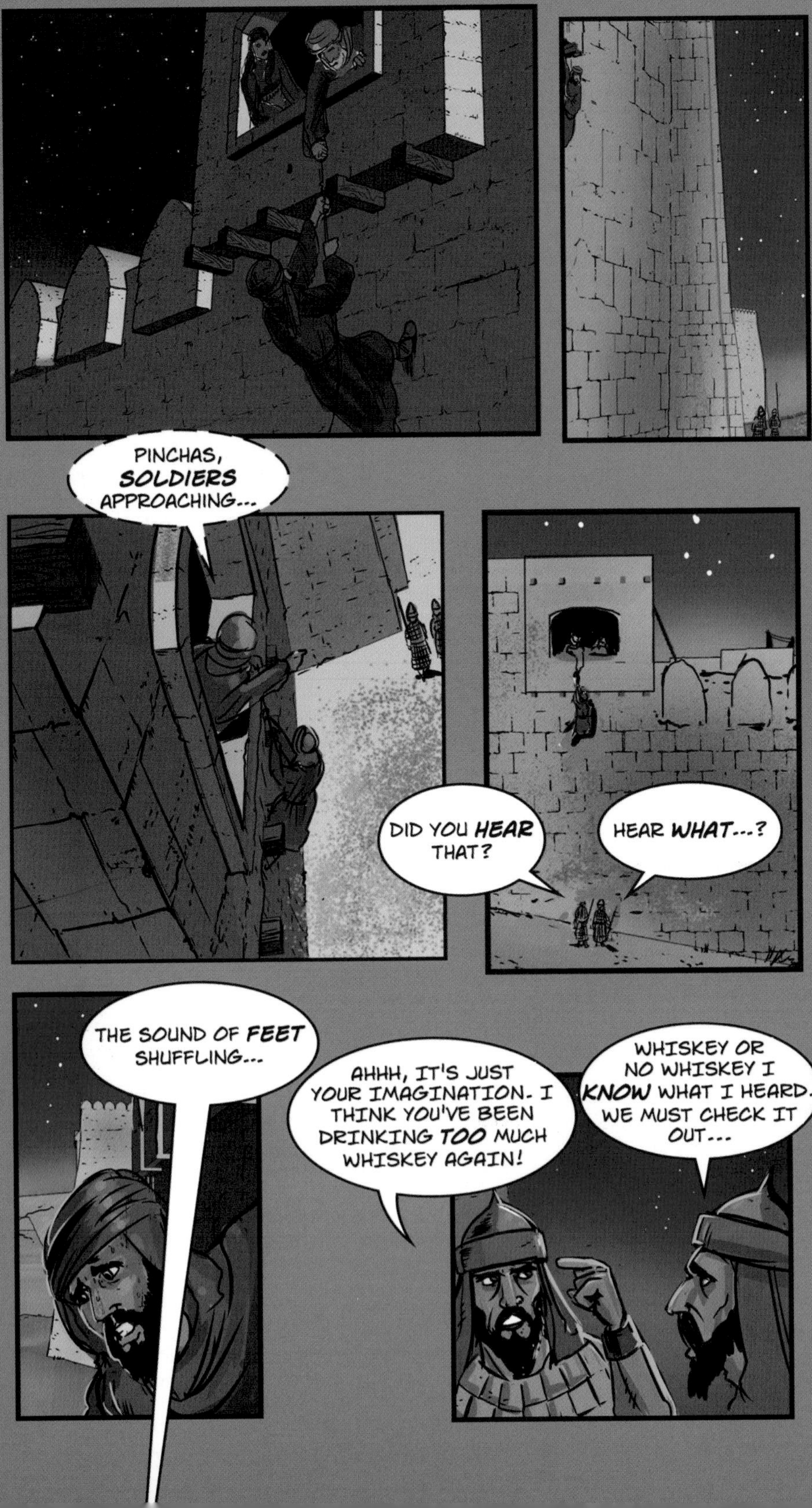
PINCHAS, SOLDIERS APPROACHING...
DID YOU HEAR THAT?
HEAR WHAT...?
THE SOUND OF FEET SHUFFLING...
AHHH, IT'S JUST YOUR IMAGINATION. I THINK YOU'VE BEEN DRINKING TOO MUCH WHISKEY AGAIN!
WHISKEY OR NO WHISKEY I KNOW WHAT I HEARD. WE MUST CHECK IT OUT...

WE'RE DOING NO SUCH THING! YOU'RE JUST GETTING SPOOKED LIKE THE REST OF US BECAUSE YISRAEL IS RIGHT AT OUR DOORSTEP, READY TO ATTACK...
I SUPPOSE YOU ARE RIGHT; I HAVE BEEN ON EDGE LATELY. C'MON, LET'S HAVE A SHOT OF THAT WHISKEY.
- - AND SHE SENT THEM AWAY, AND THEY DEPARTED.
RACHAV WAS RIGHT, IT'S TIME TO GET OUT OF YERICHO. THE SOLDIERS THINK WE ARE EN ROUTE TO THE YARDEN. WE SHOULD HEAD IN THE OPPOSITE DIRECTION TOWARD THE MOUNTAINS AND LAY LOW FOR A LITTLE WHILE.
AND SHE BOUND THE SCARLET CORD TO THE WINDOW.
– וַתְּשַׁלְּחֵם וַיֵּלֵכוּ וַתִּקְשֹׁר אֶת תִּקְוַת הַשָּׁנִי בַּחַלּוֹן.

22 AND THEY LEFT, AND CAME TO THE MOUNTAIN - -
MEANWHILE NEAR THE YARDEN...
I WANT YOU MEN TO **SEARCH** THIS ENTIRE AREA...
WE HAVE TO **CATCH** THOSE SPIES AND FORCE THEM TO TELL US YISRAEL'S **WAR** PLANS...
I HAVEN'T SEEN ANYONE, I'VE BEEN WALKING UP AND DOWN THIS **RIVERBANK** AND ALL I SEE ARE SHEEP...
... I UNDERSTAND YOU'RE LOOKING FOR TWO FOREIGNERS, BUT NO UNFAMILIAR FACES HAVE **PASSED** THROUGH THIS AREA.
I HATE COMING UP EMPTY-HANDED, BUT WE SEARCHED THIS AREA HIGH AND LOW AND NOT A **SINGLE** TRACE OF THESE PEOPLE...
IT'S LIKE THEY **VANISHED** INTO THIN AIR...
כב. וַיֵּלְכוּ וַיָּבֹאוּ הָהָרָה - -

- - AND STAYED THERE THREE DAYS, UNTIL THE PURSUERS RETURNED (TO YERICHO). THE PURSUERS SEARCHED ALONG THE ENTIRE WAY, BUT THEY DID NOT FIND THEM.
PINCHAS WE'VE BEEN OUT HERE FOR THREE DAYS. I THINK IT IS SAFE TO GO BACK TO YEHOSHUA...
I AGREE. HASHEM HAS BEEN WITH US THIS ENTIRE TIME. WE SHOULD HEAD BACK IN THE MORNING...
I THINK WHEN WE GET DOWN FROM THE MOUNTAIN WE SHOULD SPLIT UP.
THE CAANANIM ARE LOOKING FOR TWO MEN, NOT ONE...
THIS IS WHERE WE DEPART. MAY HASHEM GIVE YOU SAFE PASSAGE...
YOU, AS WELL, STAY SAFE. I WILL SEE YOU ON THE OTHER SIDE OF THE YARDEN.
- - וַיֵּשְׁבוּ שָׁם שְׁלֹשֶׁת יָמִים עַד שָׁבוּ הָרֹדְפִים וַיְבַקְשׁוּ הָרֹדְפִים בְּכָל הַדֶּרֶךְ וְלֹא מָצָאוּ.

SOMETIME LATER...
PINCHAS...?
KALEV...?
PINCHAS, I AM OVER HERE...
OK KALEV, I WILL BE RIGHT DOWN...
23 SO THE TWO MEN WERE REUNITED, AND DESCENDED FROM THE MOUNTAIN, AND CROSSED OVER (THE YARDEN) - -
כג. וַיָּשֻׁבוּ שְׁנֵי הָאֲנָשִׁים וַיֵּרְדוּ מֵהָהָר וַיַּעַבְרוּ - -

- - וַיָּבֹאוּ אֶל יְהוֹשֻׁעַ בִּן נוּן וַיְסַפְּרוּ לוֹ אֵת כָּל הַמֹּצְאוֹת אוֹתָם. **כד.** וַיֹּאמְרוּ
אֶל יְהוֹשֻׁעַ כִּי נָתַן ה' בְּיָדֵנוּ אֶת כָּל הָאָרֶץ וְגַם נָמֹגוּ כָּל יֹשְׁבֵי הָאָרֶץ מִפָּנֵינוּ.

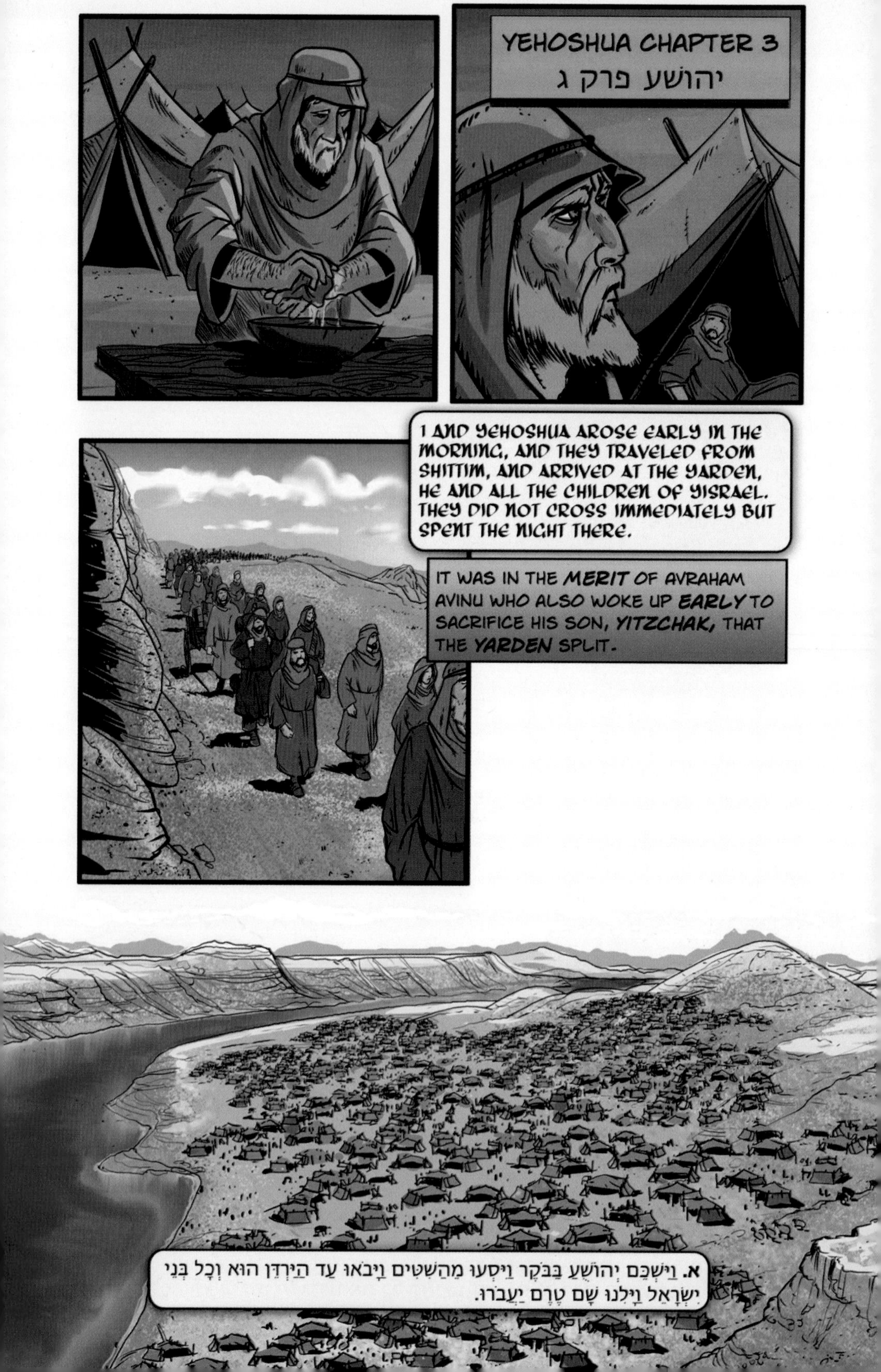
YEHOSHUA CHAPTER 3
יהושע פרק ג
1 AND YEHOSHUA AROSE EARLY IN THE MORNING, AND THEY TRAVELED FROM SHITTIM, AND ARRIVED AT THE YARDEN, HE AND ALL THE CHILDREN OF YISRAEL. THEY DID NOT CROSS IMMEDIATELY BUT SPENT THE NIGHT THERE.
IT WAS IN THE MERIT OF AVRAHAM AVINU WHO ALSO WOKE UP EARLY TO SACRIFICE HIS SON, YITZCHAK, THAT THE YARDEN SPLIT.
א. וַיַּשְׁכֵּם יְהוֹשֻׁעַ בַּבֹּקֶר וַיִּסְעוּ מֵהַשִּׁטִּים וַיָּבֹאוּ עַד הַיַּרְדֵּן הוּא וְכָל בְּנֵי
יִשְׂרָאֵל וַיָּלִנוּ שָׁם טֶרֶם יַעֲבֹרוּ.

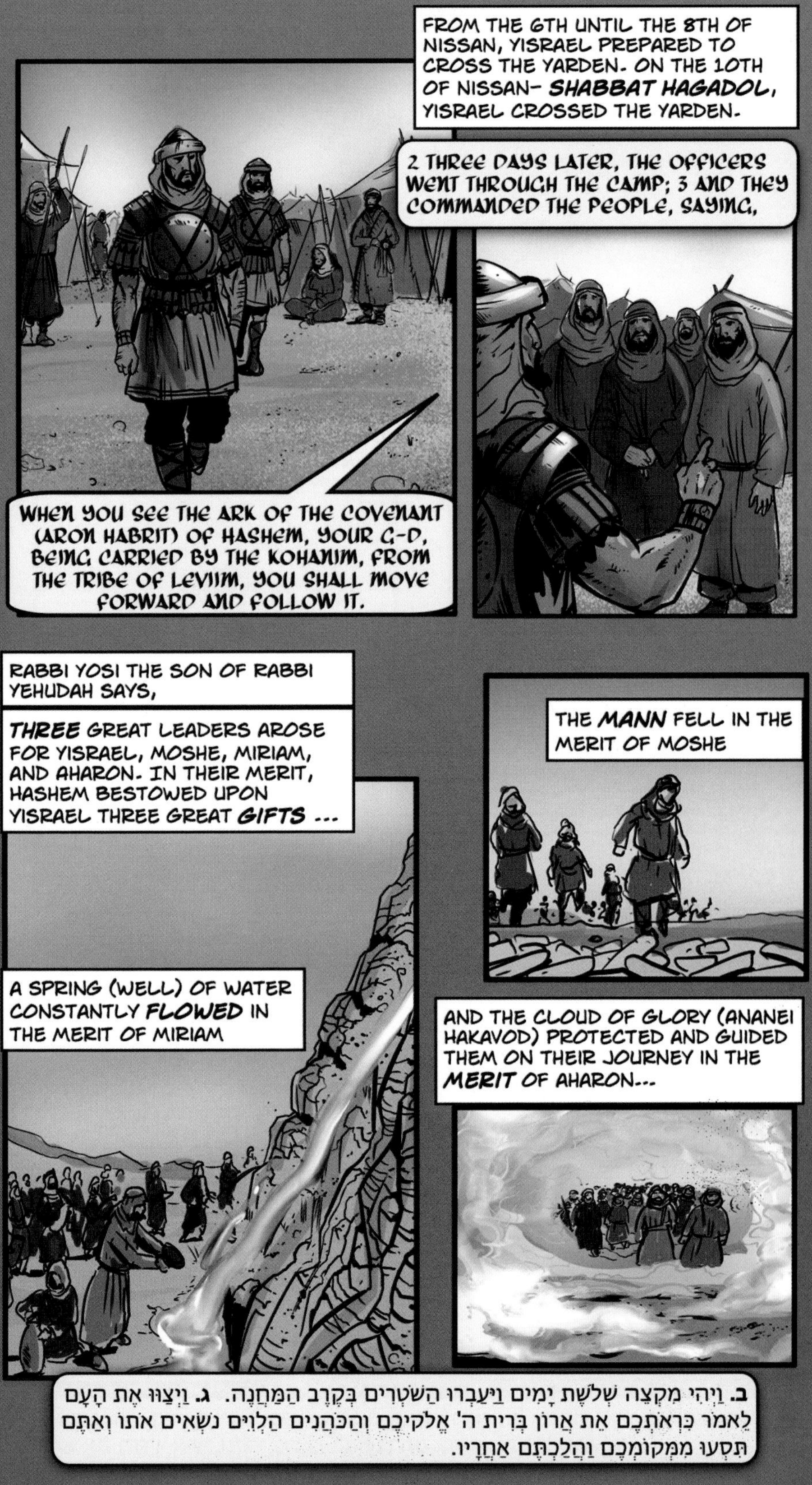
FROM THE 6TH UNTIL THE 8TH OF NISSAN, YISRAEL PREPARED TO CROSS THE YARDEN. ON THE 10TH OF NISSAN- SHABBAT HAGADOL, YISRAEL CROSSED THE YARDEN.
2 THREE DAYS LATER, THE OFFICERS WENT THROUGH THE CAMP; 3 AND THEY COMMANDED THE PEOPLE, SAYING,
WHEN YOU SEE THE ARK OF THE COVENANT (ARON HABRIT) OF HASHEM, YOUR G-D, BEING CARRIED BY THE KOHANIM, FROM THE TRIBE OF LEVIIM, YOU SHALL MOVE FORWARD AND FOLLOW IT.
RABBI YOSI THE SON OF RABBI YEHUDAH SAYS,
THREE GREAT LEADERS AROSE FOR YISRAEL, MOSHE, MIRIAM, AND AHARON. IN THEIR MERIT, HASHEM BESTOWED UPON YISRAEL THREE GREAT GIFTS ...
THE MANN FELL IN THE MERIT OF MOSHE
A SPRING (WELL) OF WATER CONSTANTLY FLOWED IN THE MERIT OF MIRIAM
AND THE CLOUD OF GLORY (ANANEI HAKAVOD) PROTECTED AND GUIDED THEM ON THEIR JOURNEY IN THE MERIT OF AHARON...

ב. וַיְהִי מִקְצֵה שְׁלֹשֶׁת יָמִים וַיַּעַבְרוּ הַשֹּׁטְרִים בְּקֶרֶב הַמַּחֲנֶה. **ג.** וַיְצַוּוּ אֶת הָעָם
לֵאמֹר כִּרְאֹתְכֶם אֵת אֲרוֹן בְּרִית ה' אֱלֹקֵיכֶם וְהַכֹּהֲנִים הַלְוִיִּם נֹשְׂאִים אֹתוֹ וְאַתֶּם
תִּסְעוּ מִמְּקוֹמְכֶם וַהֲלַכְתֶּם אַחֲרָיו.

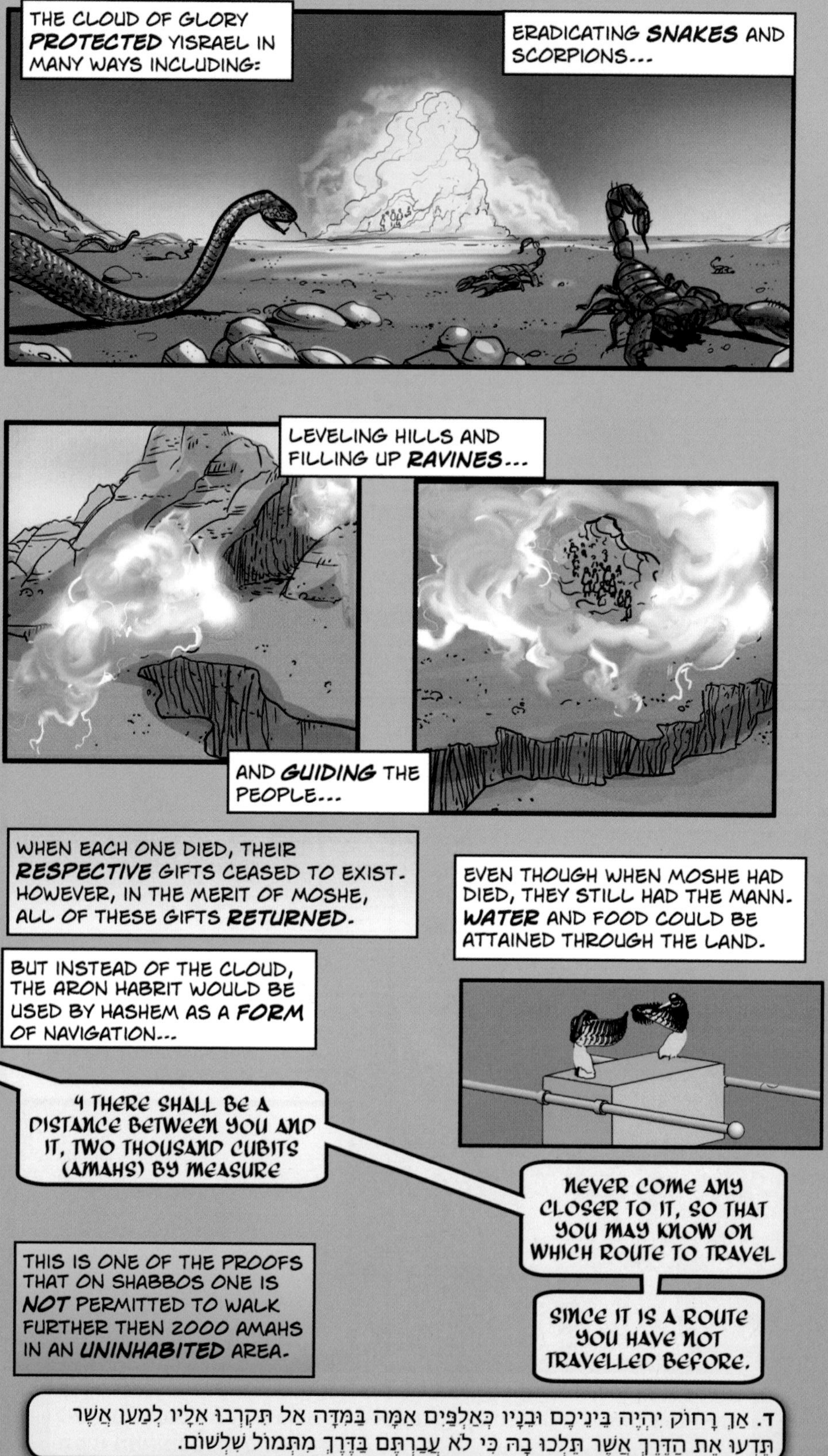

THE CLOUD OF GLORY PROTECTED YISRAEL IN MANY WAYS INCLUDING:
ERADICATING SNAKES AND SCORPIONS...
LEVELING HILLS AND FILLING UP RAVINES...
AND GUIDING THE PEOPLE...
WHEN EACH ONE DIED, THEIR RESPECTIVE GIFTS CEASED TO EXIST. HOWEVER, IN THE MERIT OF MOSHE, ALL OF THESE GIFTS RETURNED.
EVEN THOUGH WHEN MOSHE HAD DIED, THEY STILL HAD THE MANN. WATER AND FOOD COULD BE ATTAINED THROUGH THE LAND.
BUT INSTEAD OF THE CLOUD, THE ARON HABRIT WOULD BE USED BY HASHEM AS A FORM OF NAVIGATION...
4 THERE SHALL BE A DISTANCE BETWEEN YOU AND IT, TWO THOUSAND CUBITS (AMAHS) BY MEASURE
NEVER COME ANY CLOSER TO IT, SO THAT YOU MAY KNOW ON WHICH ROUTE TO TRAVEL
SINCE IT IS A ROUTE YOU HAVE NOT TRAVELLED BEFORE.
THIS IS ONE OF THE PROOFS THAT ON SHABBOS ONE IS NOT PERMITTED TO WALK FURTHER THEN 2000 AMAHS IN AN UNINHABITED AREA.
ד. אַךְ רָחוֹק יִהְיֶה בֵּינֵיכֶם וּבֵנָיו כְּאַלְפַּיִם אַמָּה בַּמִּדָּה אַל תִּקְרְבוּ אֵלָיו לְמַעַן אֲשֶׁר
תֵּדְעוּ אֶת הַדֶּרֶךְ אֲשֶׁר תֵּלְכוּ בָהּ כִּי לֹא עֲבַרְתֶּם בַּדֶּרֶךְ מִתְּמוֹל שִׁלְשׁוֹם.

5 AND YEHOSHUA SAID TO THE PEOPLE
SANCTIFY YOURSELVES; FOR TOMORROW HASHEM WILL DO WONDERS AMONG YOU.
6 AND YEHOSHUA SPOKE TO THE KOHANIM, SAYING:
WHEN YISRAEL WOULD TRAVEL IN THE DESERT, THE TRIBES (SHEVATIM) WERE DIVIDED INTO GROUPS OF THREE, SURROUNDING THE FOUR SIDES OF THE LEVIIM/KOHANIM WHO WERE CARRYING THE ARON. HOWEVER, DURING THE CROSSING OF THE YARDEN, THE KOHANIM AND LEVIIM LED.
EAST-YEHUDA, YISSASCHAR, ZEVULUN
SOUTH-REUVEN, SHIMON, GAD
WEST-EPHRAIM, MENASHE, BINYAMIN
NORTH-DAN, ASHER, NAFTALI
CENTER-LEVIIM/KOHANIM AND ARON HABRIT
CARRY THE ARON HABRIT, AND ADVANCE AHEAD OF THE PEOPLE.
ACCORDING TO THE RAMBAM, THE ARON HABRIT WAS ONLY CARRIED BY THE KOHANIM. THE RAMBAN'S OPINION IS THAT BOTH THE KOHANIM AND LEVIIM WERE ALLOWED TO CARRY THE ARON EXCEPT IN THREE CASES WHERE THE KOHANIM WERE REQUIRED TO CARRY THE ARON.
1. CROSSING THE YARDEN.
2. CIRCLING YERICHO, AND
3. ENTERING THE BEIT HAMIKDASH IN SHLOMO HAMELECH'S TIME.
AND THEY TOOK THE ARON HABRIT, AND MARCHED AHEAD OF THE PEOPLE

ה. וַיֹּאמֶר יְהוֹשֻׁעַ אֶל הָעָם הִתְקַדָּשׁוּ כִּי מָחָר יַעֲשֶׂה ה' בְּקִרְבְּכֶם נִפְלָאוֹת. **ו.** וַיֹּאמֶר
יְהוֹשֻׁעַ אֶל הַכֹּהֲנִים לֵאמֹר שְׂאוּ אֶת אֲרוֹן הַבְּרִית וְעִבְרוּ לִפְנֵי הָעָם וַיִּשְׂאוּ אֶת אֲרוֹן
הַבְּרִית וַיֵּלְכוּ לִפְנֵי הָעָם.

7 AND HASHEM SAID TO YEHOSHUA,
THIS DAY I WILL BEGIN TO MAKE YOU GREAT IN THE EYES OF ALL YISRAEL THAT THEY MAY KNOW THAT JUST AS I WAS WITH MOSHE, SO I WILL BE WITH YOU.
JUST AS I SPLIT THE SEA DURING MOSHE'S TIME, SO I WILL SPLIT THE YARDEN FOR YOU...
AND JUST AS THE SUN STOOD STILL FOR MOSHE DURING THE WAR AGAINST SICHON, SO TOO THE SUN WILL STAND STILL DURING YOUR WAR AGAINST GIVON...
8 AND YOU WILL COMMAND THE KOHANIM THAT CARRY THE ARON HABRIT SAYING: WHEN YOU REACH THE EDGE OF THE WATERS OF THE YARDEN, YOU WILL STAND STILL IN THE YARDEN.
CHRONOLOGICALLY THIS SHOULD HAVE BEEN WRITTEN IN THE FIRST CHAPTER OF YEHOSHUA. THIS IS ONE EXAMPLE THAT THE TORAH IS NOT NECESSARILY IN CHRONOLOGICAL ORDER...

ז. וַיֹּאמֶר ה' אֶל יְהוֹשֻׁעַ הַיּוֹם הַזֶּה אָחֵל גַּדֶּלְךָ בְּעֵינֵי כָּל יִשְׂרָאֵל אֲשֶׁר יֵדְעוּן כִּי כַּאֲשֶׁר הָיִיתִי
עִם מֹשֶׁה אֶהְיֶה עִמָּךְ. **ח.** וְאַתָּה תְּצַוֶּה אֶת הַכֹּהֲנִים נֹשְׂאֵי אֲרוֹן הַבְּרִית לֵאמֹר כְּבֹאֲכֶם עַד
קְצֵה מֵי הַיַּרְדֵּן בַּיַּרְדֵּן תַּעֲמֹדוּ.

9 AND YEHOSHUA SAID TO THE CHILDREN OF YISRAEL
COME CLOSE, AND HEAR THE WORDS OF HASHEM, YOUR G-D.'
HE CONFINED THEM ALL BETWEEN THE TWO STAVES OF THE ARON HABRIT. THIS MIRACLE THAT THE ENTIRE NATION STOOD BETWEEN THE POLES OF THE ARON WAS THE RESULT OF HASHEM'S PRESENCE (THE SHECHINA) EMBRACING AND BEING TOGETHER WITH YISRAEL. THIS MIRACLE ALSO OCCURRED WHEN ALL OF YISRAEL STOOD TOGETHER IN A CONFINED SPACE (WITH ROOM TO SPARE) IN THE BEIT HAMIKDASH WHERE THE SHECHINA IS PRESENT.
10 AND YEHOSHUA SAID,
FROM THIS YOU SHALL KNOW THAT THE LIVING G-D IS WITH YOU - -
ט. וַיֹּאמֶר יְהוֹשֻׁעַ אֶל בְּנֵי יִשְׂרָאֵל גֹּשׁוּ הֵנָּה וְשִׁמְעוּ אֶת דִּבְרֵי ה'
אֱלֹקֵיכֶם. י. וַיֹּאמֶר יְהוֹשֻׁעַ בְּזֹאת תֵּדְעוּן כִּי קֵל חַי בְּקִרְבְּכֶם - -

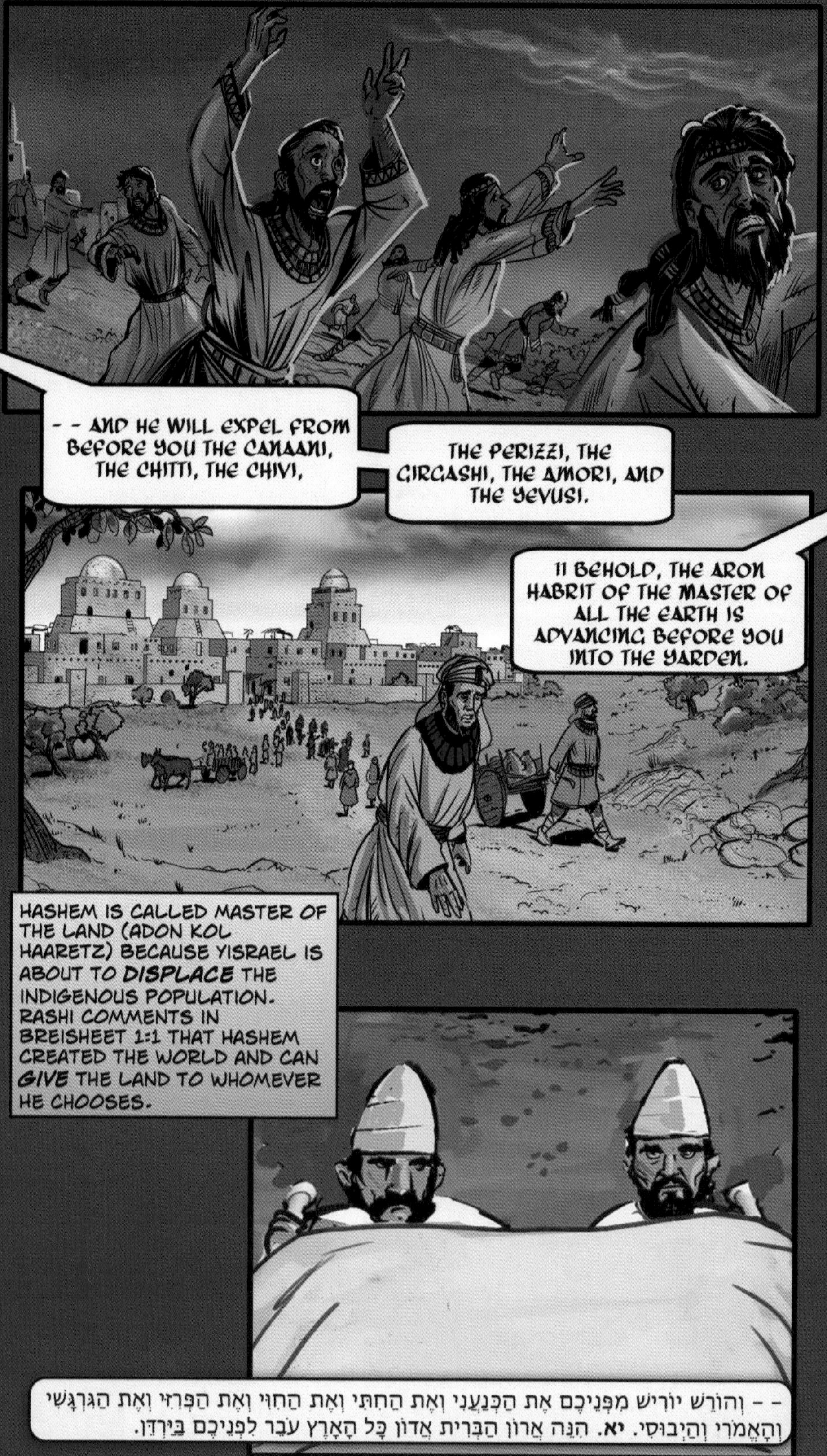
- - AND HE WILL EXPEL FROM BEFORE YOU THE CANAANI, THE CHITTI, THE CHIVI,
THE PERIZZI, THE GIRGASHI, THE AMORI, AND THE YEVUSI.
11 BEHOLD, THE ARON HABRIT OF THE MASTER OF ALL THE EARTH IS ADVANCING BEFORE YOU INTO THE YARDEN.
HASHEM IS CALLED MASTER OF THE LAND (ADON KOL HAARETZ) BECAUSE YISRAEL IS ABOUT TO *DISPLACE* THE INDIGENOUS POPULATION. RASHI COMMENTS IN BREISHEET 1:1 THAT HASHEM CREATED THE WORLD AND CAN *GIVE* THE LAND TO WHOMEVER HE CHOOSES.
– – וְהוֹרֵשׁ יוֹרִישׁ מִפְּנֵיכֶם אֶת הַכְּנַעֲנִי וְאֶת הַחִתִּי וְאֶת הַחִוִּי וְאֶת הַפְּרִזִּי וְאֶת הַגִּרְגָּשִׁי
וְהָאֱמֹרִי וְהַיְבוּסִי. יא. הִנֵּה אֲרוֹן הַבְּרִית אֲדוֹן כָּל הָאָרֶץ עֹבֵר לִפְנֵיכֶם בַּיַּרְדֵּן.

12 NOW TAKE TWELVE MEN OUT OF THE TRIBES OF YISRAEL, ONE MAN FROM EACH TRIBE.
AT THIS POINT THEY HAVE NO IDEA **WHY** OR WHAT THESE TWELVE MEN ARE SUPPOSED TO DO...

13 WHEN THE FEET OF THE KOHANIM CARRYING THE ARON OF HASHEM, MASTER OF THE EARTH, COME TO REST IN THE WATERS OF THE YARDEN, THEN THE WATERS OF THE YARDEN - THE WATERS COMING FROM UPSTREAM - WILL BE CUT OFF AND STAND IN A SINGLE MASS.
THE YARDEN ONLY SPLIT ON **ONE** SIDE. THE RIVER ON THE NORTH SIDE CONTINUED FLOWING HIGHER AND HIGHER CREATING A CONTINUOUS **COLUMN** OF WATER, WHILE THE SOUTH SIDE **EMPTIED** INTO THE DEAD SEA.

THIS IS IN **CONTRAST** TO THE YAM SUF THAT SPLIT DOWN THE **CENTER** WITH WATER ON EACH SIDE, STANDING IN TWO COLUMNS...

יב. וְעַתָּה קְחוּ לָכֶם שְׁנֵי עָשָׂר אִישׁ מִשִּׁבְטֵי יִשְׂרָאֵל אִישׁ אֶחָד אִישׁ אֶחָד לַשָּׁבֶט. **יג.** וְהָיָה
כְּנוֹחַ כַּפּוֹת רַגְלֵי הַכֹּהֲנִים נֹשְׂאֵי אֲרוֹן ה' אֲדוֹן כָּל הָאָרֶץ בְּמֵי הַיַּרְדֵּן מֵי הַיַּרְדֵּן יִכָּרֵתוּן הַמַּיִם
הַיֹּרְדִים מִלְמָעְלָה וְיַעַמְדוּ נֵד אֶחָד.

LOOKS LIKE TODAY IS THE **BIG** DAY. WE FINALLY GET TO **ENTER** THE LAND!
14 WHEN THE NATION SET OUT FROM THEIR ENCAMPMENT, TO CROSS OVER THE YARDEN, THE KOHANIM CARRYING THE ARON HABRIT WERE LEADING THE NATION.

יד. וַיְהִי בִּנְסֹעַ הָעָם מֵאָהֳלֵיהֶם לַעֲבֹר אֶת הַיַּרְדֵּן וְהַכֹּהֲנִים נֹשְׂאֵי
הָאָרוֹן הַבְּרִית לִפְנֵי הָעָם.

I DON'T UNDERSTAND, WE'RE SUPPOSED TO WALK **FORWARD**, BUT THE RIVER DIDN'T SPLIT YET!
15 NOW THE YARDEN KEEPS FLOWING ENTIRELY OVER ITS BANKS THROUGHOUT THE HARVEST SEASON. BUT AS SOON AS THE CARRIERS OF THE ARK REACHED THE YARDEN, AND THE FEET OF THE KOHANIM CARRYING THE ARK DIPPED INTO THE WATER AT ITS EDGE.
THIS IS THE **POWER** OF HASHEM.
I CAN'T BELIEVE I AM WORTHY ENOUGH TO BE A PART OF THIS **SPECTACULAR** MIRACLE...!
16 AND THE WATERS COMING DOWN FROM UPSTREAM ROSE INTO A SINGLE MASS A GREAT WAY OFF, AT ADAM, THE CITY NEXT TO TZARTHAN: AND THE WATERS FLOWING DOWNSTREAM TO THE SEA OF THE ARAVA (THE DEAD SEA) WERE CUT OFF COMPLETELY. SO THE NATION CROSSED OPPOSITE YERICHO.
טו. וּכְבוֹא נֹשְׂאֵי הָאָרוֹן עַד הַיַּרְדֵּן וְרַגְלֵי הַכֹּהֲנִים נֹשְׂאֵי הָאָרוֹן נִטְבְּלוּ בִּקְצֵה הַמָּיִם
וְהַיַּרְדֵּן מָלֵא עַל כָּל גְּדוֹתָיו כֹּל יְמֵי קָצִיר. **טז.** וַיַּעַמְדוּ הַמַּיִם הַיֹּרְדִים מִלְמַעְלָה קָמוּ נֵד
אֶחָד הַרְחֵק מְאֹד באדם (מֵאָדָם) הָעִיר אֲשֶׁר מִצַּד צָרְתָן וְהַיֹּרְדִים עַל יָם הָעֲרָבָה יָם
הַמֶּלַח תַּמּוּ נִכְרָתוּ וְהָעָם עָבְרוּ נֶגֶד יְרִיחוֹ.

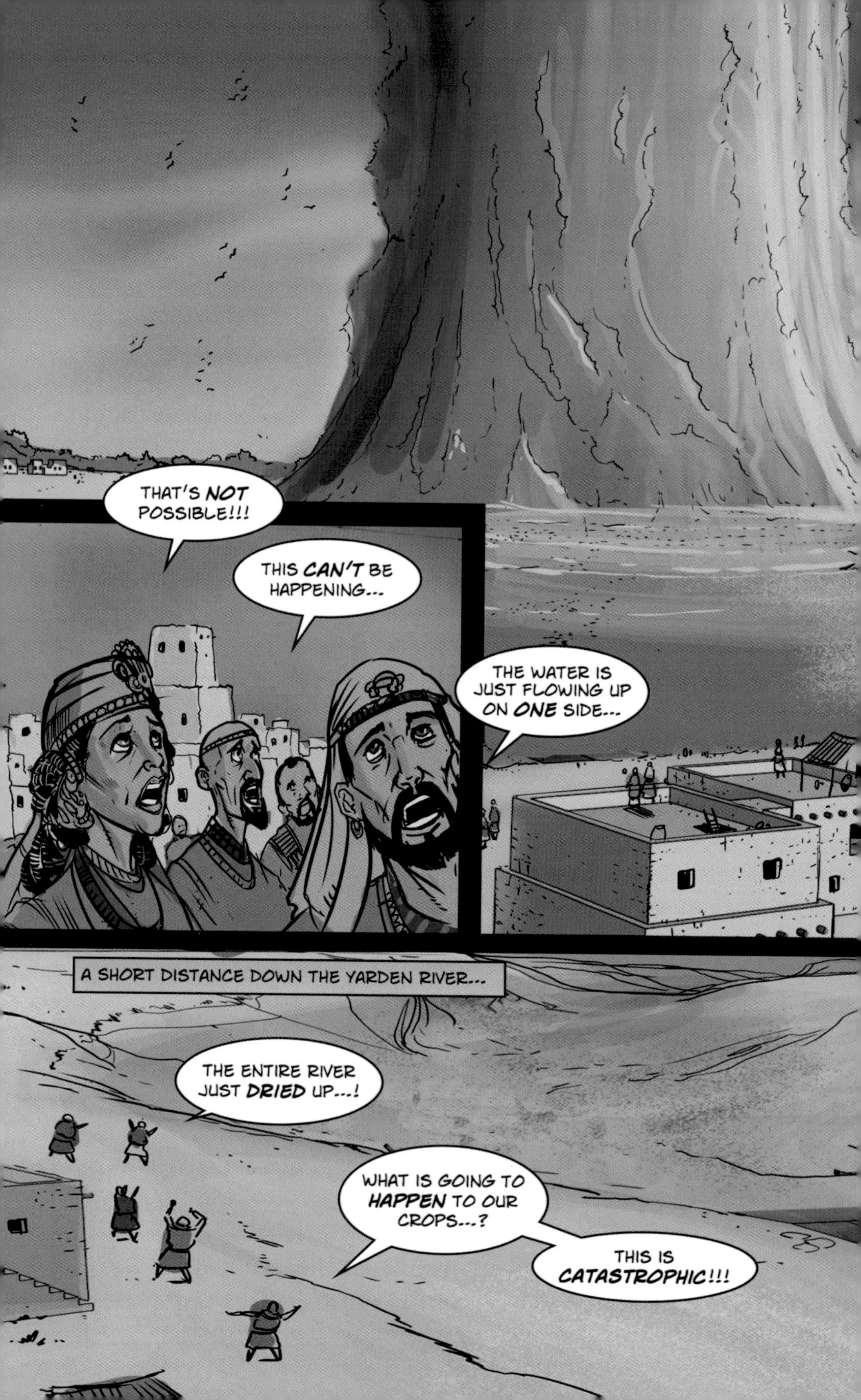

THAT'S **NOT** POSSIBLE!!!
THIS **CAN'T** BE HAPPENING...
THE WATER IS JUST FLOWING UP ON **ONE** SIDE...
A SHORT DISTANCE DOWN THE YARDEN RIVER...
THE ENTIRE RIVER JUST **DRIED** UP...!
WHAT IS GOING TO **HAPPEN** TO OUR CROPS...?
THIS IS **CATASTROPHIC**!!!

17 AND THE KOHANIM WHO CARRIED THE ARON HABRIT OF HASHEM, STOOD ON DRY LAND PRECISELY IN THE MIDST OF THE YARDEN, WHILE ALL OF YISRAEL CROSSED OVER ON DRY LAND, UNTIL THE ENTIRE NATION HAD FINISHED CROSSING THE YARDEN.
THE WATER IN THE YARDEN COMPLETELY DRIED UP (NOT MUDDY) TO ALLOW YISRAEL TO CROSS WITH EASE.
יז. וַיַּעַמְדוּ הַכֹּהֲנִים נֹשְׂאֵי הָאָרוֹן בְּרִית ה' בֶּחָרָבָה בְּתוֹךְ הַיַּרְדֵּן הָכֵן וְכָל יִשְׂרָאֵל עֹבְרִים
בֶּחָרָבָה עַד אֲשֶׁר תַּמּוּ כָּל הַגּוֹי לַעֲבֹר אֶת הַיַּרְדֵּן.

YEHOSHUA CHAPTER 4
יהושע פרק ד

1 AND IT WAS WHEN ALL THE NATION COMPLETELY PASSED THROUGH THE YARDEN, HASHEM SPOKE TO YEHOSHUA, SAYING 2 SELECT TWELVE MEN FROM THE PEOPLE, ONE MAN FROM EVERY TRIBE.
3. AND INSTRUCT THEM AS FOLLOWS: PICK UP TWELVE STONES FROM THE SPOT EXACTLY IN THE MIDDLE OF THE YARDEN, WHERE THE KOHANIM'S FEET ARE STANDING; TAKE THEM ALONG WITH YOU AND PLACE THEM AT THE LOCATION WHERE YOU WILL SPEND THE NIGHT.
א וַיְהִי כַּאֲשֶׁר תַּמּוּ כָל הַגּוֹי לַעֲבוֹר אֶת הַיַּרְדֵּן וַיֹּאמֶר ה' אֶל יְהוֹשֻׁעַ לֵאמֹר. **ב** קְחוּ
לָכֶם מִן הָעָם שְׁנֵים עָשָׂר אֲנָשִׁים אִישׁ אֶחָד אִישׁ אֶחָד מִשָּׁבֶט. **ג** וְצַוּוּ אוֹתָם לֵאמֹר שְׂאוּ
לָכֶם מִזֶּה מִתּוֹךְ הַיַּרְדֵּן מִמַּצַּב רַגְלֵי הַכֹּהֲנִים הָכִין שְׁתֵּים עֶשְׂרֵה אֲבָנִים וְהַעֲבַרְתֶּם
אוֹתָם עִמָּכֶם וְהִנַּחְתֶּם אוֹתָם בַּמָּלוֹן אֲשֶׁר-תָּלִינוּ בוֹ הַלָּיְלָה.

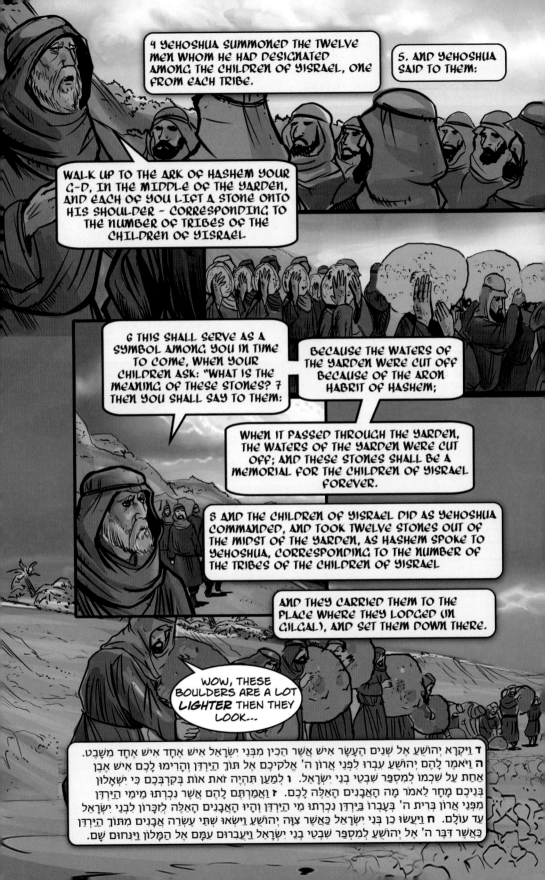

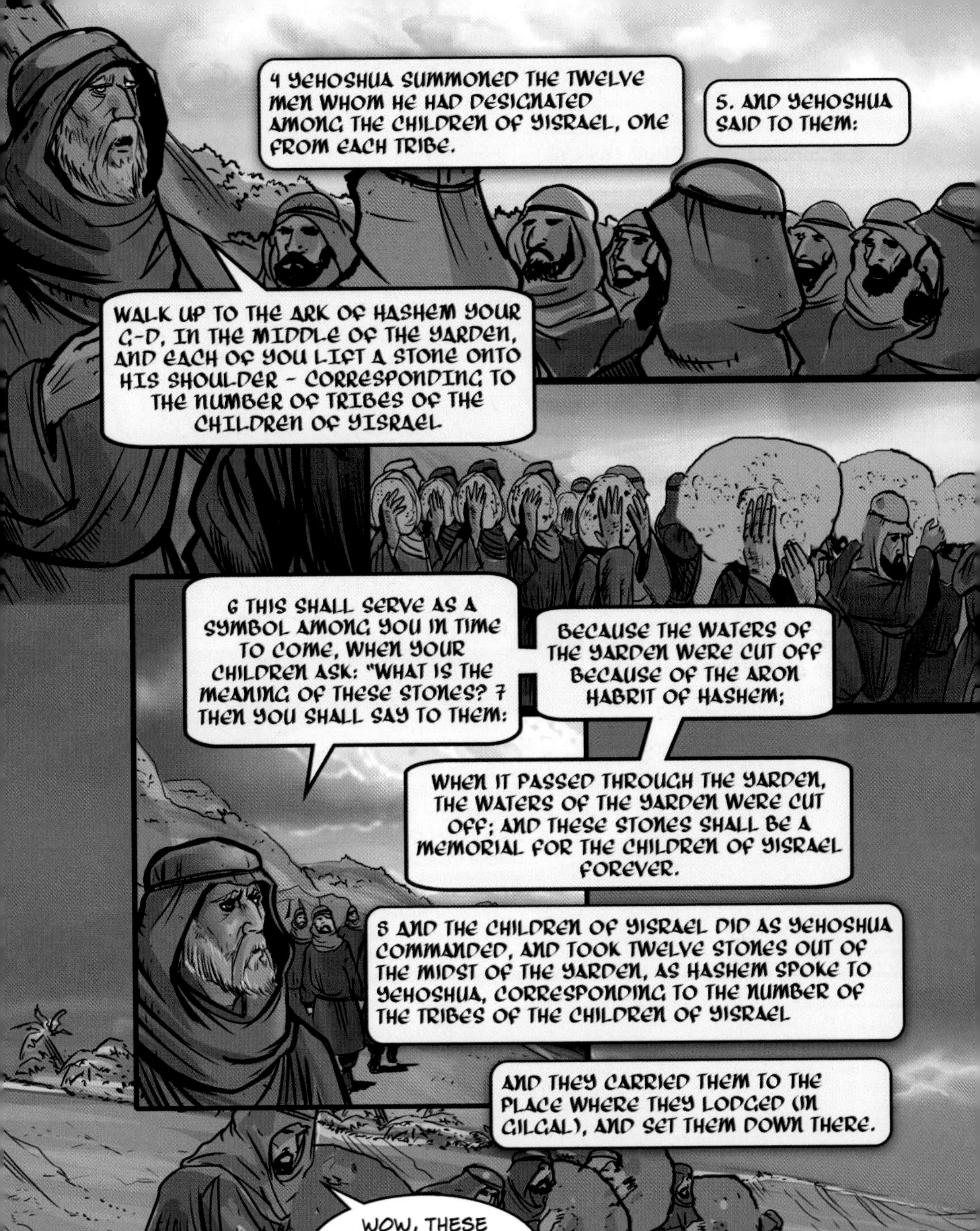
4 YEHOSHUA SUMMONED THE TWELVE MEN WHOM HE HAD DESIGNATED AMONG THE CHILDREN OF YISRAEL, ONE FROM EACH TRIBE.
5. AND YEHOSHUA SAID TO THEM:
WALK UP TO THE ARK OF HASHEM YOUR G-D, IN THE MIDDLE OF THE YARDEN, AND EACH OF YOU LIFT A STONE ONTO HIS SHOULDER - CORRESPONDING TO THE NUMBER OF TRIBES OF THE CHILDREN OF YISRAEL
6 THIS SHALL SERVE AS A SYMBOL AMONG YOU IN TIME TO COME, WHEN YOUR CHILDREN ASK: "WHAT IS THE MEANING OF THESE STONES? 7 THEN YOU SHALL SAY TO THEM:
BECAUSE THE WATERS OF THE YARDEN WERE CUT OFF BECAUSE OF THE ARON HABRIT OF HASHEM;
WHEN IT PASSED THROUGH THE YARDEN, THE WATERS OF THE YARDEN WERE CUT OFF; AND THESE STONES SHALL BE A MEMORIAL FOR THE CHILDREN OF YISRAEL FOREVER.
8 AND THE CHILDREN OF YISRAEL DID AS YEHOSHUA COMMANDED, AND TOOK TWELVE STONES OUT OF THE MIDST OF THE YARDEN, AS HASHEM SPOKE TO YEHOSHUA, CORRESPONDING TO THE NUMBER OF THE TRIBES OF THE CHILDREN OF YISRAEL
AND THEY CARRIED THEM TO THE PLACE WHERE THEY LODGED (IN GILGAL), AND SET THEM DOWN THERE.
WOW, THESE BOULDERS ARE A LOT **LIGHTER** THEN THEY LOOK...

ד וַיִּקְרָא יְהוֹשֻׁעַ אֶל שְׁנֵים הֶעָשָׂר אִישׁ אֲשֶׁר הֵכִין מִבְּנֵי יִשְׂרָאֵל אִישׁ אֶחָד אִישׁ אֶחָד מִשָּׁבֶט.
ה וַיֹּאמֶר לָהֶם יְהוֹשֻׁעַ עִבְרוּ לִפְנֵי אֲרוֹן ה' אֱלֹקיכֶם אֶל תּוֹךְ הַיַּרְדֵּן וְהָרִימוּ לָכֶם אִישׁ אֶבֶן
אַחַת עַל שִׁכְמוֹ לְמִסְפַּר שִׁבְטֵי בְנֵי יִשְׂרָאֵל. ו לְמַעַן תִּהְיֶה זֹאת אוֹת בְּקִרְבְּכֶם כִּי יִשְׁאָלוּן
בְּנֵיכֶם מָחָר לֵאמֹר מָה הָאֲבָנִים הָאֵלֶּה לָכֶם. ז וַאֲמַרְתֶּם לָהֶם אֲשֶׁר נִכְרְתוּ מֵימֵי הַיַּרְדֵּן
מִפְּנֵי אֲרוֹן בְּרִית ה' בְּעָבְרוֹ בַּיַּרְדֵּן נִכְרְתוּ מֵי הַיַּרְדֵּן וְהָיוּ הָאֲבָנִים הָאֵלֶּה לְזִכָּרוֹן לִבְנֵי יִשְׂרָאֵל
עַד עוֹלָם. ח וַיַּעֲשׂוּ כֵן בְּנֵי יִשְׂרָאֵל כַּאֲשֶׁר צִוָּה יְהוֹשֻׁעַ וַיִּשְׂאוּ שְׁתֵּי עֶשְׂרֵה אֲבָנִים מִתּוֹךְ הַיַּרְדֵּן
כַּאֲשֶׁר דִּבֶּר ה' אֶל יְהוֹשֻׁעַ לְמִסְפַּר שִׁבְטֵי בְנֵי יִשְׂרָאֵל וַיַּעֲבִרוּם עִמָּם אֶל הַמָּלוֹן וַיַּנִּחוּם שָׁם.

STILL IN THE YARDEN, PRIOR TO GOING TO GILGAL...
9. YEHOSHUA ALSO SET UP TWELVE (OTHER) STONES WITHIN THE YARDEN, IN THE PLACE WHERE THE FEET OF THE KOHANIM THAT BORE THE ARON HABRIT STOOD; AND THEY REMAIN THERE TO THIS DAY.
THESE **ADDITIONAL** TWELVE STONES THAT YEHOSHUA SET UP WITHIN THE YARDEN ARE A **SEPARATE** MEMORIAL...
A MONUMENT TO PUBLICIZE TO THE WORLD, THAT THIS IS THE PLACE THAT THE KOHANIM **STOOD** AS YISRAEL CROSSED THROUGH THE YARDEN.
10 AND THE KOHANIM, THE BEARERS OF THE ARON HABRIT, WERE STANDING IN THE MIDDLE OF THE YARDEN UNTIL ALL THE INSTRUCTIONS THAT HASHEM HAD ORDERED YEHOSHUA TO CONVEY TO THE PEOPLE HAD BEEN CARRIED OUT. AND SO THE PEOPLE SPEEDILY CROSSED OVER, JUST AS MOSHE HAD ASSURED YEHOSHUA IN HIS CHARGE TO HIM. – –
KNOW **WHY** YOU ARE CROSSING THE YARDEN; IT IS ON CONDITION THAT YOU DISPOSSESS THE INHABITANTS OF THE **LAND** FROM BEFORE YOU; AS IT IS STATED IN BAMIDBAR 33:52
YOU SHALL DRIVE OUT **ALL** THE INHABITANTS OF THE LAND FROM BEFORE YOU, **DESTROY** ALL THEIR TEMPLES, DESTROY THEIR MOLTEN IDOLS, AND **DEMOLISH** THEIR HIGH PLACES.
IF YOU ACCEPT THIS UPON YOURSELVES, **WELL** AND GOOD OTHERWISE THE WATER WILL **RETURN** AND DROWN YOU (RIGHT HERE, RIGHT NOW...)
ט. וּשְׁתֵּים עֶשְׂרֵה אֲבָנִים הֵקִים יְהוֹשֻׁעַ בְּתוֹךְ הַיַּרְדֵּן תַּחַת מַצַּב רַגְלֵי הַכֹּהֲנִים נֹשְׂאֵי אֲרוֹן
הַבְּרִית וַיִּהְיוּ שָׁם עַד הַיּוֹם הַזֶּה. י וְהַכֹּהֲנִים נֹשְׂאֵי הָאָרוֹן עֹמְדִים בְּתוֹךְ הַיַּרְדֵּן עַד תֹּם כָּל
הַדָּבָר אֲשֶׁר צִוָּה ה' אֶת יְהוֹשֻׁעַ לְדַבֵּר אֶל הָעָם כְּכֹל אֲשֶׁר צִוָּה מֹשֶׁה אֶת יְהוֹשֻׁעַ – –

- - AND THE PEOPLE HURRIED AND PASSED THROUGH.
11 AND IT WAS WHEN ALL THE PEOPLE FINISHED CROSSING, THAT THE ARON HABRIT OF HASHEM AND THE KOHANIM ADVANCED TO THE HEAD OF THE PEOPLE.
12 AND THE CHILDREN OF REUVEN, THE CHILDREN OF GAD, AND THE HALF TRIBE OF MENASHE, PASSED OVER, ARMED BEFORE THE CHILDREN OF YISRAEL, AS MOSHE HAD SPOKEN TO THEM; 13 ABOUT FORTY THOUSAND ARMED FOR WAR, WENT FOR THE SAKE OF HASHEM TO DO BATTLE, AT THE PLAINS OF YERICHO.
- - וַיְמַהֲרוּ הָעָם וַיַּעֲבֹרוּ. **יא** וַיְהִי כַּאֲשֶׁר תַּם כָּל הָעָם לַעֲבוֹר וַיַּעֲבֹר
אֲרוֹן ה' וְהַכֹּהֲנִים לִפְנֵי הָעָם. **יב** וַיַּעַבְרוּ בְּנֵי רְאוּבֵן וּבְנֵי גָד וַחֲצִי שֵׁבֶט
הַמְנַשֶּׁה חֲמֻשִׁים לִפְנֵי בְּנֵי יִשְׂרָאֵל כַּאֲשֶׁר דִּבֶּר אֲלֵיהֶם מֹשֶׁה. **יג** כְּאַרְבָּעִים
אֶלֶף חֲלוּצֵי הַצָּבָא עָבְרוּ לִפְנֵי ה' לַמִּלְחָמָה אֶל עַרְבוֹת יְרִיחוֹ.

14 ON THAT DAY HASHEM EXALTED YEHOSHUA IN THE SIGHT OF ALL YISRAEL; AND THEY REVERED HIM, AS THEY REVERED MOSHE, ALL THE DAYS OF HIS LIFE.
THE *PREVIOUS* VERSES WERE THE GENERAL ACCOUNTING OF THE YARDEN CROSSING. THE NEXT VERSES WILL GIVE A MORE *DETAILED* UNDERSTANDING...
יד בַּיּוֹם הַהוּא גִּדַּל ה' אֶת יְהוֹשֻׁעַ בְּעֵינֵי כָּל יִשְׂרָאֵל וַיִּרְאוּ אֹתוֹ כַּאֲשֶׁר יָרְאוּ
אֶת מֹשֶׁה כָּל יְמֵי חַיָּיו.

15 AND HASHEM SPOKE TO YEHOSHUA, SAYING,
16 'COMMAND THE KOHANIM THAT BEAR THE ARK OF THE TESTIMONY TO COME UP OUT OF THE YARDEN.'
WE SEE AN INCREDIBLE INSIGHT FROM THE FACT THAT IT SAYS HERE; THAT THE KOHANIM SHOULD "COME UP" AS OPPOSED TO "CROSS THROUGH THE YARDEN"- IT IS TELLING US THAT THE KOHANIM WERE **STILL** ON THE EAST SIDE OF THE YARDEN AND NEVER CROSSED THROUGH TO THE WEST SIDE LIKE YISRAEL DID. "COME UP" NOT "CROSS THROUGH."
17 YEHOSHUA THEREFORE COMMANDED THE KOHANIM, SAYING:
COME UP OUT OF THE YARDEN
18, AS SOON AS THE KOHANIM WHO WERE CARRYING THE ARK OF HASHEM CAME UP OUT OF THE YARDEN,
AND THE FEET OF THE KOHANIM STEPPED ONTO THE DRY GROUND, THE WATERS OF THE YARDEN RESUMED THEIR COURSE, FLOWING OVER ITS ENTIRE BED AS BEFORE.
טו וַיֹּאמֶר ה' אֶל יְהוֹשֻׁעַ לֵאמֹר. **טז** צַוֵּה אֶת הַכֹּהֲנִים נֹשְׂאֵי אֲרוֹן הָעֵדוּת וְיַעֲלוּ מִן
הַיַּרְדֵּן. **יז** וַיְצַו יְהוֹשֻׁעַ אֶת הַכֹּהֲנִים לֵאמֹר עֲלוּ מִן הַיַּרְדֵּן. **יח** וַיְהִי בעלות (כַּעֲלוֹת)
הַכֹּהֲנִים נֹשְׂאֵי אֲרוֹן בְּרִית ה' מִתּוֹךְ הַיַּרְדֵּן נִתְּקוּ כַּפּוֹת רַגְלֵי הַכֹּהֲנִים אֶל הֶחָרָבָה
וַיָּשֻׁבוּ מֵי הַיַּרְדֵּן לִמְקוֹמָם וַיֵּלְכוּ כִתְמוֹל שִׁלְשׁוֹם עַל כָּל גְּדוֹתָיו.

THEY ARE ON THE OTHER SIDE OF THE YARDEN, HOW ARE THEY GOING TO CROSS OVER...?
WE'RE NOT JUST GOING TO LEAVE THEM STRANDED!
SINCE THE KOHANIM WERE LEFT ON THE EAST SIDE OF THE YARDEN, THE ARON HABRIT OF HASHEM LIFTED THE KOHANIM AND MIRACULOUSLY DELIVERED THEM TO THE WESTERN SIDE OF THE YARDEN WHERE YISRAEL WAS WAITING...
EVERYONE, HOLD ON TIGHT AND DON'T LOOK DOWN...!
WHAT A SIGHT! THE ARON CARRIES THE KOHANIM AND NOT THE OTHER WAY AROUND...

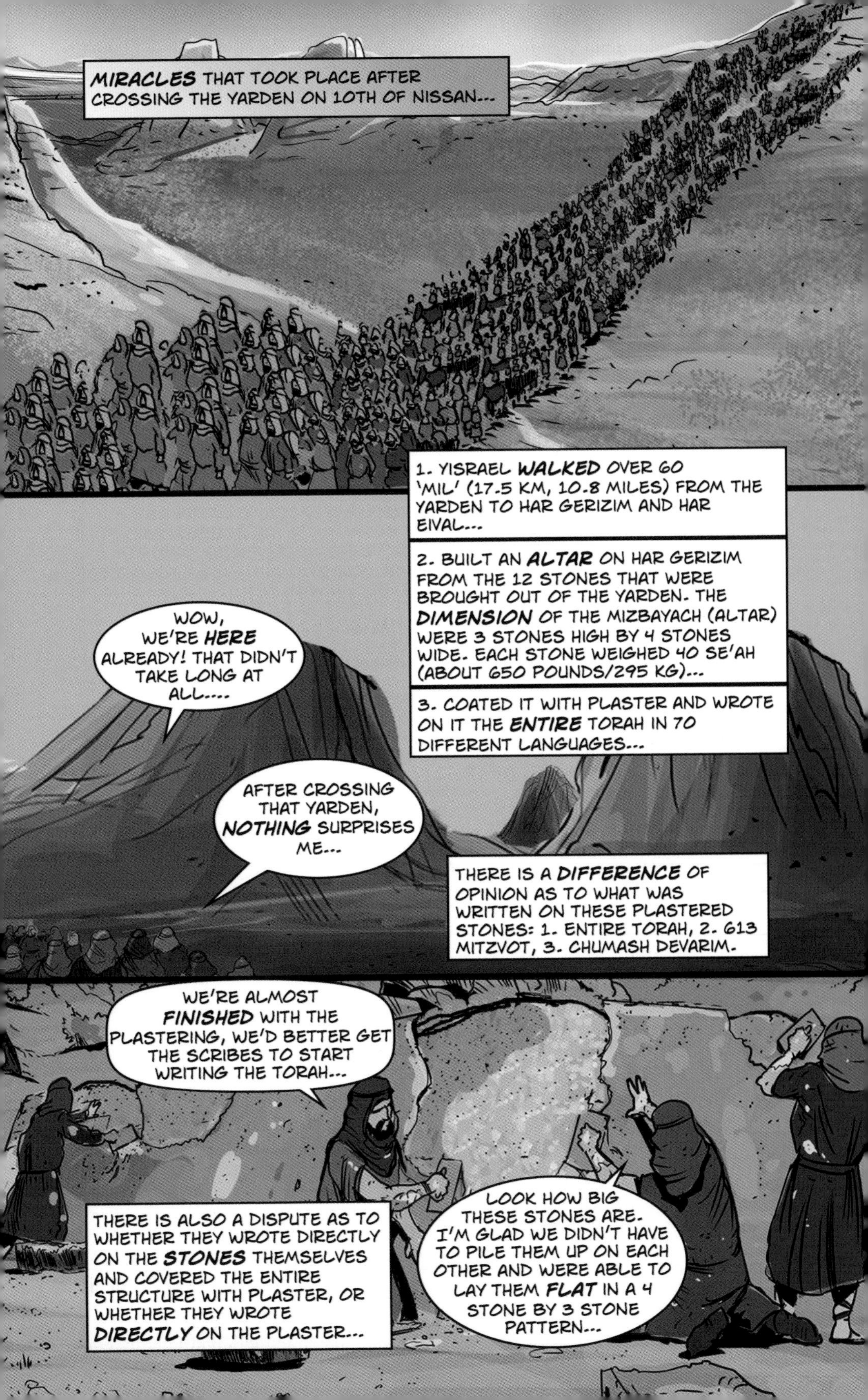
MIRACLES THAT TOOK PLACE AFTER CROSSING THE YARDEN ON 10TH OF NISSAN...
1. YISRAEL WALKED OVER 60 'MIL' (17.5 KM, 10.8 MILES) FROM THE YARDEN TO HAR GERIZIM AND HAR EIVAL...
2. BUILT AN ALTAR ON HAR GERIZIM FROM THE 12 STONES THAT WERE BROUGHT OUT OF THE YARDEN. THE DIMENSION OF THE MIZBAYACH (ALTAR) WERE 3 STONES HIGH BY 4 STONES WIDE. EACH STONE WEIGHED 40 SE'AH (ABOUT 650 POUNDS/295 KG)...
3. COATED IT WITH PLASTER AND WROTE ON IT THE ENTIRE TORAH IN 70 DIFFERENT LANGUAGES...
WOW, WE'RE HERE ALREADY! THAT DIDN'T TAKE LONG AT ALL....
AFTER CROSSING THAT YARDEN, NOTHING SURPRISES ME...
THERE IS A DIFFERENCE OF OPINION AS TO WHAT WAS WRITTEN ON THESE PLASTERED STONES: 1. ENTIRE TORAH, 2. 613 MITZVOT, 3. CHUMASH DEVARIM.
WE'RE ALMOST FINISHED WITH THE PLASTERING, WE'D BETTER GET THE SCRIBES TO START WRITING THE TORAH...
THERE IS ALSO A DISPUTE AS TO WHETHER THEY WROTE DIRECTLY ON THE STONES THEMSELVES AND COVERED THE ENTIRE STRUCTURE WITH PLASTER, OR WHETHER THEY WROTE DIRECTLY ON THE PLASTER...
LOOK HOW BIG THESE STONES ARE. I'M GLAD WE DIDN'T HAVE TO PILE THEM UP ON EACH OTHER AND WERE ABLE TO LAY THEM FLAT IN A 4 STONE BY 3 STONE PATTERN...

MORE MIRACLES THAT TOOK PLACE AFTER CROSSING THE YARDEN ON 10TH OF NISSAN...

4. ***OFFERED*** OLAH'S AND SHELOMIM ON THE MIZBAYACH, AND THEN ATE, DRANK AND REJOICED...

THIS IS A ***GREAT*** FEAST...
I KNOW, AND IT'S ***STILL*** ONLY THE MIDDLE OF THE DAY...

5. ***PRONOUNCED*** THE BLESSINGS AND CURSES ON HAR GERIZIM AND HAR EVAL...

SIX TRIBES ***ASCENDED*** TO HAR GERIZIM AND SIX TO HAR EVAL. THE KOHANIM , THE LEVIIM AND THE ARON STOOD BELOW IN THE ***MIDDLE***. THE LEVIIM ***TURNED*** THEIR FACES TOWARDS HAR GERIZIM AND BEGAN WITH THE BLESSINGS. BOTH SETS OF TRIBES ***ANSWERED*** "AMEN". THEN THE LEVIIM TURNED THEIR FACES TOWARDS HAR EVAL AND BEGAN WITH THE CURSE. AGAIN BOTH SETS OF TRIBES ANSWERED "AMEN". IT WOULD ***CONTINUE*** IN THIS MANNER UNTIL THE VERY LAST CURSE...

THERE ARE TWO OPINIONS AS TO WHEN THE BLESSING AND CURSES OF HAR GERIZIM AND HAR EVAL TOOK PLACE.

ONE STATES IT TOOK PLACE AFTER THE CROSSING OF THE YARDEN, AND THE OTHER STATES IT TOOK PLACE AFTER THE BATTLE OF AI IN CHAPTER 8.

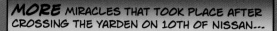

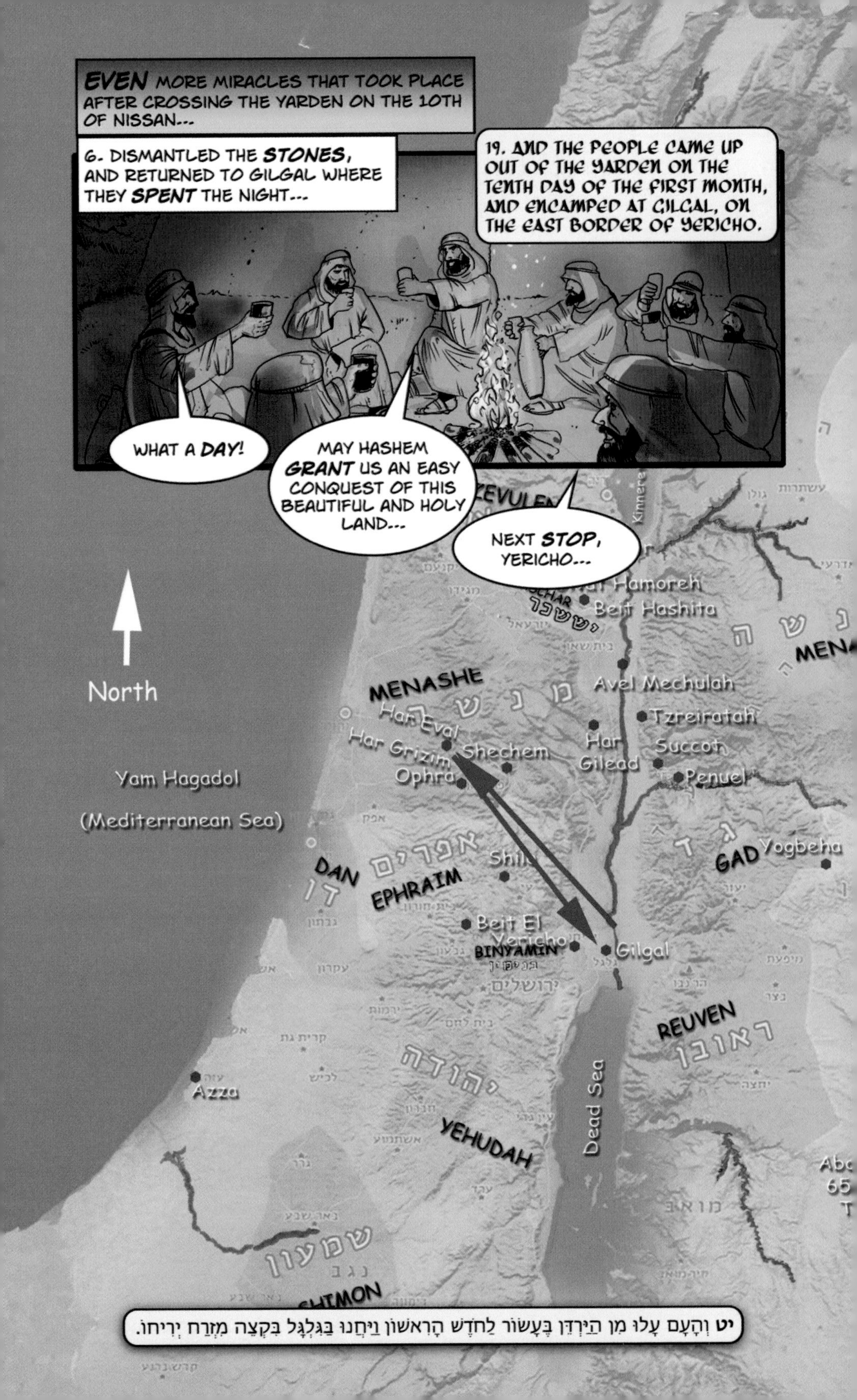

EVEN MORE MIRACLES THAT TOOK PLACE AFTER CROSSING THE YARDEN ON THE 10TH OF NISSAN...
6. DISMANTLED THE STONES, AND RETURNED TO GILGAL WHERE THEY SPENT THE NIGHT...
19. AND THE PEOPLE CAME UP OUT OF THE YARDEN ON THE TENTH DAY OF THE FIRST MONTH, AND ENCAMPED AT GILGAL, ON THE EAST BORDER OF YERICHO.
WHAT A DAY!
MAY HASHEM GRANT US AN EASY CONQUEST OF THIS BEAUTIFUL AND HOLY LAND...
NEXT STOP, YERICHO...
North
ZEVULEN
Kinneret
Hamoreh
Beit Hashita
יששכר
MENASHE
מנשה
Avel Mechulah
Tzreiratah
Har Eval
Har Grizim
Shechem
Har Gilead
Succot
Penuel
Ophra
Yam Hagadol
(Mediterranean Sea)
DAN
דן
אפרים
EPHRAIM
Shiloh
GAD
גד
Yogbeha
Beit El
Yericho
BINYAMIN
Gilgal
ירושלים
REUVEN
ראובן
יהודה
Azza
YEHUDAH
Dead Sea
מואב
שמעון
SHIMON
יט וְהָעָם עָלוּ מִן הַיַּרְדֵּן בֶּעָשׂוֹר לַחֹדֶשׁ הָרִאשׁוֹן וַיַּחֲנוּ בַּגִּלְגָּל בִּקְצֵה מִזְרַח יְרִיחוֹ.

20 AND THOSE TWELVE STONES, WHICH THEY TOOK OUT OF THE YARDEN, YEHOSHUA SET UP IN GILGAL.
21 AND HE SPOKE TO THE CHILDREN OF YISRAEL, SAYING
IN TIME TO COME, WHEN YOUR CHILDREN WILL ASK THEIR FATHERS SAYING, "WHAT IS THE MEANING OF THESE STONES?"
22 THEN YOU SHALL LET YOUR CHILDREN KNOW, SAYING,
"YISRAEL CROSSED THE YARDEN ON DRY LAND.
23 FOR HASHEM YOUR G-D DRIED UP THE WATERS OF YARDEN FROM BEFORE YOU, UNTIL YOU CROSSED.
AS HASHEM YOUR G-D DID TO THE REED SEA, WHICH HE DRIED UP FROM BEFORE US, UNTIL WE CROSSED,
24 THAT ALL THE PEOPLE OF THE EARTH MAY KNOW HOW MIGHTY IS THE HAND OF HASHEM; THAT YOU WILL FEAR HASHEM YOUR G-D FOREVER."

כ וְאֵת שְׁתֵּים עֶשְׂרֵה הָאֲבָנִים הָאֵלֶּה אֲשֶׁר לָקְחוּ מִן הַיַּרְדֵּן הֵקִים יְהוֹשֻׁעַ בַּגִּלְגָּל. **כא**
וַיֹּאמֶר אֶל בְּנֵי יִשְׂרָאֵל לֵאמֹר אֲשֶׁר יִשְׁאָלוּן בְּנֵיכֶם מָחָר אֶת אֲבוֹתָם לֵאמֹר מָה הָאֲבָנִים
הָאֵלֶּה. **כב** וְהוֹדַעְתֶּם אֶת בְּנֵיכֶם לֵאמֹר בַּיַּבָּשָׁה עָבַר יִשְׂרָאֵל אֶת הַיַּרְדֵּן הַזֶּה. **כג** אֲשֶׁר
הוֹבִישׁ ה' אֱלֹקֵיכֶם אֶת מֵי הַיַּרְדֵּן מִפְּנֵיכֶם עַד עָבְרְכֶם כַּאֲשֶׁר עָשָׂה ה' אֱלֹקֵיכֶם לְיַם סוּף
אֲשֶׁר הוֹבִישׁ מִפָּנֵינוּ עַד עָבְרֵנוּ. **כד** לְמַעַן דַּעַת כָּל עַמֵּי הָאָרֶץ אֶת יַד ה' כִּי חֲזָקָה הִיא
לְמַעַן יְרָאתֶם אֶת ה' אֱלֹקֵיכֶם כָּל הַיָּמִים.

YEHOSHUA CHAPTER 5
יהושע פרק ה

LOOK AT THAT...! THE RIVER IS RISING ON ONE SIDE. IT'S GROWING HIGHER AND HIGHER LIKE A BIG COLUMN OF WATER...
I HAVE SOME DISTURBING NEWS YOUR MAJESTY. YISRAEL HAS CROSSED OVER THE YARDEN.
EVEN THOUGH THEY WERE IN THE DESERT FOR 40 YEARS, WE KNEW THIS DAY WOULD COME...
IT IS MUCH WORSE THAN THAT. OUR PEOPLE ARE PANICKING ABOUT HOW THEY CROSSED OVER THE YARDEN...
I KNOW, I HEARD G-D CREATED A MIRACULOUS EVENT BY SPLITTING THE YARDEN, AND NOW THE WHOLE NATION IS FILLED WITH TERROR...
1 AND IT CAME TO PASS, WHEN ALL THE KINGS OF THE AMORI, ON THE WESTERN SIDE OF THE YARDEN,
AND WHEN ALL THE KINGS OF THE CANAANI, THAT WERE BY THE SEA, HEARD THAT HASHEM HAD DRIED UP THE WATERS OF THE YARDEN FOR THE SAKE OF THE CHILDREN OF YISRAEL, UNTIL THEY CROSSED OVER. THEIR HEARTS MELTED, AND NO SPIRIT WAS LEFT IN THEM BECAUSE OF YISRAEL.
SIRE, WE NEED NOT WORRY ABOUT YISRAEL... NO ONE HAS EVER PENETRATED THE WALLS OF YERICHO...
I KNOW ABOUT OUR WALLS AND OUR PAST, BUT WE HAVE NEVER GONE TO BATTLE WITH THE G-D OF YISRAEL!

א וַיְהִי כִשְׁמֹעַ כָּל מַלְכֵי הָאֱמֹרִי אֲשֶׁר בְּעֵבֶר הַיַּרְדֵּן יָמָּה וְכָל מַלְכֵי הַכְּנַעֲנִי אֲשֶׁר עַל הַיָּם
אֵת אֲשֶׁר הוֹבִישׁ ה' אֶת מֵי הַיַּרְדֵּן מִפְּנֵי בְנֵי יִשְׂרָאֵל עַד עברנו (עָבְרָם) וַיִּמַּס לְבָבָם וְלֹא הָיָה
בָם עוֹד רוּחַ מִפְּנֵי בְּנֵי יִשְׂרָאֵל.

2 AT THAT TIME HASHEM SAID TO YEHOSHUA: 'MAKE KNIVES OF STONE,
THIS ONE IS FOR ME, I AM GOING TO MAKE IT **EXTRA** SHARP...
AND CIRCUMCISE THE CHILDREN OF YISRAEL A SECOND TIME.
THE **FIRST** TIME YISRAEL CIRCUMCISED THEMSELVES WAS THE NIGHT BEFORE THEY LEFT MITZRAYIM...
YISRAEL **NEVER** RECEIVED THEIR CIRCUMCISION IN THE DESERT FOR THEY NEVER KNEW WHEN THEY WOULD DISMANTLE THE CAMP AND TRAVEL TO ANOTHER LOCATION, AND ONE NEEDS THREE DAYS TO RECUPERATE FROM A BRIT MILAH (BRIS).
ARE YOU **NERVOUS**? I KNOW I AM.
I SURE AM, EVEN THOUGH IT'S A **BIG** MITZVAH, I WISH I HAD IT DONE WHEN I WAS **EIGHT** DAYS OLD...
JUST REMEMBER AVRAHAM AVINU WAS 99 YEARS OLD WHEN HE GOT HIS BRIS. NOW IT'S **OUR** TURN TO DO THIS GREAT MITZVAH.
ב בָּעֵת הַהִיא אָמַר ה' אֶל יְהוֹשֻׁעַ עֲשֵׂה לְךָ חַרְבוֹת צֻרִים וְשׁוּב מֹל אֶת בְּנֵי יִשְׂרָאֵל שֵׁנִית.

ג וַיַּעַשׂ לוֹ יְהוֹשֻׁעַ חַרְבוֹת צֻרִים וַיָּמָל אֶת בְּנֵי יִשְׂרָאֵל אֶל גִּבְעַת הָעֲרָלוֹת.

4 AND THIS IS THE REASON WHY YEHOSHUA HAD THE CIRCUMCISION PERFORMED: ALL THE PEOPLE THAT CAME OUT OF MITZRAYIM, THAT WERE MALES OF MILITARY AGE, HAD DIED WHILE WANDERING IN THE DESERT AFTER LEAVING MITZRAYIM.

5 FOR ALL THE PEOPLE THAT CAME OUT WERE CIRCUMCISED, BUT NONE OF THE PEOPLE BORN AFTER THE EXODUS, WHILE WANDERING IN THE DESERT HAD BEEN CIRCUMCISED. 6 FOR THE CHILDREN OF YISRAEL WALKED FORTY YEARS IN THE DESERT, UNTIL ALL THE PEOPLE, THE MEN OF WAR (BETWEEN 20 AND 60 YEARS OLD) THAT CAME OUT OF MITZRAYIM PERISHED, BECAUSE THEY DID NOT LISTEN TO THE VOICE OF HASHEM; TO WHOM HASHEM SWORE THAT HE WOULD NOT LET THEM SEE THE LAND WHICH HASHEM SWORE TO THEIR FATHERS THAT HE WOULD GIVE US, A LAND FLOWING WITH MILK AND HONEY.

IN THE SINAI DESERT, DUE TO THE SIN OF THE SPIES (MERAGLIM), HASHEM PUNISHED YISRAEL BY MAKING THEM WANDER IN THE DESERT FOR 40 YEARS... (BAMIDBAR 13:31 – 14:3)
31. ...WE ARE UNABLE TO GO UP AGAINST THE PEOPLE, FOR THEY ARE STRONGER THAN US. 32...THE LAND WE PASSED THROUGH TO EXPLORE IS A LAND THAT CONSUMES ITS INHABITANTS,
AND ALL THE PEOPLE WE SAW IN IT ARE MEN OF GREAT SIZE. 33. THERE WE SAW THE GIANTS, THE SONS OF ANAK, DESCENDED FROM THE GIANTS. IN OUR EYES, WE SEEMED LIKE GRASSHOPPERS, AND SO WE WERE IN THEIR EYES. (BAMIDBAR 13:31-33)

1. THE ENTIRE COMMUNITY RAISED THEIR VOICES IN LOUD CRIES, AND THE PEOPLE WEPT ON THAT NIGHT. 2. ALL THE CHILDREN OF YISRAEL COMPLAINED AGAINST MOSHE AND AHARON, AND THE ENTIRE CONGREGATION SAID,
IF ONLY WE HAD DIED IN THE LAND OF EGYPT, OR IF ONLY WE HAD DIED IN THIS DESERT.
3. WHY DOES HASHEM BRING US TO THIS LAND TO FALL BY THE SWORD; OUR WIVES AND CHILDREN WILL BE AS SPOILS. IS IT NOT BETTER FOR US TO RETURN TO EGYPT? (BAMIDBAR 14:1-3)

7 BUT HE RAISED THEIR CHILDREN IN THEIR STEAD, AND IT WAS THESE THAT YEHOSHUA CIRCUMCISED; FOR THEY WERE UNCIRCUMCISED, BECAUSE THEY HAD NOT BEEN CIRCUMCISED ALONG THE WAY.

ד וְזֶה הַדָּבָר אֲשֶׁר מָל יְהוֹשֻׁעַ כָּל הָעָם הַיֹּצֵא מִמִּצְרַיִם הַזְּכָרִים כֹּל אַנְשֵׁי הַמִּלְחָמָה מֵתוּ
בַמִּדְבָּר בַּדֶּרֶךְ בְּצֵאתָם מִמִּצְרָיִם. ה כִּי מֻלִים הָיוּ כָּל הָעָם הַיֹּצְאִים וְכָל הָעָם הַיִּלֹּדִים
בַּמִּדְבָּר בַּדֶּרֶךְ בְּצֵאתָם מִמִּצְרַיִם לֹא מָלוּ. ו כִּי אַרְבָּעִים שָׁנָה הָלְכוּ בְנֵי יִשְׂרָאֵל בַּמִּדְבָּר עַד
תֹּם כָּל הַגּוֹי אַנְשֵׁי הַמִּלְחָמָה הַיֹּצְאִים מִמִּצְרַיִם אֲשֶׁר לֹא שָׁמְעוּ בְּקוֹל ה' אֲשֶׁר נִשְׁבַּע ה'
לָהֶם לְבִלְתִּי הַרְאוֹתָם אֶת הָאָרֶץ אֲשֶׁר נִשְׁבַּע ה' לַאֲבוֹתָם לָתֶת לָנוּ אֶרֶץ זָבַת חָלָב וּדְבָשׁ.
ז וְאֶת בְּנֵיהֶם הֵקִים תַּחְתָּם אֹתָם מָל יְהוֹשֻׁעַ כִּי עֲרֵלִים הָיוּ כִּי לֹא מָלוּ אוֹתָם בַּדָּרֶךְ.

THANK YOU FOR VISITING ME, I AM FEELING MUCH BETTER TODAY...
8 AND IT CAME TO PASS, WHEN ALL THE NATION WAS CIRCUMCISED, THAT THEY REMAINED IN THEIR PLACES IN THE CAMP, UNTIL THEY RECOVERED.
IT'S NICE TO GET OUT IN THE FRESH AIR AFTER BEING COOPED UP INSIDE FOR THE PAST FEW DAYS...
SLAVES, WHEN ARE YOU GOING TO BEGIN WORKING? YOU ARE ALL LAZY...
9 AND HASHEM SAID TO YEHOSHUA: 'THIS DAY I HAVE ROLLED AWAY FROM YOU THE DISGRACE OF MITZRAYIM.' THEREFORE THE NAME OF THAT PLACE WAS CALLED GILGAL (TO ROLL), TO THIS DAY.
MITZRAYIM AT THE TIME FORESAW THAT BLOOD WAS IN YISRAELS FUTURE. LITTLE DID THEY KNOW THAT THE BLOOD REFERENCE, WAS THIS BRIT MILAH.
ח וַיְהִי כַּאֲשֶׁר תַּמּוּ כָל הַגּוֹי לְהִמּוֹל וַיֵּשְׁבוּ תַחְתָּם בַּמַּחֲנֶה עַד
חֲיוֹתָם. ט וַיֹּאמֶר ה' אֶל יְהוֹשֻׁעַ הַיּוֹם גַּלּוֹתִי אֶת חֶרְפַּת מִצְרַיִם
מֵעֲלֵיכֶם וַיִּקְרָא שֵׁם הַמָּקוֹם הַהוּא גִּלְגָּל עַד הַיּוֹם הַזֶּה.

10 AND THE CHILDREN OF YISRAEL ENCAMPED IN GILGAL; AND THEY BROUGHT THE KORBAN PESACH (PESACH SACRIFICE) ON THE FOURTEENTH DAY OF THE MONTH (NISSAN) AT EVENING IN THE PLAINS OF YERICHO.
AND HASHEM TOOK US OUT OF MITZRAYIM... HE DID GREAT MIRACLES FOR US...
MY FATHER TOLD ME FIRSTHAND THAT HE WITNESSED ALL OF THE 10 PLAGUES...
AND HOW THE MITZRIM HAD TO BUY WATER WHEN THE NILE TURNED TO BLOOD...!

י וַיַּחֲנוּ בְנֵי יִשְׂרָאֵל בַּגִּלְגָּל וַיַּעֲשׂוּ אֶת הַפֶּסַח בְּאַרְבָּעָה עָשָׂר יוֹם לַחֹדֶשׁ בָּעֶרֶב
בְּעַרְבוֹת יְרִיחוֹ.

11 ON THE DAY AFTER THE PESACH SACRIFICE, ON THAT VERY SAME DAY, THEY ATE OF THE PRODUCE OF THE COUNTRY, MATZAHS AND PARCHED GRAIN.
YISRAEL ARE **FORBIDDEN** TO EAT FROM NEWLY GROWN GRAINS: WHEAT, BARLEY, OATS, RYE, AND SPELT. THEY MUST WAIT UNTIL THE 16TH OF NISSAN, WHEN THE KORBAN **OMER** IS OFFERED.
THE PROHIBITION OF EATING **NEW** GRAIN APPLIES TO:
RAW
ROASTED
OR GROUND...
THE KORBAN OMER COULD ONLY BE BROUGHT FROM BARLEY WHICH GREW IN A FIELD **OWNED** BY A YISRAEL.
EVEN THOUGH THE CHILDREN OF YISRAEL HAD **JUST** ENTERED THE LAND, THEY WERE STILL ABLE TO BRING THE OMER FROM BARLEY. ALTHOUGH ITS GRAIN HAD ONLY GROWN ONE THIRD OF ITS SIZE UNDER THE CANAANIM, IT MIRACULOUSLY GREW TO ITS **FULL** MATURITY IN THE SIX DAYS SINCE THE CHILDREN OF YISRAEL OCCUPIED THE LAND.
12 AND THE MANN STOPPED ON THE NEXT DAY, AFTER THEY HAD EATEN OF THE PRODUCE OF THE LAND; THE CHILDREN OF YISRAEL DID NOT HAVE MANN ANY MORE. BUT THEY DID EAT FROM THE FRUIT OF THE LAND OF CANAAN THAT YEAR.
יא וַיֹּאכְלוּ מֵעֲבוּר הָאָרֶץ מִמָּחֳרַת הַפֶּסַח מַצּוֹת וְקָלוּי בְּעֶצֶם הַיּוֹם הַזֶּה. **יב** וַיִּשְׁבֹּת
הַמָּן מִמָּחֳרָת בְּאָכְלָם מֵעֲבוּר הָאָרֶץ וְלֹא הָיָה עוֹד לִבְנֵי יִשְׂרָאֵל מָן וַיֹּאכְלוּ מִתְּבוּאַת אֶרֶץ
כְּנַעַן בַּשָּׁנָה הַהִיא.

יג וַיְהִי בִּהְיוֹת יְהוֹשֻׁעַ בִּירִיחוֹ וַיִּשָּׂא עֵינָיו וַיַּרְא וְהִנֵּה אִישׁ עֹמֵד לְנֶגְדּוֹ וְחַרְבּוֹ
שְׁלוּפָה בְּיָדוֹ - -

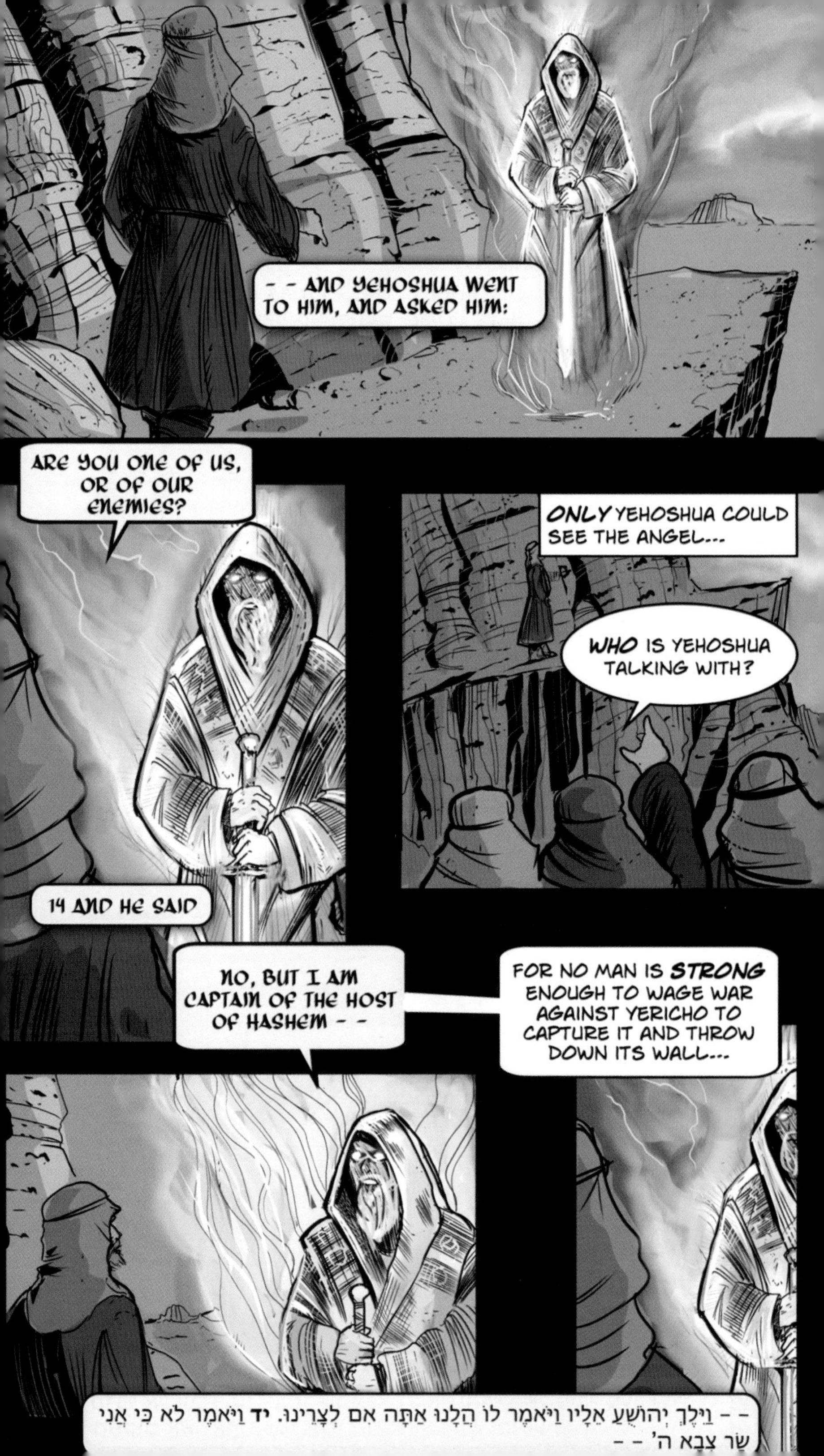

- - AND YEHOSHUA WENT TO HIM, AND ASKED HIM:
ARE YOU ONE OF US, OR OF OUR ENEMIES?
ONLY YEHOSHUA COULD SEE THE ANGEL...
WHO IS YEHOSHUA TALKING WITH?
14 AND HE SAID
NO, BUT I AM CAPTAIN OF THE HOST OF HASHEM - -
FOR NO MAN IS STRONG ENOUGH TO WAGE WAR AGAINST YERICHO TO CAPTURE IT AND THROW DOWN ITS WALL...
- - וַיֵּלֶךְ יְהוֹשֻׁעַ אֵלָיו וַיֹּאמֶר לוֹ הֲלָנוּ אַתָּה אִם לְצָרֵינוּ. יד וַיֹּאמֶר לֹא כִּי אֲנִי
שַׂר צְבָא ה' - -

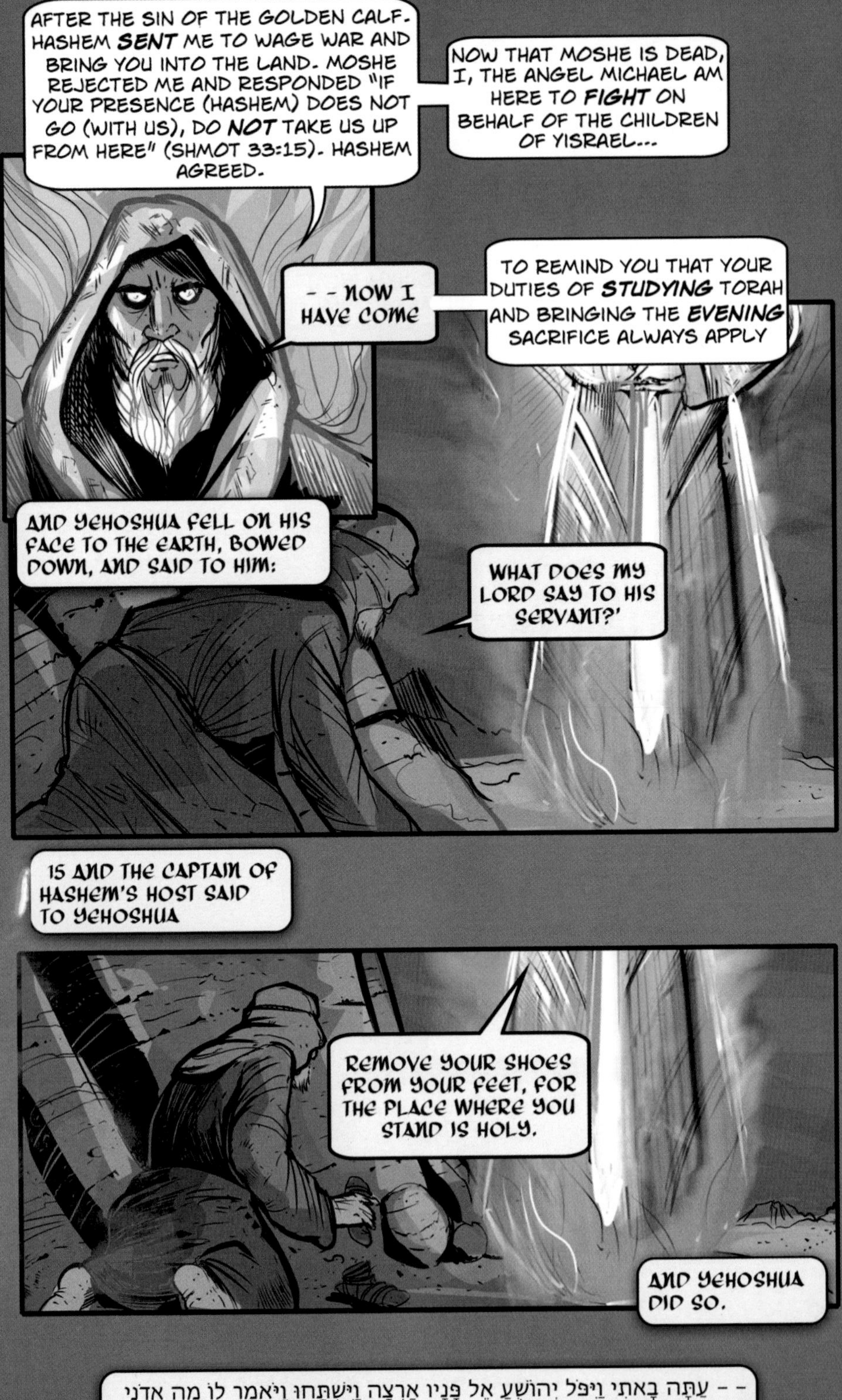
AFTER THE SIN OF THE GOLDEN CALF. HASHEM **SENT** ME TO WAGE WAR AND BRING YOU INTO THE LAND. MOSHE REJECTED ME AND RESPONDED "IF YOUR PRESENCE (HASHEM) DOES NOT GO (WITH US), DO **NOT** TAKE US UP FROM HERE" (SHMOT 33:15). HASHEM AGREED.
NOW THAT MOSHE IS DEAD, I, THE ANGEL MICHAEL AM HERE TO **FIGHT** ON BEHALF OF THE CHILDREN OF YISRAEL...
- - NOW I HAVE COME
TO REMIND YOU THAT YOUR DUTIES OF **STUDYING** TORAH AND BRINGING THE **EVENING** SACRIFICE ALWAYS APPLY
AND YEHOSHUA FELL ON HIS FACE TO THE EARTH, BOWED DOWN, AND SAID TO HIM:
WHAT DOES MY LORD SAY TO HIS SERVANT?'
15 AND THE CAPTAIN OF HASHEM'S HOST SAID TO YEHOSHUA
REMOVE YOUR SHOES FROM YOUR FEET, FOR THE PLACE WHERE YOU STAND IS HOLY.
AND YEHOSHUA DID SO.

- - עַתָּה בָאתִי וַיִּפֹּל יְהוֹשֻׁעַ אֶל פָּנָיו אַרְצָה וַיִּשְׁתָּחוּ וַיֹּאמֶר לוֹ מָה אֲדֹנִי
מְדַבֵּר אֶל עַבְדּוֹ. **טו** וַיֹּאמֶר שַׂר צְבָא ה' אֶל יְהוֹשֻׁעַ שַׁל נַעַלְךָ מֵעַל רַגְלֶךָ כִּי
הַמָּקוֹם אֲשֶׁר אַתָּה עֹמֵד עָלָיו קֹדֶשׁ הוּא וַיַּעַשׂ יְהוֹשֻׁעַ כֵּן.

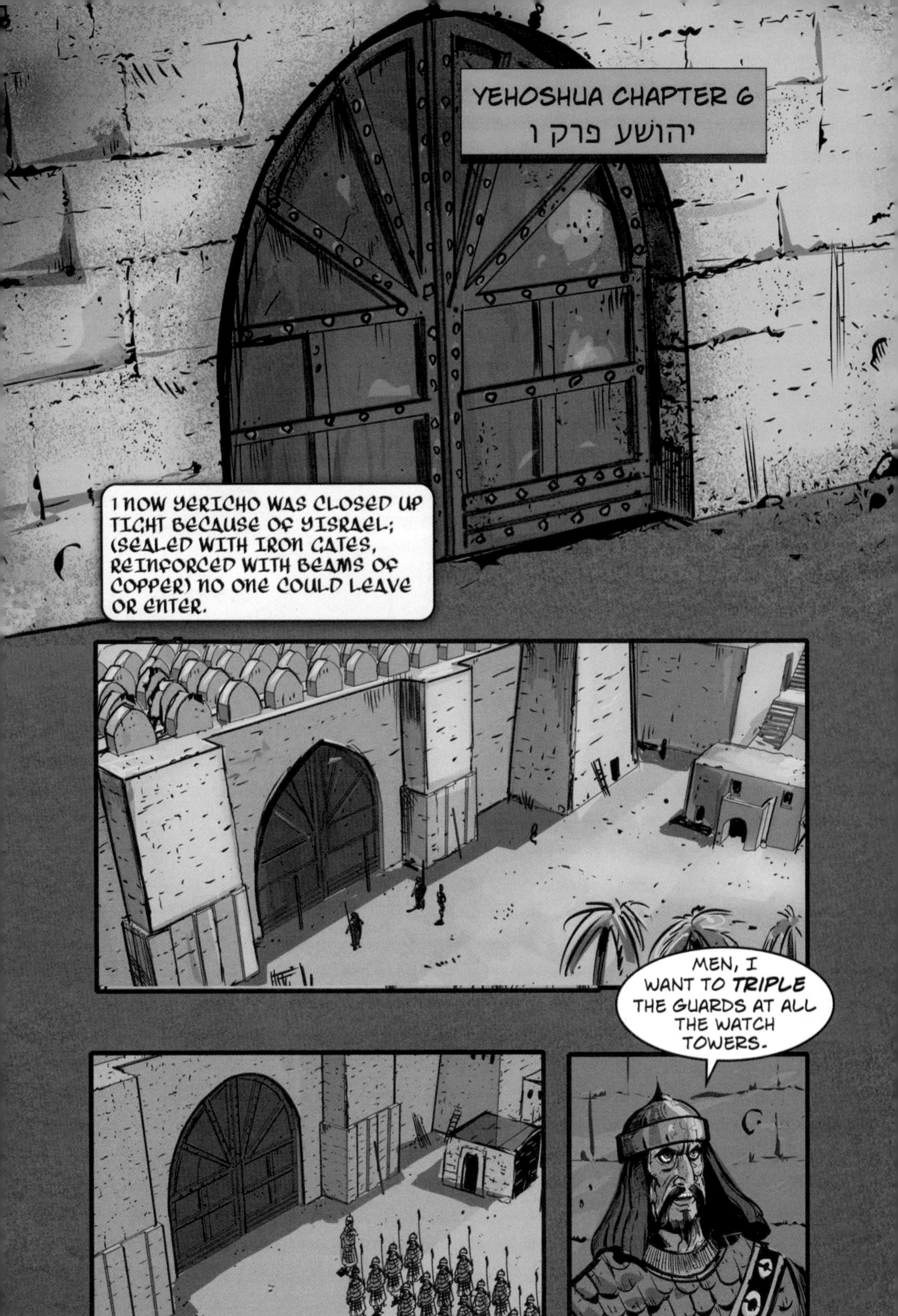
YEHOSHUA CHAPTER 6
יהושע פרק ו
1 NOW YERICHO WAS CLOSED UP TIGHT BECAUSE OF YISRAEL; (SEALED WITH IRON GATES, REINFORCED WITH BEAMS OF COPPER) NO ONE COULD LEAVE OR ENTER.
MEN, I WANT TO TRIPLE THE GUARDS AT ALL THE WATCH TOWERS.

א וִירִיחוֹ סֹגֶרֶת וּמְסֻגֶּרֶת מִפְּנֵי בְּנֵי יִשְׂרָאֵל אֵין יוֹצֵא וְאֵין בָּא.

YISRAEL IS NEARBY, AND EVERYONE IS AFRAID...
DID YOU HEAR WHAT THEY DID TO THE EMORI'S BEFORE THEY CROSSED THE YARDEN...?
AT FIRST THEY ASKED TO JUST PASS THROUGH THE LAND. THEY PROMISED NOT TO WALK THROUGH THEIR FIELDS AND VINEYARDS,
THEY WOULD JUST STAY ON THE KINGS HIGHWAY. THEY ALSO STATED THEY WOULD NOT DRINK ANY OF THEIR WATER.
AND THEN WHAT HAPPENED?
SICHON WAS NOT OK WITH YISRAEL'S CONDITIONS. HE WAS BEING PAID OFF BY ALL THE CANAANI KINGS TO PROTECT THE BORDERS.
INSTEAD HE CHOSE TO WAGE WAR. HE MET YISRAEL AT YAHTZA AND WAS TOTALLY ANNIHILATED...
YISRAEL ENDED UP CONQUERING ALL OF THEIR LAND....

OBVIOUSLY YOU CAN'T ATTACK YISRAEL HEAD ON...
WE HAVE THE MOST SECURE CITY IN THE REGION. WE ARE SURROUNDED BY SEVEN WALLS AND EACH WALL IS AS THICK AS ITS HEIGHT...
I UNDERSTAND WHAT YOU ARE SAYING. DON'T WORRY I WILL PASS THE WORD AROUND THAT WE ARE WELL FORTIFIED AND THERE IS NOTHING TO BE CONCERNED ABOUT.
DO SO IMMEDIATELY, I NEED THE TROOPS SPIRITS TO BE HIGH...
THE CITY IS IN COMPLETE LOCKDOWN. I HAVE NEVER SEEN THEM DO THIS BEFORE TO SUCH A GREAT EXTENT...

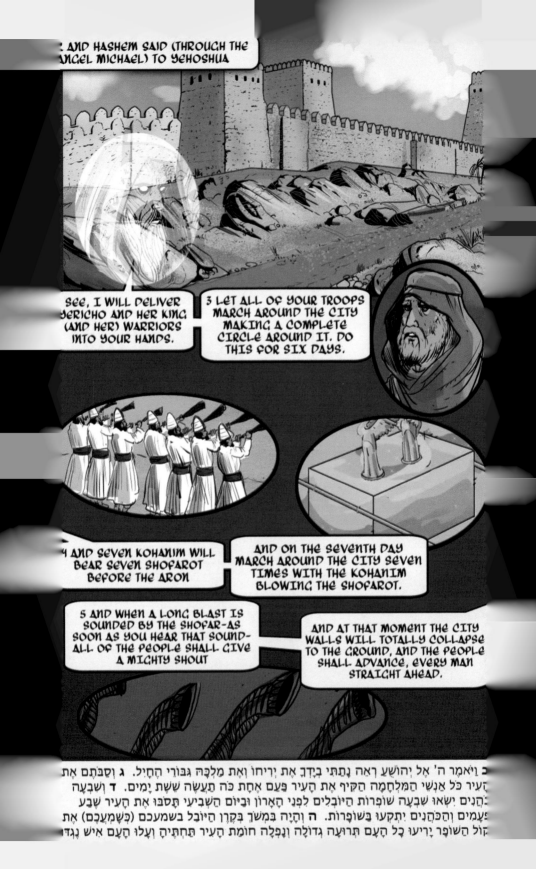

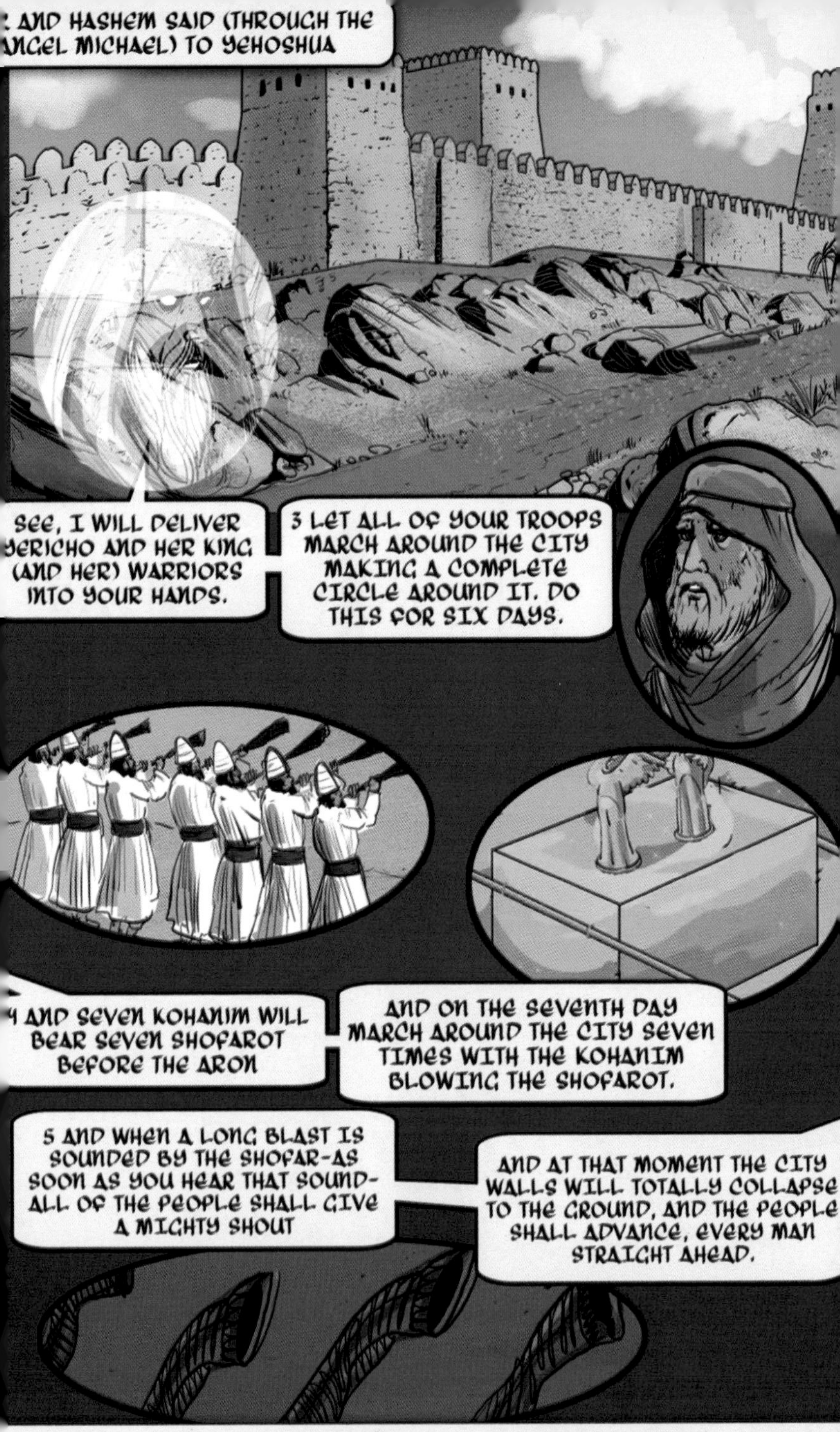

ב וַיֹּאמֶר ה' אֶל יְהוֹשֻׁעַ רְאֵה נָתַתִּי בְיָדְךָ אֶת יְרִיחוֹ וְאֶת מַלְכָּהּ גִּבּוֹרֵי הֶחָיִל. ג וְסַבֹּתֶם אֶת
עִיר כֹּל אַנְשֵׁי הַמִּלְחָמָה הַקֵּיף אֶת הָעִיר פַּעַם אֶחָת כֹּה תַעֲשֶׂה שֵׁשֶׁת יָמִים. ד וְשִׁבְעָה
הֲנִים יִשְׂאוּ שִׁבְעָה שׁוֹפְרוֹת הַיּוֹבְלִים לִפְנֵי הָאָרוֹן וּבַיּוֹם הַשְּׁבִיעִי תָּסֹבּוּ אֶת הָעִיר שֶׁבַע
עָמִים וְהַכֹּהֲנִים יִתְקְעוּ בַּשּׁוֹפָרוֹת. ה וְהָיָה בִּמְשֹׁךְ בְּקֶרֶן הַיּוֹבֵל בשמעכם (כְּשָׁמְעֲכֶם) אֶת
קוֹל הַשּׁוֹפָר יָרִיעוּ כָל הָעָם תְּרוּעָה גְדוֹלָה וְנָפְלָה חוֹמַת הָעִיר תַּחְתֶּיהָ וְעָלוּ הָעָם אִישׁ נֶגְדּו

6 AND YEHOSHUA THE SON OF NUN CALLED THE KOHANIM, AND SAID TO THEM:
TAKE UP THE ARK OF THE COVENANT (ARON HABRIT, ARON OF HASHEM), AND LET SEVEN KOHANIM CARRYING SEVEN SHOFAROT PRECEDE THE ARON OF HASHEM.
7 AND HE SAID TO THE PEOPLE
GO FORWARD, MARCH AROUND THE CITY AND LET THE ARMED MEN MARCH IN FRONT OF THE ARON OF HASHEM.

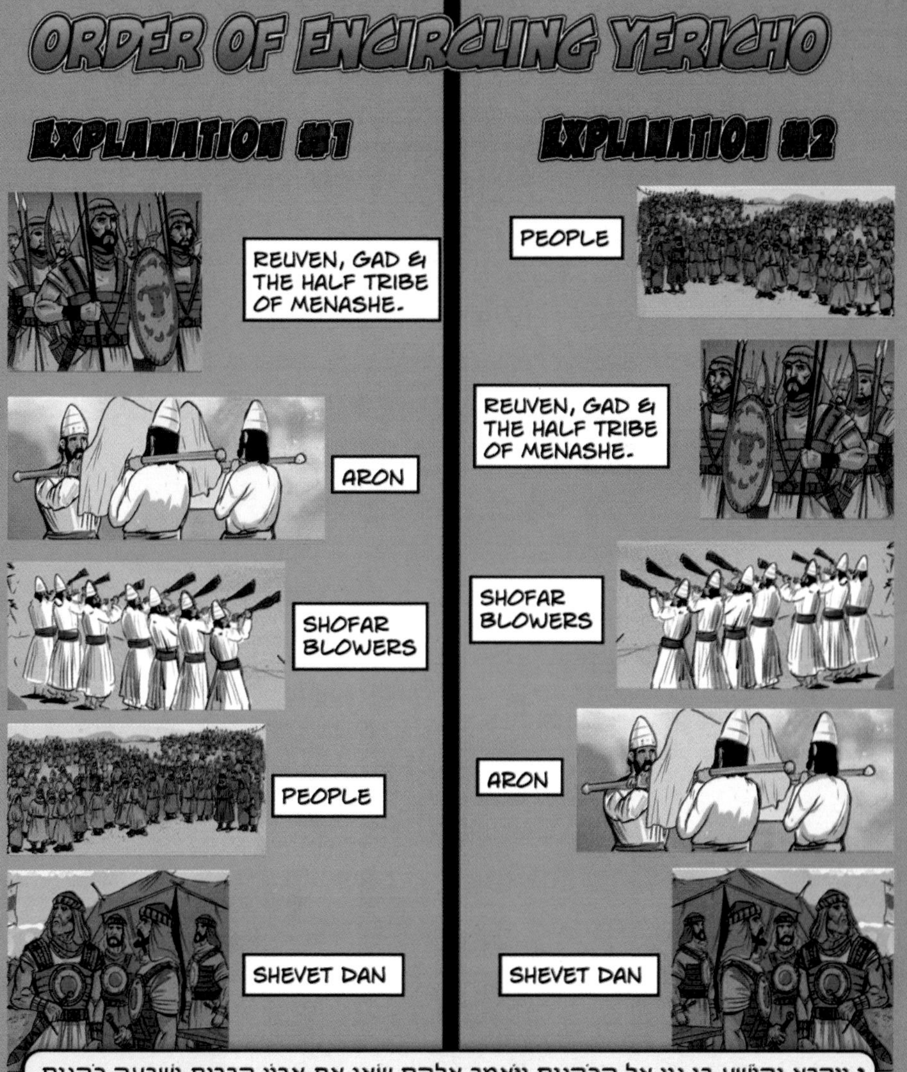
ORDER OF ENCIRCLING YERICHO
EXPLANATION #1
REUVEN, GAD & THE HALF TRIBE OF MENASHE.
ARON
SHOFAR BLOWERS
PEOPLE
SHEVET DAN
EXPLANATION #2
PEOPLE
REUVEN, GAD & THE HALF TRIBE OF MENASHE.
SHOFAR BLOWERS
ARON
SHEVET DAN

ו וַיִּקְרָא יְהוֹשֻׁעַ בִּן נוּן אֶל הַכֹּהֲנִים וַיֹּאמֶר אֲלֵהֶם שְׂאוּ אֶת אֲרוֹן הַבְּרִית וְשִׁבְעָה כֹהֲנִים
יִשְׂאוּ שִׁבְעָה שׁוֹפְרוֹת יוֹבְלִים לִפְנֵי אֲרוֹן ה'. **ז** ויאמרו (וַיֹּאמֶר) אֶל הָעָם עִבְרוּ וְסֹבּוּ אֶת
הָעִיר וְהֶחָלוּץ יַעֲבֹר לִפְנֵי אֲרוֹן ה'.

8 WHEN YEHOSHUA HAD INSTRUCTED THE PEOPLE, THE SEVEN KOHANIM CARRYING THE SEVEN SHOFAROT ADVANCED BEFORE HASHEM, BLOWING THEIR SHOFAROT AND THE ARON OF THE COVENANT OF HASHEM FOLLOWED THEM.
9 AND THE ARMED MEN MARCHED IN FRONT OF THE KOHANIM WHO WERE BLOWING THE SHOFAROT, AND THE REAR GUARD MARCHED BEHIND THE ARON WITH THE SHOFAROT SOUNDING ALL THE TIME.
10 AND YEHOSHUA COMMANDED THE PEOPLE, SAYING
DO NOT SHOUT, DO NOT LET YOUR VOICES BE HEARD, AND DO NOT LET A SOUND COME OUT FROM YOUR MOUTHS UNTIL THE MOMENT THAT I COMMAND YOU [TO], "SHOUT!" THEN YOU WILL SHOUT.
ח וַיְהִי כֶּאֱמֹר יְהוֹשֻׁעַ אֶל הָעָם וְשִׁבְעָה הַכֹּהֲנִים נֹשְׂאִים שִׁבְעָה שׁוֹפְרוֹת הַיּוֹבְלִים לִפְנֵי ה' עָבְרוּ וְתָקְעוּ בַּשּׁוֹפָרוֹת וַאֲרוֹן בְּרִית ה' הֹלֵךְ אַחֲרֵיהֶם. ט וְהֶחָלוּץ הֹלֵךְ לִפְנֵי הַכֹּהֲנִים תקעו (תֹּקְעֵי) הַשּׁוֹפָרוֹת וְהַמְאַסֵּף הֹלֵךְ אַחֲרֵי הָאָרוֹן הָלוֹךְ וְתָקוֹעַ בַּשּׁוֹפָרוֹת. י וְאֶת הָעָם צִוָּה יְהוֹשֻׁעַ לֵאמֹר לֹא תָרִיעוּ וְלֹא תַשְׁמִיעוּ אֶת קוֹלְכֶם וְלֹא יֵצֵא מִפִּיכֶם דָּבָר עַד יוֹם אָמְרִי אֲלֵיכֶם הָרִיעוּ וַהֲרֵיעֹתֶם.

11 SO HE HAD THE ARON OF HASHEM GO AROUND THE CITY AND COMPLETE ONE CIRCLE.
AND THEY RETURNED TO THE CAMP AND SLEPT THERE FOR THE NIGHT.
TODAY WAS SOME DAY. THE *TENSION* IN THE AIR WAS SO THICK, YOU COULD CUT IT WITH A KNIFE.

יא וַיַּסֵּב אֲרוֹן ה' אֶת הָעִיר הַקֵּף פַּעַם אֶחָת וַיָּבֹאוּ הַמַּחֲנֶה וַיָּלִינוּ בַּמַּחֲנֶה.

DAY 2
12 AND YEHOSHUA ROSE EARLY IN THE MORNING, AND THE KOHANIM TOOK UP THE ARON OF HASHEM. 13 AND THE SEVEN KOHANIM BEARING THE SEVEN SHOFAROT BEFORE THE ARON OF HASHEM WENT ON CONTINUALLY, AND BLEW WITH THE SHOFAROT; AND THE ARMED MEN WENT BEFORE THEM AND THE REAR GUARD (TRIBE OF DAN) CAME AFTER THE ARON OF HASHEM, [THE KOHANIM] BLOWING WITH THE SHOFAROT CONTINUALLY. 14 AND THE SECOND DAY THEY COMPASSED THE CITY ONCE, AND RETURNED INTO THE CAMP. - -
THEY'VE COME BACK, I THOUGHT THEY WENT HOME LAST NIGHT FIGURING IT WAS IMPOSSIBLE TO BREAK THROUGH THESE WALLS...
DAY 3
LOOK AT THE FOOLS... THEY THINK THEY CAN SCARE US BY WALKING AROUND OUR CITY AND BLOWING A FEW HORNS...
BOO YISRAEL... GO BACK TO THE DESERT WHERE YOU BELONG!!!
SIRE, I DON'T KNOW WHY THEY KEEP CIRCLING THE CITY EVERY DAY AND THEN RETURN TO THEIR BASE CAMP.
DAY 4
GENERAL, YOU ARE THE BEST WAR STRATEGIST ON THIS CONTINENT, I PAY YOU HANDSOMELY. I WANT ANSWERS, AND I WANT THEM NOW!!!
יב וַיַּשְׁכֵּם יְהוֹשֻׁעַ בַּבֹּקֶר וַיִּשְׂאוּ הַכֹּהֲנִים אֶת אֲרוֹן ה'. **יג** וְשִׁבְעָה הַכֹּהֲנִים נֹשְׂאִים
שִׁבְעָה שׁוֹפְרוֹת הַיֹּבְלִים לִפְנֵי אֲרוֹן ה' הֹלְכִים הָלוֹךְ וְתָקְעוּ בַּשּׁוֹפָרוֹת וְהֶחָלוּץ הֹלֵךְ
לִפְנֵיהֶם וְהַמְאַסֵּף הֹלֵךְ אַחֲרֵי אֲרוֹן ה' הולך (הָלוֹךְ) וְתָקוֹעַ בַּשּׁוֹפָרוֹת. **יד** וַיָּסֹבּוּ אֶת
הָעִיר בַּיּוֹם הַשֵּׁנִי פַּעַם אַחַת וַיָּשֻׁבוּ הַמַּחֲנֶה - -

DAY 5
HERE WE ARE AGAIN GENTLEMEN, AND I STILL DON'T HAVE ANY ANSWERS. GENERAL, ANY SUGGESTIONS ON A PREEMPTIVE ATTACK?
SIRE THAT IS EXACTLY WHAT THEY ARE EXPECTING US TO DO. THE BEST PLAN IS TO REMAIN WITHIN THESE FORTIFIED WALLS.
DAY 6
SIX DAYS OF THIS... WHAT ARE THEY UP TO? IT'S GOT TO BE SOMETHING, I CAN FEEL IT IN MY BONES...
IT'S ALWAYS THE SAME FORMATION OF ONLY MEN, THEY NEVER SPEAK A WORD, AND THEY BLOW THOSE BLASTED HORNS.
OUR ONLY CHOICE FOR NOW IS TO WAIT AND SEE...!
- - SO THEY DID FOR SIX DAYS.
- - כֹּה עָשׂוּ שֵׁשֶׁת יָמִים.

15 ON THE SEVENTH DAY (SHABBAT) THEY ROSE EARLY AT DAYBREAK.
AND MARCHED AROUND THE CITY, IN THE SAME MANNER, SEVEN TIMES. THIS WAS THE ONLY DAY THAT THEY MARCHED AROUND THE CITY SEVEN TIMES.

טו וַיְהִי בַּיּוֹם הַשְּׁבִיעִי וַיַּשְׁכִּמוּ כַּעֲלוֹת הַשַּׁחַר וַיָּסֹבּוּ אֶת הָעִיר כַּמִּשְׁפָּט הַזֶּה
שֶׁבַע פְּעָמִים רַק בַּיּוֹם הַהוּא סָבְבוּ אֶת הָעִיר שֶׁבַע פְּעָמִים.

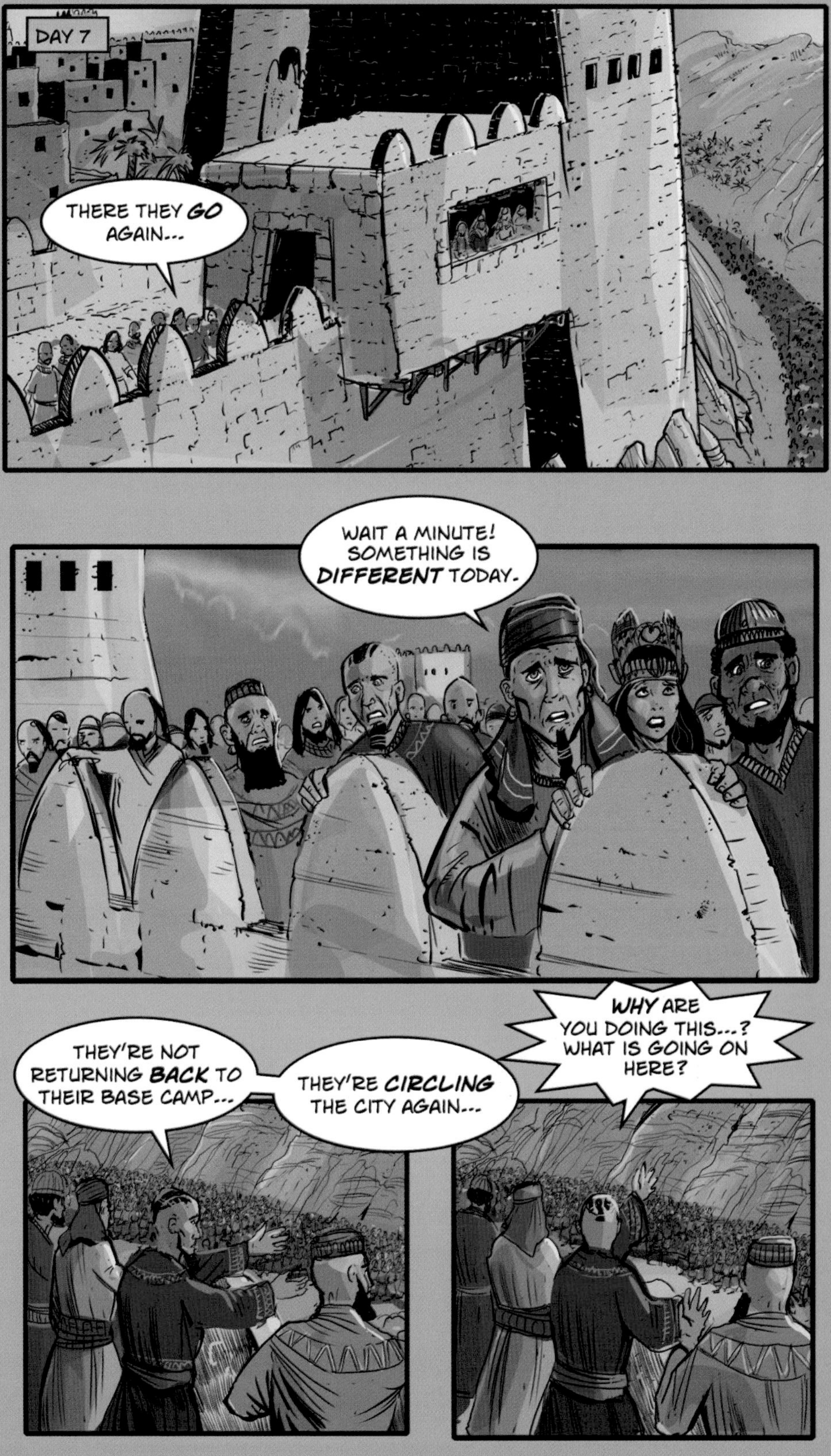
DAY 7
THERE THEY GO AGAIN...
WAIT A MINUTE! SOMETHING IS DIFFERENT TODAY.
THEY'RE NOT RETURNING BACK TO THEIR BASE CAMP...
THEY'RE CIRCLING THE CITY AGAIN...
WHY ARE YOU DOING THIS...? WHAT IS GOING ON HERE?

SIRE THEY HAVE ALREADY ENCIRCLED THE CITY FIVE TIMES. I DO NOT KNOW WHAT THEY ARE UP TO...
IT'S REALLY HAPPENING. I WILL GO DOWN IN HISTORY AS THE LAST KING OF YERICHO, THE MIGHTIEST CITY OF CANAAN...
GENERAL, PUT THE TROOPS ON HIGH ALERT! I WANT EVERY AVAILABLE MAN READY FOR WAR...
YES, YOUR HIGHNESS.
16 ON THE SEVENTH ROUND, AS THE KOHANIM BLEW THE SHOFAROT, YEHOSHUA COMMANDED THE PEOPLE:
SHOUT! FOR HASHEM HAS GIVEN YOU THE CITY.
טז וַיְהִי בַּפַּעַם הַשְּׁבִיעִית תָּקְעוּ הַכֹּהֲנִים בַּשּׁוֹפָרוֹת וַיֹּאמֶר יְהוֹשֻׁעַ אֶל הָעָם
הָרִיעוּ כִּי נָתַן ה' לָכֶם אֶת הָעִיר.

17 AND THE CITY AND ALL THAT IS IN IT, WILL BE CONSECRATED FOR HASHEM
ONLY RACHAV THE INNKEEPER WILL LIVE, SHE AND ALL WHO ARE WITH HER IN THE HOUSE,
BECAUSE SHE HID THE MESSENGERS THAT WE SENT.
18 BUT YOU MUST BE AWARE (NOT TO TAKE) OF THAT WHICH IS SANCTIFIED, OR ELSE YOU WILL BE BANISHED: IF YOU TAKE ANYTHING FROM THAT WHICH IS SANCTIFIED YOU WILL CAUSE THE CAMP OF YISRAEL TO BE BANISHED, AND YOU WILL BRING CALAMITY ON IT.
19 AND ALL THE SILVER, AND GOLD, AND VESSELS OF BRASS AND IRON, ARE HOLY TO HASHEM. THEY MUST GO INTO THE TREASURY OF HASHEM.

יז וְהָיְתָה הָעִיר חֵרֶם הִיא וְכָל אֲשֶׁר בָּהּ לַה׳ רַק רָחָב הַזּוֹנָה תִּחְיֶה הִיא וְכָל אֲשֶׁר
אִתָּהּ בַּבַּיִת כִּי הֶחְבְּאַתָה אֶת הַמַּלְאָכִים אֲשֶׁר שָׁלָחְנוּ. **יח** וְרַק אַתֶּם שִׁמְרוּ מִן
הַחֵרֶם פֶּן תַּחֲרִימוּ וּלְקַחְתֶּם מִן הַחֵרֶם וְשַׂמְתֶּם אֶת מַחֲנֵה יִשְׂרָאֵל לְחֵרֶם וַעֲכַרְתֶּם
אוֹתוֹ. **יט** וְכֹל כֶּסֶף וְזָהָב וּכְלֵי נְחֹשֶׁת וּבַרְזֶל קֹדֶשׁ הוּא לַה׳ אוֹצַר ה׳ יָבוֹא.

כ וַיָּרַע הָעָם וַיִּתְקְעוּ בַּשֹּׁפָרוֹת וַיְהִי כִשְׁמֹעַ הָעָם אֶת קוֹל הַשּׁוֹפָר וַיָּרִיעוּ
הָעָם תְּרוּעָה גדולה --

THE WALLS ARE COLLAPSING!!!
HELLLLLLP!!!
AAAHHHH!!!

- - AND THE WALL TOTALLY COLLAPSED AND THE PEOPLE RUSHED INTO THE CITY. EVERY MAN WENT STRAIGHT AHEAD AND THEY CAPTURED THE CITY.
THE WALLS JUST SANK INTO THE EARTH!!!
YISRAEL IS COMING... WE'RE DEAD, WE'RE ALL DEAD!
THAT'S RIGHT, YOU ARE ALL DEAD...
WE'RE BEING ATTACKED, DEFEND YOURSELVES!!!
KILL EVERY IDOL WORSHIPPING HEATHEN...
CHARGE!!!
- - וַתִּפֹּל הַחוֹמָה תַּחְתֶּיהָ וַיַּעַל הָעָם הָעִירָה אִישׁ נֶגְדּוֹ, וַיִּלְכְּדוּ אֶת-הָעִיר.

ARGH!!!!
I AM OFF TO FIND MORE HEATHENS...
WOOOSH
THANK YOU... THAT WAS A CLOSE ONE!
WHERE ARE THE REST OF YOU HIDING?

UH, OH! THREE AGAINST ONE, I'M NOT SURE I LIKE THESE ODDS!!! PLEASE HASHEM, HELP ME OUT HERE...
WELL WELL, WHAT DO WE HAVE HERE? IT LOOKS LIKE A LOST YISRAEL.
THIS LITTLE SHEEP MUST HAVE STRAYED AWAY FROM HIS PACK...
HEY YISRAEL, ARE YOU LOST? DO YOU NEED SOME DIRECTIONS?
MAYBE WE CAN HELP YOU. GET OVER HERE, SO WE CAN CARVE A MAP INTO YOUR HEART...
I LIKE MY HEART JUST THE WAY IT IS, THANK YOU VERY MUCH. BUT FROM WHAT I SEE, YOUR HEARTS WILL STOP BEATING IN JUST A FEW MOMENTS...
WHAT ARE YOU TALKING ABOUT, WE OUTNUMBER YOU...?
I SUGGEST YOU LOOK UP...

WHY? WHA, **WHAT'S** GOING ON...!
TIMBERRR!!
AHHHH!!!
SPLAT!
UGG, WHAT A HORRIBLE WAY TO **GO...**

21 AND THEY COMPLETELY DESTROYED ALL THAT WAS IN THE CITY, BOTH MAN AND WOMAN, YOUNG AND OLD, OX, SHEEP, AND DONKEY, BY THE SWORD.
22 AND YEHOSHUA SAID TO THE TWO MEN THAT HAD SPIED OUT THE LAND: '
GO INTO THE INNKEEPER'S HOUSE, AND BRING OUT FROM THERE THE WOMAN, AND ALL THAT SHE HAS, AS YOU SWORE TO HER.'
WE JUST HAVE TO FIND THE HOUSE WITH THE RED CORD...

כא וַיַּחֲרִימוּ אֶת כָּל אֲשֶׁר בָּעִיר מֵאִישׁ וְעַד אִשָּׁה מִנַּעַר וְעַד זָקֵן וְעַד שׁוֹר וָשֶׂה וַחֲמוֹר
לְפִי חָרֶב. **כב** וְלִשְׁנַיִם הָאֲנָשִׁים הַמְרַגְּלִים אֶת הָאָרֶץ אָמַר יְהוֹשֻׁעַ בֹּאוּ בֵּית הָאִשָּׁה
הַזּוֹנָה וְהוֹצִיאוּ מִשָּׁם אֶת הָאִשָּׁה וְאֶת כָּל אֲשֶׁר לָהּ כַּאֲשֶׁר נִשְׁבַּעְתֶּם לָהּ.

THIS IS THE PLACE. I RECOGNIZE THE HOUSE. BESIDES, THERE IS THE RED CORD HANGING OUTSIDE THE WINDOW.
WHAT IS THIS? IT LOOKS LIKE HALF THE CITY IS IN HER HOUSE...
WHO ARE ALL THESE PEOPLE?
WHAT DID YOU DO? YOU WERE ONLY SUPPOSED TO BRING IN YOUR IMMEDIATE HOUSEHOLD.
WHAT DO YOU MEAN, THIS IS MY FAMILY!

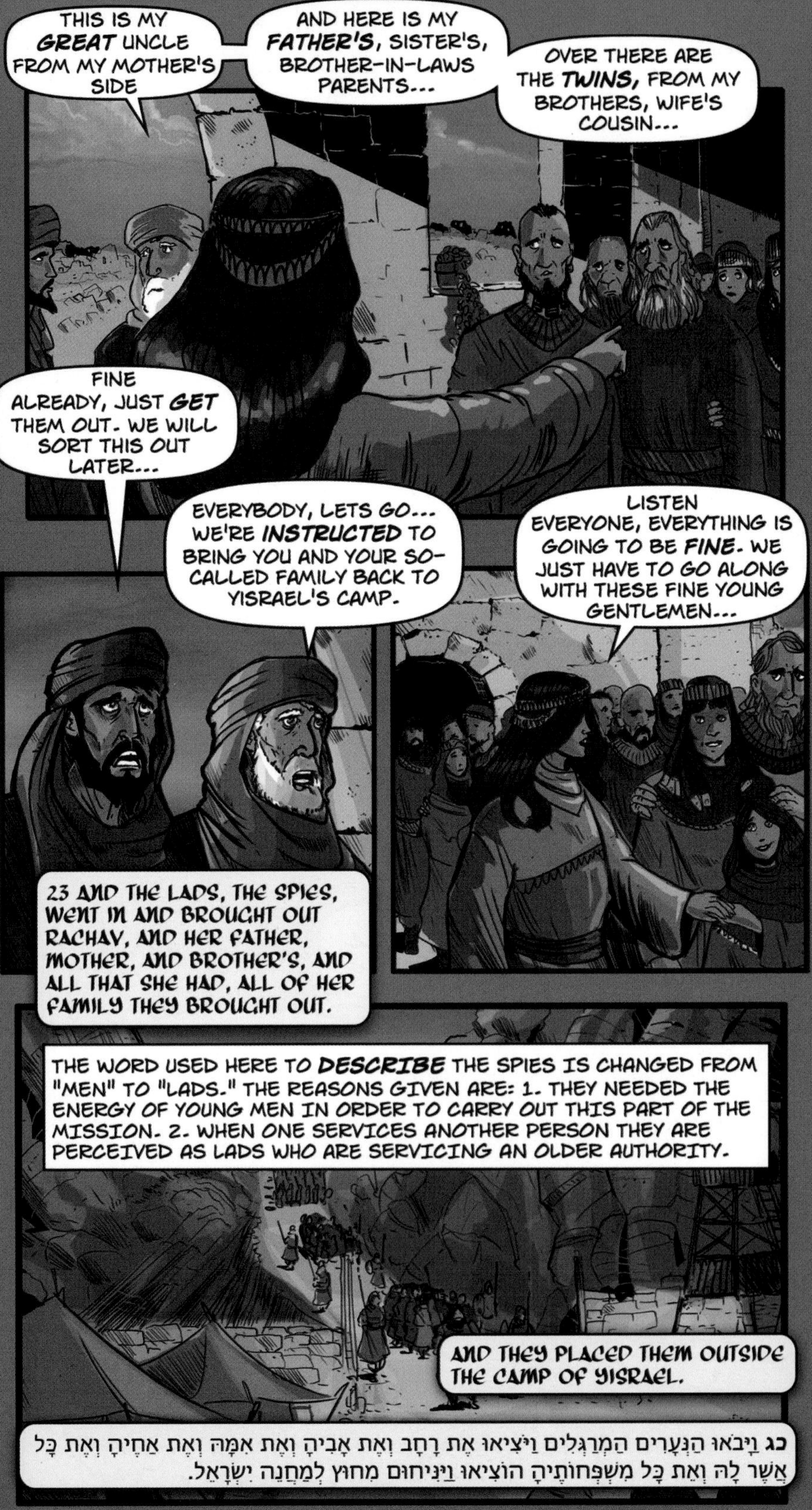
THIS IS MY GREAT UNCLE FROM MY MOTHER'S SIDE
AND HERE IS MY FATHER'S, SISTER'S, BROTHER-IN-LAWS PARENTS...
OVER THERE ARE THE TWINS, FROM MY BROTHERS, WIFE'S COUSIN...
FINE ALREADY, JUST GET THEM OUT. WE WILL SORT THIS OUT LATER...
EVERYBODY, LETS GO... WE'RE INSTRUCTED TO BRING YOU AND YOUR SO-CALLED FAMILY BACK TO YISRAEL'S CAMP.
LISTEN EVERYONE, EVERYTHING IS GOING TO BE FINE. WE JUST HAVE TO GO ALONG WITH THESE FINE YOUNG GENTLEMEN...
23 AND THE LADS, THE SPIES, WENT IN AND BROUGHT OUT RACHAV, AND HER FATHER, MOTHER, AND BROTHER'S, AND ALL THAT SHE HAD, ALL OF HER FAMILY THEY BROUGHT OUT.
THE WORD USED HERE TO DESCRIBE THE SPIES IS CHANGED FROM "MEN" TO "LADS." THE REASONS GIVEN ARE: 1. THEY NEEDED THE ENERGY OF YOUNG MEN IN ORDER TO CARRY OUT THIS PART OF THE MISSION. 2. WHEN ONE SERVICES ANOTHER PERSON THEY ARE PERCEIVED AS LADS WHO ARE SERVICING AN OLDER AUTHORITY.
AND THEY PLACED THEM OUTSIDE THE CAMP OF YISRAEL.
כג וַיָּבֹאוּ הַנְּעָרִים הַמְרַגְּלִים וַיֹּצִיאוּ אֶת רָחָב וְאֶת אָבִיהָ וְאֶת אִמָּהּ וְאֶת אַחֶיהָ וְאֶת כָּל אֲשֶׁר לָהּ וְאֵת כָּל מִשְׁפְּחוֹתֶיהָ הוֹצִיאוּ וַיַּנִּיחוּם מִחוּץ לְמַחֲנֵה יִשְׂרָאֵל.

24 THEY BURNED DOWN THE CITY AND EVERYTHING IN IT.
LOOK AT ALL THIS STUFF. I COULD REALLY USE JUST ONE OF THESE VESSELS.
BUT THE TRUTH IS, I'M GLAD WE ARE DEDICATING THIS FIRST CITY TO HASHEM...
I BET WE CAN BUILD THE BEIT HAMIKDASH WITH THE FORTUNE OBTAINED FROM THIS ONE CITY ALONE...
BUT THE SILVER AND GOLD AND THE OBJECTS OF COPPER AND IRON WERE DEPOSITED IN THE TREASURY OF THE HOUSE OF HASHEM.
כד וְהָעִיר שָׂרְפוּ בָאֵשׁ וְכָל אֲשֶׁר בָּהּ רַק הַכֶּסֶף וְהַזָּהָב וּכְלֵי הַנְּחֹשֶׁת
וְהַבַּרְזֶל נָתְנוּ אוֹצַר בֵּית ה'.

RACHAV AND HER FAMILY ARE APPROACHING
YEHOSHUA SENT FOR US.
YES I KNOW, I WILL TELL HIM YOU ARE HERE...
BECAUSE YOU SAVED OUR SPIES, PINCHAS AND KALEV, YOU AND YOUR FAMILY, IF YOU WISH, ARE WELCOME TO CONVERT AND BECOME A MEMBER OF YISRAEL.
25 ONLY RACHAV THE INNKEEPER AND HER FATHER'S FAMILY WERE SPARED BY YEHOSHUA ALONG WITH ALL THAT BELONGED TO HER. AND SHE LIVED AMONG YISRAEL UNTIL TODAY. FOR SHE HAD HIDDEN THE MESSENGERS THAT YEHOSHUA SENT TO SPY OUT YERICHO.
THE SAGES TELL US THAT YEHOSHUA MARRIED RACHAV AND ONE OF THE SPECIAL DESCENDANT'S OF THAT MARRIAGE WAS YERMIYAHU THE PROPHET...
BEHOLD YOU ARE 'MEKUDESHET' TO ME... ACCORDING TO MOSHE AND YISRAEL
כה וְאֶת רָחָב הַזּוֹנָה וְאֶת בֵּית אָבִיהָ וְאֶת כָּל אֲשֶׁר לָהּ הֶחֱיָה יְהוֹשֻׁעַ וַתֵּשֶׁב בְּקֶרֶב
יִשְׂרָאֵל עַד הַיּוֹם הַזֶּה כִּי הֶחְבִּיאָה אֶת הַמַּלְאָכִים אֲשֶׁר שָׁלַח יְהוֹשֻׁעַ לְרַגֵּל אֶת יְרִיחוֹ.

26 AND AT THAT TIME YEHOSHUA MADE AN OATH, SAYING:
THE CURSE OF HASHEM WILL BE ON THE MAN THAT RISES UP AND BUILDS THIS CITY, YERICHO.
WITH THE LOSS OF HIS FIRST-BORN WILL HE LAY THE FOUNDATION AND WITH THE LOSS OF HIS YOUNGEST SON WILL HE SET UP ITS GATES.

27 SO HASHEM WAS WITH YEHOSHUA AND HIS FAME SPREAD THROUGHOUT THE LAND.

YEHOSHUA BEGAN MINTING COINS BASED ON THE BLESSING FROM MOSHE (SEE DEVARIM 33:17). ON ONE SIDE WAS AN OX WHO HAS GREAT **STRENGTH** AND ON THE OTHER SIDE IS AN ORYX WHOSE HORNS ARE VERY **BEAUTIFUL** AND MAJESTIC...

כו וַיַּשְׁבַּע יְהוֹשֻׁעַ בָּעֵת הַהִיא לֵאמֹר אָרוּר הָאִישׁ לִפְנֵי ה' אֲשֶׁר יָקוּם וּבָנָה אֶת
הָעִיר הַזֹּאת אֶת יְרִיחוֹ בִּבְכֹרוֹ יְיַסְּדֶנָּה וּבִצְעִירוֹ יַצִּיב דְּלָתֶיהָ. **כז** וַיְהִי ה' אֶת יְהוֹשֻׁעַ
וַיְהִי שָׁמְעוֹ בְּכָל הָאָרֶץ.

YEHOSHUA CHAPTER 7
יהושע פרק ז
1 AND THE CHILDREN OF YISRAEL DEFIED AND DISOBEYED THE INSTRUCTIONS OF YEHOSHUA AND TOOK FROM THE ITEMS THAT WERE SANCTIFIED FOR HASHEM.
FOR ACHAN, THE SON OF CARMI, THE SON OF ZABDI, THE SON OF ZERAH, OF THE TRIBE OF YEHUDAH, TOOK OF THE ITEMS THAT WERE SANCTIFIED FOR HASHEM.
AND HASHEM WAS EXTREMELY ANGRY WITH THE CHILDREN OF YISRAEL.
א וַיִּמְעֲלוּ בְנֵי יִשְׂרָאֵל מַעַל בַּחֵרֶם וַיִּקַּח עָכָן בֶּן כַּרְמִי בֶן זַבְדִּי בֶן זֶרַח לְמַטֵּה יְהוּדָה מִן
הַחֵרֶם וַיִּחַר אַף ה' בִּבְנֵי יִשְׂרָאֵל.

2 AND YEHOSHUA SENT MEN FROM YERICHO TO AI, WHICH IS CLOSE TO BEIT AVEN, ON THE EAST SIDE OF BEIT EL,
North
Beit El
בית-אל
Ai
עי
Yericho
יריחו
Yarden
Beit Aven
בית און
גבעון
Gilgal
גלגל
Yerushalayim
ירושלים
Dead Sea
AND SPOKE TO THEM, SAYING:
GO UP AND SPY OUT THE LAND.
YEHOSHUA WANTS TO KNOW EVERYTHING ABOUT AI. HOW LARGE IS THEIR ARMY. HOW MANY CITIZENS. IS THE CITY WELL FORTIFIED ETC.
AND THE MEN WENT UP AND SPIED OUT AI.
FROM THE OUTSIDE, THE CITY DOESN'T LOOK LIKE ANYTHING SPECIAL...
IT DOESN'T SEEM VERY THREATENING. IT ACTUALLY LOOKS LIKE A VERY ORDINARY SMALL CITY.

ב וַיִּשְׁלַח יְהוֹשֻׁעַ אֲנָשִׁים מִירִיחוֹ הָעַי אֲשֶׁר עִם בֵּית אָוֶן מִקֶּדֶם לְבֵית אֵל וַיֹּאמֶר אֲלֵיהֶם
לֵאמֹר עֲלוּ וְרַגְּלוּ אֶת הָאָרֶץ וַיַּעֲלוּ הָאֲנָשִׁים וַיְרַגְּלוּ, אֶת הָעָי.

JUST PEACEFUL FARMERS.
DON'T BE FOOLED. THEY WORSHIP THE IDOL MOLECH... YOU KNOW, THE PEOPLE PUT THEIR OWN CHILDREN THROUGH FIRE AS A SIGN OF DEVOTION.
UUCH! THAT IS HORRIFYING!!
TRY THESE FIGS! I AM TELLING YOU THEY ARE THE BEST IN THE LAND...
VERY WELL, YOU USUALLY GIVE ME GOOD PRODUCE, BUT I MUST TELL YOU, THE LAST TIME I BOUGHT SOMETHING FROM YOU, ALL THE FRUIT SPOILED!
I HOPE I BOUGHT THE RIGHT THING? I CAN'T REMEMBER IF MY WIFE TOLD ME TO BUY A SACK OF OATS OR BARLEY...
THIS IS JUST A SIMPLE SMALL MARKET... THEY DON'T SEEM VERY SCARY...
DOESN'T SEEM LIKE MUCH OF AN ARMY. THEY ARE JUST STANDING AROUND, KEEPING THE PEACE...
TIME TO HEAD BACK AND REPORT EVERYTHING WE HAVE SEEN.

ג וַיָּשֻׁבוּ אֶל יְהוֹשֻׁעַ וַיֹּאמְרוּ אֵלָיו אַל יַעַל כָּל הָעָם כְּאַלְפַּיִם אִישׁ אוֹ כִּשְׁלֹשֶׁת אֲלָפִים
אִישׁ יַעֲלוּ וְיַכּוּ אֶת הָעָי אַל תְּיַגַּע שָׁמָּה אֶת כָּל הָעָם כִּי מְעַט הֵמָּה. **ד** וַיַּעֲלוּ מִן הָעָם
שָׁמָּה כִּשְׁלֹשֶׁת אֲלָפִים אִישׁ --

SUDDENLY...
ATTACK!!!
TROOPS MAINTAIN FORMATION!!!
ARGH!!!
THIS IS AN AMBUSH, THEY'RE COMING FROM EVERYWHERE!!!
RETREAT, THERE ARE TOO MANY OF THEM!!!
-- AND THEY FLED BEFORE THE MEN OF AI
5 THE MEN OF AI KILLED ABOUT THIRTY-SIX OF THEM, PURSUING THEM OUTSIDE THE GATE AS FAR AS SHEVARIM, AND CUTTING THEM DOWN ALONG THE DESCENT.
-- וַיָּנֻסוּ לִפְנֵי אַנְשֵׁי הָעָי. ה וַיַּכּוּ מֵהֶם אַנְשֵׁי הָעַי כִּשְׁלֹשִׁים וְשִׁשָּׁה אִישׁ
וַיִּרְדְּפוּם לִפְנֵי הַשַּׁעַר עַד הַשְּׁבָרִים וַיַּכּוּם בַּמּוֹרָד --

THIS IS A COMPLETE DISASTER! HOW COULD THIS HAVE HAPPENED? WE JUST DESTROYED YERICHO WITHOUT ANY LOSS OF LIFE.
THE SAGES QUESTION WHETHER THE FALLEN SOLDIERS WERE 36 RIGHTEOUS MEN OR YAIR SON OF MENASHE WHO WAS COMPARED TO THE 36 RIGHTEOUS PEOPLE.
-- AND THE HEARTS OF THE NATION MELTED, AND BECAME LIKE WATER.
WE WERE COMPLETELY TAKEN BY SURPRISE, WE DIDN'T HAVE A CHANCE...
WE LOST 36 MEN...!
6 AND YEHOSHUA TORE HIS CLOTHES
WHYYYY!!!
--וַיִּמַּס לְבַב הָעָם וַיְהִי לְמָיִם. ו וַיִּקְרַע יְהוֹשֻׁעַ שִׂמְלֹתָיו --

- - HE AND THE ELDERS OF YISRAEL LAY UNTIL EVENING WITH THEIR FACES TO THE GROUND IN FRONT OF THE ARON OF HASHEM, AND THEY PUT DIRT ON THEIR HEADS.

7 AND YEHOSHUA SAID
WOE HASHEM, G-D, WHY DID YOU LEAD THIS PEOPLE ACROSS THE YARDEN ONLY TO DELIVER US INTO THE HANDS OF THE AMORI, TO BE DESTROYED BY THEM? IF ONLY WE HAD BEEN CONTENT TO REMAIN ON THE OTHER SIDE OF THE YARDEN.
8 PLEASE, HASHEM, WHAT WILL I SAY, AFTER YISRAEL HAS TURNED THEIR BACKS (BECAUSE YISRAEL IS FEELING TOTALLY DEFEATED) BEFORE THEIR ENEMIES! 9 FOR WHEN THE CANAANI AND ALL THE INHABITANTS OF THE LAND HEAR OF THIS, THEY WILL SURROUND US, AND WIPE OUT OUR NAME FROM THE EARTH. AND WHAT WILL YOU DO FOR YOUR GREAT NAME?'

10 AND HASHEM SAID TO YEHOSHUA

GET UP; WHY DO YOU FALL ON YOUR FACE?

EXPLANATION #1: ***GET UP***, YOUR WORDS ARE ACCEPTED.

EXPLANATION #2: WHY DIDN'T YOU ***GET UP*** AND LEAD THE TROOPS INTO BATTLE?

EXPLANATION #3: WHY DID YOU ***GET UP*** AND INSTITUTE A BAN ON THE SPOILS OF YERICHO? IN DOING SO, I WAS COMPELLED TO ENFORCE YOUR EDICT.

11 YISRAEL HAS SINNED,

EVEN THOUGH ONLY ONE PERSON, ACHAN BEN CARMI, SINNED, ALL OF YISRAEL MUST BARE ***RESPONSIBILITY***. YISRAEL IS ONE NATION, ONE PEOPLE, COMPLETELY ENTWINED WITHIN ONE ANOTHER AND RESPONSIBLE FOR EACH OTHER.

AND THEY ALSO TRANSGRESSED MY COVENANT WHICH I COMMANDED THEM

YISRAEL IS ***NOW*** RESPONSIBLE TO OBEY ALL OF THE DIRECTIVES GIVEN BY THE PROPHETS...

AND THEY ALSO HAVE TAKEN OF THE CONSECRATED ITEMS

THEY ***PROFANED*** THE NAME OF HASHEM BY TAKING THE SANCTIFIED ITEMS...

AND HAVE ALSO STOLEN

THEY STOLE ***SECRETLY,*** THINKING THEY COULD HIDE FROM HASHEM...

AND ALSO CONCEALED THE TRUTH,

PERHAPS SOMEONE WAS ***AWARE*** OF THE CULPRITS ACTIONS...

AND ALSO THEY HAVE EVEN PUT IT WITHIN THEIR OWN CONTAINERS.

TO FURTHER ***HIDE*** IT...

THE REASON וְגַם IS REPEATED FIVE TIME IN VERSE 11 IS TO REPRESENT THAT THEY ***TRANSGRESSED*** THE FIVE BOOKS OF MOSHE...

-- וַיִּפֹּל עַל פָּנָיו אַרְצָה לִפְנֵי אֲרוֹן ה' עַד הָעֶרֶב הוּא וְזִקְנֵי יִשְׂרָאֵל וַיַּעֲלוּ עָפָר עַל רֹאשָׁם. **ז** וַיֹּאמֶר
יְהוֹשֻׁעַ אֲהָהּ אֲד'נָי ה' לָמָה הֵעֲבַרְתָּ הַעֲבִיר אֶת הָעָם הַזֶּה אֶת הַיַּרְדֵּן לָתֵת אֹתָנוּ בְּיַד הָאֱמֹרִי
לְהַאֲבִידֵנוּ וְלוּ הוֹאַלְנוּ וַנֵּשֶׁב בְּעֵבֶר הַיַּרְדֵּן. **ח** בִּי אֲד'נָי מָה אֹמַר אַחֲרֵי אֲשֶׁר הָפַךְ יִשְׂרָאֵל עֹרֶף לִפְנֵי
אֹיְבָיו. **ט** וְיִשְׁמְעוּ הַכְּנַעֲנִי וְכֹל יֹשְׁבֵי הָאָרֶץ וְנָסַבּוּ עָלֵינוּ וְהִכְרִיתוּ אֶת שְׁמֵנוּ מִן הָאָרֶץ וּמַה תַּעֲשֶׂה
לְשִׁמְךָ הַגָּדוֹל. **י** וַיֹּאמֶר ה' אֶל יְהוֹשֻׁעַ קֻם לָךְ לָמָּה זֶּה אַתָּה נֹפֵל עַל פָּנֶיךָ. **יא** חָטָא יִשְׂרָאֵל וְגַם
עָבְרוּ אֶת בְּרִיתִי אֲשֶׁר צִוִּיתִי אוֹתָם וְגַם לָקְחוּ מִן הַחֵרֶם וְגַם גָּנְבוּ וְגַם כִּחֲשׁוּ וְגַם שָׂמוּ בִכְלֵיהֶם.

12 THE CHILDREN OF YISRAEL WILL NOT BE ABLE TO HOLD THEIR GROUND AGAINST THEIR ENEMIES. THEY WILL HAVE TO TURN THEIR BACKS BEFORE THEIR ENEMIES, FOR THEY HAVE BEEN CONDEMNED. I WILL NOT BE WITH YOU ANYMORE UNLESS YOU DESTROY THE PERPETRATOR AND CONSECRATED THINGS FROM AMONG YOU.

13 GO, PURIFY THE PEOPLE, AND SAY, 'PURIFY YOURSELVES FOR TOMORROW, FOR SO SAYS HASHEM, THE G-D OF YISRAEL, THERE IS SOMETHING THAT IS CONDEMNED IN YOUR MIDST. YISRAEL, YOU WILL NOT BE ABLE TO STAND BEFORE YOUR ENEMIES, UNTIL YOU REMOVE THE CONDEMNED ELEMENT FROM AMONG YOU.

14 TOMORROW MORNING YOU WILL PRESENT YOURSELVES BY TRIBES. WHICHEVER TRIBE HASHEM INDICATES SHALL COME FORWARD BY FAMILIES, THE FAMILY THAT HASHEM INDICATES SHALL COME FORWARD BY THE ANCESTRAL LINE, AND THE THE ANCESTRAL LINE THAT HASHEM INDICATES SHALL COME FORWARD BY THE HEAD OF THAT FAMILY.

15 THEN HE WHO IS INDICATED AS THE CONDEMNED ONE, AND ALL THAT IS HIS, SHALL BE BURNED BY FIRE BECAUSE HE HAS VIOLATED THE COVENANT OF HASHEM AND BECAUSE HE HAS CAUSED A HORRENDOUS THING IN YISRAEL.'

יב וְלֹא יֻכְלוּ בְּנֵי יִשְׂרָאֵל לָקוּם לִפְנֵי אֹיְבֵיהֶם עֹרֶף יִפְנוּ לִפְנֵי אֹיְבֵיהֶם כִּי הָיוּ לְחֵרֶם לֹא
אוֹסִיף לִהְיוֹת עִמָּכֶם אִם לֹא תַשְׁמִידוּ הַחֵרֶם מִקִּרְבְּכֶם. **יג** קֻם קַדֵּשׁ אֶת הָעָם וְאָמַרְתָּ
הִתְקַדְּשׁוּ לְמָחָר כִּי כֹה אָמַר ה' אֱלֹקֵי יִשְׂרָאֵל חֵרֶם בְּקִרְבְּךָ יִשְׂרָאֵל לֹא תוּכַל לָקוּם
לִפְנֵי אֹיְבֶיךָ עַד הֲסִירְכֶם הַחֵרֶם מִקִּרְבְּכֶם. **יד** וְנִקְרַבְתֶּם בַּבֹּקֶר לְשִׁבְטֵיכֶם וְהָיָה הַשֵּׁבֶט
אֲשֶׁר יִלְכְּדֶנּוּ ה' יִקְרַב לַמִּשְׁפָּחוֹת וְהַמִּשְׁפָּחָה אֲשֶׁר יִלְכְּדֶנָּה ה' תִּקְרַב לַבָּתִּים וְהַבַּיִת
אֲשֶׁר יִלְכְּדֶנּוּ ה' יִקְרַב לַגְּבָרִים. **טו** וְהָיָה הַנִּלְכָּד בַּחֵרֶם יִשָּׂרֵף בָּאֵשׁ אֹתוֹ וְאֶת כָּל אֲשֶׁר
לוֹ כִּי עָבַר אֶת בְּרִית ה' וְכִי עָשָׂה נְבָלָה בְּיִשְׂרָאֵל.

16 SO YEHOSHUA ROSE UP EARLY IN THE MORNING, AND BROUGHT YISRAEL FORWARD BY TRIBES.
THE HEADS OF EACH TRIBE WERE BROUGHT BEFORE THE KOHEN GADOL (HIGH PRIEST) AND THE ARON HABRIT (ARK OF COVENANT)
THE CHOSHEN (BREASTPLATE) WAS ONE OF THE SACRED GARMENTS WORN BY THE KOHEN GADOL. THE DIVINE DECISIONS WERE GIVEN THROUGH THE LETTERS INSCRIBED ON THE CHOSHEN.
אברהם יצחק יעקב
ראובן
שמעון
לוי
יהודה
יששכר
זבולן
דן
נפתלי
גד
אשר
יוסף
בנימין
שבטי ישרון
AND THE TRIBE OF YEHUDAH WAS INDICATED.
YEHUDAH WAS SELECTED IN ONE OF TWO WAYS. THE NAME OF YEHUDAH FADED ON THE CHOSHEN THAT THE KOHEN GADOL WAS WEARING. OR YEHUDAH'S ELDER FROZE WHILE PASSING BY THE ARON HABRIT.
טז וַיַּשְׁכֵּם יְהוֹשֻׁעַ בַּבֹּקֶר וַיַּקְרֵב אֶת יִשְׂרָאֵל לִשְׁבָטָיו וַיִּלָּכֵד שֵׁבֶט יְהוּדָה.

ONCE THE TRIBE OF YEHUDAH WAS INDICATED, YEHOSHUA USED A SERIES OF LOTTERIES TO FIND WHO WAS THE GUILTY ONE. HE PLACED ALL THE NAMES OF THE FAMILIES OF YEHUDAH INTO A CONTAINER, AND PULLED OUT A FAMILY NAME. THEN HE PLACED ALL THE NAMES OF THE MEN FROM THAT FAMILY INTO THE CONTAINER AND PULLED OUT A NAME.
ALL OF THE MALE HOUSEHOLD HEADS FROM ZARCHI, PLEASE STEP FORWARD...
ZAVDI, YOU ARE NOW CHOSEN, PLEASE BRING YOUR MALE CHILDREN FORWARD...
THE NEXT NAME I CHOOSE WILL BE THE GUILTY PARTY...
17 HE THEN HAD THE FAMILY OF YEHUDA COME FORWARD, AND FROM THEM, THE FAMILY OF ZARCHI WAS INDICATED. THEN HE HAD THE FAMILY OF ZARCHI COME FORWARD, AND FROM THOSE MEN, ZAVDI WAS INDICATED. 18 HE THEN HAD THE MEN OF THAT FAMILY COME FORWARD- -
יז וַיַּקְרֵב אֶת מִשְׁפַּחַת יְהוּדָה וַיִּלְכֹּד אֵת מִשְׁפַּחַת הַזַּרְחִי וַיַּקְרֵב אֶת מִשְׁפַּחַת
הַזַּרְחִי לַגְּבָרִים וַיִּלָּכֵד זַבְדִּי. יח וַיַּקְרֵב אֶת בֵּיתוֹ לַגְּבָרִים - -

- - AND ACHAN, THE SON OF CARMI, THE SON OF ZAVDI, THE SON OF ZERACH, OF THE TRIBE OF YEHUDAH, WAS INDICATED.
THIS IS AN OUTRAGE! IF I PLACED INTO THE CONTAINER YOUR NAME AND ELIEZER THE KOHEN GADOL, THE TWO GREATEST PEOPLE OF THIS GENERATION, ONE OF YOU WOULD BE CHOSEN...!
THE LOTTERY SYSTEM WILL BE USED TO DIVIDE THE LAND. PLEASE DO NOT CAST DOUBTS ON THIS METHOD...
19 AND YEHOSHUA SAID TO ACHAN
MY SON, GIVE HONOR TO HASHEM, THE G-D OF YISRAEL
AND CONFESS TO HIM. TELL ME WHAT YOU HAVE DONE; DO NOT HIDE ANY DETAILS FROM ME.
THE TORAH LAID DOWN AN IMPORTANT EDICT; BEFORE SOMEONE IS EXECUTED, HE IS IMPLORED TO DO VIDUY (CONFESSION) ON HIS SINS...

THERE ARE **FOUR** CATEGORIES OF EXECUTION:

STRANGULATION...

THE CONVICTED PERSON WAS BURIED UP TO HIS KNEES. A CLOTH WAS THEN **WRAPPED** AROUND HIS NECK, WHERE TWO MEN WOULD PULL ON THE CLOTH FROM BOTH SIDES UNTIL HE DIED.

STONING...

THE CONVICTED PERSON WAS **THROWN** OFF A SMALL CLIFF. IF THE FALL DID NOT KILL HIM, A ROCK WAS **DROPPED** ON HIM. IF THIS TOO FAILED, THE PEOPLE WOULD THEN **PELT** HIM WITH STONES.

DECAPITATION...

THE CONVICTED PERSON'S HEAD IS CUT OFF BY A SWORD.

BURNIING...

THE CONVICTED PERSON'S MOUTH WAS **FORCED** OPEN AND MOLTEN METAL WAS POURED DOWN HIS THROAT.

IT IS BETTER AND MORE SATISFACTORY TO ACQUIT A THOUSAND **GUILTY** PEOPLE THAN TO PUT A SINGLE INNOCENT PERSON TO DEATH.

THE RABBIS OF THE COURTS WOULD **FAST** ON THE DAY THEY HAD TO CARRY OUT THE CAPITAL PUNISHMENT ON SOMEONE. IT WAS A VERY **SAD** AND SOLEMN DAY FOR EVERYONE.

- - וַיִּלָּכֵד עָכָן בֶּן כַּרְמִי בֶן זַבְדִּי בֶּן זֶרַח לְמַטֵּה יְהוּדָה. **יט** וַיֹּאמֶר יְהוֹשֻׁעַ אֶל עָכָן בְּנִי
שִׂים נָא כָבוֹד לַה' אֱלֹקֵי יִשְׂרָאֵל וְתֶן לוֹ תוֹדָה וְהַגֶּד נָא לִי מֶה עָשִׂיתָ אַל תְּכַחֵד מִמֶּנִּי.

YEHOSHUA IS TRYING TO PIN THE BLAME ON ONE OF OUR OWN.
REALLY, THE FAULT LIES WITH HIM ALONE. HE SHOULD HAVE LED THE TROOPS IN BATTLE LIKE HASHEM INSTRUCTED HIM TO DO.
DOES HE REALLY THINK THAT WE, THE TRIBE OF YEHUDAH, WILL SIT BACK AND DO NOTHING!
WE MUST ARM OURSELVES SO THE LEADERSHIP TAKES US SERIOUSLY...
WE WANT ACHAN TO GO FREE...!
YEAH!!
LOOK AT WHAT I'VE DONE! WE JUST ENTERED THE LAND, AND I WILL GO DOWN IN HISTORY AS THE CAUSE OF THE FIRST CIVIL WAR IN YISRAEL.

כ וַיַּעַן עָכָן אֶת יְהוֹשֻׁעַ וַיֹּאמַר אָמְנָה אָנֹכִי חָטָאתִי לַה' אֱלֹקֵי יִשְׂרָאֵל וְכָזֹאת וְכָזֹאת
עָשִׂיתִי. **כא** ואראה (וָאֵרֶא) בַשָּׁלָל אַדֶּרֶת שִׁנְעָר אַחַת טוֹבָה וּמָאתַיִם שְׁקָלִים כֶּסֶף - -

- - AND A WEDGE OF GOLD WEIGHING FIFTY SHEKELS, AND I CRAVED THEM, AND TOOK THEM.
FURTHERMORE, I IGNORED THE BAN DECREED BY MOSHE IN THE DESERT.
YOU REMEMBER, THE WARS WITH ARAD, SICHON, OG AND MIDYAN.
I ACCUMULATED SO MUCH BOOTY, I CAN'T EVEN REMEMBER WHERE I TOOK IT FROM...
THEY ARE BURIED IN THE GROUND UNDER MY TENT, WITH THE SILVER UNDER IT.
- - וּלְשׁוֹן זָהָב אֶחָד חֲמִשִּׁים שְׁקָלִים מִשְׁקָלוֹ וָאֶחְמְדֵם וָאֶקָּחֵם וְהִנָּם
טְמוּנִים בָּאָרֶץ בְּתוֹךְ הָאָהֳלִי וְהַכֶּסֶף תַּחְתֶּיהָ.

כב וַיִּשְׁלַח יְהוֹשֻׁעַ מַלְאָכִים וַיָּרֻצוּ הָאֹהֱלָה וְהִנֵּה טְמוּנָה בְּאָהֳלוֹ וְהַכֶּסֶף תַּחְתֶּיהָ.

23 AND THEY TOOK THEM FROM THE TENT, AND BROUGHT THEM TO YEHOSHUA, AND TO ALL THE CHILDREN OF YISRAEL
HERE THEY ARE, JUST AS ACHAN DESCRIBED...
MASTER OF THE UNIVERSE, FOR THESE, YOU WOULD HAVE HAD YOUR CHILDREN BE HARMED?
ALL OF YISRAEL ARE WELCOME TO INSPECT THE GOLD AND SILVER TAKEN BY ACHAN FROM THE CONSECRATED CITY OF YERICHO...
AND THEY LAID THEM DOWN BEFORE HASHEM.

כג וַיִּקָּחוּם מִתּוֹךְ הָאֹהֶל וַיְבִאוּם אֶל יְהוֹשֻׁעַ וְאֶל כָּל בְּנֵי יִשְׂרָאֵל וַיַּצִּקֻם לִפְנֵי ה'.

24 AND YEHOSHUA, AND ALL YISRAEL WITH HIM, TOOK ACHAN THE SON OF ZERACH, THE SILVER, THE GARMENTS, AND WEDGE OF GOLD, HIS SONS AND DAUGHTERS, HIS OX, HIS DONKEY, HIS FLOCK, HIS TENT, AND ALL HIS BELONGINGS,
I CAN'T BELIEVE HE TOOK **SO** MUCH STUFF...
ACHAN, BECAUSE YOU **CONFESSED** TO YOUR WRONGDOINGS, YOU WILL HAVE ATONEMENT FOR ALL OF YOUR TRANSGRESSIONS...
WHY IS ACHAN'S **WHOLE** FAMILY ALSO BEING TAKEN TO ACHOR?
YEHOSHUA WANTS THEM TO **WITNESS** THE PUNISHMENT SO THEY SHOULD BE DETERRED FROM ANY FUTURE SINS..
AND THEY BROUGHT THEM UP TO THE VALLEY OF ACHOR.
THE ROAD TO ACHOR WENT THROUGH **HILLS**, THAT'S WHY THE VERSE STATES "THEY BROUGHT THEM UP TO THE VALLEY OF ACHOR.
כד וַיִּקַּח יְהוֹשֻׁעַ אֶת עָכָן בֶּן זֶרַח וְאֶת הַכֶּסֶף וְאֶת הָאַדֶּרֶת וְאֶת לְשׁוֹן הַזָּהָב וְאֶת בָּנָיו
וְאֶת בְּנֹתָיו וְאֶת שׁוֹרוֹ וְאֶת חֲמֹרוֹ וְאֶת צֹאנוֹ וְאֶת אָהֳלוֹ וְאֶת כָּל אֲשֶׁר לוֹ וְכָל יִשְׂרָאֵל עִמּוֹ
וַיַּעֲלוּ אֹתָם עֵמֶק עָכוֹר.

25 AND YEHOSHUA SAID
WHAT A HORRIFYING CALAMITY YOU HAVE BROUGHT UPON US?
NOW HASHEM WILL BRING A HORRIFYING CALAMITY UPON YOU THIS DAY!!
ACHAN WAS PUT TO DEATH BECAUSE HE DISOBEYED YEHOSHUA'S COMMAND AND STOLE WHAT WAS SANCTIFIED FOR HASHEM. HIS DEATH BY STONING WAS BECAUSE HE DESECRATED THE SHABBOS WHEN HE STOLE THE SPOILS IN YERICHO....
AND ALL YISRAEL PELTED HIM WITH STONES - -
AND THEY BURNED THEM WITH FIRE (HIS TENT AND MOVABLE OBJECTS), AND PELTED THEM (THE ANIMALS AS WELL) WITH STONES.
26 THEY RAISED A HUGE MOUND OF STONES OVER HIM, WHICH IS STILL THERE TO THIS DAY, AND HASHEM TURNED FROM THE FIERCENESS OF HIS ANGER. THEREFORE THE NAME OF THAT PLACE WAS NAMED THE VALLEY OF ACHOR, TO THIS DAY.
THE AREA WAS NAMED ACHOR FROM WHAT YEHOSHUA SAID IN VERSE 25, THAT ACHAN CAUSED A "CALAMITY" IN YISRAEL...
WE SAY THE PRAYER 'ALEINU' THREE TIMES DAILY, EVERY SINGLE DAY OF THE YEAR. YEHOSHUA COMPOSED ALEINU, AND ACHAN COMPOSED THE SECOND STANZA. IMPLIED WITHIN THE FIRST THREE WORDS OF 'AL KAIN NEKAVEH' על כן נקוה, IS ACHAN'S NAME (ע-כ-ן) OUR SAGES REVEALED TO US THAT THIS IS THE SOURCE THAT ACHAN WAS INDEED THE AUTHOR.
EVEN THOUGH ACHAN REBELLED AGAINST HASHEM AND YEHOSHUA, AND CAUSED DEATH TO YISRAEL, WHO WERE NOT TO SUFFER ANY CASUALTIES DURING WARTIME, HE WILL BE REMEMBERED FOR DOING TESHUVA WITH HIS WHOLE HEART AND SOUL AND BE WORTHY OF COAUTHORING ONE OF THE GREATEST PRAYERS OF ALL TIME.

כה וַיֹּאמֶר יְהוֹשֻׁעַ מֶה עֲכַרְתָּנוּ יַעְכָּרְךָ ה' בַּיּוֹם הַזֶּה וַיִּרְגְּמוּ אֹתוֹ כָל יִשְׂרָאֵל אֶבֶן
וַיִּשְׂרְפוּ אֹתָם בָּאֵשׁ וַיִּסְקְלוּ אֹתָם בָּאֲבָנִים. **כו** וַיָּקִימוּ עָלָיו גַּל אֲבָנִים גָּדוֹל עַד הַיּוֹם
הַזֶּה וַיָּשָׁב ה' מֵחֲרוֹן אַפּוֹ עַל כֵּן קָרָא שֵׁם הַמָּקוֹם הַהוּא עֵמֶק עָכוֹר עַד הַיּוֹם הַזֶּה.

YEHOSHUA CHAPTER 8
יהושע פרק ח
1 AND HASHEM SAID TO YEHOSHUA,
FEAR NOT, AND BE NOT DISMAYED; TAKE ALL THE FIGHTING TROOPS WITH YOU, AND GO AND MARCH AGAINST AI.
SEE, I WILL DELIVER THE KING OF AI, HIS PEOPLE, HIS CITY, AND HIS LAND INTO YOUR HANDS.
2 AND YOU WILL DO TO AI AND HER KING AS YOU DID TO YERICHO AND HER KING; HOWEVER, YOU MAY TAKE THE SPOILS AND THE CATTLE AS BOOTY FOR YOURSELVES; SET UP AN AMBUSH AGAINST THE CITY FROM BEHIND.
PRIOR TO THE SIN OF ACHAN, YISRAEL CAPTURED A KINGDOM BY BASICALLY WALKING AROUND THE CITY AND BLOWING A FEW SHOFAROT. NOW THINGS WILL CHANGE. EVEN THOUGH HASHEM WILL STILL FIGHT THE WAR FOR YISRAEL, THEY WILL, HOWEVER, BE REQUIRED TO IMPLEMENT STRATEGIES TO DEFEAT THEIR ENEMIES.
MEANWHILE...
JUST IN CASE YISRAEL DECIDES TO STRIKE AGAIN. I WANT MEN STATIONED HERE AND HERE...
AFTER OUR VICTORY LAST TIME, G-D IS OBVIOUSLY NOT WITH THEM!
THIS TIME I WANT TO GO ON THE OFFENSE. SHOULD THEY ATTACK, I WANT EVERY AVAILABLE SOLDIER TO CHASE THEM DOWN AND KILL ALL OF THEIR TROOPS...

א וַיֹּאמֶר ה' אֶל יְהוֹשֻׁעַ אַל תִּירָא וְאַל תֵּחָת קַח עִמְּךָ אֵת כָּל עַם הַמִּלְחָמָה וְקוּם עֲלֵה
הָעָי רְאֵה נָתַתִּי בְיָדְךָ אֶת מֶלֶךְ הָעַי וְאֶת עַמּוֹ וְאֶת עִירוֹ וְאֶת אַרְצוֹ. ב וְעָשִׂיתָ לָעַי וּלְמַלְכָּהּ
כַּאֲשֶׁר עָשִׂיתָ לִירִיחוֹ וּלְמַלְכָּהּ רַק שְׁלָלָהּ וּבְהֶמְתָּהּ תָּבֹזּוּ לָכֶם שִׂים לְךָ אֹרֵב לָעִיר מֵאַחֲרֶיהָ.

ג וַיָּקָם יְהוֹשֻׁעַ וְכָל עַם הַמִּלְחָמָה לַעֲלוֹת הָעָי וַיִּבְחַר יְהוֹשֻׁעַ שְׁלֹשִׁים אֶלֶף אִישׁ גִּבּוֹרֵי הַחַיִל
וַיִּשְׁלָחֵם לָיְלָה. **ד** וַיְצַו אֹתָם לֵאמֹר רְאוּ אַתֶּם אֹרְבִים לָעִיר מֵאַחֲרֵי הָעִיר אַל תַּרְחִיקוּ מִן
הָעִיר מְאֹד וִהְיִיתֶם כֻּלְּכֶם נְכֹנִים. **ה** וַאֲנִי וְכָל הָעָם אֲשֶׁר אִתִּי נִקְרַב אֶל הָעִיר - -

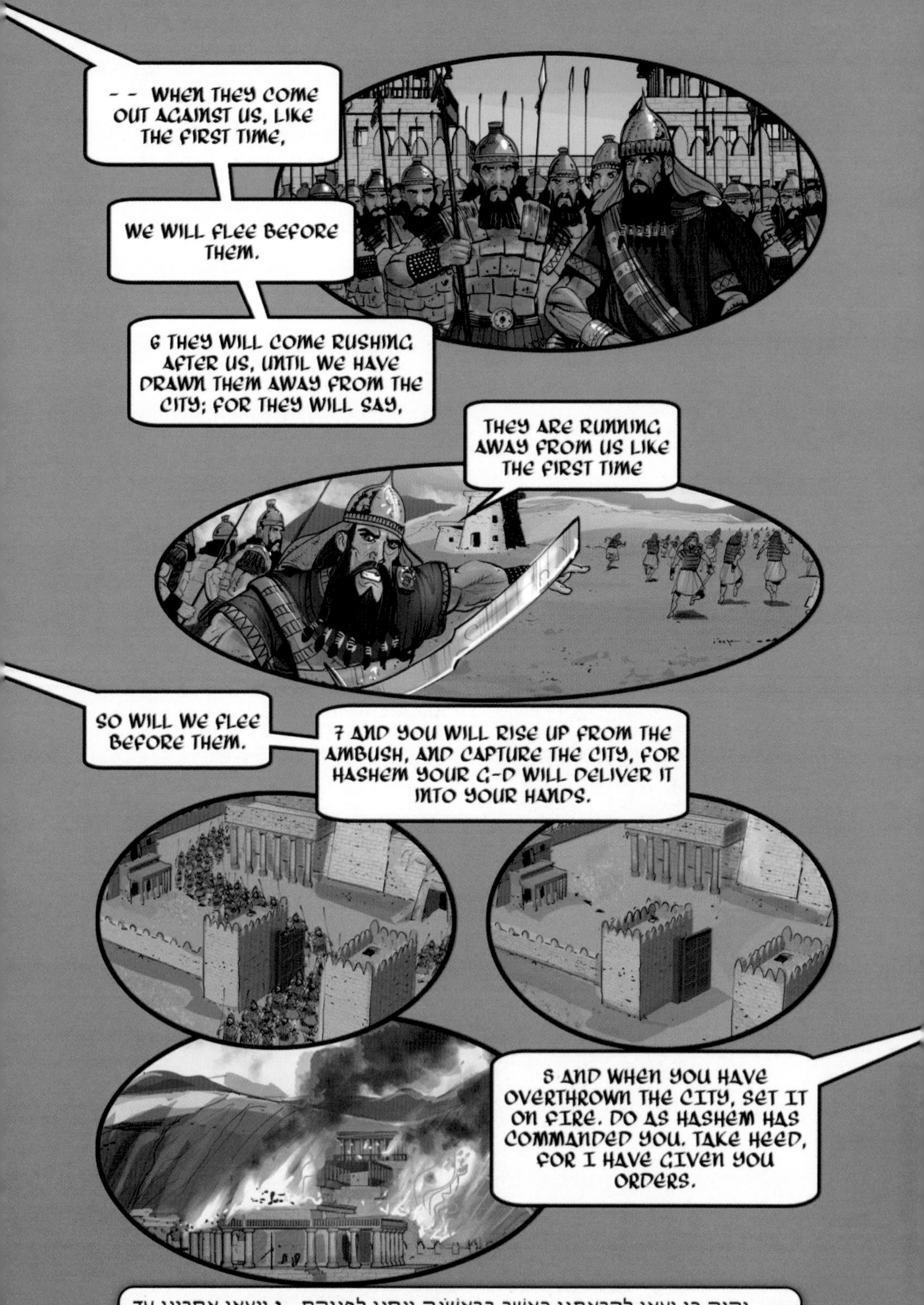
- - WHEN THEY COME OUT AGAINST US, LIKE THE FIRST TIME,
WE WILL FLEE BEFORE THEM.
6 THEY WILL COME RUSHING AFTER US, UNTIL WE HAVE DRAWN THEM AWAY FROM THE CITY; FOR THEY WILL SAY,
THEY ARE RUNNING AWAY FROM US LIKE THE FIRST TIME
SO WILL WE FLEE BEFORE THEM.
7 AND YOU WILL RISE UP FROM THE AMBUSH, AND CAPTURE THE CITY, FOR HASHEM YOUR G-D WILL DELIVER IT INTO YOUR HANDS.
8 AND WHEN YOU HAVE OVERTHROWN THE CITY, SET IT ON FIRE. DO AS HASHEM HAS COMMANDED YOU. TAKE HEED, FOR I HAVE GIVEN YOU ORDERS.

-- וְהָיָה כִּי יֵצְאוּ לִקְרָאתֵנוּ כַּאֲשֶׁר בָּרִאשֹׁנָה וְנַסְנוּ לִפְנֵיהֶם. **ו** וְיָצְאוּ אַחֲרֵינוּ עַד
הַתִּיקֵנוּ אוֹתָם מִן הָעִיר כִּי יֹאמְרוּ נָסִים לְפָנֵינוּ כַּאֲשֶׁר בָּרִאשֹׁנָה וְנַסְנוּ לִפְנֵיהֶם. **ז**
וְאַתֶּם תָּקֻמוּ מֵהָאוֹרֵב וְהוֹרַשְׁתֶּם אֶת הָעִיר וּנְתָנָהּ ה' אֱלֹקֵיכֶם בְּיֶדְכֶם. **ח** וְהָיָה
כְּתָפְשְׂכֶם אֶת הָעִיר תַּצִּיתוּ אֶת הָעִיר בָּאֵשׁ כִּדְבַר ה' תַּעֲשׂוּ רְאוּ צִוִּיתִי אֶתְכֶם.

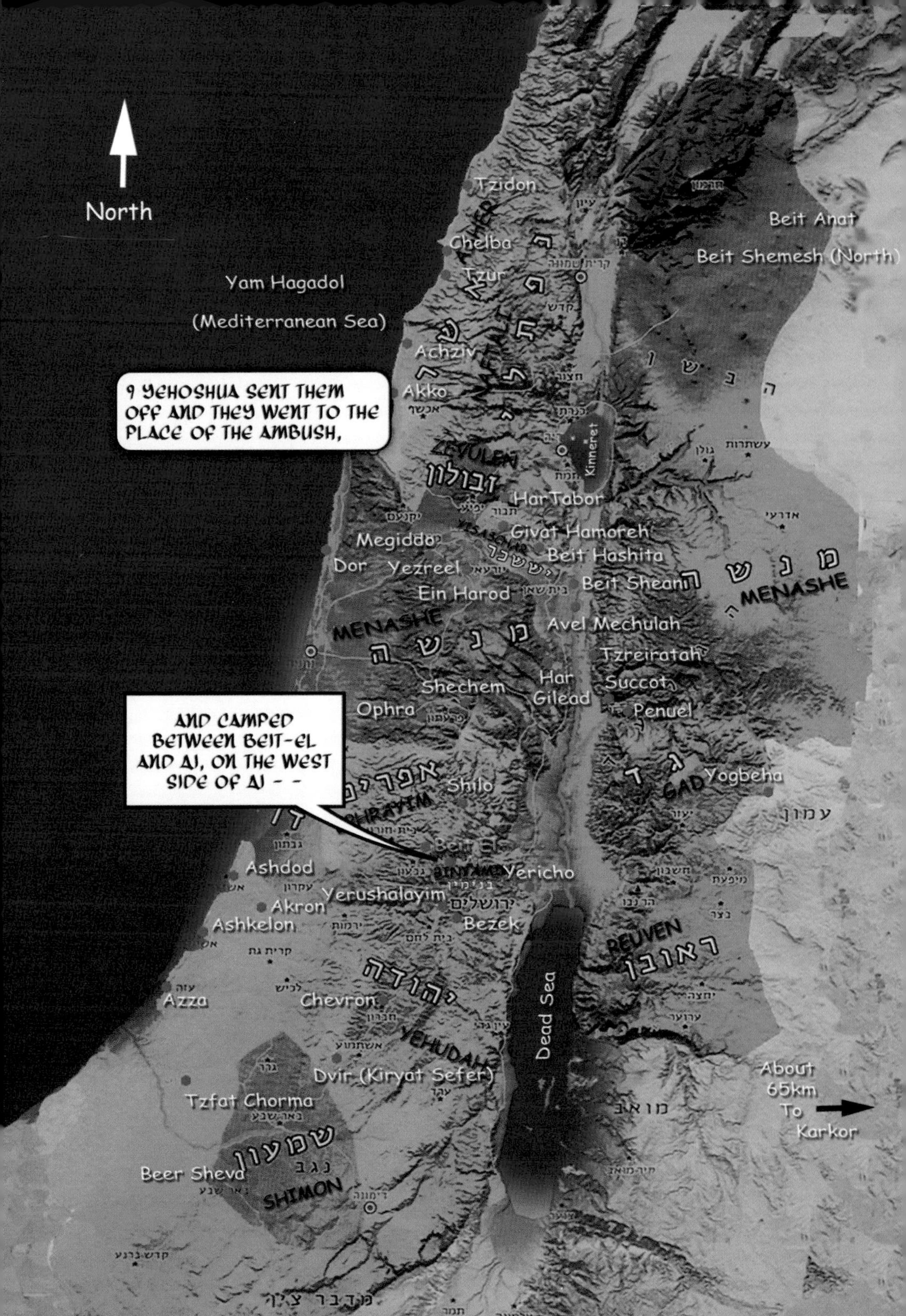

ט וַיִּשְׁלָחֵם יְהוֹשֻׁעַ וַיֵּלְכוּ אֶל הַמַּאְרָב וַיֵּשְׁבוּ בֵּין בֵּית אֵל וּבֵין הָעַי מִיָּם לָעָי - -

- - AND YEHOSHUA SLEPT THAT NIGHT WITH THE REST OF THE SOLDIERS.
10 AND YEHOSHUA ROSE UP EARLY IN THE MORNING, AND ASSEMBLED THE PEOPLE.
YEHOSHUA INSPECTED THE TROOPS IN PREPARATION FOR WAR.
THIS TIME AND EVERY TIME FROM NOW ON, I WILL LEAD YOU INTO BATTLE.
AND HE AND THE ELDERS OF YISRAEL WENT UP BEFORE THE PEOPLE TO AI.
11 ALL THE FIGHTING MEN THAT WERE WITH HIM ADVANCED NEAR THE CITY AND CAMPED TO THE NORTH OF AI, WITH A VALLEY BETWEEN THEM AND AI.
12 AND HE TOOK ABOUT FIVE THOUSAND MEN, AND STATIONED THEM AS AN AMBUSH BETWEEN BEIT EL AND AI, WEST OF THE CITY.

– – וַיָּלֶן יְהוֹשֻׁעַ בַּלַּיְלָה הַהוּא בְּתוֹךְ הָעָם. **י** וַיַּשְׁכֵּם יְהוֹשֻׁעַ בַּבֹּקֶר וַיִּפְקֹד אֶת הָעָם
וַיַּעַל הוּא וְזִקְנֵי יִשְׂרָאֵל לִפְנֵי הָעָם הָעָי. **יא** וְכָל הָעָם הַמִּלְחָמָה אֲשֶׁר אִתּוֹ עָלוּ וַיִּגְּשׁוּ
וַיָּבֹאוּ נֶגֶד הָעִיר וַיַּחֲנוּ מִצְּפוֹן לָעַי וְהַגַּי בֵּינָו וּבֵין הָעָי. **יב** וַיִּקַּח כַּחֲמֵשֶׁת אֲלָפִים אִישׁ
וַיָּשֶׂם אוֹתָם אֹרֵב בֵּין בֵּית אֵל וּבֵין הָעַי מִיָּם לָעִיר.

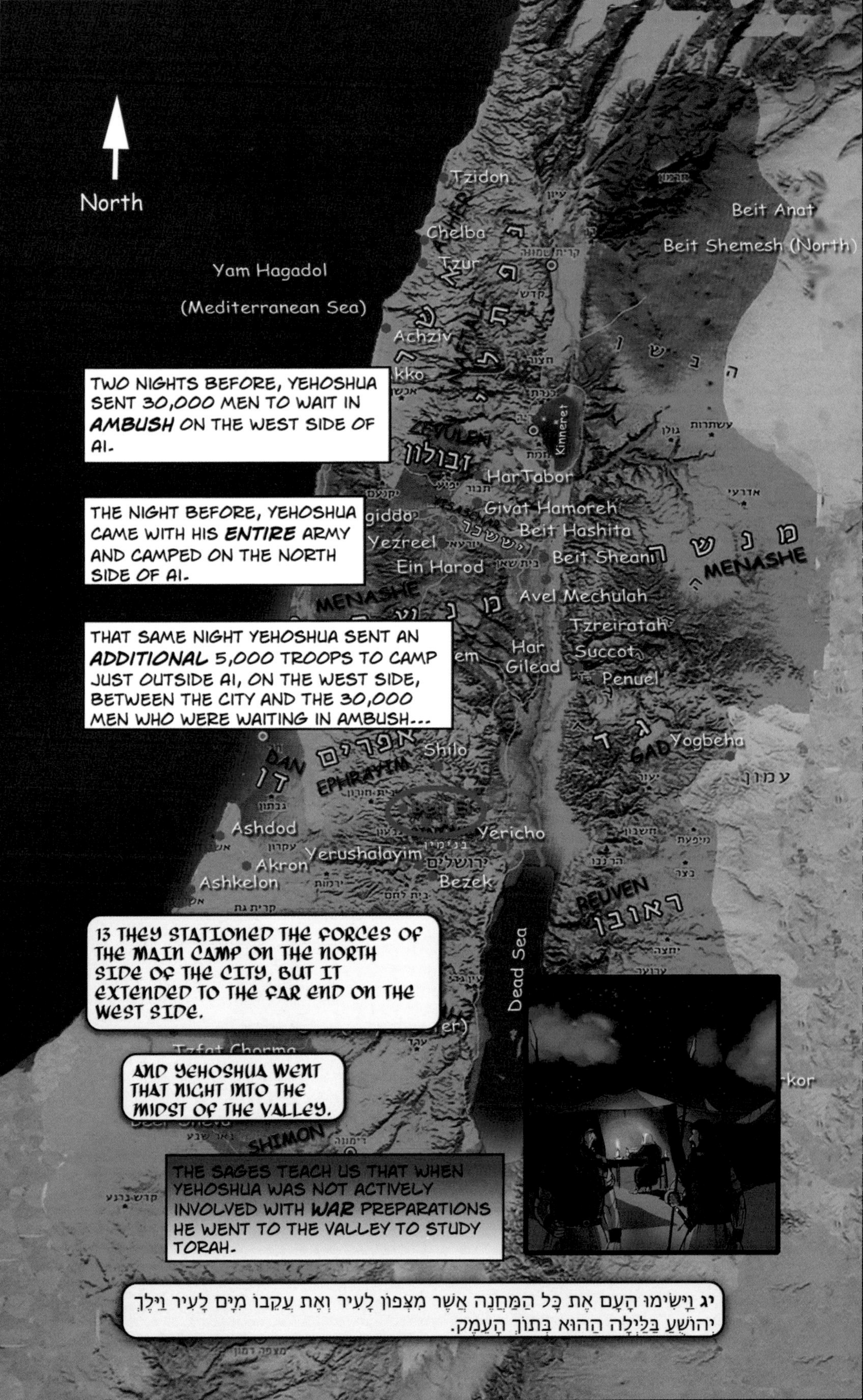
North
Yam Hagadol
(Mediterranean Sea)
Tzidon
Beit Anat
Chelba
Beit Shemesh (North)
Tzur
Achziv
Kinneret
ZEVULEN
זבולון
Har Tabor
Givat Hamoreh
Beit Hashita
Yezreel
Beit Shean
Ein Harod
MENASHE
Avel Mechulah
Tzreiratah
Har Gilead
Succot
Penuel
Shilo
GAD
Yogbeha
DAN
EPHRAYIM
אפרים
Ashdod
Yericho
Yerushalayim
ירושלים
Akron
Ashkelon
Bezek
REUVEN
ראובן
Dead Sea
SHIMON
TWO NIGHTS BEFORE, YEHOSHUA SENT 30,000 MEN TO WAIT IN AMBUSH ON THE WEST SIDE OF AI.
THE NIGHT BEFORE, YEHOSHUA CAME WITH HIS ENTIRE ARMY AND CAMPED ON THE NORTH SIDE OF AI.
THAT SAME NIGHT YEHOSHUA SENT AN ADDITIONAL 5,000 TROOPS TO CAMP JUST OUTSIDE AI, ON THE WEST SIDE, BETWEEN THE CITY AND THE 30,000 MEN WHO WERE WAITING IN AMBUSH...
13 THEY STATIONED THE FORCES OF THE MAIN CAMP ON THE NORTH SIDE OF THE CITY, BUT IT EXTENDED TO THE FAR END ON THE WEST SIDE.
AND YEHOSHUA WENT THAT NIGHT INTO THE MIDST OF THE VALLEY.
THE SAGES TEACH US THAT WHEN YEHOSHUA WAS NOT ACTIVELY INVOLVED WITH WAR PREPARATIONS HE WENT TO THE VALLEY TO STUDY TORAH.
יג וַיָּשִׂימוּ הָעָם אֶת כָּל הַמַּחֲנֶה אֲשֶׁר מִצְּפוֹן לָעִיר וְאֶת עֲקֵבוֹ מִיָּם לָעִיר וַיֵּלֶךְ
יְהוֹשֻׁעַ בַּלַּיְלָה הַהוּא בְּתוֹךְ הָעֵמֶק.

REMEMBER, STICK TO THE PLAN. FIRST, WE WILL FACE THE TROOPS OF AI AS IF WE ARE ABOUT TO ATTACK. THEN ON MY ORDERS YOU ARE TO RETREAT...
DO NOT FEAR BECAUSE HASHEM AS ALREADY GIVEN AI INTO OUR HANDS.
MEANWHILE...
YOUR HIGHNESS, YISRAEL IS PLANNING A FRONTAL ASSAULT AGAIN AT PRECISELY THE SAME TIME OF DAY THEY WERE DEFEATED LAST TIME.
I SUGGEST WE SEND OUT THE NECESSARY MEN TO MEET THEM IN BATTLE...
I AGREE, HOWEVER, THIS TIME I WANT THEM COMPLETELY DECIMATED...
FURTHERMORE, I PLAN ON GOING INTO BATTLE WITH THE TROOPS. INFORM MY SQUIRE TO PREPARE MY ARMOR FOR COMBAT!

I WANT MEN IN FORMATION THERE, THERE AND OVER THERE...
14 WHEN THE KING OF AI SAW THEM (YEHOSHUA'S ARMY) HE AND ALL THE MEN OF THE CITY RUSHED OUT EARLY IN THE MORNING AND WENT WITH HIS ENTIRE ARMY AT THE APPOINTED TIME FACING THE PLAINS TO WAGE WAR WITH YISRAEL.
BUT HE DID NOT KNOW THAT THERE WAS AN AMBUSH WAITING FOR HIM BEHIND THE CITY.
I CAN SEE IT IN YEHOSHUA'S EYES, HE'S AFRAID...
GIVE THE ORDER TO ATTACK!!!

יד וַיְהִי כִּרְאוֹת מֶלֶךְ הָעַי וַיְמַהֲרוּ וַיַּשְׁכִּימוּ וַיֵּצְאוּ אַנְשֵׁי הָעִיר לִקְרַאת יִשְׂרָאֵל
לַמִּלְחָמָה הוּא וְכָל עַמּוֹ לַמּוֹעֵד לִפְנֵי הָעֲרָבָה וְהוּא לֹא יָדַע כִּי אֹרֵב לוֹ מֵאַחֲרֵי הָעִיר.

15 AND YEHOSHUA AND ALL YISRAEL PRETENDED AS IF THEY WERE BEATEN BEFORE THEM, AND THEY FLED BY THE WAY OF THE WILDERNESS.

טו וַיִּנָּגְעוּ יְהוֹשֻׁעַ וְכָל יִשְׂרָאֵל לִפְנֵיהֶם וַיָּנֻסוּ דֶּרֶךְ הַמִּדְבָּר.

טז וַיִּזָּעֲקוּ כָּל הָעָם אֲשֶׁר בעיר (בָּעַי) לִרְדֹּף אַחֲרֵיהֶם וַיִּרְדְּפוּ אַחֲרֵי יְהוֹשֻׁעַ וַיִּנָּתְקוּ
ן הָעִיר. יז וְלֹא נִשְׁאַר אִישׁ בָּעַי וּבֵית אֵל אֲשֶׁר לֹא יָצְאוּ אַחֲרֵי יִשְׂרָאֵל וַיַּעַזְבוּ אֶת
הָעִיר פְּתוּחָה וַיִּרְדְּפוּ אַחֲרֵי יִשְׂרָאֵל.

18 AND HASHEM SAID TO YEHOSHUA 'STRETCH OUT THE JAVELIN THAT IS IN YOUR HAND TOWARD AI, FOR I WILL GIVE IT INTO YOUR HAND.'
AND YEHOSHUA STRETCHED OUT THE JAVELIN THAT WAS IN HIS HAND TOWARD THE CITY.
MEANWHILE AT THE AMBUSH CAMP OF 30,000 YISRAEL SOLDIERS...
THERE'S YEHOSHUA'S SIGNAL. ARISE UP AND DESTROY THE CITY...
REMEMBER, KILL EVERYONE AND SET THE THE ENTIRE CITY ON FIRE!!!
WHILE THE 30,000 TROOPS WERE ATTACKING AI, THE SECOND CAMP OF 5000 YISRAEL SOLDIERS WERE ADVANCING ON BEIT EL.
19 AS SOON AS HE HELD OUT HIS HAND THE MEN WAITING TO AMBUSH, CAME RUSHING OUT OF THEIR POSITION. AND RAN TO THE CITY - -

יח וַיֹּאמֶר ה' אֶל יְהוֹשֻׁעַ נְטֵה בַּכִּידוֹן אֲשֶׁר בְּיָדְךָ אֶל הָעַי כִּי בְיָדְךָ אֶתְּנֶנָּה וַיֵּט יְהוֹשֻׁעַ בַּכִּידוֹן
אֲשֶׁר בְּיָדוֹ אֶל הָעִיר. **יט** וְהָאוֹרֵב קָם מְהֵרָה מִמְּקוֹמוֹ וַיָּרוּצוּ כִּנְטוֹת יָדוֹ וַיָּבֹאוּ הָעִיר – –

BACK IN AI...
AAGGHH!
- - AND CAPTURED IT, AND QUICKLY SET THE CITY ON FIRE.
MEANWHILE
SIRE, OUR CITY IS ON FIRE...!
- - וַיִּלְכְּדוּהָ וַיְמַהֲרוּ וַיַּצִּיתוּ אֶת-הָעִיר בָּאֵשׁ.

WHAT HAS YEHOSHUA DONE?!
ATTACK---
RETREAT!!!
20 AND WHEN THE MEN OF AI LOOKED BEHIND THEM, THEY SAW, THE SMOKE OF THE CITY ASCENDING UP TO HEAVEN, AND THEY HAD NO PLACE TO FLEE IN ANY DIRECTION; AND THE PEOPLE WHO HAD BEEN FLEEING TO THE DESERT (YISRAEL) NOW BECAME THE PURSUERS.
כ וַיִּפְנוּ אַנְשֵׁי הָעַי אַחֲרֵיהֶם וַיִּרְאוּ וְהִנֵּה עָלָה עֲשַׁן הָעִיר הַשָּׁמַיְמָה וְלֹא הָיָה בָהֶם יָדַיִם לָנוּס הֵנָּה וָהֵנָּה וְהָעָם הַנָּס הַמִּדְבָּר נֶהְפַּךְ אֶל הָרוֹדֵף.

LET'S SEE WHAT THE MEN OF AI THINK OF US NOW...
GOT TO GET OUT OF THIS TRAP...!
I CAN'T HOLD THEM BACK!!!
FINALLY, OUR TURN TO FIGHT BACK...
OWFFF!!!
THERE IS JUST TOO MANY...
THEY ARE KILLING US OFF ONE BY ONE!
21 AND WHEN YEHOSHUA AND ALL YISRAEL SAW THAT THE AMBUSH SUCCEEDED IN TAKING THE CITY, AND THAT THE SMOKE OF THE CITY ASCENDED, THEN THEY TURNED AROUND AND SLEW THE MEN OF AI.
כא וִיהוֹשֻׁעַ וְכָל יִשְׂרָאֵל רָאוּ כִּי לָכַד הָאֹרֵב אֶת-הָעִיר
וְכִי עָלָה עֲשַׁן הָעִיר וַיָּשֻׁבוּ וַיַּכּוּ אֶת אַנְשֵׁי הָעָי.

כב וְאֵלֶּה יָצְאוּ מִן הָעִיר לִקְרָאתָם וַיִּהְיוּ לְיִשְׂרָאֵל בַּתָּוֶךְ אֵלֶּה מִזֶּה וְאֵלֶּה מִזֶּה וַיַּכּוּ אוֹתָם
עַד בִּלְתִּי הִשְׁאִיר לוֹ שָׂרִיד וּפָלִיט. כג וְאֶת מֶלֶךְ הָעַי תָּפְשׂוּ חָי וַיַּקְרִבוּ אֹתוֹ אֶל-יְהוֹשֻׁעַ.

24 WHEN YISRAEL HAD KILLED ALL THE INHABITANTS OF AI WHO HAD PURSUED THEM INTO THE DESERT, AND ALL OF THEM, TO THE LAST MAN, HAD FALLEN BY THE SWORD, ALL OF YISRAEL TURNED BACK TO GO TO AI AND PUT IT TO THE SWORD (DESTROY THE REST BY THE SWORD).
25 THE TOTAL AMOUNT OF PEOPLE WHO WERE KILLED THAT DAY, MEN, WOMEN, AND THE ENTIRE POPULATION OF AI, CAME TO TWELVE THOUSAND. 26 FOR YEHOSHUA DID NOT DRAW BACK HIS HAND THAT HE STRETCHED OUT WITH THE JAVELIN, UNTIL HE HAD UTTERLY DESTROYED ALL THE INHABITANTS OF AI.
DIFFERENCE BETWEEN STAFF AND JAVELIN:
THE STAFF WAS AN INSTRUMENT USED BY HASHEM TO PERFORM MIRACLES. THEY PASSED THIS STAFF DOWN TO THE PROPHETS. EVEN YEHOSHUA, WHO WAS THE STUDENT OF MOSHE RABBEINU AND RECEIVED THE STAFF FROM HIM, DID NOT USE IT. HE ONLY USED THE JAVELIN. THE IDEA OF THE STAFF WAS TO SHOW MASTERY AND POWER OF CAPABILITY. HOWEVER, THE JAVELIN WAS ALL ABOUT LEADERSHIP ON THE BATTLEFIELD. THAT IS WHY HASHEM TOLD YEHOSHUA TO USE IT.

ד וַיְהִי כְּכַלּוֹת יִשְׂרָאֵל לַהֲרֹג אֶת כָּל יֹשְׁבֵי הָעַי בַּשָּׂדֶה בַּמִּדְבָּר אֲשֶׁר רְדָפוּם בּוֹ וַיִּפְּלוּ
לָּם לְפִי חֶרֶב עַד תֻּמָּם וַיָּשֻׁבוּ כָל יִשְׂרָאֵל הָעַי וַיַּכּוּ אֹתָהּ לְפִי חָרֶב. **כה** וַיְהִי כָל
נֹּפְלִים בַּיּוֹם הַהוּא מֵאִישׁ וְעַד אִשָּׁה שְׁנֵים עָשָׂר אָלֶף כֹּל אַנְשֵׁי הָעָי. **כו** וִיהוֹשֻׁעַ
א הֵשִׁיב יָדוֹ אֲשֶׁר נָטָה בַּכִּידוֹן עַד אֲשֶׁר הֶחֱרִים אֵת כָּל יֹשְׁבֵי הָעָי.

27 YISRAEL ONLY TOOK THE CATTLE AND THE SPOIL OF THE CITY AS THEIR BOOTY, ACCORDING TO THE WORD OF HASHEM WHICH HE COMMANDED YEHOSHUA. 28 SO YEHOSHUA BURNT AI, AND TURNED IT INTO A MOUND OF RUINS FOR ALL TIME, A DESOLATION TO THIS DAY.
THIS TIME WE ARE ALLOWED TO TAKE THE SPOILS OF WAR.
WE HAVE TO ALWAYS REMEMBER, THAT WE ARE A NATION, WE ARE ONE, AND MUST BE RESPONSIBLE FOR EACH OTHER.
WHEN WE FOLLOW IN THE WAYS OF HASHEM AND ARE GOOD TO EACH OTHER. HASHEM WILL ALWAYS BE THERE FOR US.
THAT'S RIGHT, THIS IS THE PROMISE OF HASHEM TO YISRAEL. WHEN THE ENEMIES OF YISRAEL FIGHT AGAINST US, THEY WILL ULTIMATELY BE DESTROYED...
כז רַק הַבְּהֵמָה וּשְׁלַל הָעִיר הַהִיא בָּזְזוּ לָהֶם יִשְׂרָאֵל כִּדְבַר ה' אֲשֶׁר צִוָּה אֶת
יְהוֹשֻׁעַ. **כח** וַיִּשְׂרֹף יְהוֹשֻׁעַ אֶת הָעָי וַיְשִׂימֶהָ תֵּל עוֹלָם שְׁמָמָה עַד הַיּוֹם הַזֶּה.

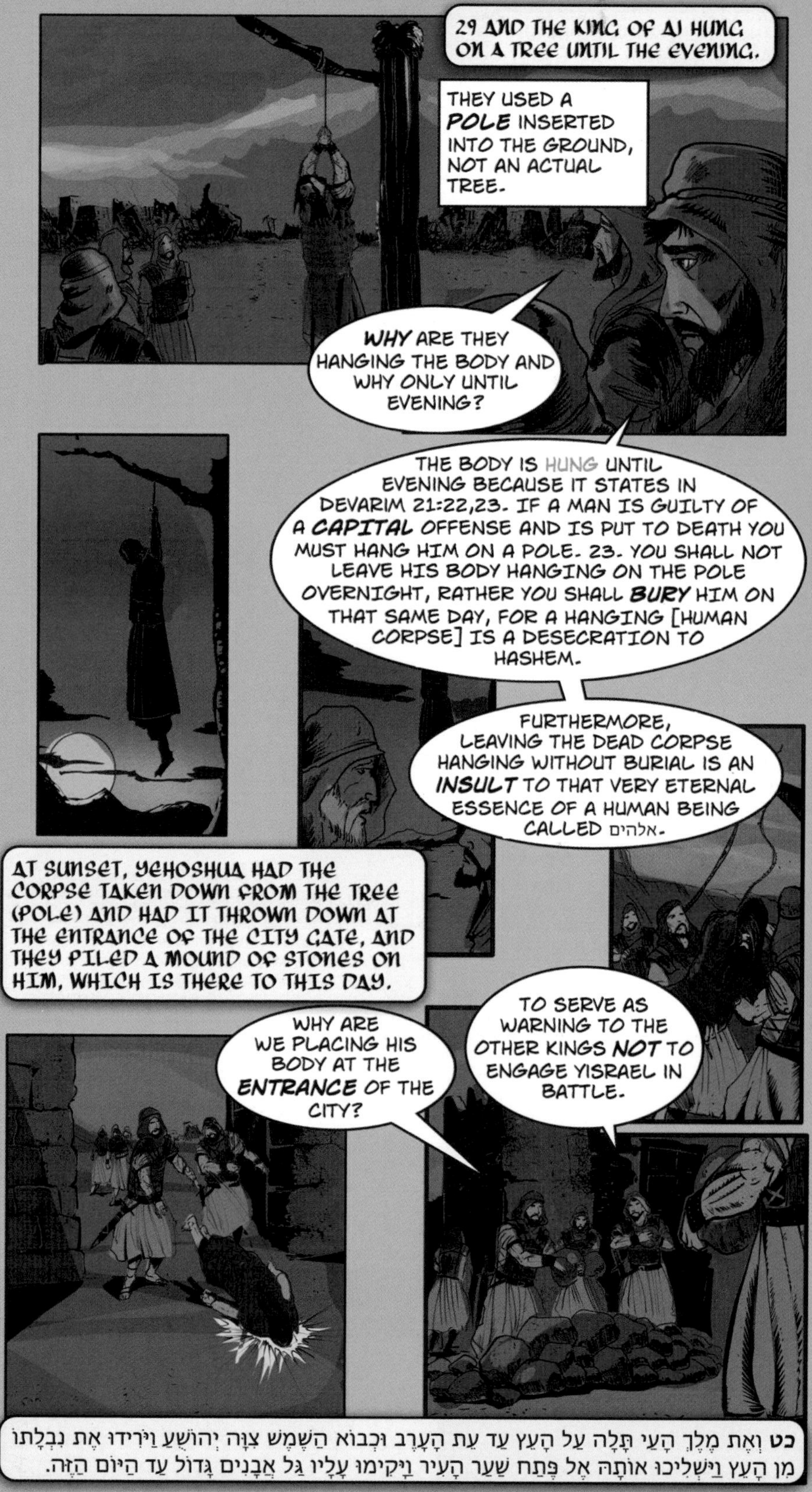
29 AND THE KING OF AI HUNG ON A TREE UNTIL THE EVENING.
THEY USED A POLE INSERTED INTO THE GROUND, NOT AN ACTUAL TREE.
WHY ARE THEY HANGING THE BODY AND WHY ONLY UNTIL EVENING?
THE BODY IS HUNG UNTIL EVENING BECAUSE IT STATES IN DEVARIM 21:22,23. IF A MAN IS GUILTY OF A CAPITAL OFFENSE AND IS PUT TO DEATH YOU MUST HANG HIM ON A POLE. 23. YOU SHALL NOT LEAVE HIS BODY HANGING ON THE POLE OVERNIGHT, RATHER YOU SHALL BURY HIM ON THAT SAME DAY, FOR A HANGING [HUMAN CORPSE] IS A DESECRATION TO HASHEM.
FURTHERMORE, LEAVING THE DEAD CORPSE HANGING WITHOUT BURIAL IS AN INSULT TO THAT VERY ETERNAL ESSENCE OF A HUMAN BEING CALLED אלהים.
AT SUNSET, YEHOSHUA HAD THE CORPSE TAKEN DOWN FROM THE TREE (POLE) AND HAD IT THROWN DOWN AT THE ENTRANCE OF THE CITY GATE, AND THEY PILED A MOUND OF STONES ON HIM, WHICH IS THERE TO THIS DAY.
WHY ARE WE PLACING HIS BODY AT THE ENTRANCE OF THE CITY?
TO SERVE AS WARNING TO THE OTHER KINGS NOT TO ENGAGE YISRAEL IN BATTLE.

כט וְאֶת מֶלֶךְ הָעַי תָּלָה עַל הָעֵץ עַד עֵת הָעָרֶב וּכְבוֹא הַשֶּׁמֶשׁ צִוָּה יְהוֹשֻׁעַ וַיֹּרִידוּ אֶת נִבְלָתוֹ
מִן הָעֵץ וַיַּשְׁלִיכוּ אוֹתָהּ אֶל פֶּתַח שַׁעַר הָעִיר וַיָּקִימוּ עָלָיו גַּל אֲבָנִים גָּדוֹל עַד הַיּוֹם הַזֶּה.

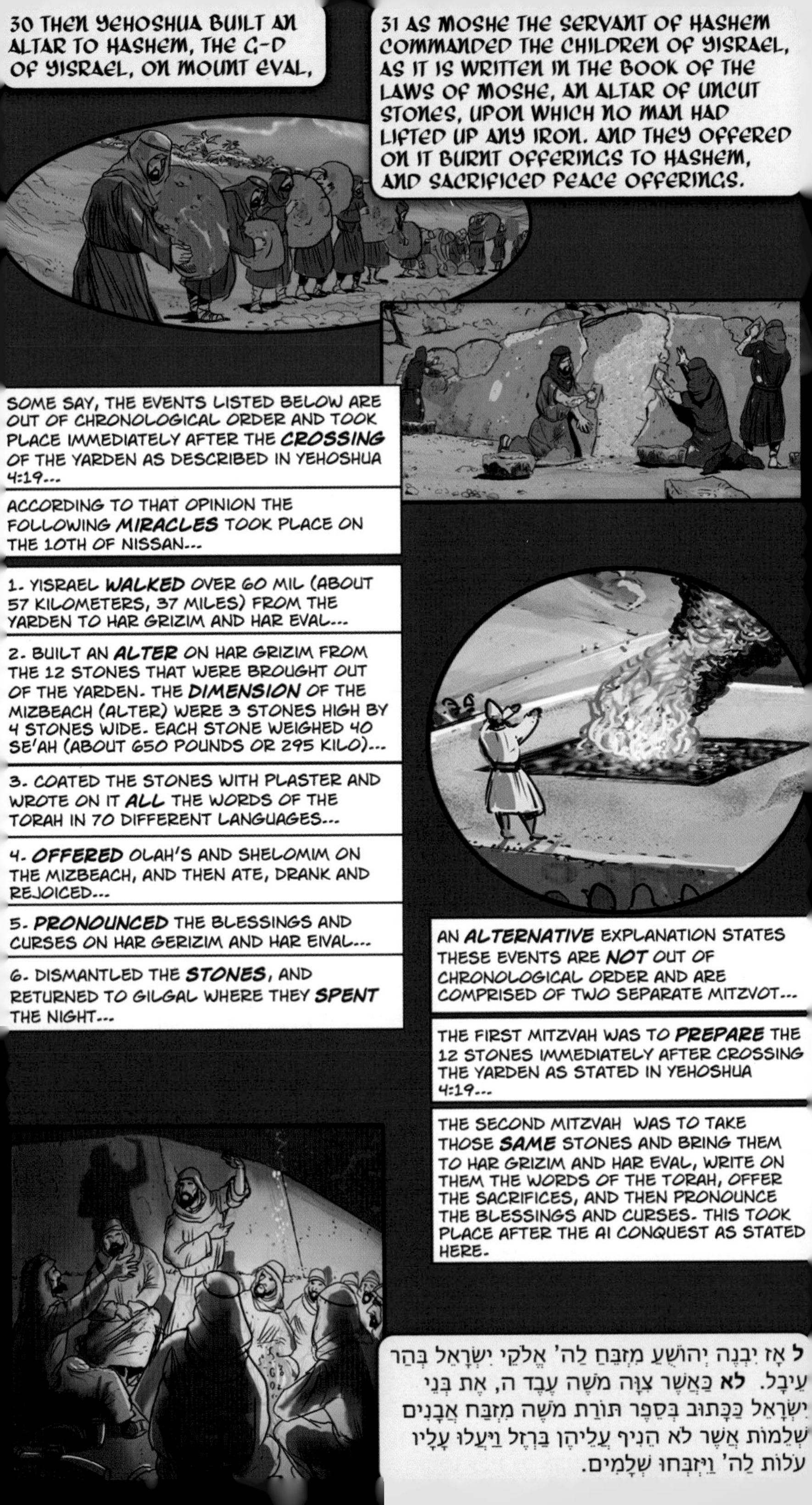
30 THEN YEHOSHUA BUILT AN ALTAR TO HASHEM, THE G-D OF YISRAEL, ON MOUNT EVAL,
31 AS MOSHE THE SERVANT OF HASHEM COMMANDED THE CHILDREN OF YISRAEL, AS IT IS WRITTEN IN THE BOOK OF THE LAWS OF MOSHE, AN ALTAR OF UNCUT STONES, UPON WHICH NO MAN HAD LIFTED UP ANY IRON. AND THEY OFFERED ON IT BURNT OFFERINGS TO HASHEM, AND SACRIFICED PEACE OFFERINGS.
SOME SAY, THE EVENTS LISTED BELOW ARE OUT OF CHRONOLOGICAL ORDER AND TOOK PLACE IMMEDIATELY AFTER THE CROSSING OF THE YARDEN AS DESCRIBED IN YEHOSHUA 4:19...
ACCORDING TO THAT OPINION THE FOLLOWING MIRACLES TOOK PLACE ON THE 10TH OF NISSAN...
1. YISRAEL WALKED OVER 60 MIL (ABOUT 57 KILOMETERS, 37 MILES) FROM THE YARDEN TO HAR GRIZIM AND HAR EVAL...
2. BUILT AN ALTER ON HAR GRIZIM FROM THE 12 STONES THAT WERE BROUGHT OUT OF THE YARDEN. THE DIMENSION OF THE MIZBEACH (ALTER) WERE 3 STONES HIGH BY 4 STONES WIDE. EACH STONE WEIGHED 40 SE'AH (ABOUT 650 POUNDS OR 295 KILO)...
3. COATED THE STONES WITH PLASTER AND WROTE ON IT ALL THE WORDS OF THE TORAH IN 70 DIFFERENT LANGUAGES...
4. OFFERED OLAH'S AND SHELOMIM ON THE MIZBEACH, AND THEN ATE, DRANK AND REJOICED...
5. PRONOUNCED THE BLESSINGS AND CURSES ON HAR GERIZIM AND HAR EIVAL...
6. DISMANTLED THE STONES, AND RETURNED TO GILGAL WHERE THEY SPENT THE NIGHT...
AN ALTERNATIVE EXPLANATION STATES THESE EVENTS ARE NOT OUT OF CHRONOLOGICAL ORDER AND ARE COMPRISED OF TWO SEPARATE MITZVOT...
THE FIRST MITZVAH WAS TO PREPARE THE 12 STONES IMMEDIATELY AFTER CROSSING THE YARDEN AS STATED IN YEHOSHUA 4:19...
THE SECOND MITZVAH WAS TO TAKE THOSE SAME STONES AND BRING THEM TO HAR GRIZIM AND HAR EVAL, WRITE ON THEM THE WORDS OF THE TORAH, OFFER THE SACRIFICES, AND THEN PRONOUNCE THE BLESSINGS AND CURSES. THIS TOOK PLACE AFTER THE AI CONQUEST AS STATED HERE.
ל אָז יִבְנֶה יְהוֹשֻׁעַ מִזְבֵּחַ לַה' אֱלֹקֵי יִשְׂרָאֵל בְּהַר עֵיבָל. לא כַּאֲשֶׁר צִוָּה מֹשֶׁה עֶבֶד ה, אֶת בְּנֵי יִשְׂרָאֵל כַּכָּתוּב בְּסֵפֶר תּוֹרַת מֹשֶׁה מִזְבַּח אֲבָנִים שְׁלֵמוֹת אֲשֶׁר לֹא הֵנִיף עֲלֵיהֶן בַּרְזֶל וַיַּעֲלוּ עָלָיו עֹלוֹת לַה' וַיִּזְבְּחוּ שְׁלָמִים.

32 AND HE WROTE THERE UPON THE STONES THE LAWS OF MOSHE, WHICH HE WROTE BEFORE THE CHILDREN OF YISRAEL.
THERE IS A DIFFERENCE OF OPINION AS TO WHETHER THEY WROTE THE ENTIRE TORAH, OR SEFER DEVARIM OR JUST SOME FORM OF THE SEFER HAMITZVOT, ETC.
THERE IS ALSO A DISPUTE AS TO WHETHER THEY WROTE DIRECTLY ON THE STONES THEMSELVES AND COVERED THE ENTIRE STRUCTURE WITH PLASTER OR WHETHER THEY WROTE DIRECTLY ON THE PLASTER...
WHATEVER WAS ACTUALLY WRITTEN ON THE STONES WAS ALSO TRANSLATED INTO SEVENTY LANGUAGES. THIS GAVE THE NATIONS OF THE LAND THE OPPORTUNITY TO LEARN THE TORAH OF HASHEM, GIVEN TO MOSHE...
לב וַיִּכְתָּב שָׁם עַל הָאֲבָנִים אֵת מִשְׁנֵה תּוֹרַת מֹשֶׁה אֲשֶׁר כָּתַב לִפְנֵי בְּנֵי יִשְׂרָאֵל.

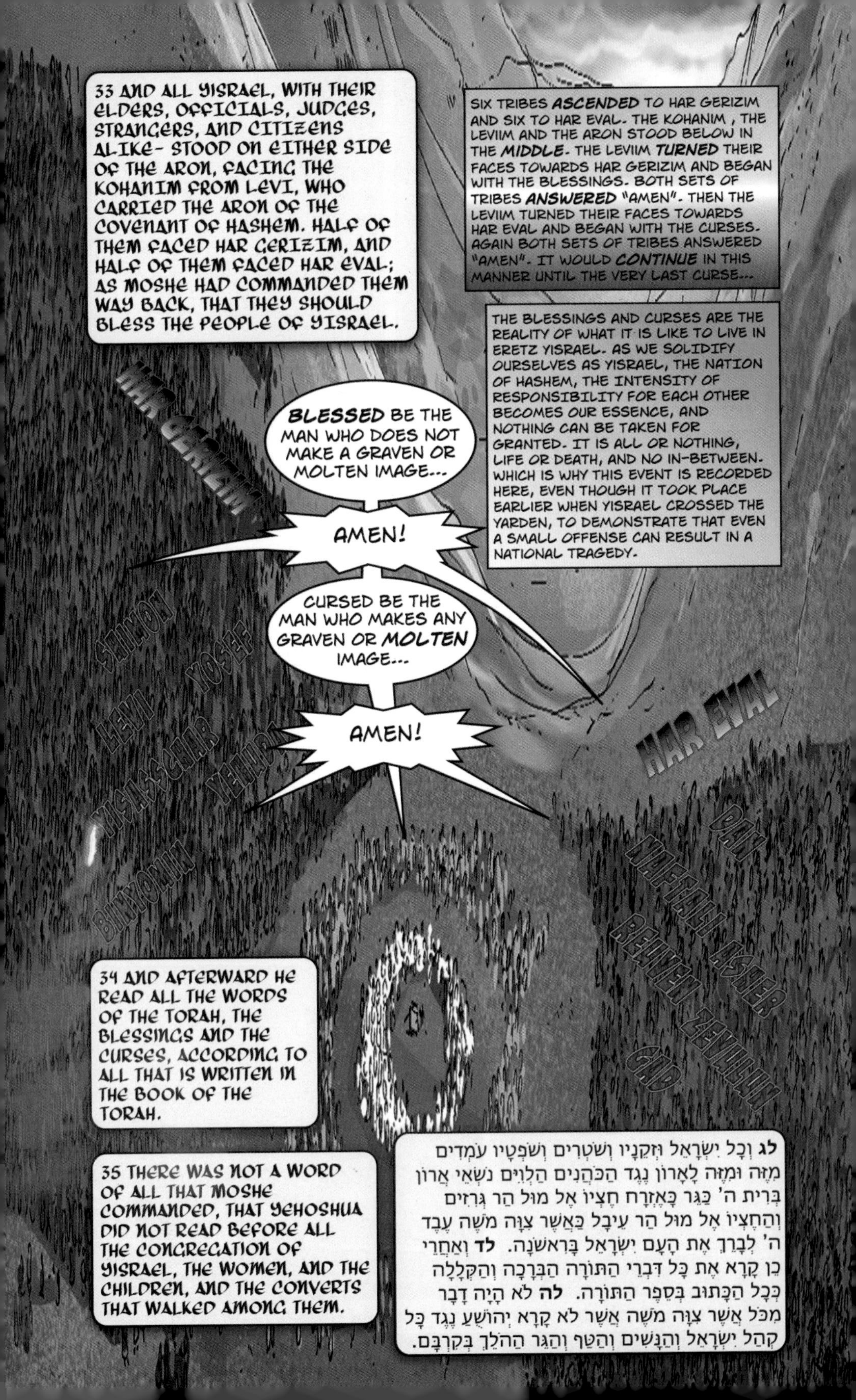
33 AND ALL YISRAEL, WITH THEIR ELDERS, OFFICIALS, JUDGES, STRANGERS, AND CITIZENS ALIKE- STOOD ON EITHER SIDE OF THE ARON, FACING THE KOHANIM FROM LEVI, WHO CARRIED THE ARON OF THE COVENANT OF HASHEM. HALF OF THEM FACED HAR GERIZIM, AND HALF OF THEM FACED HAR EVAL; AS MOSHE HAD COMMANDED THEM WAY BACK, THAT THEY SHOULD BLESS THE PEOPLE OF YISRAEL.
SIX TRIBES **ASCENDED** TO HAR GERIZIM AND SIX TO HAR EVAL. THE KOHANIM , THE LEVIIM AND THE ARON STOOD BELOW IN THE **MIDDLE**. THE LEVIIM **TURNED** THEIR FACES TOWARDS HAR GERIZIM AND BEGAN WITH THE BLESSINGS. BOTH SETS OF TRIBES **ANSWERED** "AMEN". THEN THE LEVIIM TURNED THEIR FACES TOWARDS HAR EVAL AND BEGAN WITH THE CURSES. AGAIN BOTH SETS OF TRIBES ANSWERED "AMEN". IT WOULD **CONTINUE** IN THIS MANNER UNTIL THE VERY LAST CURSE...
THE BLESSINGS AND CURSES ARE THE REALITY OF WHAT IT IS LIKE TO LIVE IN ERETZ YISRAEL. AS WE SOLIDIFY OURSELVES AS YISRAEL, THE NATION OF HASHEM, THE INTENSITY OF RESPONSIBILITY FOR EACH OTHER BECOMES OUR ESSENCE, AND NOTHING CAN BE TAKEN FOR GRANTED. IT IS ALL OR NOTHING, LIFE OR DEATH, AND NO IN-BETWEEN. WHICH IS WHY THIS EVENT IS RECORDED HERE, EVEN THOUGH IT TOOK PLACE EARLIER WHEN YISRAEL CROSSED THE YARDEN, TO DEMONSTRATE THAT EVEN A SMALL OFFENSE CAN RESULT IN A NATIONAL TRAGEDY.
HAR GERIZIM
BLESSED BE THE MAN WHO DOES NOT MAKE A GRAVEN OR MOLTEN IMAGE...
AMEN!
CURSED BE THE MAN WHO MAKES ANY GRAVEN OR **MOLTEN** IMAGE...
AMEN!
HAR EVAL
SHIMON
LEVI
YOSEF
BINYOMIN
DAN
ASHER
REUVEN
GAD
34 AND AFTERWARD HE READ ALL THE WORDS OF THE TORAH, THE BLESSINGS AND THE CURSES, ACCORDING TO ALL THAT IS WRITTEN IN THE BOOK OF THE TORAH.
35 THERE WAS NOT A WORD OF ALL THAT MOSHE COMMANDED, THAT YEHOSHUA DID NOT READ BEFORE ALL THE CONGREGATION OF YISRAEL, THE WOMEN, AND THE CHILDREN, AND THE CONVERTS THAT WALKED AMONG THEM.
לג וְכָל יִשְׂרָאֵל וּזְקֵנָיו וְשֹׁטְרִים וְשֹׁפְטָיו עֹמְדִים מִזֶּה וּמִזֶּה לָאָרוֹן נֶגֶד הַכֹּהֲנִים הַלְוִיִּם נֹשְׂאֵי אֲרוֹן בְּרִית ה' כַּגֵּר כָּאֶזְרָח חֶצְיוֹ אֶל מוּל הַר גְּרִזִים וְהַחֶצְיוֹ אֶל מוּל הַר עֵיבָל כַּאֲשֶׁר צִוָּה מֹשֶׁה עֶבֶד ה' לְבָרֵךְ אֶת הָעָם יִשְׂרָאֵל בָּרִאשֹׁנָה. **לד** וְאַחֲרֵי כֵן קָרָא אֶת כָּל דִּבְרֵי הַתּוֹרָה הַבְּרָכָה וְהַקְּלָלָה כְּכָל הַכָּתוּב בְּסֵפֶר הַתּוֹרָה. **לה** לֹא הָיָה דָבָר מִכֹּל אֲשֶׁר צִוָּה מֹשֶׁה אֲשֶׁר לֹא קָרָא יְהוֹשֻׁעַ נֶגֶד כָּל קְהַל יִשְׂרָאֵל וְהַנָּשִׁים וְהַטַּף וְהַגֵּר הַהֹלֵךְ בְּקִרְבָּם.

YEHOSHUA CHAPTER 9
יהושע פרק ט
WE MUST HURRY... PRIOR TO ATTACKING ANY POPULACE, WE MUST PRESENT THIS PROPOSAL TO ALL THE SEVEN NATIONS OF THE LAND...
DO YOU THINK THEY WILL TAKE US SERIOUSLY?
AFTER WHAT WE DID TO YERICHO AND AI THEY WOULD BE FOOLISH NOT TO...
WE COME AS A REPRESENTATIVE OF YEHOSHUA, LEADER OF YISRAEL.
SPEAK!
YOU ARE HEREBY GIVEN THREE CHOICES ...
1. LEAVE THE COUNTRY.
2. REMAIN IN THE LAND AND BECOME AN ALIEN RESIDENT...
AN ALIEN RESIDENT IS ONE WHO IS DESIGNATED THE LEGAL STATUS OF A NON-JEW LIVING IN THE LAND OF ISRAEL WHO DOESN'T WANT TO CONVERT TO JUDAISM BUT AGREES TO OBSERVE THE SEVEN LAWS OF NOACH.

3. ENTER INTO A WAR WITH YISRAEL AND BECOME UTTERLY DESTROYED...!
ONE MORE THING. SHOULD YOU DECIDE TO BECOME AN ALIEN RESIDENT AND LIVE IN PEACE WITH YISRAEL. YOU MUST ADHERE TO THREE CONDITIONS...
1. KEEP THE SEVEN NOAHIDE LAWS. 2. ACCEPT NO POSITIONS OF LEADERSHIP AND 3. BE WILLING TO ASSIST THE FUTURE KING OF YISRAEL THROUGH LABOR AND CONTRIBUTIONS..
WE ARE WAITING, SO DO NOT DELAY IN GIVING US YOUR ANSWER!!!

ELSEWHERE IN THE LAND OF GIRGASHIE...
REMEMBER, DO NOT HESITATE IN GIVING YEHOSHUA YOUR ANSWER...
MY LAND, MY INHERITANCE, MY PEOPLE... WE HAVE BEEN HERE FOR SO LONG!
SIRE, YOU MUST CONSIDER THEIR OFFER. THINK OF THE PEOPLE... WE ARE NO MATCH FOR THE NATION OF YISRAEL WHO DEFEATED THE TWO STRONGEST KINGDOMS IN THE REGION...
I KNOW WHAT I MUST DO. THE G-D OF YISRAEL WILL NOT ALLOW US TO REMAIN HERE. PREPARE THE PEOPLE. WE ARE RELOCATING. WE ARE GOING TO RESETTLE IN ANOTHER LAND...
I CAN'T BELIEVE THAT AFTER DECADES OF LIVING HERE WE MUST JUST PICK UP AND LEAVE!
WE HAVE LEFT EVERYTHING BEHIND, ALL THAT WE BUILT, OUR FERTILE LAND....
I HEAR AFRICA IS LOVELY THIS TIME OF YEAR...

1 WHEN ALL THE KINGS WEST OF THE YARDEN–IN THE MOUNTAINS, IN THE LOWLANDS, AND ALONG THE ENTIRE COAST OF THE MEDITERRANEAN SEA UP TO THE BEGINNING OF LEVANON, THE CHITTE, AMORIE, CANAANIE, PERIZZIE, CHIVIE, AND YEVUSIE–LEARNED OF THIS,
THEY HEARD OF ALL THAT **HAPPENED** TO YERICHO AND AI, AND OF THEIR THREE OPTIONS.
א וַיְהִי כִשְׁמֹעַ כָּל הַמְּלָכִים אֲשֶׁר בְּעֵבֶר הַיַּרְדֵּן בָּהָר
וּבַשְּׁפֵלָה וּבְכֹל חוֹף הַיָּם הַגָּדוֹל אֶל מוּל הַלְּבָנוֹן
הַחִתִּי וְהָאֱמֹרִי הַכְּנַעֲנִי הַפְּרִזִּי הַחִוִּי וְהַיְבוּסִי.

GENTLEMEN, WE ALL KNOW WHY WE ARE HERE...
WE HAVE AN ENORMOUS PROBLEM, AND THAT PROBLEM IS YISRAEL!
THE FLOOR IS NOW OPEN FOR DISCUSSION...
YOUR EXCELLENCY, I WOULD LIKE TO BEGIN.
WHAT GIVES YISRAEL THE RIGHT TO WALTZ INTO OUR COUNTRY AND TAKE OVER OUR LAND?
THE G-D OF YISRAEL IS WITH THEM. HE IS THE ONE WHO CREATED THIS WORLD AND HE IS THE ONE WHO CAN GIVE THE LAND TO WHOMEVER HE WISHES...
YES, BUT HOW DO WE KNOW THIS IS THE WILL OF G-D... CLEARLY YOU REMEMBER YISRAEL LOST THE FIRST BATTLE WITH AI...
GOOD POINT...

2 THEY GATHERED TOGETHER AS ONE TO FIGHT AGAINST YEHOSHUA AND YISRAEL.

ב וַיִּתְקַבְּצוּ יַחְדָּו לְהִלָּחֵם עִם
יְהוֹשֻׁעַ וְעִם יִשְׂרָאֵל פֶּה אֶחָד.

MEANWHILE WITHIN GIVON TERRITORY...
3 THE INHABITANTS OF GIVON HEARD WHAT YEHOSHUA HAD DONE TO YERICHO AND TO AI.
CAN YOU BELIEVE WHAT IS HAPPENING. OUR KING IS MEETING WITH THE OTHER THIRTY ONE KINGS TO DISCUSS THE ULTIMATUM GIVEN BY YEHOSHUA...
THEY ARE ACTUALLY CONSIDERING BANDING TOGETHER TO FIGHT YISRAEL...
DID YOU HEAR, WHAT THEY DID TO YERICHO AND AI...?
YES I SURE DID! I AGREE, THIS WOULD BE CATASTROPHIC!
WHAT WE NEED IS AN ALTERNATIVE PLAN...
WHAT DO YOU SUGGEST?
I RECOMMEND WE CREATE A RUSE...
ג וְיֹשְׁבֵי גִבְעוֹן שָׁמְעוּ אֵת אֲשֶׁר עָשָׂה יְהוֹשֻׁעַ לִירִיחוֹ וְלָעָי.

YEHOSHUA GAVE ALL THE NATIONS OF CANAAN THREE CHOICES. I SUGGEST WE ACCEPT THE CHOICE OF LIVING IN THIS LAND. ALL THIS IDOL WORSHIP IS NONSENSE, G-D OF YISRAEL HAS PROVEN HIMSELF TO BE THE REAL G-D.
I AM HAPPY TO ACCEPT THE NOAHIDE LAWS. AS FAR AS THE OTHER TWO CONDITIONS ARE CONCERNED, WE HAVE NEVER TAKEN LEADERSHIP ROLES BEFORE AND ARE ALREADY SUBSERVIENT TO A KING.
AREN'T YOU FORGETTING WE COME FROM GIVON AND OUR KING WILL NEVER BE SUBSERVIENT TO ANYONE, AND FOR SURE NOT TO YISRAEL...
THAT'S MY NEXT POINT, NO ONE WILL KNOW THAT WE ARE FROM GIVON BECAUSE NOBODY REALLY KNOWS WHAT WE LOOK LIKE.
AS FAR AS YEHOSHUA IS CONCERNED, ALL MIDDLE EASTERN PEOPLE LOOK ALIKE...
I SAY WE DRESS UP AS A GROUP OF WONDERERS WHO COME FROM OUTSIDE CANAAN. WE APPROACH YISRAEL'S CAMP AND TELL THEM WE ARE STRANGERS FROM A DISTANT LAND AND WISH TO RESIDE IN THIS LAND.
WE MAKE A COVENANT WITH THEM ACCEPTING ALL THEIR TERMS AND CONDITIONS. BY THE TIME THEY FIND OUT WHO WE REALLY ARE, IT WILL BE TOO LATE...
YOU KNOW, AS NUTTY AS THIS SOUNDS, IT ACTUALLY HAS POTENTIAL AND JUST MIGHT WORK... HOWEVER, WE ARE GOING TO NEED A LOT OF PREPARATION...

4 AND THEY ACTED WITH CRAFTINESS AND WENT AND DISGUISED (THEMSELVES) AS AMBASSADORS (OF THE CHITTIE)
YOU LOOK LIKE A REAL DIGNITARY...
WHEN I WENT TO THE MARKET, THEY COULDN'T BELIEVE I WAS SPECIFICALLY LOOKING FOR BAGS IN THE WORST CONDITION...
AND TOOK OLD SACKS UPON THEIR DONKEYS AND WORN WINE SKINS, FRAYED AND PATCHED UP.
THE WINE SACKS HAVE TO BE PATCHED UP, THEY CAN'T HAVE HOLES IN THEM...
WHAT ARE YOU DOING LAZYING AROUND? WE HAVE SO MUCH WORK TO DO!
WE ARE WORKING... YOU WANT IT TO LOOK LIKE WE'VE BEEN TRAVELING IN THE HOT SUN FOR A LONG TIME.
SO, WE'RE GETTING A TAN; THIS WAY, WE LOOK MORE AUTHENTIC...
ד וַיַּעֲשׂוּ גַם הֵמָּה בְּעָרְמָה וַיֵּלְכוּ וַיִּצְטַיָּרוּ וַיִּקְחוּ שַׂקִּים
בָּלִים לַחֲמוֹרֵיהֶם וְנֹאדוֹת יַיִן בָּלִים וּמְבֻקָּעִים וּמְצֹרָרִים.

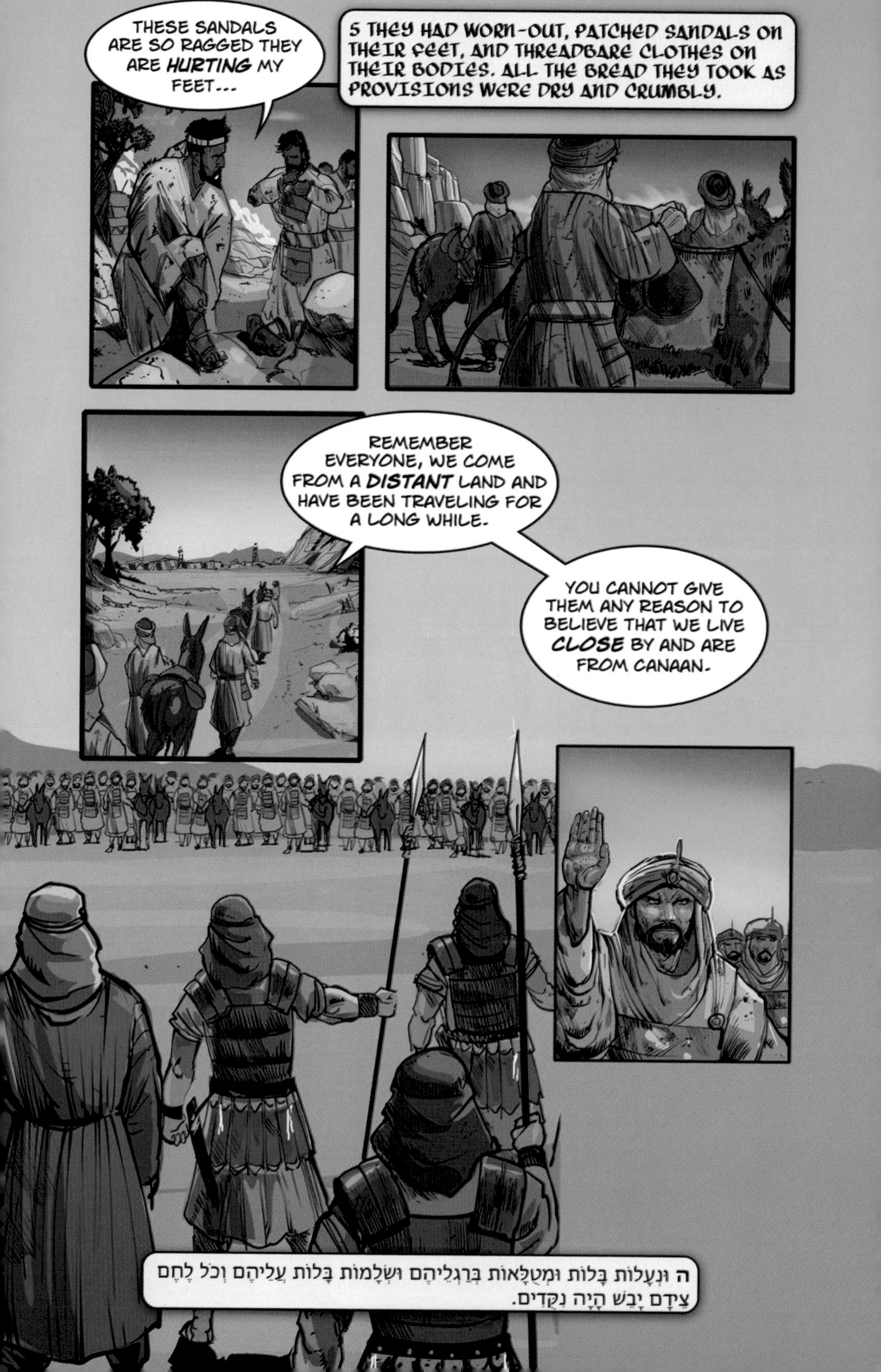
THESE SANDALS ARE SO RAGGED THEY ARE HURTING MY FEET...
5 THEY HAD WORN-OUT, PATCHED SANDALS ON THEIR FEET, AND THREADBARE CLOTHES ON THEIR BODIES. ALL THE BREAD THEY TOOK AS PROVISIONS WERE DRY AND CRUMBLY.
REMEMBER EVERYONE, WE COME FROM A DISTANT LAND AND HAVE BEEN TRAVELING FOR A LONG WHILE.
YOU CANNOT GIVE THEM ANY REASON TO BELIEVE THAT WE LIVE CLOSE BY AND ARE FROM CANAAN.
ה וּנְעָלוֹת בָּלוֹת וּמְטֻלָּאוֹת בְּרַגְלֵיהֶם וּשְׂלָמוֹת בָּלוֹת עֲלֵיהֶם וְכֹל לֶחֶם
צֵידָם יָבֵשׁ הָיָה נִקֻּדִים.

6 AND THEY WENT TO YEHOSHUA, TO THE CAMP AT GILGAL AND SAID TO HIM AND TO THE MEN OF YISRAEL:
WE COME FROM A DISTANT LAND, WE PROPOSE THAT YOU MAKE A PACT WITH US.
7 AND THE MEN OF YISRAEL SAID UNTO THE CHIVIE:
GIVON COMES FROM CHIVIE.
CHIVIE IS USED HERE BECAUSE THEY FIGURED IF YAAKOV'S SONS (SHIMON AND LEVI) DEALT CUNNINGLY WITH CHAMOR, THE FATHER OF SHECHEM, FROM CHIVIE, WHY CAN'T WE...
BUT PERHAPS YOU LIVE AMONG US, HOW THEN CAN WE MAKE A PACT WITH YOU?

ו וַיֵּלְכוּ אֶל יְהוֹשֻׁעַ אֶל הַמַּחֲנֶה הַגִּלְגָּל וַיֹּאמְרוּ אֵלָיו וְאֶל אִישׁ יִשְׂרָאֵל
מֵאֶרֶץ רְחוֹקָה בָּאנוּ וְעַתָּה כִּרְתוּ לָנוּ בְרִית. ז ויאמרו (וַיֹּאמֶר) אִישׁ יִשְׂרָאֵל
אֶל הַחִוִּי אוּלַי בְּקִרְבִּי אַתָּה יוֹשֵׁב וְאֵיךְ אכרות (אֶכְרָת) לְךָ בְרִית.

ח וַיֹּאמְרוּ אֶל יְהוֹשֻׁעַ עֲבָדֶיךָ אֲנָחְנוּ וַיֹּאמֶר אֲלֵיהֶם יְהוֹשֻׁעַ מִי אַתֶּם וּמֵאַיִן תָּבֹאוּ.
ט וַיֹּאמְרוּ אֵלָיו מֵאֶרֶץ רְחוֹקָה מְאֹד בָּאוּ עֲבָדֶיךָ לְשֵׁם ה' אֱלֹקֶיךָ כִּי שָׁמַעְנוּ שָׁמְעוֹ
וְאֵת כָּל אֲשֶׁר עָשָׂה בְּמִצְרָיִם. **י** וְאֵת כָּל אֲשֶׁר עָשָׂה לִשְׁנֵי מַלְכֵי הָאֱמֹרִי אֲשֶׁר בְּעֵבֶר
הַיַּרְדֵּן לְסִיחוֹן מֶלֶךְ חֶשְׁבּוֹן וּלְעוֹג מֶלֶךְ הַבָּשָׁן אֲשֶׁר בְּעַשְׁתָּרוֹת.

יא וַיֹּאמְרוּ אֵלֵינוּ זְקֵינֵינוּ וְכָל יֹשְׁבֵי אַרְצֵנוּ לֵאמֹר קְחוּ בְיֶדְכֶם צֵידָה לַדֶּרֶךְ וּלְכוּ לִקְרָאתָם
וַאֲמַרְתֶּם אֲלֵיהֶם עַבְדֵיכֶם אֲנַחְנוּ וְעַתָּה כִּרְתוּ לָנוּ בְרִית. **יב** זֶה לַחְמֵנוּ חָם הִצְטַיַּדְנוּ אֹתוֹ
מִבָּתֵּינוּ בְּיוֹם צֵאתֵנוּ לָלֶכֶת אֲלֵיכֶם וְעַתָּה הִנֵּה יָבֵשׁ וְהָיָה נִקֻּדִים. **יג** וְאֵלֶּה נֹאדוֹת הַיַּיִן
אֲשֶׁר מִלֵּאנוּ חֲדָשִׁים וְהִנֵּה הִתְבַּקָּעוּ וְאֵלֶּה שַׂלְמוֹתֵינוּ וּנְעָלֵינוּ בָּלוּ מֵרֹב הַדֶּרֶךְ מְאֹד.

14 AND THE MEN ACCEPTED THEIR DECEIT AND DID NOT ASK (THROUGH THE URIM V'TUMIM) COUNSEL FROM HASHEM.
15 AND YEHOSHUA MADE PEACE WITH THEM AND MADE A PACT WITH THEM TO LET THEM LIVE AND THE PRINCES OF THE CONGREGATION SWORE TO THEM.

יד וַיִּקְחוּ הָאֲנָשִׁים מִצֵּידָם וְאֶת פִּי ה' לֹא שָׁאָלוּ. **טו** וַיַּעַשׂ לָהֶם יְהוֹשֻׁעַ
שָׁלוֹם וַיִּכְרֹת לָהֶם בְּרִית לְחַיּוֹתָם וַיִּשָּׁבְעוּ לָהֶם נְשִׂיאֵי הָעֵדָה.

16 AND IT CAME TO PASS THREE DAYS AFTER THEY MADE THE PACT WITH THEM, THEY LEARNED THAT THEY WERE THEIR NEIGHBORS AND THAT THEY DWELLED AMONG THEM.
DID YOU HEAR THAT THE GIVONIM ARE ACTUALLY FROM CHIVIE AND ONLY LIVE A FEW MILES AWAY...
I KNEW THERE WAS SOMETHING WRONG ABOUT THEM. I COULD FEEL IT IN MY BONES...
THE GIVONIM ARE CHARLATANS, WHY DID THE ELDERS MAKE A PACT WITH THEM?
WE SHOULD HAVE TAKEN OUR TIME AND INVESTIGATED THEM THOROUGHLY...
WHAT CAN WE DO NOW? THE DEED IS DONE, THE OATH IS SWORN...
PREPARE THE TROOPS, WE HAVE TO SEE FOR OURSELVES...
טז וַיְהִי מִקְצֵה שְׁלֹשֶׁת יָמִים אַחֲרֵי אֲשֶׁר כָּרְתוּ לָהֶם בְּרִית וַיִּשְׁמְעוּ כִּי
קְרֹבִים הֵם אֵלָיו וּבְקִרְבּוֹ הֵם יֹשְׁבִים.

17 AND THE CHILDREN OF YISRAEL JOURNEYED AND CAME TO THEIR CITIES ON THE THIRD DAY. THESE CITIES WERE GIVON AND CHEPHIRAH AND BEEROT AND KIRYAT YEARIM.
WELL, THERE THEY ARE RIGHT BEFORE OUR EYES. THEY DECEIVED US AND *TRICKED* US INTO MAKING A FALSE OATH...
PREPARE THE TROOPS. WE *CAN'T* LET THEM GET AWAY WITH THIS...
יז וַיִּסְעוּ בְנֵי יִשְׂרָאֵל וַיָּבֹאוּ אֶל עָרֵיהֶם בַּיּוֹם הַשְּׁלִישִׁי וְעָרֵיהֶם גִּבְעוֹן
וְהַכְּפִירָה וּבְאֵרוֹת וְקִרְיַת יְעָרִים.

יח וְלֹא הִכּוּם בְּנֵי יִשְׂרָאֵל כִּי נִשְׁבְּעוּ לָהֶם נְשִׂיאֵי הָעֵדָה בַּה' אֱלֹקֵי יִשְׂרָאֵל – –

- - וַיִּלֹּנוּ כָל הָעֵדָה עַל הַנְּשִׂיאִים. **יט** וַיֹּאמְרוּ כָל הַנְּשִׂיאִים אֶל כָּל הָעֵדָה אֲנַחְנוּ
נִשְׁבַּעְנוּ לָהֶם בַּה' אֱלֹקֵי יִשְׂרָאֵל וְעַתָּה לֹא נוּכַל לִנְגֹּעַ בָּהֶם. **כ** זֹאת נַעֲשֶׂה לָהֶם וְהַחֲיֵה
אוֹתָם וְלֹא יִהְיֶה עָלֵינוּ קֶצֶף עַל הַשְּׁבוּעָה אֲשֶׁר נִשְׁבַּעְנוּ לָהֶם. **כא** וַיֹּאמְרוּ אֲלֵיהֶם
הַנְּשִׂיאִים יִחְיוּ וַיִּהְיוּ חֹטְבֵי עֵצִים וְשֹׁאֲבֵי מַיִם לְכָל הָעֵדָה כַּאֲשֶׁר דִּבְּרוּ לָהֶם הַנְּשִׂיאִים.

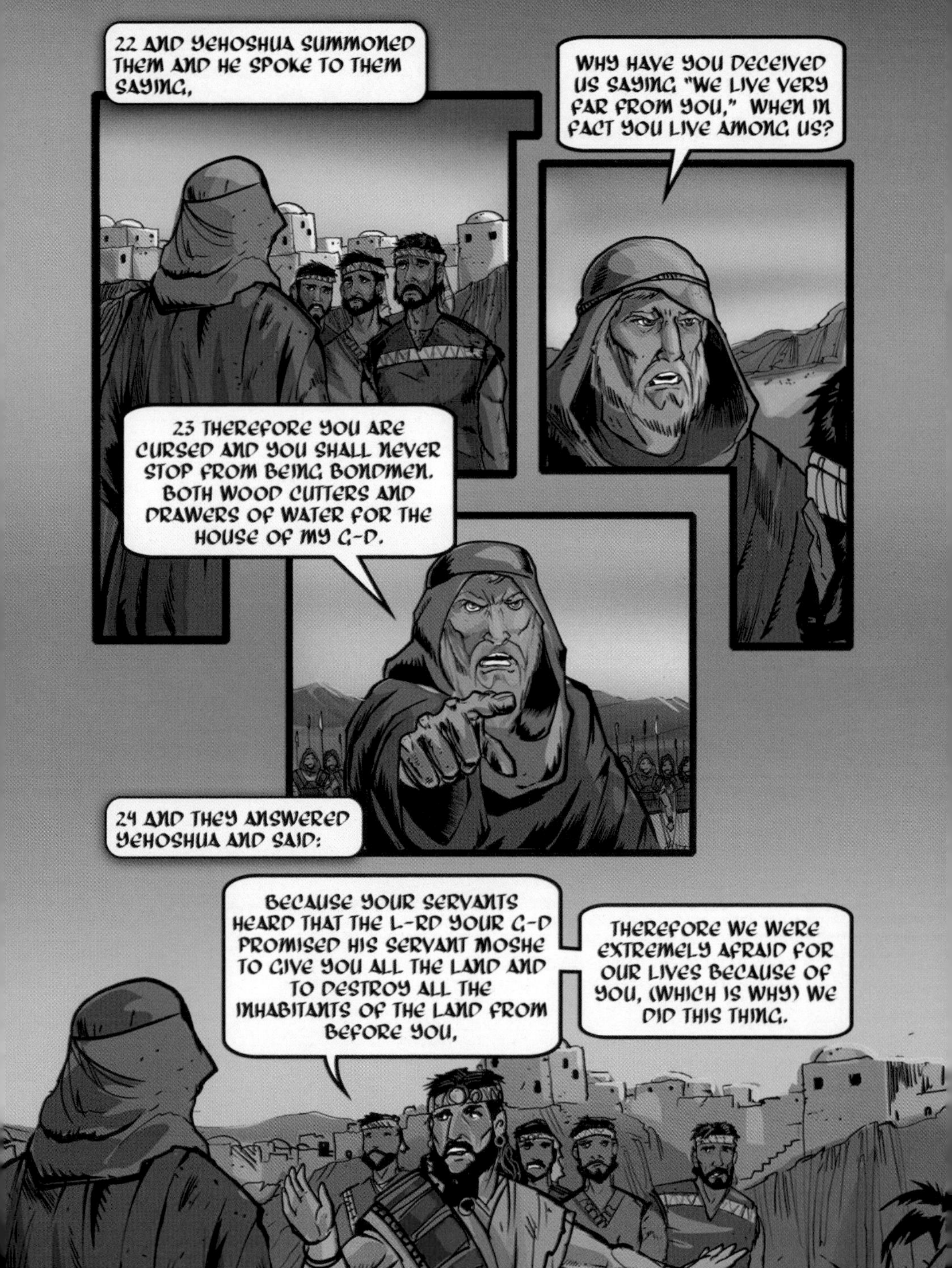

כב וַיִּקְרָא לָהֶם יְהוֹשֻׁעַ וַיְדַבֵּר אֲלֵיהֶם לֵאמֹר לָמָּה רִמִּיתֶם אֹתָנוּ לֵאמֹר רְחוֹקִים אֲנַחְנוּ
מִכֶּם מְאֹד וְאַתֶּם בְּקִרְבֵּנוּ יֹשְׁבִים. **כג** וְעַתָּה אֲרוּרִים אַתֶּם וְלֹא יִכָּרֵת מִכֶּם עֶבֶד וְחֹטְבֵי
עֵצִים וְשֹׁאֲבֵי מַיִם לְבֵית אֱלֹקָי. **כד** וַיַּעֲנוּ אֶת יְהוֹשֻׁעַ וַיֹּאמְרוּ כִּי הֻגֵּד הֻגַּד לַעֲבָדֶיךָ אֵת
אֲשֶׁר צִוָּה ה' אֱלֹקֶיךָ אֶת מֹשֶׁה עַבְדּוֹ לָתֵת לָכֶם אֶת כָּל הָאָרֶץ וּלְהַשְׁמִיד אֶת כָּל יֹשְׁבֵי
הָאָרֶץ מִפְּנֵיכֶם וַנִּירָא מְאֹד לְנַפְשֹׁתֵינוּ מִפְּנֵיכֶם וַנַּעֲשֵׂה אֶת הַדָּבָר הַזֶּה.

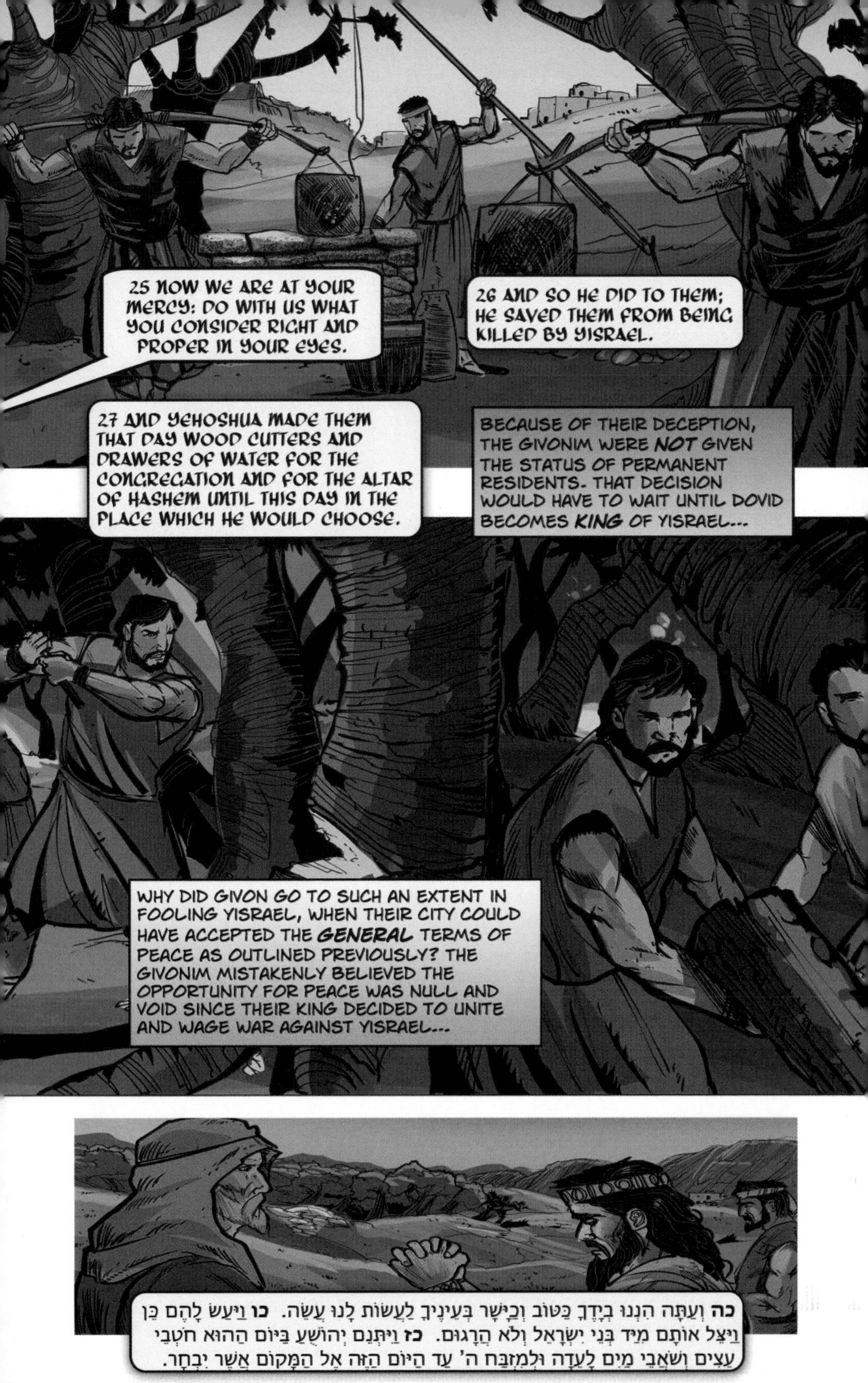
25 NOW WE ARE AT YOUR MERCY: DO WITH US WHAT YOU CONSIDER RIGHT AND PROPER IN YOUR EYES.
26 AND SO HE DID TO THEM; HE SAVED THEM FROM BEING KILLED BY YISRAEL.
27 AND YEHOSHUA MADE THEM THAT DAY WOOD CUTTERS AND DRAWERS OF WATER FOR THE CONGREGATION AND FOR THE ALTAR OF HASHEM UNTIL THIS DAY IN THE PLACE WHICH HE WOULD CHOOSE.
BECAUSE OF THEIR DECEPTION, THE GIVONIM WERE **NOT** GIVEN THE STATUS OF PERMANENT RESIDENTS. THAT DECISION WOULD HAVE TO WAIT UNTIL DOVID BECOMES **KING** OF YISRAEL...
WHY DID GIVON GO TO SUCH AN EXTENT IN FOOLING YISRAEL, WHEN THEIR CITY COULD HAVE ACCEPTED THE **GENERAL** TERMS OF PEACE AS OUTLINED PREVIOUSLY? THE GIVONIM MISTAKENLY BELIEVED THE OPPORTUNITY FOR PEACE WAS NULL AND VOID SINCE THEIR KING DECIDED TO UNITE AND WAGE WAR AGAINST YISRAEL...
כה וְעַתָּה הִנְנוּ בְיָדֶךָ כַּטּוֹב וְכַיָּשָׁר בְּעֵינֶיךָ לַעֲשׂוֹת לָנוּ עֲשֵׂה. **כו** וַיַּעַשׂ לָהֶם כֵּן
וַיַּצֵּל אוֹתָם מִיַּד בְּנֵי יִשְׂרָאֵל וְלֹא הֲרָגוּם. **כז** וַיִּתְּנֵם יְהוֹשֻׁעַ בַּיּוֹם הַהוּא חֹטְבֵי
עֵצִים וְשֹׁאֲבֵי מַיִם לָעֵדָה וּלְמִזְבַּח ה' עַד הַיּוֹם הַזֶּה אֶל הַמָּקוֹם אֲשֶׁר יִבְחָר.

YEHOSHUA CHAPTER 10
יהושע פרק י

1 AND IT WAS WHEN KING ADONI TZEDEK OF YERUSHALAYIM LEARNED YEHOSHUA HAD CAPTURED AI AND UTTERLY DESTROYED IT, TREATING AI AND ITS KING LIKE IT TREATED YERICHO AND ITS KING, AND THAT THE PEOPLE OF GIVON HAD COME TO TERMS WITH YISRAEL AND REMAINED AMONG THEM.
BRING ME MY SCRIBE!
2 THE KING WAS VERY FRIGHTENED. FOR GIVON WAS A LARGE CITY, LIKE ONE OF THE ROYAL CITIES. IN FACT LARGER THAN AI AND ALL ITS MEN WERE WARRIORS.
3 SO THE KING ADONI TZEDEK OF YERUSHALAYIM SENT THIS MESSAGE TO HOHAM KING OF CHEVRON AND TO PIRAM KING OF YARMUT AND TO YAPHIA KING OF LACHISH AND TO DEVIR KING OF EGLON.
YOU SUMMONED ME YOUR HIGHNESS...
SEND THIS MESSAGE OUT TO THE OTHER FOUR KINGS
SAYING:
4 COME UP AND HELP ME DEFEAT GIVON, FOR IT HAS MADE PEACE WITH YEHOSHUA AND WITH THE CHILDREN OF YISRAEL.

א וַיְהִי כִשְׁמֹעַ אֲדֹנִי צֶדֶק מֶלֶךְ יְרוּשָׁלַםִ כִּי לָכַד יְהוֹשֻׁעַ אֶת הָעַי וַיַּחֲרִימָהּ כַּאֲשֶׁר עָשָׂה
לִירִיחוֹ וּלְמַלְכָּהּ כֵּן עָשָׂה לָעַי וּלְמַלְכָּהּ וְכִי הִשְׁלִימוּ יֹשְׁבֵי גִבְעוֹן אֶת יִשְׂרָאֵל וַיִּהְיוּ בְּקִרְבָּם.
ב וַיִּירְאוּ מְאֹד כִּי עִיר גְּדוֹלָה גִּבְעוֹן כְּאַחַת עָרֵי הַמַּמְלָכָה וְכִי הִיא גְדוֹלָה מִן הָעַי וְכָל
אֲנָשֶׁיהָ גִּבֹּרִים. **ג** וַיִּשְׁלַח אֲדֹנִי צֶדֶק מֶלֶךְ יְרוּשָׁלַםִ אֶל הוֹהָם מֶלֶךְ חֶבְרוֹן וְאֶל פִּרְאָם מֶלֶךְ
יַרְמוּת וְאֶל יָפִיעַ מֶלֶךְ לָכִישׁ וְאֶל דְּבִיר מֶלֶךְ עֶגְלוֹן לֵאמֹר. **ד** עֲלוּ אֵלַי וְעִזְרֻנִי וְנַכֶּה אֶת גִּבְעוֹן
כִּי הִשְׁלִימָה אֶת יְהוֹשֻׁעַ וְאֶת בְּנֵי יִשְׂרָאֵל.

5 THE FIVE KINGS OF THE AMORI, THE KING OF YERUSHALAYIM, THE KING OF CHEVRON, THE KING OF YARMUT, THE KING OF LACHISH, AND THE KING OF EGLON WITH ALL THEIR ARMIES - JOINED FORCES AND MARCHED ON GIVON, AND ENCAMPED AGAINST IT AND ATTACKED IT.

THIS DOES NOT LOOK GOOD...
WE HAVE TO SEND WORD TO YEHOSHUA...

ה וַיֵּאָסְפוּ וַיַּעֲלוּ חֲמֵשֶׁת מַלְכֵי הָאֱמֹרִי מֶלֶךְ יְרוּשָׁלַםִ מֶלֶךְ חֶבְרוֹן מֶלֶךְ יַרְמוּת
מֶלֶךְ לָכִישׁ מֶלֶךְ עֶגְלוֹן הֵם וְכָל מַחֲנֵיהֶם וַיַּחֲנוּ עַל גִּבְעוֹן וַיִּלָּחֲמוּ עָלֶיהָ.

6 AND THE MEN OF GIVON SENT TO YEHOSHUA IN THE CAMP AT GILGAL SAYING,
DO NOT FAIL YOUR SERVANTS, COME TO US QUICKLY AND SAVE US AND HELP US, FOR ALL THE KINGS OF THE AMORI THAT DWELL IN THE HILL COUNTRY ARE GATHERED TOGETHER AGAINST US.
7 SO YEHOSHUA MARCHED UP FROM GILGAL, WITH HIS ENTIRE FIGHTING FORCE, AND ALL THE TRAINED WARRIORS.
8 AND HASHEM SAID TO YEHOSHUA: 'DO NOT FEAR THEM, FOR I HAVE DELIVERED THEM INTO YOUR HAND NO MAN WILL STAND AGAINST YOU.'

ו וַיִּשְׁלְחוּ אַנְשֵׁי גִבְעוֹן אֶל יְהוֹשֻׁעַ אֶל הַמַּחֲנֶה הַגִּלְגָּלָה לֵאמֹר אַל תֶּרֶף יָדֶיךָ
מֵעֲבָדֶיךָ עֲלֵה אֵלֵינוּ מְהֵרָה וְהוֹשִׁיעָה לָּנוּ וְעָזְרֵנוּ כִּי נִקְבְּצוּ אֵלֵינוּ כָּל מַלְכֵי הָאֱמֹרִי
יֹשְׁבֵי הָהָר. **ז** וַיַּעַל יְהוֹשֻׁעַ מִן הַגִּלְגָּל הוּא וְכָל עַם הַמִּלְחָמָה עִמּוֹ וְכֹל גִּבּוֹרֵי הֶחָיִל.
ח וַיֹּאמֶר ה' אֶל יְהוֹשֻׁעַ אַל תִּירָא מֵהֶם כִּי בְיָדְךָ נְתַתִּים לֹא יַעֲמֹד אִישׁ מֵהֶם בְּפָנֶיךָ.

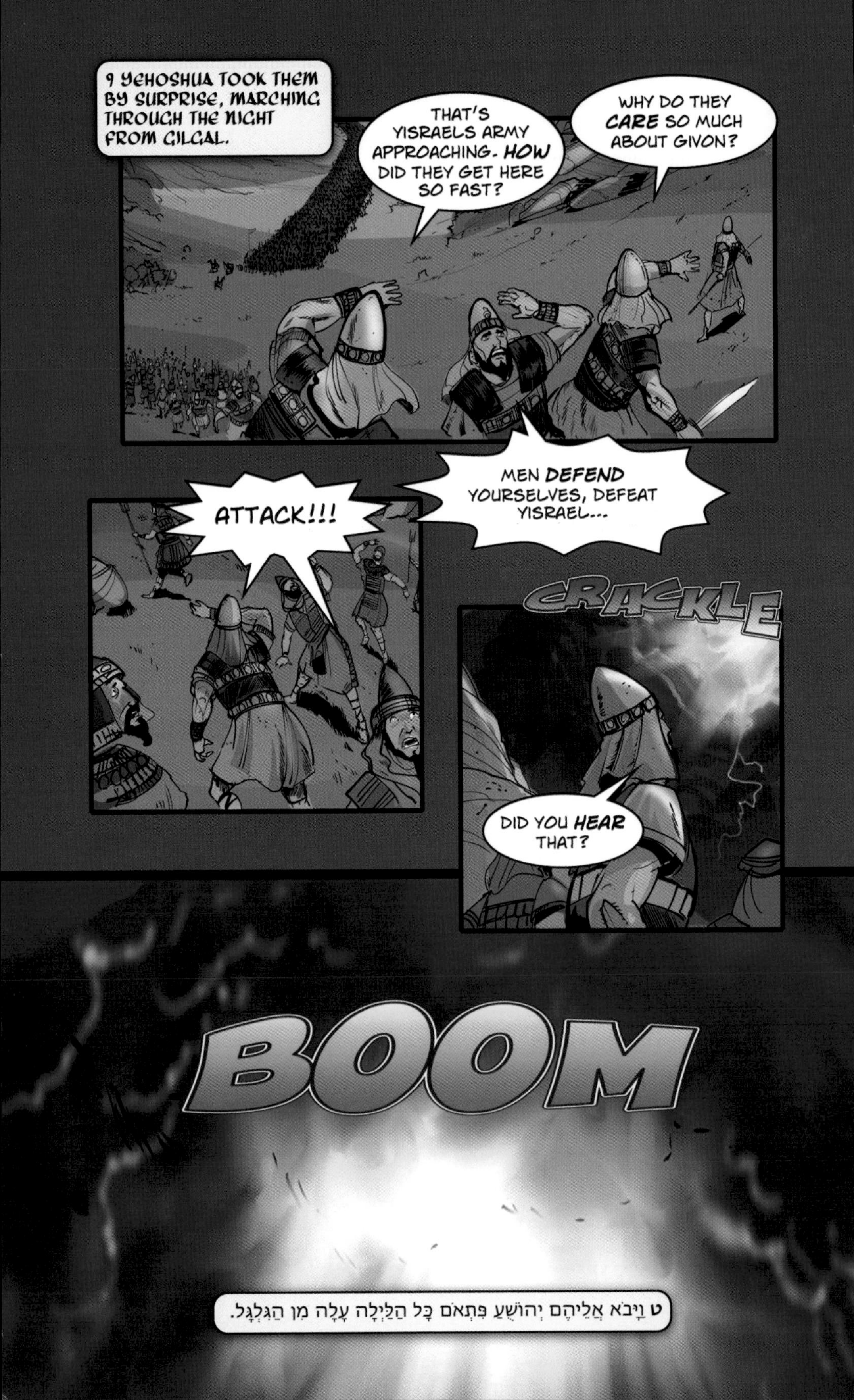
9 YEHOSHUA TOOK THEM BY SURPRISE, MARCHING THROUGH THE NIGHT FROM GILGAL.
THAT'S YISRAELS ARMY APPROACHING. HOW DID THEY GET HERE SO FAST?
WHY DO THEY CARE SO MUCH ABOUT GIVON?
MEN DEFEND YOURSELVES, DEFEAT YISRAEL...
ATTACK!!!
CRACKLE
DID YOU HEAR THAT?
BOOM
ט וַיָּבֹא אֲלֵיהֶם יְהוֹשֻׁעַ פִּתְאֹם כָּל הַלַּיְלָה עָלָה מִן הַגִּלְגָּל.

WHAT IS HAPPENING?
THAT THUNDERING SOUND JUST CAME OUT OF NOWHERE!
IT MUST BE YISRAEL'S ARMY SURROUNDING US. THERE MUST BE A MILLION SOLDIERS!!!
10 AND HASHEM CONFUSED THEM BEFORE YISRAEL
IT'S A TRAP... RETREAT!!!
ARGH!!!
AND INFLICTED A CRUSHING DEFEAT ON THEM AT GIVON. (THEY FURTHER) PURSUED THEM IN THE DIRECTION OF BEIT CHORON AND CRUSHED THEM ALL THE WAY TO AZEKAH AND MAKKEDAH.
THREE TIMES HASHEM USED ויהמם (PANIC, CONFUSION) TO WAGE WAR. THE OTHER TIMES WAS THE WAR AGAINST THE PLISHTIM, (SHMUEL I, 7:10) AND THE WAR AGAINST SISERA. (SHOFTIM, 4:15)
י וַיְהֻמֵּם ה' לִפְנֵי יִשְׂרָאֵל וַיַּכֵּם מַכָּה גְדוֹלָה בְּגִבְעוֹן וַיִּרְדְּפֵם דֶּרֶךְ מַעֲלֵה בֵית
חוֹרֹן וַיַּכֵּם עַד עֲזֵקָה וְעַד מַקֵּדָה.

HEY! WHAT'S HAPPENING NOW?!!!

יא וַיְהִי בְּנֻסָם מִפְּנֵי יִשְׂרָאֵל הֵם בְּמוֹרַד בֵּית חוֹרֹן וַה' הִשְׁלִיךְ עֲלֵיהֶם אֲבָנִים גְּדֹלוֹת מִן
הַשָּׁמַיִם עַד עֲזֵקָה וַיָּמֻתוּ רַבִּים אֲשֶׁר מֵתוּ בְּאַבְנֵי הַבָּרָד מֵאֲשֶׁר הָרְגוּ בְּנֵי יִשְׂרָאֵל בֶּחָרֶב.

יב אָז יְדַבֵּר יְהוֹשֻׁעַ לַה' בְּיוֹם תֵּת ה' אֶת הָאֱמֹרִי לִפְנֵי בְּנֵי יִשְׂרָאֵל וַיֹּאמֶר לְעֵינֵי
יִשְׂרָאֵל שֶׁמֶשׁ בְּגִבְעוֹן דּוֹם וְיָרֵחַ בְּעֵמֶק אַיָּלוֹן.

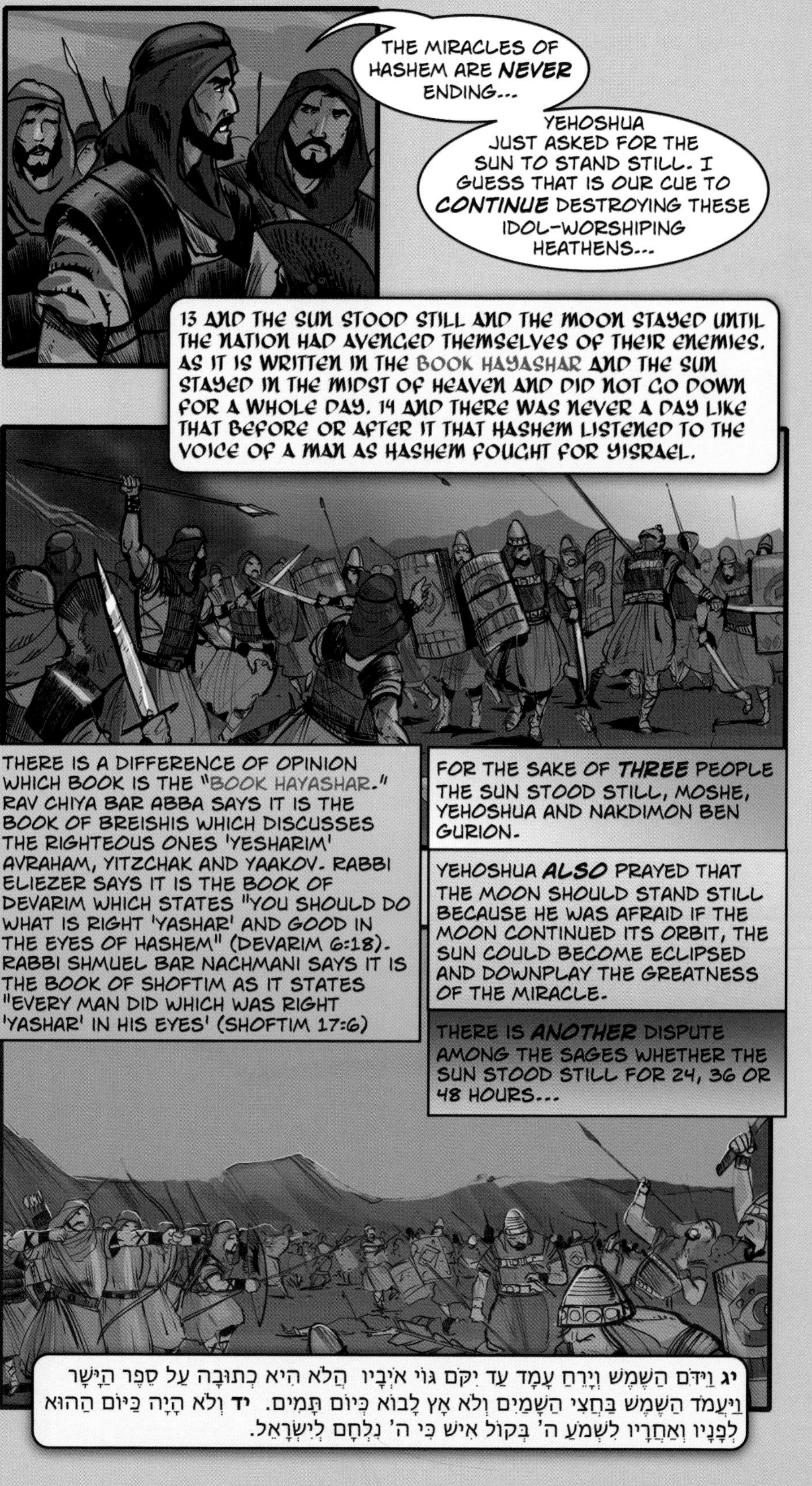
THE MIRACLES OF HASHEM ARE NEVER ENDING...
YEHOSHUA JUST ASKED FOR THE SUN TO STAND STILL. I GUESS THAT IS OUR CUE TO CONTINUE DESTROYING THESE IDOL-WORSHIPING HEATHENS...
13 AND THE SUN STOOD STILL AND THE MOON STAYED UNTIL THE NATION HAD AVENGED THEMSELVES OF THEIR ENEMIES. AS IT IS WRITTEN IN THE BOOK HAYASHAR AND THE SUN STAYED IN THE MIDST OF HEAVEN AND DID NOT GO DOWN FOR A WHOLE DAY. 14 AND THERE WAS NEVER A DAY LIKE THAT BEFORE OR AFTER IT THAT HASHEM LISTENED TO THE VOICE OF A MAN AS HASHEM FOUGHT FOR YISRAEL.
THERE IS A DIFFERENCE OF OPINION WHICH BOOK IS THE "BOOK HAYASHAR." RAV CHIYA BAR ABBA SAYS IT IS THE BOOK OF BREISHIS WHICH DISCUSSES THE RIGHTEOUS ONES 'YESHARIM' AVRAHAM, YITZCHAK AND YAAKOV. RABBI ELIEZER SAYS IT IS THE BOOK OF DEVARIM WHICH STATES "YOU SHOULD DO WHAT IS RIGHT 'YASHAR' AND GOOD IN THE EYES OF HASHEM" (DEVARIM 6:18). RABBI SHMUEL BAR NACHMANI SAYS IT IS THE BOOK OF SHOFTIM AS IT STATES "EVERY MAN DID WHICH WAS RIGHT 'YASHAR' IN HIS EYES' (SHOFTIM 17:6)
FOR THE SAKE OF THREE PEOPLE THE SUN STOOD STILL, MOSHE, YEHOSHUA AND NAKDIMON BEN GURION.
YEHOSHUA ALSO PRAYED THAT THE MOON SHOULD STAND STILL BECAUSE HE WAS AFRAID IF THE MOON CONTINUED ITS ORBIT, THE SUN COULD BECOME ECLIPSED AND DOWNPLAY THE GREATNESS OF THE MIRACLE.
THERE IS ANOTHER DISPUTE AMONG THE SAGES WHETHER THE SUN STOOD STILL FOR 24, 36 OR 48 HOURS...
יג וַיִּדֹּם הַשֶּׁמֶשׁ וְיָרֵחַ עָמָד עַד יִקֹּם גּוֹי אֹיְבָיו הֲלֹא הִיא כְתוּבָה עַל סֵפֶר הַיָּשָׁר
וַיַּעֲמֹד הַשֶּׁמֶשׁ בַּחֲצִי הַשָּׁמַיִם וְלֹא אָץ לָבוֹא כְּיוֹם תָּמִים. יד וְלֹא הָיָה כַּיּוֹם הַהוּא
לְפָנָיו וְאַחֲרָיו לִשְׁמֹעַ ה' בְּקוֹל אִישׁ כִּי ה' נִלְחָם לְיִשְׂרָאֵל.

15 THEN YEHOSHUA TOGETHER WITH ALL OF YISRAEL RETURNED TO THE CAMP AT GILGAL.
THE SAGES COMMENT THAT YEHOSHUA RETURNED TO GILGAL AFTER THE EVENTS OF THE UPCOMING VERSES...
SOMEWHERE IN MAKKEDAH WHILE THE WAR IS STILL RAGING ON...
16 AND THESE FIVE KINGS FLED AND HID THEMSELVES IN THE CAVE AT MAKKEDAH.
IT LOOKS LIKE WE WILL BE SAFE IN HERE.
WHEN IT GETS DARK, WE WILL BE ABLE TO REGROUP AND COME UP WITH A NEW STRATEGY...
SPEAKING ABOUT DARK, DID YOU NOTICE HOW LONG THE SUN IS STAYING UP IN THE SKY. IT SEEMS LIKE IT IS NEVER GOING TO SET...
17 AND IT WAS REPORTED TO YEHOSHUA SAYING:
THE FIVE KINGS HAVE BEEN DISCOVERED HIDING IN THE CAVE IN MAKKEDAH.
18 YEHOSHUA SAID:
ROLL BIG STONES UP AGAINST THE ENTRANCE TO THE CAVE AND POST MEN OVER IT TO GUARD THEM. 19 BUT AS FOR THE REST OF YOU, DON'T STOP, PURSUE THE ENEMIES AND KILL THE ONES LAGGING BEHIND. DO NOT LET THEM ENTER THEIR CITIES FOR HASHEM YOUR G-D HAS DELIVERED THEM INTO YOUR HAND.

טו וַיָּשָׁב יְהוֹשֻׁעַ וְכָל יִשְׂרָאֵל עִמּוֹ אֶל הַמַּחֲנֶה הַגִּלְגָּלָה. **טז** וַיָּנֻסוּ חֲמֵשֶׁת הַמְּלָכִים
הָאֵלֶּה וַיֵּחָבְאוּ בַמְּעָרָה בְּמַקֵּדָה. **יז** וַיֻּגַּד לִיהוֹשֻׁעַ לֵאמֹר נִמְצְאוּ חֲמֵשֶׁת הַמְּלָכִים
נֶחְבְּאִים בַּמְּעָרָה בְּמַקֵּדָה. **יח** וַיֹּאמֶר יְהוֹשֻׁעַ גֹּלּוּ אֲבָנִים גְּדֹלוֹת אֶל פִּי הַמְּעָרָה
וְהַפְקִידוּ עָלֶיהָ אֲנָשִׁים לְשָׁמְרָם. **יט** וְאַתֶּם אַל תַּעֲמֹדוּ רִדְפוּ אַחֲרֵי אֹיְבֵיכֶם וְזִנַּבְתֶּם
אוֹתָם אַל תִּתְּנוּם לָבוֹא אֶל עָרֵיהֶם כִּי נְתָנָם ה' אֱלֹקֵיכֶם בְּיֶדְכֶם.

LATER AT THE CAVE OF MAKKEDAH...
I HEAR SOMETHING GOING ON OUTSIDE...
IT SOUNDS LIKE A RUMBLING NOISE...
I LIKE THE IDEA THAT WE ARE TRAPPING THEM LIKE THE RATS THAT THEY ARE...
IT SHOULDN'T BE TOO DIFFICULT TO COVER THIS CAVE...
MAYBE ITS AN AVALANCHE!
QUIET! I HEAR VOICES COMING FROM THE OUTSIDE OF THE CAVE.
THEY ARE SPEAKING HEBREW.
YISRAEL IS SEALING OFF THE ENTRANCE...
THIS IS REALLY BAD!
WHAT ON EARTH! THERE IS NO WAY OUT, WE ARE DOOMED!

THIS SHOULD KEEP THE KINGS SAFE AND SOUND FOR A LITTLE WHILE...
TIME NOW TO FINISH THE JOB OF DESTROYING THE REST OF OUR ENEMIES...
OVER THIS RIDGE SHOULD BE THE TAIL END OF THE ARMY...
REMEMBER, WE CAN'T ALLOW ANYONE TO RETURN TO THEIR CITIES.
THERE THEY ARE, AFTER THEM...
GET EVERY LAST ONE OF THEM, DON'T LET ANY OF THEM GET AWAY!
RRROOOMMM
IDOL WORSHIPING HEATHEN...!
ARGH!!!

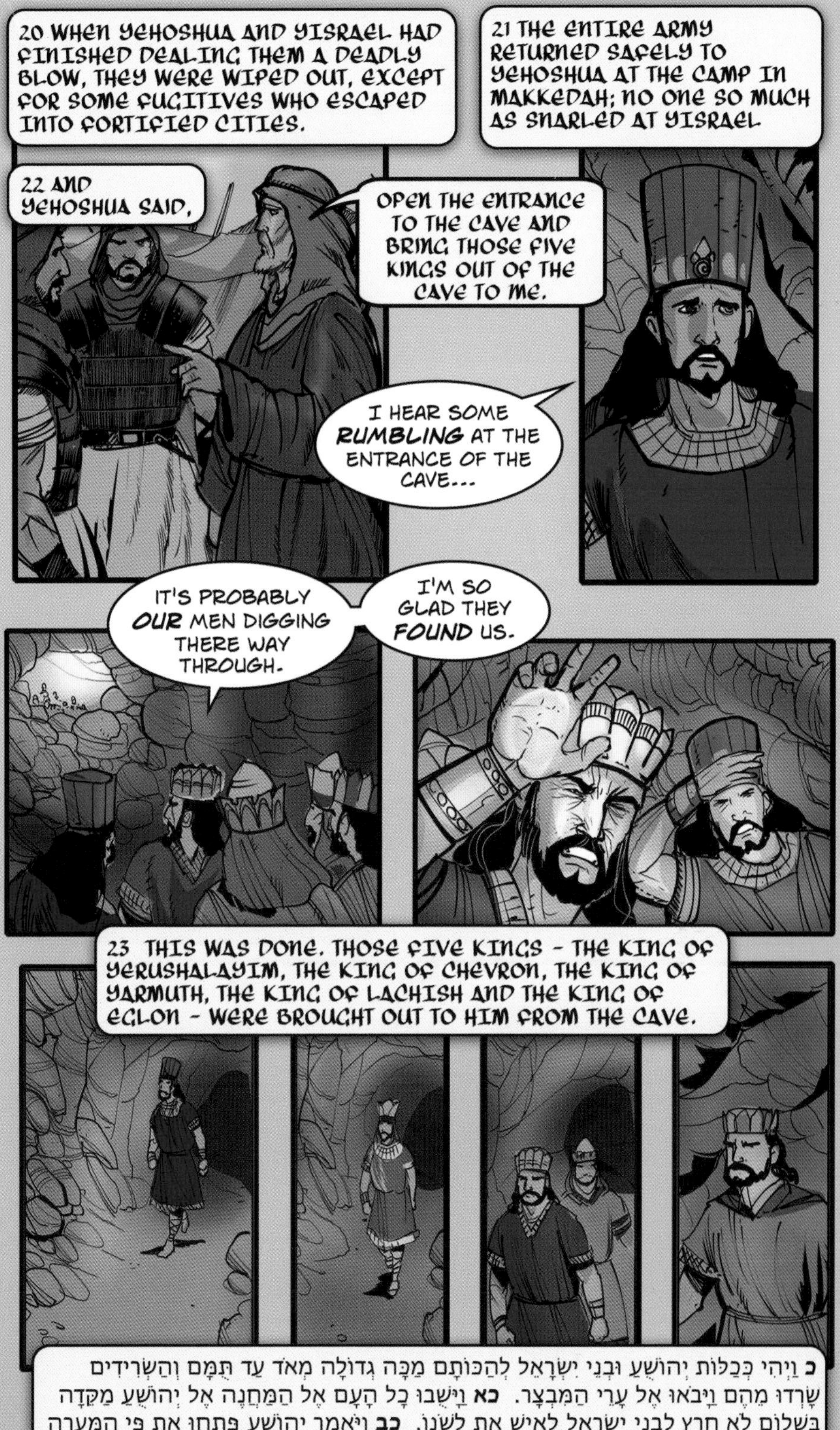
20 WHEN YEHOSHUA AND YISRAEL HAD FINISHED DEALING THEM A DEADLY BLOW, THEY WERE WIPED OUT, EXCEPT FOR SOME FUGITIVES WHO ESCAPED INTO FORTIFIED CITIES.
21 THE ENTIRE ARMY RETURNED SAFELY TO YEHOSHUA AT THE CAMP IN MAKKEDAH; NO ONE SO MUCH AS SNARLED AT YISRAEL
22 AND YEHOSHUA SAID,
OPEN THE ENTRANCE TO THE CAVE AND BRING THOSE FIVE KINGS OUT OF THE CAVE TO ME.
I HEAR SOME RUMBLING AT THE ENTRANCE OF THE CAVE...
IT'S PROBABLY OUR MEN DIGGING THERE WAY THROUGH.
I'M SO GLAD THEY FOUND US.
23 THIS WAS DONE. THOSE FIVE KINGS - THE KING OF YERUSHALAYIM, THE KING OF CHEVRON, THE KING OF YARMUTH, THE KING OF LACHISH AND THE KING OF EGLON - WERE BROUGHT OUT TO HIM FROM THE CAVE.

כ וַיְהִי כְּכַלּוֹת יְהוֹשֻׁעַ וּבְנֵי יִשְׂרָאֵל לְהַכּוֹתָם מַכָּה גְדוֹלָה מְאֹד עַד תֻּמָּם וְהַשְּׂרִידִים
שָׂרְדוּ מֵהֶם וַיָּבֹאוּ אֶל עָרֵי הַמִּבְצָר. **כא** וַיָּשֻׁבוּ כָל הָעָם אֶל הַמַּחֲנֶה אֶל יְהוֹשֻׁעַ מַקֵּדָה
בְּשָׁלוֹם לֹא חָרַץ לִבְנֵי יִשְׂרָאֵל לְאִישׁ אֶת לְשֹׁנוֹ. **כב** וַיֹּאמֶר יְהוֹשֻׁעַ פִּתְחוּ אֶת פִּי הַמְּעָרָה
וְהוֹצִיאוּ אֵלַי אֶת חֲמֵשֶׁת הַמְּלָכִים הָאֵלֶּה מִן הַמְּעָרָה. **כג** וַיַּעֲשׂוּ כֵן וַיֹּצִיאוּ אֵלָיו אֶת
חֲמֵשֶׁת הַמְּלָכִים הָאֵלֶּה מִן הַמְּעָרָה אֵת מֶלֶךְ יְרוּשָׁלַםִ אֶת מֶלֶךְ חֶבְרוֹן אֶת מֶלֶךְ יַרְמוּת
אֶת מֶלֶךְ לָכִישׁ אֶת מֶלֶךְ עֶגְלוֹן.

24 AND WHEN THE KINGS WERE BROUGHT OUT TO YEHOSHUA, YEHOSHUA SUMMONED ALL THE MEN OF YISRAEL AND ORDERED THE ARMY OFFICERS WHO HAD ACCOMPANIED HIM,
COME FORWARD PUT YOUR FEET UPON THE NECKS OF THESE KINGS.
TO STRIKE **FEAR** INTO THE HEARTS OF THE CANAANIM. THAT THEY SHOULD THINK TWICE BEFORE WAGING WAR AGAINST YISRAEL...
ARRR
AND THEY CAME FORWARD AND PUT THEIR FEET ON THEIR NECKS.
25 AND YEHOSHUA SAID TO THEM, - -
כד וַיְהִי כְּהוֹצִיאָם אֶת הַמְּלָכִים הָאֵלֶּה אֶל יְהוֹשֻׁעַ וַיִּקְרָא יְהוֹשֻׁעַ אֶל כָּל אִישׁ יִשְׂרָאֵל
וַיֹּאמֶר אֶל קְצִינֵי אַנְשֵׁי הַמִּלְחָמָה הֶהָלְכוּא אִתּוֹ קִרְבוּ שִׂימוּ אֶת רַגְלֵיכֶם עַל צַוְּארֵי
הַמְּלָכִים הָאֵלֶּה וַיִּקְרְבוּ וַיָּשִׂימוּ אֶת רַגְלֵיהֶם עַל צַוְּארֵיהֶם. **כה** וַיֹּאמֶר אֲלֵיהֶם יְהוֹשֻׁעַ - -

- - FEAR NOT AND DO NOT BE DISMAYED, BE STRONG AND COURAGEOUS, FOR THUS SHALL HASHEM DO TO ALL YOUR ENEMIES WITH WHOM YOU ARE AT WAR.
26 AND AFTERWARD YEHOSHUA STRUCK THEM AND PUT THEM TO DEATH
AND HANGED THEM ON FIVE TREES (POLES) - -
TO THINK, HERE ARE THE FIVE MOST POWERFUL KINGS IN ALL OF CANAAN...
THEY COULD ONLY HAVE BEEN DEFEATED WITH THE HELP OF HASHEM...

- - אַל תִּירְאוּ וְאַל תֵּחָתּוּ חִזְקוּ וְאִמְצוּ כִּי כָכָה יַעֲשֶׂה ה' לְכָל אֹיְבֵיכֶם אֲשֶׁר אַתֶּם
נִלְחָמִים אוֹתָם. **כו** וַיַּכֵּם יְהוֹשֻׁעַ אַחֲרֵי כֵן וַיְמִיתֵם וַיִּתְלֵם עַל חֲמִשָּׁה עֵצִים - -

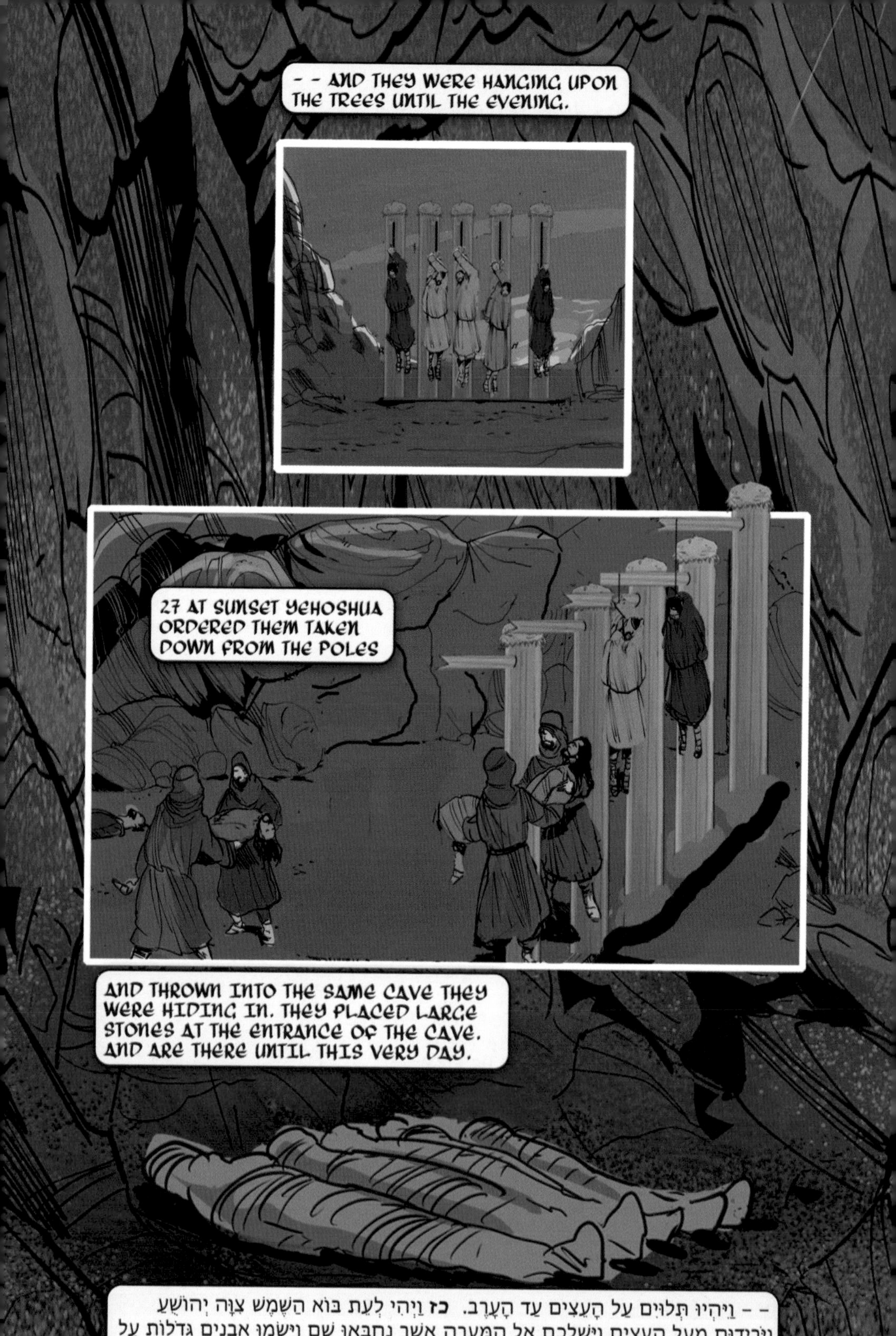

– – וַיִּהְיוּ תְּלוּיִם עַל הָעֵצִים עַד הָעָרֶב. **כז** וַיְהִי לְעֵת בּוֹא הַשֶּׁמֶשׁ צִוָּה יְהוֹשֻׁעַ
וַיֹּרִידוּם מֵעַל הָעֵצִים וַיַּשְׁלִכֻם אֶל הַמְּעָרָה אֲשֶׁר נֶחְבְּאוּ שָׁם וַיָּשִׂמוּ אֲבָנִים גְּדֹלוֹת עַל
פִּי הַמְּעָרָה עַד עֶצֶם הַיּוֹם הַזֶּה.

AND THE WAR CONTINUES...
KLING
KLANK
28 ON THAT DAY YEHOSHUA CAPTURED MAKKEDAH AND PUT IT AND IT'S KING TO DEATH BY SWORD, DESTROYING IT AND EVERY PERSON IN IT; LEAVING NO ONE TO ESCAPE.
THERE GOES THE KING, AFTER HIM...
I HAVE TO SAY, HE RAN PRETTY FAST.
YEAH, BUT NOT FAST ENOUGH...
AND HE DID TO THE KING OF MAKKEDAH AS HE HAD DONE TO THE KING OF YERICHO.
THE KING OF MAKKEDAH WAS KILLED IN THE HEAT OF BATTLE AS OPPOSED TO BEING EXECUTED...
THE DAY IS STILL YOUNG... TIME TO CONTINUE ON TO LIVNAH...

כח וְאֶת מַקֵּדָה לָכַד יְהוֹשֻׁעַ בַּיּוֹם הַהוּא וַיַּכֶּהָ לְפִי חֶרֶב וְאֶת מַלְכָּהּ הֶחֱרִם אוֹתָם וְאֶת
כָּל הַנֶּפֶשׁ אֲשֶׁר בָּהּ לֹא הִשְׁאִיר שָׂרִיד וַיַּעַשׂ לְמֶלֶךְ מַקֵּדָה כַּאֲשֶׁר עָשָׂה לְמֶלֶךְ יְרִיחוֹ.

29 FROM MAKKEDAH, YEHOSHUA AND ALL OF YISRAEL PROCEEDED TO LIVNAH, AND WAGED WAR AGAINST LIVNAH.
THE SUN IS SETTING, WE SHOULD FINISH THIS BATTLE QUICKLY AND GET READY FOR SHABBAT...
GOOD IDEA, I AM STARTING TO GET TIRED...
30 AND HASHEM DELIVERED IT AND ALSO THE KING INTO THE HAND OF YISRAEL AND HE SMOTE IT WITH THE EDGE OF THE SWORD AND ALL THE SOULS THAT WERE THERE. HE LEFT NONE REMAINING IN IT AND HE DID TO THE KING AS HE HAD DONE TO THE KING OF YERICHO.
כט וַיַּעֲבֹר יְהוֹשֻׁעַ וְכָל יִשְׂרָאֵל עִמּוֹ מִמַּקֵּדָה לִבְנָה וַיִּלָּחֶם עִם לִבְנָה. ל וַיִּתֵּן
ה' גַּם אוֹתָהּ בְּיַד יִשְׂרָאֵל וְאֶת מַלְכָּהּ וַיַּכֶּהָ לְפִי חֶרֶב וְאֶת כָּל הַנֶּפֶשׁ אֲשֶׁר בָּהּ
לֹא הִשְׁאִיר בָּהּ שָׂרִיד וַיַּעַשׂ לְמַלְכָּהּ כַּאֲשֶׁר עָשָׂה לְמֶלֶךְ יְרִיחוֹ.

WHAT A DAY! WHAT A LONG DAY...
THERE WAS JUST MIRACLE AFTER MIRACLE. FINALLY IT'S SHABBAT AND WE GET TO REFLECT ON WHAT HASHEM HAS DONE FOR US...
IT'S NICE TO WASH UP...
MY FEET ARE HURTING...
TEN MINUTES TO SUNDOWN, TEN MINUTES TO SUNDOWN!
31 FROM LIVNAH, YEHOSHUA AND ALL OF YISRAEL PROCEEDED TO LACHISH, AND ENCAMPED NEXT TO IT - -
PRAISE HASHEM FOR ALL THE BLESSING'S HE HAS GIVEN US...
לא וַיַּעֲבֹר יְהוֹשֻׁעַ וְכָל יִשְׂרָאֵל עִמּוֹ מִלִּבְנָה לָכִישָׁה וַיִּחַן עָלֶיהָ - -

- - AND FOUGHT AGAINST IT (AFTER SHABBAT ON MONDAY). 32 AND HASHEM DELIVERED LACHISH INTO THE HAND OF YISRAEL AND THEY CAPTURED IT ON THE SECOND DAY AND KILLED ALL THE PEOPLE THAT WERE THERE, JUST AS THEY HAD DONE TO LIVNAH.
MEANWHILE, KING CHORAM AT GEZER...
SIRE, WE'VE JUST BEEN *INFORMED* THAT YISRAEL HAS BEGUN ATTACKING LACHISH...
THIS MADNESS HAS *GOT* TO STOP. PREPARE THE TROOPS TO MARCH AT ONCE.
WE WILL *STRIKE* YISRAEL FROM THE REAR AND OUTFLANK THEM! YEHOSHUA WON'T KNOW WHAT HIT HIM...
- - וַיִּלָּחֶם בָּהּ. **לב** וַיִּתֵּן ה' אֶת לָכִישׁ בְּיַד יִשְׂרָאֵל וַיִּלְכְּדָהּ בַּיּוֹם הַשֵּׁנִי וַיַּכֶּהָ לְפִי חֶרֶב וְאֶת כָּל הַנֶּפֶשׁ אֲשֶׁר בָּהּ כְּכֹל אֲשֶׁר עָשָׂה לְלִבְנָה.

FIGHT THEM WITH **ALL** YOUR MIGHT. DESTROY YISRAEL FOREVER!
ATTACK YISRAEL, CUT THEM ALL DOWN!
VICTORY WILL BE OURS!!!
33 AT THAT TIME KING CHORAM OF GEZER MARCHED TO HELP LACHISH; BUT YEHOSHUA DEFEATED HIM AND HIS ARMY, ALLOWING NO ONE TO ESCAPE.
ARGH...
WE SHOULD HAVE TAKEN YEHOSHUA'S **OFFER** FOR PEACE...
לג אָז עָלָה הֹרָם מֶלֶךְ גֶּזֶר לַעְזֹר אֶת לָכִישׁ וַיַּכֵּהוּ יְהוֹשֻׁעַ וְאֶת עַמּוֹ
עַד בִּלְתִּי הִשְׁאִיר לוֹ שָׂרִיד.

34 FROM LACHISH, YEHOSHUA AND ALL OF YISRAEL PROCEEDED TO EGLON, AND ENCAMPED NEXT TO IT AND ATTACKED IT. 35. THEY CAPTURED IT AND KILLED ALL THE PEOPLE THAT WERE THERE, AND ON THAT DAY THEY DESTROYED EVERYTHING, JUST LIKE THEY DID TO LACHISH.
36 AND YEHOSHUA WENT UP FROM EGLON AND ALL YISRAEL WITH HIM TO CHEVRON AND THEY FOUGHT AGAINST IT. 37 THEY CAPTURED IT AND KILLED THE KING, THE TOWNS AND EVERY PERSON IN IT WITH THE SWORD, NO ONE ESCAPED, NOTHING REMAINED, JUST LIKE THEY DID TO EGLON; THEY DESTROYED EVERYTHING AND EVERYONE.
AS SEEN IN VERSE 26, THE KINGS OF EGLON AND CHEVRON WERE PUT TO *DEATH* BY YEHOSHUA. THE KINGS MENTIONED HERE WERE MOST PROBABLY NEWLY CROWNED KINGS...
38 YEHOSHUA AND ALL OF YISRAEL WITH HIM TURNED BACK TO DEVIR AND ATTACKED IT. 39. HE CAPTURED IT AND ITS KING AND ALL THE TOWNS. THEY KILLED THEM AND DESTROYED ALL THE PEOPLE IN IT. THEY LET NO ONE ESCAPE, JUST LIKE THEY DID TO CHEVRON SO HE DID TO DEVIR AND HER KING, LIKE THEY DID TO LIVNA AND HER KING.
לד וַיַּעֲבֹר יְהוֹשֻׁעַ וְכָל יִשְׂרָאֵל עִמּוֹ מִלָּכִישׁ עֶגְלֹנָה וַיַּחֲנוּ עָלֶיהָ וַיִּלָּחֲמוּ עָלֶיהָ. **לה**
וַיִּלְכְּדוּהָ בַּיּוֹם הַהוּא וַיַּכּוּהָ לְפִי חֶרֶב וְאֵת כָּל הַנֶּפֶשׁ אֲשֶׁר בָּהּ בַּיּוֹם הַהוּא הֶחֱרִים
כְּכֹל אֲשֶׁר עָשָׂה לְלָכִישׁ. **לו** וַיַּעַל יְהוֹשֻׁעַ וְכָל יִשְׂרָאֵל עִמּוֹ מֵעֶגְלוֹנָה חֶבְרוֹנָה וַיִּלָּחֲמוּ
עָלֶיהָ. **לז** וַיִּלְכְּדוּהָ וַיַּכּוּהָ לְפִי חֶרֶב וְאֶת מַלְכָּהּ וְאֶת כָּל עָרֶיהָ וְאֶת כָּל הַנֶּפֶשׁ אֲשֶׁר
בָּהּ לֹא הִשְׁאִיר שָׂרִיד כְּכֹל אֲשֶׁר עָשָׂה לְעֶגְלוֹן וַיַּחֲרֵם אוֹתָהּ וְאֶת כָּל הַנֶּפֶשׁ אֲשֶׁר בָּהּ.
לח וַיָּשָׁב יְהוֹשֻׁעַ וְכָל יִשְׂרָאֵל עִמּוֹ דְּבִרָה וַיִּלָּחֶם עָלֶיהָ. **לט** וַיִּלְכְּדָהּ וְאֶת מַלְכָּהּ וְאֶת
כָּל עָרֶיהָ וַיַּכּוּם לְפִי חֶרֶב וַיַּחֲרִימוּ אֶת כָּל נֶפֶשׁ אֲשֶׁר בָּהּ לֹא הִשְׁאִיר שָׂרִיד כַּאֲשֶׁר
עָשָׂה לְחֶבְרוֹן כֵּן עָשָׂה לִדְבִרָה וּלְמַלְכָּהּ וְכַאֲשֶׁר עָשָׂה לְלִבְנָה וּלְמַלְכָּהּ.

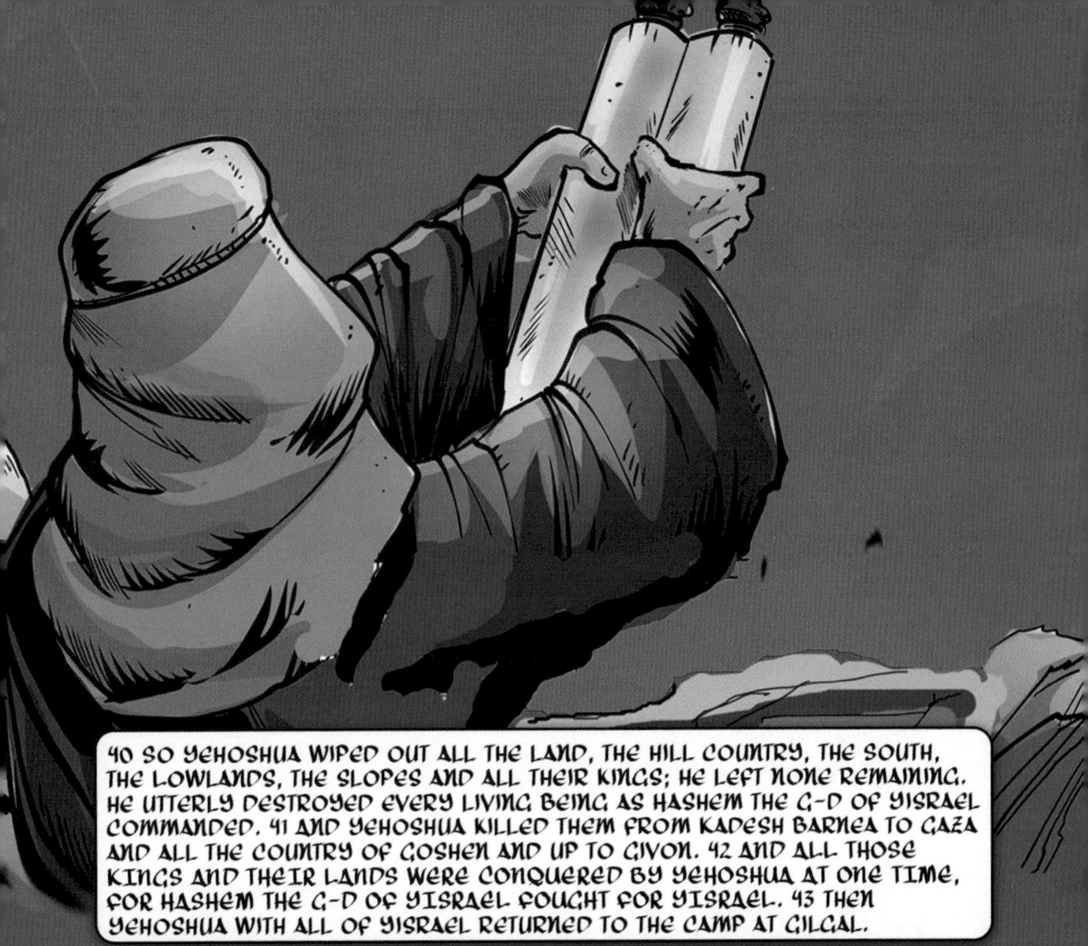
40 SO YEHOSHUA WIPED OUT ALL THE LAND, THE HILL COUNTRY, THE SOUTH, THE LOWLANDS, THE SLOPES AND ALL THEIR KINGS; HE LEFT NONE REMAINING. HE UTTERLY DESTROYED EVERY LIVING BEING AS HASHEM THE G-D OF YISRAEL COMMANDED. 41 AND YEHOSHUA KILLED THEM FROM KADESH BARNEA TO GAZA AND ALL THE COUNTRY OF GOSHEN AND UP TO GIVON. 42 AND ALL THOSE KINGS AND THEIR LANDS WERE CONQUERED BY YEHOSHUA AT ONE TIME, FOR HASHEM THE G-D OF YISRAEL FOUGHT FOR YISRAEL. 43 THEN YEHOSHUA WITH ALL OF YISRAEL RETURNED TO THE CAMP AT GILGAL.

מ וַיַּכֶּה יְהוֹשֻׁעַ אֶת כָּל הָאָרֶץ הָהָר וְהַנֶּגֶב וְהַשְּׁפֵלָה וְהָאֲשֵׁדוֹת וְאֵת כָּל מַלְכֵיהֶם לֹא
הִשְׁאִיר שָׂרִיד וְאֵת כָּל הַנְּשָׁמָה הֶחֱרִים כַּאֲשֶׁר צִוָּה ה' אֱלֹקֵי יִשְׂרָאֵל. **מא** וַיַּכֵּם יְהוֹשֻׁעַ
מִקָּדֵשׁ בַּרְנֵעַ וְעַד עַזָּה וְאֵת כָּל אֶרֶץ גֹּשֶׁן וְעַד גִּבְעוֹן. **מב** וְאֵת כָּל הַמְּלָכִים הָאֵלֶּה וְאֶת
אַרְצָם לָכַד יְהוֹשֻׁעַ פַּעַם אֶחָת כִּי ה' אֱלֹקֵי יִשְׂרָאֵל נִלְחָם לְיִשְׂרָאֵל. **מג** וַיָּשָׁב יְהוֹשֻׁעַ
וְכָל יִשְׂרָאֵל עִמּוֹ אֶל הַמַּחֲנֶה הַגִּלְגָּלָה.

YEHOSHUA CHAPTER 11
יהושע פרק יא
REMEMBER, YOU ARE DOING ALL THE TALKING. BE CONCISE AND DIRECT...
SIRE, WE BRING YOU DIRE NEWS...
SPEAK!
YEHOSHUA HAS DECIMATED THE ENTIRE SOUTHERN REGION.

IF HE COULD CONQUER THE FIVE KINGS, HE COULD SURELY OBLITERATE US.
YOU ARE MY ADVISERS, WHAT DO YOU SAY!
YISRAEL IS CURRENTLY CAMPED IN GILGAL. PERHAPS THEY ARE FINISHED WITH THEIR MILITARY CAMPAIGN...
YOU IGNORAMUS! WITH ADVICE LIKE THAT I WILL HAVE YOU CUT UP INTO LITTLE PIECES AND FED TO MY DOGS.
WHAT I MEANT TO SAY YOUR EXCELLENCY IS, SINCE YEHOSHUA IS CAMPED IN GILGAL WE HAVE TIME TO ORGANIZE THE OTHER KINGS IN THE REGION AND COMBINE FORCES TO PUT AN END TO YISRAEL'S CONQUEST.
HMM... I AGREE.
SEND WORD TO OUR ALLIES IN THE NORTH. WE WILL BAND TOGETHER AGAINST YEHOSHUA AND ATTACK AS ONE...

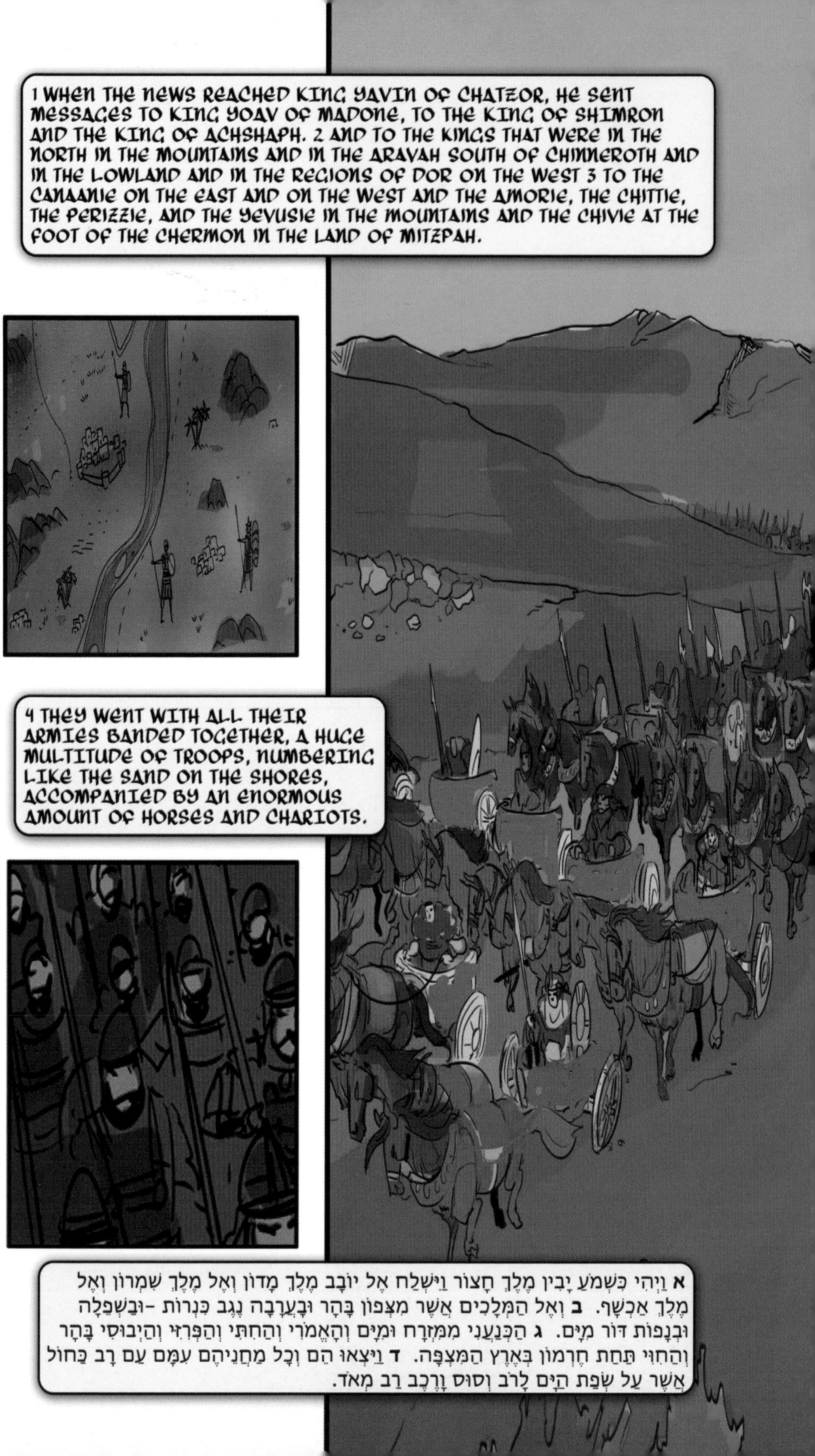
1 WHEN THE NEWS REACHED KING YAVIN OF CHATZOR, HE SENT MESSAGES TO KING YOAV OF MADONE, TO THE KING OF SHIMRON AND THE KING OF ACHSHAPH. 2 AND TO THE KINGS THAT WERE IN THE NORTH IN THE MOUNTAINS AND IN THE ARAVAH SOUTH OF CHINNEROTH AND IN THE LOWLAND AND IN THE REGIONS OF DOR ON THE WEST 3 TO THE CANAANIE ON THE EAST AND ON THE WEST AND THE AMORIE, THE CHITTIE, THE PERIZZIE, AND THE YEVUSIE IN THE MOUNTAINS AND THE CHIVIE AT THE FOOT OF THE CHERMON IN THE LAND OF MITZPAH.
4 THEY WENT WITH ALL THEIR ARMIES BANDED TOGETHER, A HUGE MULTITUDE OF TROOPS, NUMBERING LIKE THE SAND ON THE SHORES, ACCOMPANIED BY AN ENORMOUS AMOUNT OF HORSES AND CHARIOTS.
א וַיְהִי כִּשְׁמֹעַ יָבִין מֶלֶךְ חָצוֹר וַיִּשְׁלַח אֶל יוֹבָב מֶלֶךְ מָדוֹן וְאֶל מֶלֶךְ שִׁמְרוֹן וְאֶל
מֶלֶךְ אַכְשָׁף. ב וְאֶל הַמְּלָכִים אֲשֶׁר מִצְּפוֹן בָּהָר וּבָעֲרָבָה נֶגֶב כִּנְרוֹת -וּבַשְּׁפֵלָה
וּבְנָפוֹת דּוֹר מִיָּם. ג הַכְּנַעֲנִי מִמִּזְרָח וּמִיָּם וְהָאֱמֹרִי וְהַחִתִּי וְהַפְּרִזִּי וְהַיְבוּסִי בָּהָר
וְהַחִוִּי תַּחַת חֶרְמוֹן בְּאֶרֶץ הַמִּצְפָּה. ד וַיֵּצְאוּ הֵם וְכָל מַחֲנֵיהֶם עִמָּם עַם רָב כַּחוֹל
אֲשֶׁר עַל שְׂפַת הַיָּם לָרֹב וְסוּס וָרֶכֶב רַב מְאֹד.

ה וַיִּוָּעֲדוּ כֹּל הַמְּלָכִים הָאֵלֶּה וַיָּבֹאוּ וַיַּחֲנוּ יַחְדָּו אֶל מֵי מֵרוֹם לְהִלָּחֵם עִם יִשְׂרָאֵל.
ו וַיֹּאמֶר ה' אֶל יְהוֹשֻׁעַ אַל תִּירָא מִפְּנֵיהֶם כִּי מָחָר כָּעֵת הַזֹּאת אָנֹכִי נֹתֵן אֶת כֻּלָּם
חֲלָלִים לִפְנֵי יִשְׂרָאֵל אֶת סוּסֵיהֶם תְּעַקֵּר וְאֶת מַרְכְּבֹתֵיהֶם תִּשְׂרֹף בָּאֵשׁ. **ז** וַיָּבֹא
יְהוֹשֻׁעַ וְכָל עַם הַמִּלְחָמָה עִמּוֹ עֲלֵיהֶם עַל מֵי מֵרוֹם פִּתְאֹם וַיִּפְּלוּ בָּהֶם.

CHARGE!!!
RRRUMBLE
SHIMON, GET OUT OF THE WAY!!!
WHOOSH
GRRRR!

THIS TIME YOU'RE NOT GETTING AWAY...!
THAT'S WHAT YOU THINK!
ARGHH!!
SSSWISSH!
ARRRR!!!!
SHIFFF!!!
TIME TO FINISH MORE OF YOU OFF...
YOU COULD HAVE MADE PEACE. INSTEAD YOU DECIDED TO ATTACK...
NOW YOU WILL PAY THE PRICE...

FIRE AT WILL!!!
SWOOOSH
INCOMING!!!
GET DOWN!
PING
PING
PING
PING
ROARRR!!!!!
HASHEM HELP US.
TIME TO SEND YOU BACK TO THE DESERT!!!
UHHH!!!
I DON'T THINK SO! HASHEM WANTS US RIGHT HERE...

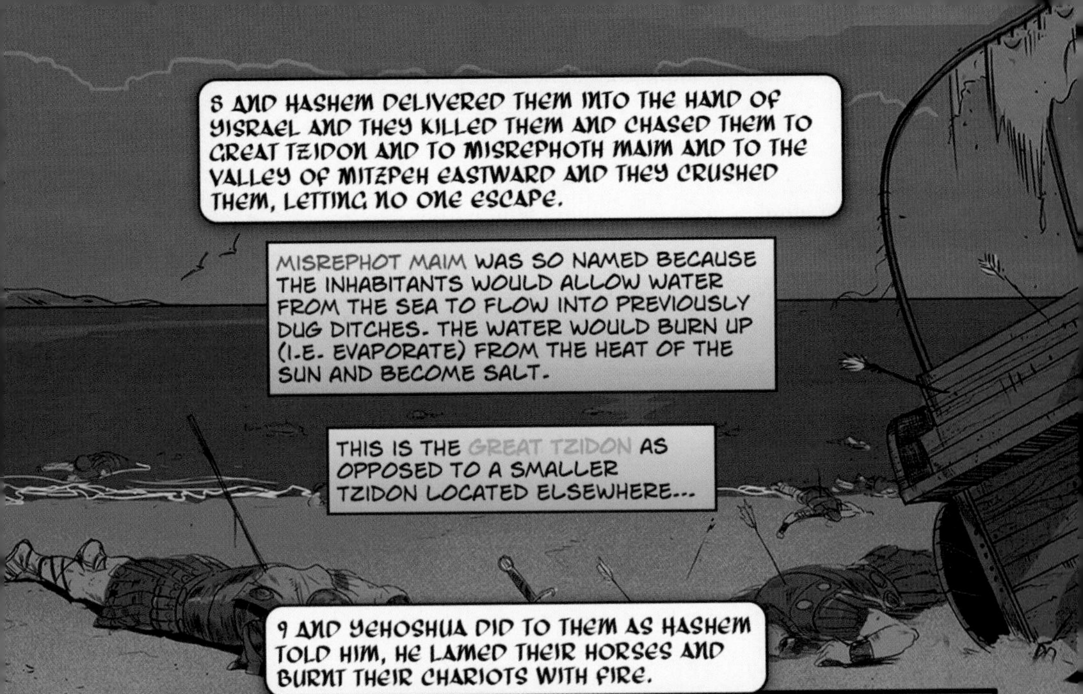
8 AND HASHEM DELIVERED THEM INTO THE HAND OF YISRAEL AND THEY KILLED THEM AND CHASED THEM TO GREAT TZIDON AND TO MISREPHOTH MAIM AND TO THE VALLEY OF MITZPEH EASTWARD AND THEY CRUSHED THEM, LETTING NO ONE ESCAPE.
MISREPHOT MAIM WAS SO NAMED BECAUSE THE INHABITANTS WOULD ALLOW WATER FROM THE SEA TO FLOW INTO PREVIOUSLY DUG DITCHES. THE WATER WOULD BURN UP (I.E. EVAPORATE) FROM THE HEAT OF THE SUN AND BECOME SALT.
THIS IS THE GREAT TZIDON AS OPPOSED TO A SMALLER TZIDON LOCATED ELSEWHERE...
9 AND YEHOSHUA DID TO THEM AS HASHEM TOLD HIM, HE LAMED THEIR HORSES AND BURNT THEIR CHARIOTS WITH FIRE.

THE NATION OF YISRAEL ***WINS*** BATTLES ONLY BECAUSE OF HASHEM AND HIS RELATIONSHIP WITH YISRAEL. HE IS THE WARRIOR OF ALL WARRIORS. IT IS HASHEM AND ABSOLUTELY NOTHING ELSE THAT WINS WARS. YEHOSHUA WAS PROCLAIMING THIS MESSAGE TO THE NATION BY MAIMING THE HORSES AND SHOWING THE NATION IT IS NOT THE HORSE THAT HELPED WIN THE BATTLE. TAKE THIS ***LESSON*** WITH YOU NOT ONLY IN THE BATTLEFIELD, BUT ALSO WHERE EVER YOU GO. HASHEM IS THE ONE, NOT US AND NOT OUR WEAPONS AND NOT OUR HORSES NOR OUR CHARIOTS.

NEVERTHELESS, HASHEM IN HIS UNFATHOMABLE WISDOM ***CREATED*** ANIMALS WITH INCREDIBLE CAPABILITIES TO SERVE HUMANITY. FOR EXAMPLE THE HORSE, WHICH IS SO CRITICAL FOR THE NEEDS OF MAN. WE NEED THEM FOR TRANSPORTATION, FOR WORK, FOR TRANSPORT, AND MOST IMPORTANT FOR WAR. WARFARE WAS THE ***PRIMARY*** REASON HASHEM CREATED THEIR ENORMOUS POWER AND STAMINA.

IN CONCLUSION, JUST AS THE NATIONS OF THE WORLD GO TO BATTLE WITH HORSE AND CHARIOT, SO TOO YOU THE NATION OF YISRAEL WILL GO TO ***BATTLE*** WITH HORSE AND CHARIOT.

ח וַיִּתְּנֵם ה' בְּיַד יִשְׂרָאֵל וַיַּכּוּם וַיִּרְדְּפוּם עַד צִידוֹן רַבָּה וְעַד מִשְׂרְפוֹת מַיִם
וְעַד בִּקְעַת מִצְפֶּה מִזְרָחָה וַיַּכֻּם עַד בִּלְתִּי הִשְׁאִיר לָהֶם שָׂרִיד. **ט** וַיַּעַשׂ לָהֶם
יְהוֹשֻׁעַ כַּאֲשֶׁר אָמַר לוֹ ה' אֶת סוּסֵיהֶם עִקֵּר וְאֶת מַרְכְּבֹתֵיהֶם שָׂרַף בָּאֵשׁ.

10 YEHOSHUA THEN TURNED BACK AND CAPTURED CHATZOR,
WHY DID WE HAVE TO RUSH BACK TO CHATZOR? THEY WERE CLEARLY DEFEATED...
WE DON'T WANT THEM TO HAVE A CHANCE TO REGROUP.
CHATZOR
WE HAVE MADE OUR ASSERTION KNOWN. LET IT BE CLEAR TO ALL THE NATIONS WHAT WILL BE THE CONSEQUENCES TO THEIR CHOICES AND DECISIONS!
AND HE KILLED THE KING WITH HIS SWORD. AS CHATZOR WAS FORMERLY THE HEAD OF ALL THOSE KINGDOMS.
YEHOSHUA COMPLETELY BURNED CHATZOR TO DETER ANY FUTURE KINGS FROM UNIFYING INTO ONE HUGE ARMY...
11 AND THEY KILLED ALL THE SOULS THAT WERE THERE BY THE SWORD, UTTERLY DESTROYING THEM AND (LEAVING) NONE LEFT AND CHATZOR WAS BURNT DOWN.

י וַיָּשָׁב יְהוֹשֻׁעַ בָּעֵת הַהִיא וַיִּלְכֹּד אֶת חָצוֹר וְאֶת מַלְכָּהּ הִכָּה בֶחָרֶב כִּי חָצוֹר לְפָנִים הִיא
רֹאשׁ כָּל הַמַּמְלָכוֹת הָאֵלֶּה. **יא** וַיַּכּוּ אֶת כָּל הַנֶּפֶשׁ אֲשֶׁר בָּהּ לְפִי חֶרֶב הַחֲרֵם לֹא נוֹתַר
כָּל נְשָׁמָה וְאֶת חָצוֹר שָׂרַף בָּאֵשׁ.

THANK YOU HASHEM FOR CONQUERING ALL THESE CITIES...

12 THOSE ROYAL CITIES AND THEIR KINGS, HE KILLED THEM WITH HIS SWORD, UTTERLY DESTROYING THEM AS WAS COMMANDED BY MOSHE THE SERVANT OF HASHEM. 13. HOWEVER, ALL THOSE CITIES STILL STANDING ON THEIR MOUNDS WERE NOT BURNED DOWN BY YISRAEL; ONLY CHATZOR ALONE DID YEHOSHUA BURN DOWN.

I AM GOING TO USE SOME OF MY SPOILS OF WAR AS A SACRIFICE TO HASHEM ACKNOWLEDGING ALL OF HIS GREATNESS AND KINDNESS.
YOU'RE RIGHT, WE SHOULD ALWAYS REMEMBER THAT WAR IS VERY DANGEROUS AND WITHOUT THE HELP OF HASHEM THE OUTCOME OF OUR BATTLES COULD BE VERY BAD.

14 AND ALL THE SPOILS AND CATTLE OF THESE CITIES THE CHILDREN OF YISRAEL TOOK FOR THEMSELVES AS BOOTY. BUT THEY CUT DOWN THEIR POPULATION WITH THE SWORD UNTIL THEY KILLED THEM ALL; THEY DID NOT SPARE A SOUL. 15 AS HASHEM COMMANDED MOSHE HIS SERVANT SO DID MOSHE COMMAND YEHOSHUA. AND SO DID YEHOSHUA. HE LEFT NOTHING UNDONE OF ALL THAT HASHEM COMMANDED MOSHE.

יב וְאֶת כָּל עָרֵי הַמְּלָכִים הָאֵלֶּה וְאֶת כָּל מַלְכֵיהֶם לָכַד יְהוֹשֻׁעַ וַיַּכֵּם לְפִי חֶרֶב
הֶחֱרִים אוֹתָם כַּאֲשֶׁר צִוָּה מֹשֶׁה עֶבֶד ה'. **יג** רַק כָּל הֶעָרִים הָעֹמְדוֹת עַל תִּלָּם לֹא
שְׂרָפָם יִשְׂרָאֵל זוּלָתִי אֶת חָצוֹר לְבַדָּהּ שָׂרַף יְהוֹשֻׁעַ. **יד** וְכֹל שְׁלַל הֶעָרִים הָאֵלֶּה
וְהַבְּהֵמָה בָּזְזוּ לָהֶם בְּנֵי יִשְׂרָאֵל רַק אֶת כָּל הָאָדָם הִכּוּ לְפִי חֶרֶב עַד הִשְׁמִדָם אוֹתָם
לֹא הִשְׁאִירוּ כָּל נְשָׁמָה. **טו** כַּאֲשֶׁר צִוָּה ה' אֶת מֹשֶׁה עַבְדּוֹ כֵּן צִוָּה מֹשֶׁה אֶת יְהוֹשֻׁעַ
וְכֵן עָשָׂה יְהוֹשֻׁעַ לֹא הֵסִיר דָּבָר מִכֹּל אֲשֶׁר צִוָּה ה' אֶת מֹשֶׁה.

THE UPCOMING VERSES SUMMARIZE THE LAND THAT YEHOSHUA HAD CONQUERED.
16 YEHOSHUA CONQUERED THIS WHOLE REGION: THE MOUNTAINS [OF YEHUDA], THE SOUTH, THE ENTIRE LAND OF GOSHEN, THE LOWLANDS, THE ARABAH, THE MOUNTAINS AND COASTAL PLAINS OF YISRAEL.
IT'S FUNNY THAT THIS LAND ALSO HAS A CITY CALLED GOSHEN. IT'S A VERY FERTILE PIECE OF LAND, I WONDER WHICH TRIBE IS GOING TO GET IT.
IT PROBABLY SHOULD BE YEHUDAH. WHEN YAAKOV AND HIS FAMILY OF 70 SOULS INITIALLY WENT DOWN TO MITZRAYIM, YEHUDAH PAVED THE WAY FOR YISRAEL TO SETTLE IN GOSHEN.
GOOD POINT, I EVEN HEARD THAT YEHUDAH MADE SURE THERE WAS A STUDY HALL TO LEARN TORAH...
17 FROM THE MOUNTAIN CALLED THE BARE MOUNTAIN, WHICH ASCENDS TO SEIR, ALL THE WAY TO BAAL-GAD, IN THE VALLEY OF LEVANON AT THE FOOT OF MOUNT CHERMON.
THIS MOUNTAIN ALSO SLOPED EVENLY TOWARD THE LAND OF YISRAEL AND TOWARD THE LAND OF SEIR.
THIS WAS REFERRED TO AS A BARE MOUNTAIN SINCE VEGETATION DID NOT GROW ON IT.
HE CAPTURED ALL THE KINGS AND KILLED THEM.

טז וַיִּקַּח יְהוֹשֻׁעַ אֶת כָּל הָאָרֶץ הַזֹּאת הָהָר וְאֶת כָּל הַנֶּגֶב וְאֵת כָּל אֶרֶץ הַגֹּשֶׁן וְאֶת
הַשְּׁפֵלָה וְאֶת הָעֲרָבָה וְאֶת הַר יִשְׂרָאֵל וּשְׁפֵלָתֹה. **יז** מִן הָהָר הֶחָלָק הָעוֹלֶה שֵׂעִיר
וְעַד בַּעַל גָּד בְּבִקְעַת הַלְּבָנוֹן תַּחַת הַר חֶרְמוֹן וְאֵת כָּל מַלְכֵיהֶם לָכַד וַיַּכֵּם וַיְמִיתֵם.

יח יָמִים רַבִּים עָשָׂה יְהוֹשֻׁעַ אֶת כָּל הַמְּלָכִים הָאֵלֶּה מִלְחָמָה. **יט** לֹא הָיְתָה עִיר
אֲשֶׁר הִשְׁלִימָה אֶל בְּנֵי יִשְׂרָאֵל בִּלְתִּי הַחִוִּי יֹשְׁבֵי גִבְעוֹן אֶת הַכֹּל לָקְחוּ בַמִּלְחָמָה.
כ כִּי מֵאֵת ה' הָיְתָה לְחַזֵּק אֶת לִבָּם לִקְרַאת הַמִּלְחָמָה אֶת יִשְׂרָאֵל לְמַעַן
הַחֲרִימָם לְבִלְתִּי הֱיוֹת לָהֶם תְּחִנָּה כִּי לְמַעַן הַשְׁמִידָם כַּאֲשֶׁר צִוָּה ה' אֶת מֹשֶׁה.

PUNY YISRAEL, YOU THINK YOU CAN DEFEAT ME! WHAT I "EAT" FOR BREAKFAST IS MORE THAN ALL OF YOU COMBINED...
ALL I KNOW IS WHEN WE BURY YOU, THE WORMS WILL HAVE ENOUGH FOOD FOR A YEAR...

SWWISSSH
WOA... THAT WAS A CLOSE ONE!
I DIDN'T THINK THESE BIG GUY'S CAN MOVE SO FAST...

KLANK!!!
HA HA! YOU'RE FINISHED!!
I DIDN'T EVEN DENT IN HIS SHIELD!

TIME FOR A DIFFERENT APPROACH...
ARGH!!!
SLASH!!!
NOW, I'M GOING TO CUT YOU UP INTO LITTLE PIECES!!!
I THINK THAT TIME WE MADE HIM MAD.
WHOOSH
AHHHH!!!
SHIFFF

21 AT THAT TIME YEHOSHUA CAME AND WIPED OUT THE GIANTS FROM THE MOUNTAIN REGION FROM CHEVRON, DEVIR, ANAV, FROM ALL THE MOUNTAINOUS AREAS OF YEHUDAH AND FROM ALL THE MOUNTAIN REGIONS OF YISRAEL, YEHOSHUA UTTERLY DESTROYED THEM ALONG WITH THEIR CITIES.

כא וַיָּבֹא יְהוֹשֻׁעַ בָּעֵת הַהִיא וַיַּכְרֵת אֶת הָעֲנָקִים מִן הָהָר מִן חֶבְרוֹן מִן דְּבִר
מִן עֲנָב וּמִכֹּל הַר יְהוּדָה וּמִכֹּל הַר יִשְׂרָאֵל עִם עָרֵיהֶם הֶחֱרִימָם יְהוֹשֻׁעַ.

22 NO GIANTS WERE LEFT IN THE LAND OF YISRAEL, BUT SOME REMAINED IN GAZA, GATH AND ASHDOD.
23 SO YEHOSHUA CONQUERED THE WHOLE LAND ACCORDING TO ALL THAT HASHEM SPOKE TO MOSHE. AND YEHOSHUA GAVE IT FOR AN INHERITANCE TO YISRAEL ACCORDING TO THEIR DIVISIONS BY THEIR TRIBES. AND THE LAND HAD REST FROM WAR.
כב לֹא נוֹתַר עֲנָקִים בְּאֶרֶץ בְּנֵי יִשְׂרָאֵל רַק בְּעַזָּה בְּגַת וּבְאַשְׁדּוֹד נִשְׁאָרוּ.
כג וַיִּקַּח יְהוֹשֻׁעַ אֶת כָּל הָאָרֶץ כְּכֹל אֲשֶׁר דִּבֶּר ה' אֶל מֹשֶׁה וַיִּתְּנָהּ יְהוֹשֻׁעַ
לְנַחֲלָה לְיִשְׂרָאֵל כְּמַחְלְקֹתָם לְשִׁבְטֵיהֶם וְהָאָרֶץ שָׁקְטָה מִמִּלְחָמָה.

YEHOSHUA CHAPTER 12
יהושע פרק יב

TO HELP IDENTIFY THE LOCATIONS ON THE MAP, THE VERSE **NUMBERS** ARE REPRESENTED IN RED.

1 THE FOLLOWING ARE THE KINGS OF THE LAND WHOM THE CHILDREN OF YISRAEL DEFEATED AND WHOSE TERRITORIES THEY TOOK POSSESSION OF EAST OF THE YARDEN, FROM THE ARNON RIVER TO MOUNT CHERMON, INCLUDING THE EASTERN HALF OF ARAVAH.

INITIALLY, THESE LANDS BELONGED TO AMMON & MOAV, HOWEVER, THE MIGHTY GIANTS, SICHON AND OG EVENTUALLY ***CONQUERED*** THIS REGION.

2 SICHON KING OF AMORIE WHO LIVED IN CHESHBON AND RULED FROM AROR ON THE BANKS OF THE ARNON RIVER, AND WITHIN THE RIVER AND HALF OF GILEAD UP UNTIL THE YAABOK RIVER ON THE BORDER OF THE NATION OF AMMON.

THE YAABOK RIVER IS WHERE YAAKOV AVINU CROSSED ALL ALONE, ***FLEEING*** FROM LAVAN AND SPENDING THE NIGHT WRESTLING WITH THE ANGEL OF EISAV.

Valley of Levanon
Baal Gad
Mount Chermon
Maacha
Beit Anat
Beit Shemesh (North)
Bashan
Geshure
Kinneret
Ashtarot
Edrei
Beit Shean
Gilead
Salcha
Yarden
Yabbok
Cheshbon
Ammon
עמון
Beit Hayesimot
ראובן
Sichon
Aroer ?
Arnon
מואב
Araba Sea / Dead Sea
North

א וְאֵלֶּה מַלְכֵי הָאָרֶץ אֲשֶׁר הִכּוּ בְנֵי יִשְׂרָאֵל וַיִּרְשׁוּ אֶת
אַרְצָם בְּעֵבֶר הַיַּרְדֵּן מִזְרְחָה הַשָּׁמֶשׁ מִנַּחַל אַרְנוֹן עַד הַר
חֶרְמוֹן וְכָל הָעֲרָבָה מִזְרָחָה. **ב** סִיחוֹן מֶלֶךְ הָאֱמֹרִי
הַיּוֹשֵׁב בְּחֶשְׁבּוֹן מֹשֵׁל מֵעֲרוֹעֵר אֲשֶׁר עַל שְׂפַת נַחַל אַרְנוֹן
וְתוֹךְ הַנַּחַל וַחֲצִי הַגִּלְעָד וְעַד יַבֹּק הַנַּחַל גְּבוּל בְּנֵי עַמּוֹן.

3 AND OVER THE EASTERN ARAVAH UP TO THE KINNERET AND SOUTHWARD THROUGH BEIT YESHIMOT AT THE FOOT OF THE SLOPES OF PISCAH ON THE EAST, DOWN TO THE ARAVAH SEA, WHICH IS THE DEAD SEA. 4 ALSO OVER THE TERRITORY OF OG, KING OF BASHAN—ONE OF THE LAST OF THE REPHAIM—WHO RESIDED IN ASHTAROT AND IN EDRI. 5 AND RULED IN MOUNT CHERMON AND IN SALCAH AND IN ALL BASHAN TO THE BORDER OF GESHURE AND THE MAACHA AND HALF GILEAD UP TO THE BORDER OF SICHON, KING OF CHESHBON.

6 THESE WERE KILLED OUT BY MOSHE, THE SERVANT OF HASHEM, AND THE CHILDREN OF YISRAEL; AND MOSHE THE SERVANT OF HASHEM, ASSIGNED THAT TERRITORY AS A POSSESSION TO REUVEN, GAD AND THE HALF-TRIBE OF MENASHE.

ORIGINALLY, THE TERRITORIES FROM AMMON AND MOAV, DESCENDANTS FROM LOT, WERE ***PROHIBITED*** FROM ANNEXATION. HOWEVER, ONCE OG AND SICHON CONQUERED THE LAND FROM AMMON AND MOAV, THE CHILDREN OF YISRAEL WERE GIVEN PERMISSION TO OVERTHROW THE GIANTS AND ***CLAIM*** THE LAND FOR THEIR OWN.

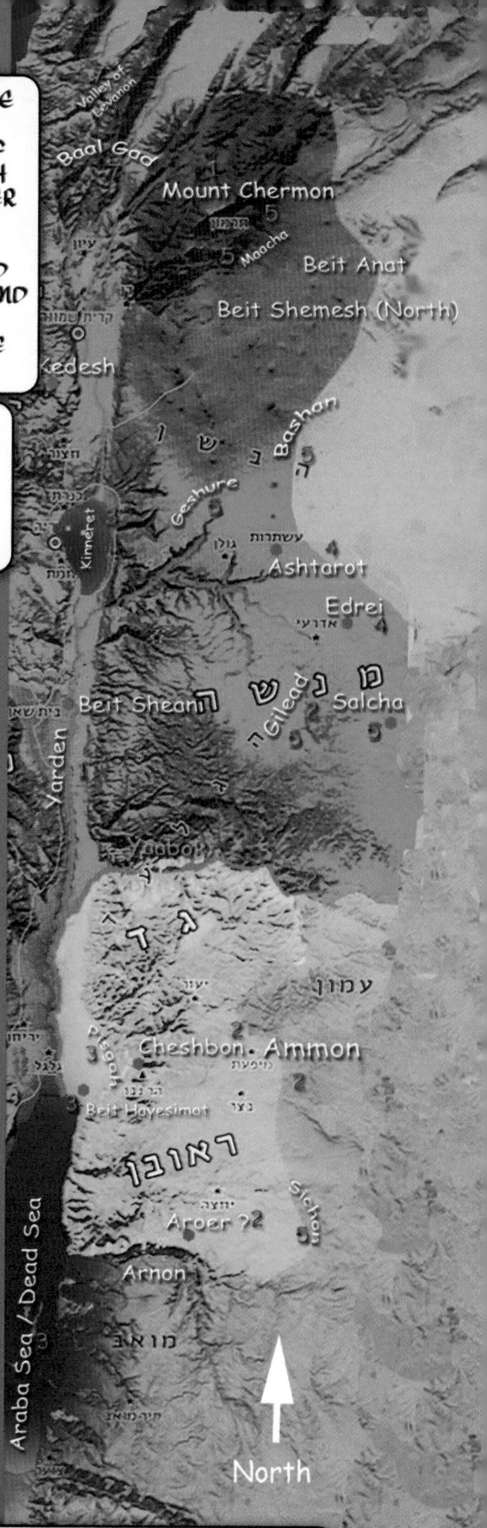

ג וְהָעֲרָבָה עַד יָם כִּנְרוֹת מִזְרָחָה וְעַד יָם הָעֲרָבָה יָם הַמֶּלַח מִזְרָחָה דֶּרֶךְ בֵּית
הַיְשִׁמוֹת וּמִתֵּימָן תַּחַת אַשְׁדּוֹת הַפִּסְגָּה. **ד** וּגְבוּל עוֹג מֶלֶךְ הַבָּשָׁן מִיֶּתֶר הָרְפָאִים
הַיּוֹשֵׁב בְּעַשְׁתָּרוֹת וּבְאֶדְרֶעִי. **ה** וּמֹשֵׁל בְּהַר חֶרְמוֹן וּבְסַלְכָה וּבְכָל הַבָּשָׁן עַד גְּבוּל
הַגְּשׁוּרִי וְהַמַּעֲכָתִי וַחֲצִי הַגִּלְעָד גְּבוּל סִיחוֹן מֶלֶךְ חֶשְׁבּוֹן. **ו** מֹשֶׁה עֶבֶד ה' וּבְנֵי
יִשְׂרָאֵל הִכּוּם וַיִּתְּנָהּ מֹשֶׁה עֶבֶד ה' יְרֻשָּׁה לָרְאוּבֵנִי וְלַגָּדִי וְלַחֲצִי שֵׁבֶט הַמְנַשֶּׁה.

APPROXIMATELY 450 YEARS EARLIER AT THE CIRCUMCISION OF YITZCHAK, AVRAHAMS SON...
I NEVER HEARD OF ANYONE DOING THIS CIRCUMCISION. WHAT DOES IT REPRESENT?
IT IS A COVENANT BETWEEN HASHEM, AND AVRAHAM AND HIS DESCENDANTS. IT SIGNIFIES THE UNIQUE RELATIONSHIP THAT AVRAHAM HAS WITH THE CREATOR OF THE WORLD.
YEAH, NINE MONTHS AGO HE EVEN DID IT TO HIMSELF, YISHMAEL AND ALL THE MALES OF HIS HOUSEHOLD.
IF YOU ASK ME, I THINK IT'S ALL IN HIS HEAD, AND IN THE END, NOTHING WILL COME OF IT...
ALL 31 KINGS WHO WITNESSED THE BIRTH OF YITZCHAK WERE EVENTUALLY CONQUERED AT THE HAND OF YEHOSHUA.

QUITE A FEAST AVRAHAM PUT TOGETHER FOR THE BIRTH OF HIS CHILD. ALL THE 31 KINGS OF CANAAN ALONG WITH THEIR GOVERNOR'S SHOWED UP...
OG, WEREN'T YOU THE ONE WHO SAID "AVRAHAM IS LIKE A BARREN MULE AND CANNOT HAVE CHILDREN."
WHAT KIND OF GIFT IS THIS? THE CHILD IS SO INSIGNIFICANT, I COULD CRUSH HIM WITH MY LITTLE FINGER...
HASHEM SAID, "OG, WHY DO YOU RIDICULE MY GIFT? BY YOUR LIFE YOU WILL SEE THOUSANDS UPON THOUSANDS OF HIS DESCENDANTS. AND YOUR FATE WILL FALL INTO THEIR HANDS." AS IT STATES, 'AND HASHEM SAID TO MOSHE, DO NOT BE AFRAID FOR I HAVE DELIVERED HIM, HIS PEOPLE, AND HIS LAND INTO YOUR HAND..."

7 AND THESE ARE THE KINGS OF THE LAND
WHOM YEHOSHUA AND THE CHILDREN OF
YISRAEL KILLED ON THE WEST SIDE OF THE
YARDEN, FROM BAAL GAD IN THE VALLEY OF
LEVANON UP TO BARE MOUNTAIN THAT GOES UP
TO SEIR; AND YEHOSHUA GAVE IT TO THE TRIBES
OF YISRAEL FOR A POSSESSION ACCORDING
TO THEIR DIVISIONS. 8 IN THE HILL COUNTRY, IN
THE LOWLANDS, IN THE ARAVAH, IN THE SLOPES,
IN THE WILDERNESS AND IN THE SOUTH; THE
CHITTIE THE AMORIE AND THE CANAANIE THE
PERIZZIE THE CHIVIE AND THE YEVUSIE. 9 THE
KING OF YERICHO ONE; THE KING OF AI WHICH
IS BESIDE BEIT EL ONE; 10 THE KING OF
YERUSHALAYIM ONE; THE KING OF CHEVRON
ONE; 11 THE KING OF YARMUTH ONE; THE KING
OF LACHISH ONE; 12 THE KING OF EGLON ONE;
THE KING OF GEZER ONE; 13 THE KING OF DEVIR
ONE; THE KING OF GEDER ONE; 14 THE KING OF
CHORMA ONE; THE KING OF ARAD ONE; 15 THE
KING OF LIVNA ONE; THE KING OF ADULLAM
ONE; 16 THE KING OF MAKKEDAH ONE; THE KING
OF BETH EL ONE; 17 THE KING OF TAPPUAH ONE;
THE KING OF CHEPHER ONE; 18 THE KING OF
APHEK ONE; THE KING OF THE SHARON ONE; 19
THE KING OF MADON ONE; THE KING OF
CHATZOR ONE; 20 THE KING OF SHIMRON
MERON ONE; THE KING OF ACHSHAPH ONE; 21
THE KING OF TAANACH ONE; THE KING OF
MEGIDDO ONE; 22 THE KING OF KEDESH ONE;
THE KING OF YOKNEAM IN CARMEL ONE; 23 THE
KING OF DOR IN THE REGION OF DOR ONE; THE
KING OF GOYIM IN THE GILGAL ONE; 24 THE
KING OF TIRTZAH ONE. TOTALING THIRTY-ONE
KINGS.

THE KINGS HAD PRIMARY LAND IN OTHER LOCATIONS. HOWEVER, AS A SIGN OF ***PRESTIGE*** IT WAS NECESSARY FOR A RULER TO CONQUER AND DOMINATE SOME PART OF THE LAND OF YISRAEL. THIS IS WHY THE KINGS ARE LISTED HERE INDIVIDUALLY AND THAT THE HOLY LAND IS SO CENTRAL.

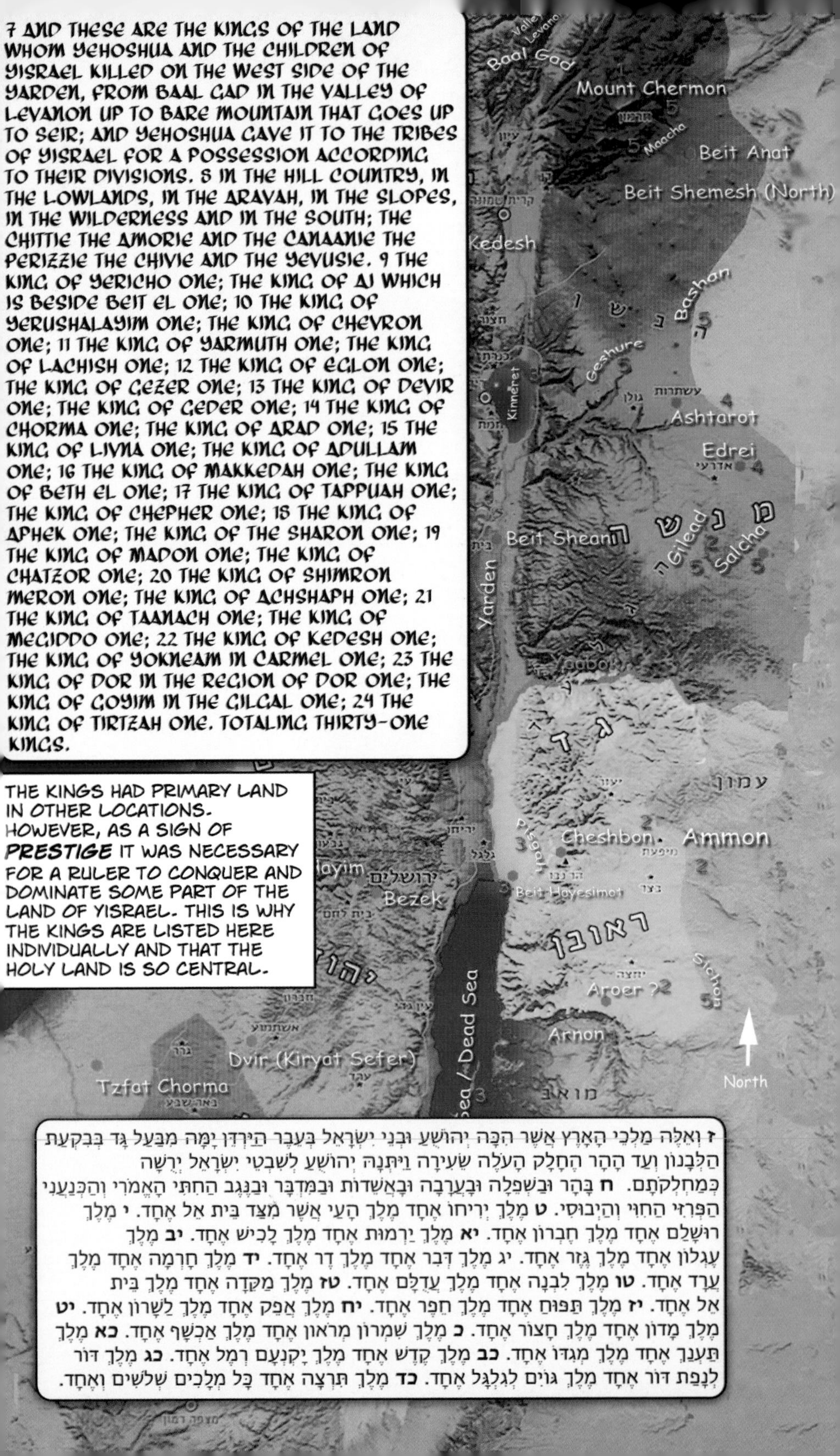

ז וְאֵלֶּה מַלְכֵי הָאָרֶץ אֲשֶׁר הִכָּה יְהוֹשֻׁעַ וּבְנֵי יִשְׂרָאֵל בְּעֵבֶר הַיַּרְדֵּן יָמָּה מִבַּעַל גָּד בְּבִקְעַת
הַלְּבָנוֹן וְעַד הָהָר הֶחָלָק הָעֹלֶה שֵׂעִירָה וַיִּתְּנָהּ יְהוֹשֻׁעַ לְשִׁבְטֵי יִשְׂרָאֵל יְרֻשָּׁה
כְּמַחְלְקֹתָם. **ח** בָּהָר וּבַשְּׁפֵלָה וּבָעֲרָבָה וּבָאֲשֵׁדוֹת וּבַמִּדְבָּר וּבַנֶּגֶב הַחִתִּי הָאֱמֹרִי וְהַכְּנַעֲנִי
הַפְּרִזִּי הַחִוִּי וְהַיְבוּסִי. **ט** מֶלֶךְ יְרִיחוֹ אֶחָד מֶלֶךְ הָעַי אֲשֶׁר מִצַּד בֵּית אֵל אֶחָד. **י** מֶלֶךְ
רוּשָׁלַם אֶחָד מֶלֶךְ חֶבְרוֹן אֶחָד. **יא** מֶלֶךְ יַרְמוּת אֶחָד מֶלֶךְ לָכִישׁ אֶחָד. **יב** מֶלֶךְ
עֶגְלוֹן אֶחָד מֶלֶךְ גֶּזֶר אֶחָד. יג מֶלֶךְ דְּבִר אֶחָד מֶלֶךְ גֶּדֶר אֶחָד. **יד** מֶלֶךְ חָרְמָה אֶחָד מֶלֶךְ
עֲרָד אֶחָד. **טו** מֶלֶךְ לִבְנָה אֶחָד מֶלֶךְ עֲדֻלָּם אֶחָד. **טז** מֶלֶךְ מַקֵּדָה אֶחָד מֶלֶךְ בֵּית
אֵל אֶחָד. **יז** מֶלֶךְ תַּפּוּחַ אֶחָד מֶלֶךְ חֵפֶר אֶחָד. **יח** מֶלֶךְ אֲפֵק אֶחָד מֶלֶךְ לַשָּׁרוֹן אֶחָד. **יט**
מֶלֶךְ מָדוֹן אֶחָד מֶלֶךְ חָצוֹר אֶחָד. **כ** מֶלֶךְ שִׁמְרוֹן מְראוֹן אֶחָד מֶלֶךְ אַכְשָׁף אֶחָד. **כא** מֶלֶךְ
תַּעְנַךְ אֶחָד מֶלֶךְ מְגִדּוֹ אֶחָד. **כב** מֶלֶךְ קֶדֶשׁ אֶחָד מֶלֶךְ יָקְנְעָם לַכַּרְמֶל אֶחָד. **כג** מֶלֶךְ דּוֹר
לְנָפַת דּוֹר אֶחָד מֶלֶךְ גּוֹיִם לְגִלְגָּל אֶחָד. **כד** מֶלֶךְ תִּרְצָה אֶחָד כָּל מְלָכִים שְׁלֹשִׁים וְאֶחָד.

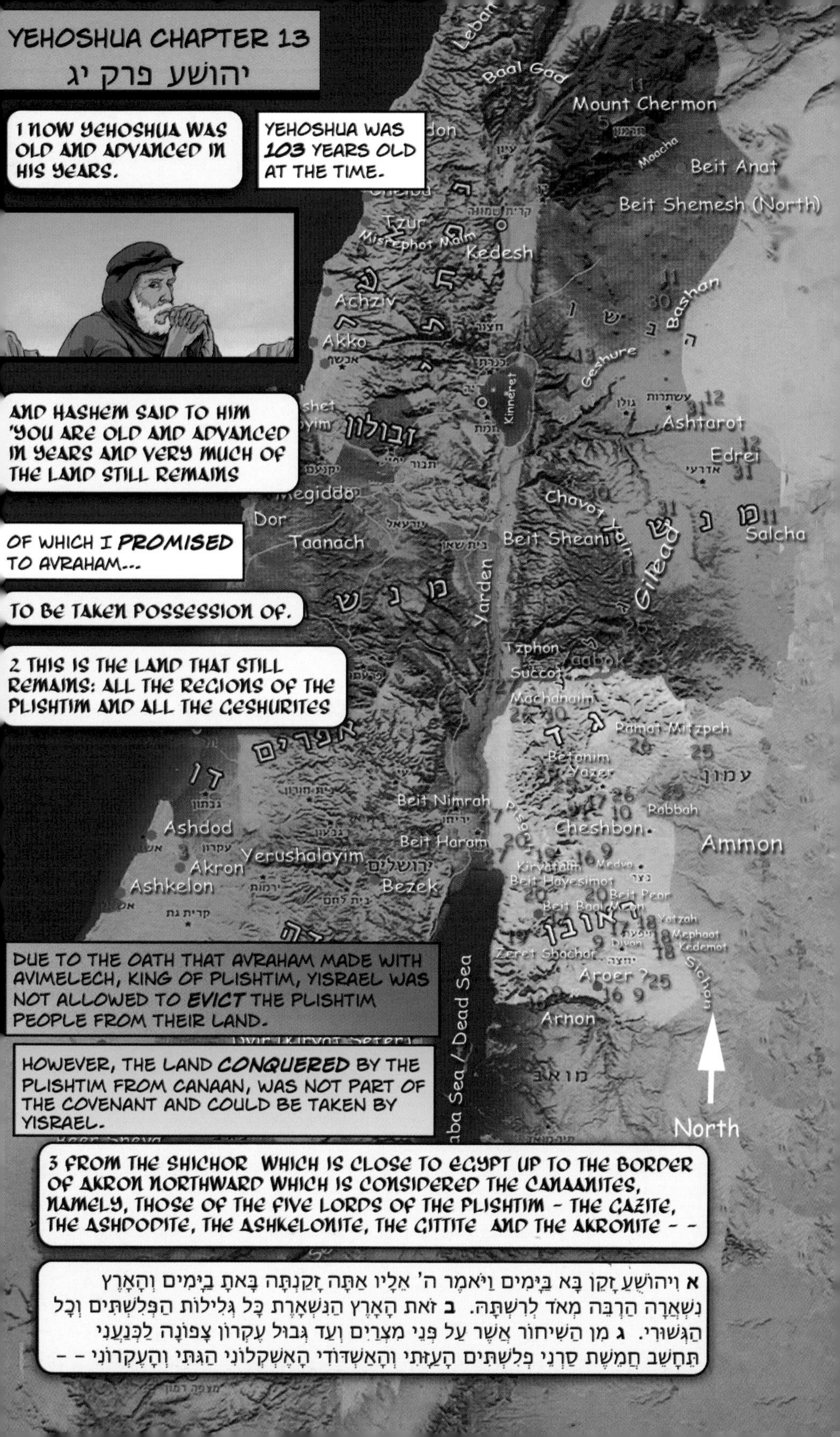
YEHOSHUA CHAPTER 13
יהושע פרק יג
1 NOW YEHOSHUA WAS OLD AND ADVANCED IN HIS YEARS.
YEHOSHUA WAS 103 YEARS OLD AT THE TIME.
AND HASHEM SAID TO HIM 'YOU ARE OLD AND ADVANCED IN YEARS AND VERY MUCH OF THE LAND STILL REMAINS
OF WHICH I PROMISED TO AVRAHAM...
TO BE TAKEN POSSESSION OF.
2 THIS IS THE LAND THAT STILL REMAINS: ALL THE REGIONS OF THE PLISHTIM AND ALL THE GESHURITES
DUE TO THE OATH THAT AVRAHAM MADE WITH AVIMELECH, KING OF PLISHTIM, YISRAEL WAS NOT ALLOWED TO EVICT THE PLISHTIM PEOPLE FROM THEIR LAND.
HOWEVER, THE LAND CONQUERED BY THE PLISHTIM FROM CANAAN, WAS NOT PART OF THE COVENANT AND COULD BE TAKEN BY YISRAEL.
3 FROM THE SHICHOR WHICH IS CLOSE TO EGYPT UP TO THE BORDER OF AKRON NORTHWARD WHICH IS CONSIDERED THE CANAANITES, NAMELY, THOSE OF THE FIVE LORDS OF THE PLISHTIM - THE GAZITE, THE ASHDODITE, THE ASHKELONITE, THE GITTITE AND THE AKRONITE - -
א וִיהוֹשֻׁעַ זָקֵן בָּא בַּיָּמִים וַיֹּאמֶר ה' אֵלָיו אַתָּה זָקַנְתָּה בָּאתָ בַיָּמִים וְהָאָרֶץ
נִשְׁאֲרָה הַרְבֵּה מְאֹד לְרִשְׁתָּהּ. ב זֹאת הָאָרֶץ הַנִּשְׁאָרֶת כָּל גְּלִילוֹת הַפְּלִשְׁתִּים וְכָל
הַגְּשׁוּרִי. ג מִן הַשִּׁיחוֹר אֲשֶׁר עַל פְּנֵי מִצְרַיִם וְעַד גְּבוּל עֶקְרוֹן צָפוֹנָה לַכְּנַעֲנִי
תֵּחָשֵׁב חֲמֵשֶׁת סַרְנֵי פְלִשְׁתִּים הָעַזָּתִי וְהָאַשְׁדּוֹדִי הָאֶשְׁקְלוֹנִי הַגִּתִּי וְהָעֶקְרוֹנִי - -
Baal Gad
Mount Chermon
Maacha
Beit Anat
Beit Shemesh (North)
Tzur
Misrephot Maim
Kedesh
Achziv
Akko
Bashan
Geshure
Kinneret
Ashtarot
Edrei
זבולון
Megiddo
Dor
Taanach
Beit Shean
Chavot Yair
Gilead
Salcha
Yarden
Tzphon
Succot
Machanaim
Ramat Mitzpeh
Betonim
Yazer
עמון
Rabbah
Beit Nimrah
Cheshbon
Ammon
Ashdod
Akron
Ashkelon
Yerushalayim
Beit Haram
Bezek
Kiryataim
Medva
Beit Hayesimot
Beit Peor
Yatzah
Mephaat
Kedemot
Zeret Shochar
Aroer ?
Sichon
Arnon
Dead Sea
מואב
North

- - ALSO THE AVVIM.
THERE ARE DIFFERENT OPINIONS ABOUT WHO THE AVVIM WERE.
SOME SAY THEY WERE ORIGINALLY FROM TEMAN, SON OF ELIPHAZ, SON OF EISAV WHO DECIDED TO LIVE AMONG THE PLISHTIM...
WHERE ARE YOU GUYS HEADED TO?
WE'RE OFF TO THE COASTLINE. WE HEAR THERE IS MORE OPPORTUNITY WITH THE PLISHTIM...
BESIDES, THE SEA AIR IS BETTER FOR MY ALLERGIES.
OTHERS SAY, THE AVVIM WERE FIERCE GIANTS WITH SIXTEEN ROWS OF TEETH...
ROARRRRR!!!
GET OUT OF MY WAY!!!
A THIRD OPINION IS, THE AVVIM ACTUALLY ARE THE PLISHTIM PEOPLE WHO INITIALLY WERE NOT ALLOWED TO BE CONQUERED BY YISRAEL. HASHEM NEVERTHELESS BROUGHT THE KAFTORITES TO DESTROY THE AVVIM, AND DWELL IN THEIR LAND; THEREBY, ALLOWING YISRAEL TO ULTIMATELY TAKE POSSESSION.
- - וְהָעַוִּים.

4 ON THE SOUTH FURTHER; IS ALL THE CANAANIE LAND FROM MEARAH OF THE TZIDONIANS TO APHEK TO THE AMORIE BORDER.

5 AND THE LAND OF THE GIVALIE AND ALL LEVANON, FROM BAAL GAD AT THE FOOT OF MOUNT CHERMON TO LEBO-CHAMAT ON THE EAST.

THE PEOPLE OF GIVAL ASSISTED IN CUTTING THE FOUNDATION STONES FOR THE **FIRST** BEIT HAMIKDASH.

6 ALL THE INHABITANTS OF THE HILL COUNTRY FROM LEVANON TO MISREPHOT MAIM EVEN ALL THE TZIDONIANS, I WILL DRIVE THEM OUT FOR THE CHILDREN OF YISRAEL.

AFTER THE DEATH OF YEHOSHUA.

YOU HAVE ONLY TO DIVIDE THE LAND BY DRAWING LOTS FOR YISRAEL AS AN INHERITANCE AS I HAVE COMMANDED YOU.

EACH TRIBE WILL HAVE TO CONQUER THE **REST** OF THEIR OWN LAND WHICH WAS ALLOTTED TO THEM.

Lebanon

Valley Levanon

Baal Gad

Mount Chermon

Tzidon

Maacha

Beit Anat

Chelba

Beit Shemesh (North)

Tzur
Misrephot Maim

Kedesh

Bashan

30

Achziv

Geshure

Akko

Ashtarot

12

Kinneret

Charoshet Hagoyim

זבולון

Chavot Yair

Edrei

31

Megiddo

Gilead

Salcha

Dor

Taanach

Beit Shean

מנשה

Yarden

Tzphon
Succot

Aphek

אפרים

Machnaim
26 30

Ramat Mitzpech

Betanim
Yazer

עמון

Beit Nimrah

26
21 10

Rabbah

Cheshbon

Ammon

Beit Haram

20 19 16 9

Yerushalayim
ירושלים

Kiryataim Medva

Bezek

Beit Hayesimot

Beit Peor

Beit Baal Meon

Yatzah

18

יהודה

Yahatz

18
Mephaot

Zeret Shachar

Kedemot

Aroer ? 25

16 9

evron

Arnon

vir (Kiryat Sefer)

מואב

Araba Sea / Dead Sea

↑

North

ד מִתֵּימָן כָּל אֶרֶץ הַכְּנַעֲנִי וּמְעָרָה אֲשֶׁר לַצִּדֹנִים עַד אֲפֵקָה עַד גְּבוּל הָאֱמֹרִי. ה וְהָאָרֶץ הַגִּבְלִי וְכָל הַלְּבָנוֹן מִזְרַח הַשֶּׁמֶשׁ מִבַּעַל גָּד תַּחַת הַר חֶרְמוֹן עַד לְבוֹא חֲמָת. ו כָּל יֹשְׁבֵי הָהָר מִן הַלְּבָנוֹן עַד מִשְׂרְפֹת מַיִם כָּל צִדֹנִים אָנֹכִי אוֹרִישֵׁם מִפְּנֵי בְּנֵי יִשְׂרָאֵל רַק הַפִּלֶהָ לְיִשְׂרָאֵל בְּנַחֲלָה כַּאֲשֶׁר צִוִּיתִיךָ.

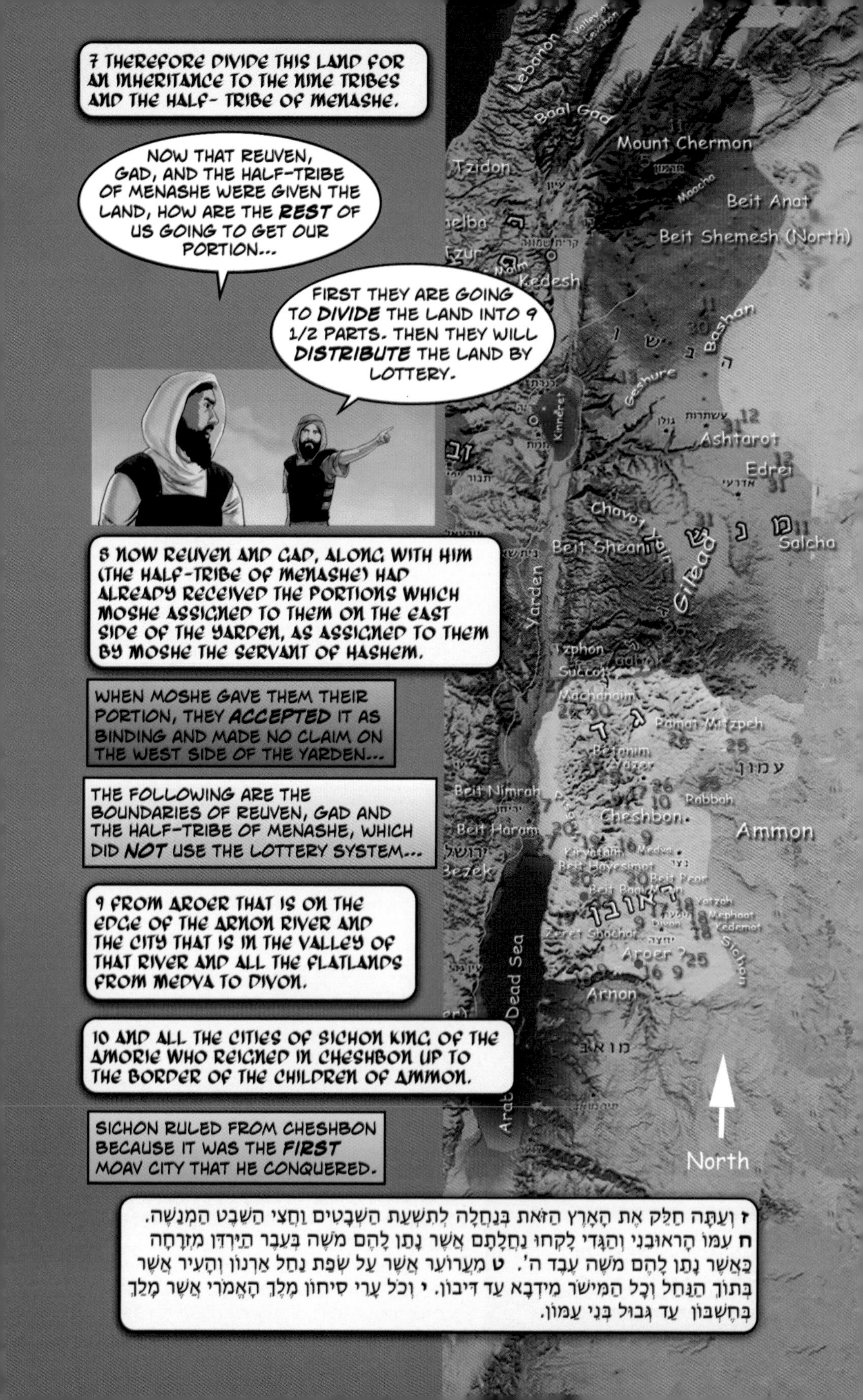

7 THEREFORE DIVIDE THIS LAND FOR AN INHERITANCE TO THE NINE TRIBES AND THE HALF- TRIBE OF MENASHE.

NOW THAT REUVEN, GAD, AND THE HALF-TRIBE OF MENASHE WERE GIVEN THE LAND, HOW ARE THE **REST** OF US GOING TO GET OUR PORTION...

FIRST THEY ARE GOING TO **DIVIDE** THE LAND INTO 9 1/2 PARTS. THEN THEY WILL **DISTRIBUTE** THE LAND BY LOTTERY.

8 NOW REUVEN AND GAD, ALONG WITH HIM (THE HALF-TRIBE OF MENASHE) HAD ALREADY RECEIVED THE PORTIONS WHICH MOSHE ASSIGNED TO THEM ON THE EAST SIDE OF THE YARDEN, AS ASSIGNED TO THEM BY MOSHE THE SERVANT OF HASHEM.

WHEN MOSHE GAVE THEM THEIR PORTION, THEY **ACCEPTED** IT AS BINDING AND MADE NO CLAIM ON THE WEST SIDE OF THE YARDEN...

THE FOLLOWING ARE THE BOUNDARIES OF REUVEN, GAD AND THE HALF-TRIBE OF MENASHE, WHICH DID **NOT** USE THE LOTTERY SYSTEM...

9 FROM AROER THAT IS ON THE EDGE OF THE ARNON RIVER AND THE CITY THAT IS IN THE VALLEY OF THAT RIVER AND ALL THE FLATLANDS FROM MEDVA TO DIVON.

10 AND ALL THE CITIES OF SICHON KING OF THE AMORIE WHO REIGNED IN CHESHBON UP TO THE BORDER OF THE CHILDREN OF AMMON.

SICHON RULED FROM CHESHBON BECAUSE IT WAS THE **FIRST** MOAV CITY THAT HE CONQUERED.

North

ז וְעַתָּה חַלֵּק אֶת הָאָרֶץ הַזֹּאת בְּנַחֲלָה לְתִשְׁעַת הַשְּׁבָטִים וַחֲצִי הַשֵּׁבֶט הַמְנַשֶּׁה.
ח עִמּוֹ הָרֹאוּבֵנִי וְהַגָּדִי לָקְחוּ נַחֲלָתָם אֲשֶׁר נָתַן לָהֶם מֹשֶׁה בְּעֵבֶר הַיַּרְדֵּן מִזְרָחָה כַּאֲשֶׁר נָתַן לָהֶם מֹשֶׁה עֶבֶד ה'. ט מֵעֲרוֹעֵר אֲשֶׁר עַל שְׂפַת נַחַל אַרְנוֹן וְהָעִיר אֲשֶׁר בְּתוֹךְ הַנַּחַל וְכָל הַמִּישֹׁר מֵידְבָא עַד דִּיבוֹן. י וְכֹל עָרֵי סִיחוֹן מֶלֶךְ הָאֱמֹרִי אֲשֶׁר מָלַךְ בְּחֶשְׁבּוֹן עַד גְּבוּל בְּנֵי עַמּוֹן.

THERE IT IS! CHESHBON.
SOON IT WILL BE ALL MINE...
WHY DOES HE BOTHER TEARING THE CITY DOWN, IF HE IS JUST GOING TO REBUILD IT...
I DON'T ASK ANY QUESTIONS OF THE BIG GUY. ALL I KNOW IS THAT HE KEEPS US EMPLOYED...

11 AND GILEAD AND THE BORDER OF THE GESHURITES AND MAACATHITES AND MOUNT CHERMON AND BASHAN TO SALCAH. 12 THE ENTIRE KINGDOM OF OG, WHO HAD REIGNED OVER BASHAN AT ASHTAROT AND AT EDREI. HE WAS THE LAST OF THE REMAINING GIANTS.

SICHON AND OG WERE THE SONS OF ACHIYAH BAR SHAMCHAZAIAND. THE BROTHERS ***BOTH*** SURVIVED THE FLOOD OF NOACH...

THESE WERE DEFEATED AND DISPOSSESSED BY MOSHE.

13 NEVERTHELESS THE CHILDREN OF YISRAEL DID NOT DRIVE OUT THE GESHURITES NOR THE MAACATHITES BUT GESHUR AND MAACATH LIVED AMONG YISRAEL UNTIL THIS DAY.

14 ONLY THE TRIBE OF LEVI HE GAVE NO INHERITANCE. THEIR PORTION BEING THE FIRE OFFERINGS OF HASHEM, THE G-D OF YISRAEL, AS HE SPOKE CONCERNING THEM.

THE TRIBE OF LEVI WAS ***NOT*** GIVEN A PORTION IN THE ACTUAL LAND OF YISRAEL. HOWEVER, YISRAEL IS COMMANDED TO ESTABLISH CITIES FOR THEM TO LIVE IN. THESE WERE THE 6 CITIES OF REFUGE AS WELL AS 42 ADDITIONAL CITIES.

LEVI WAS ***SET ASIDE*** TO SERVE HASHEM, TO ADMINISTER, AND TO TEACH THE NATION THE STRAIGHT PATHS AND RIGHTEOUS JUDGEMENTS.

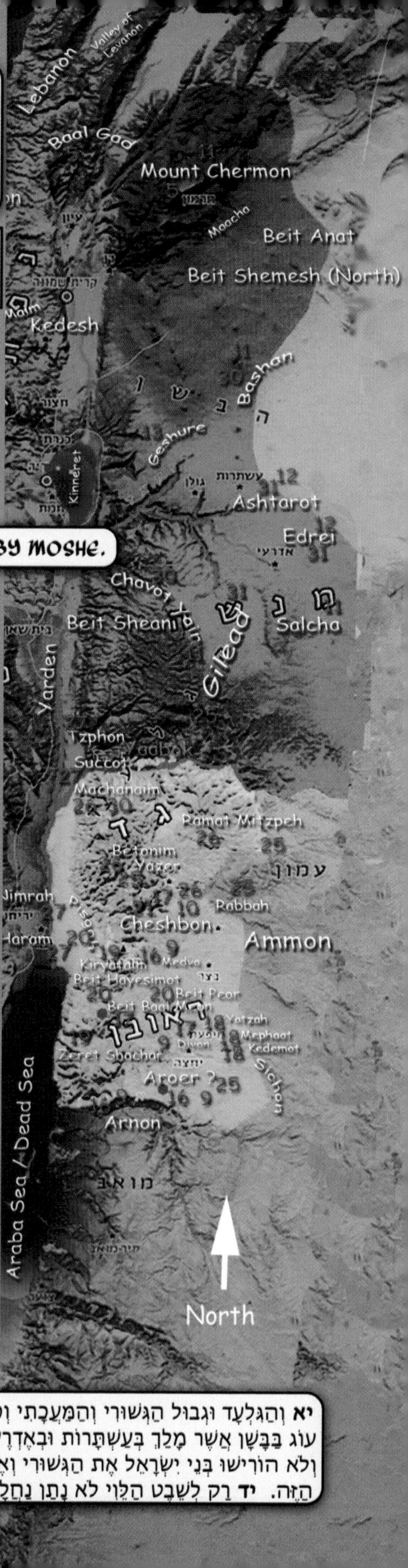

יא וְהַגִּלְעָד וּגְבוּל הַגְּשׁוּרִי וְהַמַּעֲכָתִי וְכֹל הַר חֶרְמוֹן וְכָל הַבָּשָׁן עַד סַלְכָה. **יב** כָּל מַמְלְכוּת
עוֹג בַּבָּשָׁן אֲשֶׁר מָלַךְ בְּעַשְׁתָּרוֹת וּבְאֶדְרֶעִי הוּא נִשְׁאַר מִיֶּתֶר הָרְפָאִים וַיַּכֵּם מֹשֶׁה וַיֹּרִשֵׁם. **יג**
וְלֹא הוֹרִישׁוּ בְּנֵי יִשְׂרָאֵל אֶת הַגְּשׁוּרִי וְאֶת הַמַּעֲכָתִי וַיֵּשֶׁב גְּשׁוּר וּמַעֲכַת בְּקֶרֶב יִשְׂרָאֵל עַד הַיּוֹם
הַזֶּה. **יד** רַק לְשֵׁבֶט הַלֵּוִי לֹא נָתַן נַחֲלָה אִשֵּׁי ה' אֱלֹקֵי יִשְׂרָאֵל הוּא נַחֲלָתוֹ כַּאֲשֶׁר דִּבֶּר לוֹ.

15 AND MOSHE GAVE TO THE TRIBE OF THE CHILDREN OF REUVEN ACCORDING TO THEIR FAMILIES.

MOSHE ***SUBDIVIDED*** REUVEN'S TERRITORY ACCORDING TO FAMILIES. (AS OPPOSED TO GIVING THEM THEIR ENTIRE PORTION AND ALLOWING THE TRIBE TO ALLOCATE THE SMALLER PORTIONS AMONG THEMSELVES...)

16 AND THEIR BORDER WAS FROM AROER THAT IS ON THE EDGE OF THE RIVER OF ARNON AND THE CITY THAT IS IN THE VALLEY OF THAT RIVER AND ALL THE FLATLANDS FROM MEDVA, 17 CHESHBON AND ALL HER CITIES THAT ARE IN THE FLATLANDS: DIVON, BAMOT BAAL AND BEIT BAAL MEON.

18 AND YATZAH AND KEDEMOT AND MEPHAAT.

REUVEN GAVE THESE ***THREE*** CITIES TO THE LEVIIM.

19 AND KIRYATAIM, SIVMAH AND ZERET SHAHAR IN THE MOUNT OF THE VALLEY 20 AND BEIT PEOR, THE SLOPES OF PISCAH AND BEIT HAYESHIMOT. 21 AND ALL THE CITIES OF THE FLATLANDS AND ALL THE KINGDOM OF SICHON KING OF THE AMORITES WHO REIGNED IN CHESHBON WHOM MOSHE KILLED WITH THE CHIEFS OF MIDIAN, EVI, REKEM, TZUR, CHUR AND REVA, THE DUKES OF SICHON THAT DWELLED IN THE LAND.

TZUR WAS THE ***FATHER*** OF COZBI, THE MIDIAN PRINCESS WHO WAS KILLED ALONG WITH ZIMRI BY PINCHAS... (BAMIDBAR 25:14-15)

THERE IS THE TENT OF ZIMRI, THE ***TRAITOR*** OF YISRAEL...
PINCHAS, ***WHAT*** ARE YOU DOING WITH THAT SPEAR?
AN ABOMINATION IS TAKING PLACE AND I HAVE A RESPONSIBILITY TO ***RESTORE*** THE HOLINESS AND HONOR OF HASHEM!!!

טו וַיִּתֵּן מֹשֶׁה לְמַטֵּה בְנֵי רְאוּבֵן לְמִשְׁפְּחֹתָם. **טז** וַיְהִי לָהֶם הַגְּבוּל מֵעֲרוֹעֵר אֲשֶׁר עַל
שְׂפַת נַחַל אַרְנוֹן וְהָעִיר אֲשֶׁר בְּתוֹךְ הַנַּחַל וְכָל הַמִּישֹׁר עַל מֵידְבָא. **יז** חֶשְׁבּוֹן וְכָל עָרֶיהָ
אֲשֶׁר בַּמִּישֹׁר דִּיבוֹן וּבָמוֹת בַּעַל וּבֵית בַּעַל מְעוֹן. **יח** וְיַהְצָה וּקְדֵמֹת וּמֵפָעַת. **יט** וְקִרְיָתַיִם
וְשִׂבְמָה וְצֶרֶת הַשַּׁחַר בְּהַר הָעֵמֶק. **כ** וּבֵית פְּעוֹר וְאַשְׁדּוֹת הַפִּסְגָּה וּבֵית הַיְשִׁמוֹת. **כא** וְכֹל
עָרֵי הַמִּישֹׁר וְכָל מַמְלְכוּת סִיחוֹן מֶלֶךְ הָאֱמֹרִי אֲשֶׁר מָלַךְ בְּחֶשְׁבּוֹן אֲשֶׁר הִכָּה מֹשֶׁה אֹתוֹ
וְאֶת נְשִׂיאֵי מִדְיָן אֶת אֱוִי וְאֶת רֶקֶם וְאֶת צוּר וְאֶת חוּר וְאֶת רֶבַע נְסִיכֵי סִיחוֹן יֹשְׁבֵי הָאָרֶץ.

A FEW YEARS EARLIER, AS DESCRIBED BY THE MIDRASH. BILAAM WAS IN HIS TENT PRACTICING SORCERY...
MASTER BILAAM, YISRAEL HAS BREACHED THE AREA, THEY ARE KILLING EVERY MIDIAN IN SIGHT...
I MUST INFORM THE CHIEFS OF MIDIAN OF MY ESCAPE PLAN...
YOUR EXCELLENCIES, PLEASE HURRY AND FOLLOW ME TO AVOID CAPTURE...

THIS IS THE ONLY WAY TO TRAVEL...
I THINK I SEE PINCHAS, HE IS WEARING THE KOHEN GADOL'S SPECIAL CLOTHING.
LIKE THAT WILL DO HIM ANY GOOD.
HEY PINCHAS, BETTER LUCK NEXT TIME. I'M SURE WE WILL MEET AGAIN SOON.
AND DON'T WORRY, I WILL FIND A WAY TO DESTROY YOU AND ALL OF YISRAEL...
THOSE WICKED KINGS, USING DARK MAGIC TO GET AWAY...
I CANNOT LET THEM GET AWAY!

OHH NOOO!!!
I THINK I SPOKE TOO SOON...
22 TOGETHER WITH THE OTHERS THAT THEY KILLED, THE CHILDREN OF YISRAEL PUT BILAAM THE SON OF BEOR, THE SOOTHSAYER TO DEATH BY THE SWORD. 23 AND AS FOR THE BORDER OF THE CHILDREN OF REUVEN THE YARDEN WAS THEIR BORDER. THIS WAS THE INHERITANCE OF THE CHILDREN OF REUVEN ACCORDING TO THEIR FAMILIES THEIR CITIES AND THEIR TOWNS.
WITH THE HELP OF HASHEM, PINCHAS USED THE GOLDEN PLATE THAT WAS ON HIS FOREHEAD WITH THE WORDS "HOLY TO HASHEM" WRITTEN ON IT, TO BRING BILAAM AND THE FIVE KINGS BACK DOWN TO EARTH...
SPLAT
כב וְאֶת בִּלְעָם בֶּן בְּעוֹר הַקּוֹסֵם הָרְגוּ בְנֵי יִשְׂרָאֵל בַּחֶרֶב אֶל חַלְלֵיהֶם. כג וַיְהִי
גְּבוּל בְּנֵי רְאוּבֵן הַיַּרְדֵּן וּגְבוּל זֹאת נַחֲלַת בְּנֵי רְאוּבֵן לְמִשְׁפְּחֹתָם הֶעָרִים וְחַצְרֵיהֶן.

24 AND MOSHE GAVE TO THE TRIBE OF GAD AND THE CHILDREN OF GAD ACCORDING TO THEIR FAMILIES.

25 AND THEIR BORDER WAS YAZER AND ALL THE CITIES OF GILEAD AND HALF THE LAND OF THE CHILDREN OF AMMON UNTIL AROER THAT IS NEXT TO RABBAH. 26 AND FROM CHESHBON UNTIL RAMAT MIZPEH, BETONIM AND FROM MACHANAIM UNTIL THE BORDER OF DVIR.

MACHANAIM WAS NAMED BY YAAKOV AVINU AND WAS THE CITY THAT DOVID HAMELECH ***FLED*** FOR SAFETY, FROM AVSHALOM. (SEE SHMUEL II, 17:24)

27 AND IN THE VALLEY OF BEIT HARAM, BEIT NIMRAH, SUCCOT AND TZAPHON THE REST OF THE KINGDOM OF SICHON KING OF CHESHBON. THE YARDEN THEIR BORDER UNTIL THE TIP OF THE KINNERET SEA ON THE EAST SIDE OF THE YARDEN. 28 THIS IS THE INHERITANCE OF THE CHILDREN OF GAD ACCORDING TO THEIR FAMILIES THE CITIES AND THEIR TOWNS.

29 AND MOSHE GAVE INHERITANCE TO THE HALF-TRIBE OF MENASHE AND IT WAS FOR THE HALF-TRIBE OF THE CHILDREN OF MENASHE ACCORDING TO THEIR FAMILIES. 30 AND THEIR BORDER WAS FROM MACHANAIM ALL OF BASHAN, THE ENTIRE KINGDOM OF OG, KING OF BASHAN AND ALL OF CHAVAS-YAIR IN BASHAN, SIXTY CITIES.

31 AND HALF OF GILEAD, ASHTAROT AND EDRI THE ROYAL CITIES OF OG IN BASHAN, WERE ASSIGNED TO THE DESCENDANTS OF MACHIR THE SON OF MENASHE-TO A PART OF THE DESCENDANTS OF MACHIR- AND THEIR FAMILIES. 32 THESE ARE THE INHERITANCES WHICH MOSHE DISTRIBUTED IN THE PLAINS OF MOAV BEYOND THE YARDEN EAST OF YERICHO. 33 BUT TO THE TRIBE OF LEVI MOSHE GAVE NO INHERITANCE, HASHEM THE G-D OF YISRAEL IS THEIR INHERITANCE AS HE SPOKE TO THEM.

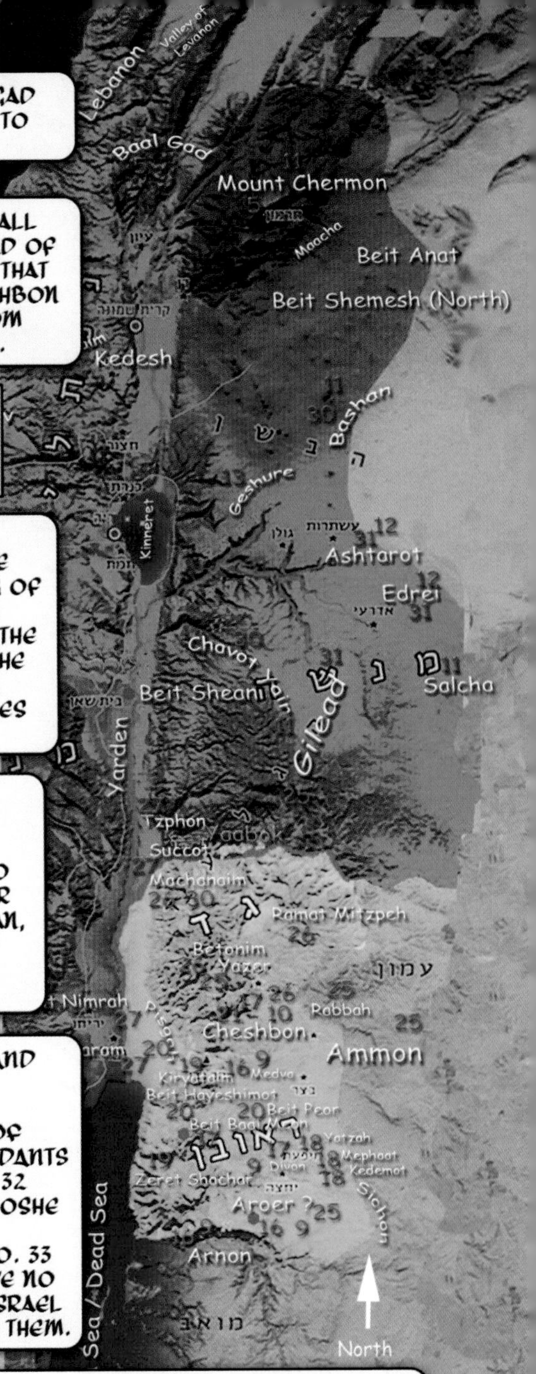

Valley of Levanon
Lebanon
Baal Gad
Mount Chermon
Maacha
Beit Anat
Beit Shemesh (North)
Kedesh
Bashan
Geshure
Kinneret
Ashtarot
Edrei
Chavot Yair
Beit Sheani
Gilead
Salcha
Yarden
Tzphon
Succot
Machanaim
Ramat Mitzpeh
Betonim
Yazer
Cheshbon
Rabbah
Ammon
Kiryataim
Medva
Beit Hayeshimot
Beit Peor
Yatzah
Mephaat
Kedemot
Dead Sea
Zeret Shachar
Aroer ?
Sichon
Arnon
מואב
עמון
North

כד וַיִּתֵּן מֹשֶׁה לְמַטֵּה גָד לִבְנֵי גָד לְמִשְׁפְּחֹתָם. **כה** וַיְהִי לָהֶם הַגְּבוּל יַעְזֵר וְכָל עָרֵי
הַגִּלְעָד וַחֲצִי אֶרֶץ בְּנֵי עַמּוֹן: עַד עֲרוֹעֵר אֲשֶׁר עַל פְּנֵי רַבָּה. **כו** וּמֵחֶשְׁבּוֹן עַד רָמַת
הַמִּצְפֶּה וּבְטֹנִים וּמִמַּחֲנַיִם עַד גְּבוּל לִדְבִר. **כז** וּבָעֵמֶק בֵּית הָרָם וּבֵית נִמְרָה וְסֻכּוֹת
וְצָפוֹן יֶתֶר מַמְלְכוּת סִיחוֹן מֶלֶךְ חֶשְׁבּוֹן הַיַּרְדֵּן וּגְבֻל עַד קְצֵה יָם כִּנֶּרֶת עֵבֶר הַיַּרְדֵּן
מִזְרָחָה. **כח** זֹאת נַחֲלַת בְּנֵי גָד לְמִשְׁפְּחֹתָם הֶעָרִים וְחַצְרֵיהֶם. **כט** וַיִּתֵּן מֹשֶׁה לַחֲצִי
שֵׁבֶט מְנַשֶּׁה וַיְהִי לַחֲצִי מַטֵּה בְנֵי מְנַשֶּׁה לְמִשְׁפְּחוֹתָם. **ל** וַיְהִי גְבוּלָם מִמַּחֲנַיִם כָּל הַבָּשָׁן
כָּל מַמְלְכוּת עוֹג מֶלֶךְ הַבָּשָׁן וְכָל חַוֹּת יָאִיר אֲשֶׁר בַּבָּשָׁן שִׁשִּׁים עִיר. **לא** וַחֲצִי הַגִּלְעָד
וְעַשְׁתָּרוֹת וְאֶדְרֶעִי עָרֵי מַמְלְכוּת עוֹג בַּבָּשָׁן לִבְנֵי מָכִיר בֶּן מְנַשֶּׁה לַחֲצִי בְנֵי מָכִיר
לְמִשְׁפְּחוֹתָם. **לב** אֵלֶּה אֲשֶׁר נִחַל מֹשֶׁה בְּעַרְבוֹת מוֹאָב מֵעֵבֶר לְיַרְדֵּן יְרִיחוֹ מִזְרָחָה. לג
וּלְשֵׁבֶט הַלֵּוִי לֹא נָתַן מֹשֶׁה נַחֲלָה ה' אֱלֹהֵי יִשְׂרָאֵל הוּא נַחֲלָתָם כַּאֲשֶׁר דִּבֶּר לָהֶם.

YEHOSHUA CHAPTER 14
יהושע פרק יד

WHAT HAPPENED SO FAR?
THEY ARE USING THE LOTTERY AND JUST FINISHED DOLING OUT THE LAND PORTIONS FOR YEHUDAH, EPHRAIM, AND THE OTHER HALF OF THE TRIBE OF MENASHE.
SO WHY ARE THEY STOPPING?
BECAUSE THERE ARE STILL MANY ENEMY OUTPOSTS THAT NEED TO BE DEFEATED, THE REMAINING TRIBES ARE AFRAID THAT ONCE THE PORTIONS OF LAND ARE ASSIGNED, EACH WILL CONQUER THEIR OWN PARTICULAR TERRITORY AND NO ONE WILL BE WILLING TO HELP THE OTHER IF NEEDED.
AS YOU KNOW, FOR THE PAST SEVEN YEARS WE HAVE BEEN FREEING THE LAND FROM THE MAJOR DOMINATING KINGDOMS.
THEREFORE, WITH OUR HELP, YEHUDAH WILL CONTINUE CONQUERING THE SOUTH AND EPHRAIM AND MENASHE WILL CAPTURE THE NORTH...
WHEN THEY ARE FINISHED, THE REST OF THE LAND WILL BE PORTIONED OUT TO THE REMAINING TRIBES USING THIS LOTTERY SYSTEM.

FOR FURTHER INFORMATION ON *HOW* THE LOTTERY WAS CONDUCTED, PLEASE REFER TO CHAPTER 18...

1 AND THESE ARE THE INHERITANCES WHICH THE CHILDREN OF YISRAEL ACQUIRED IN THE LAND OF CANAAN, WHICH ELAZAR, THE KOHEN, AND YEHOSHUA, THE SON OF NUN, AND THE HEADS OF THE FATHERS' HOUSES OF THE TRIBES OF THE CHILDREN OF YISRAEL, DISTRIBUTED TO THEM.

א וְאֵלֶּה אֲשֶׁר נָחֲלוּ בְנֵי יִשְׂרָאֵל בְּאֶרֶץ כְּנָעַן אֲשֶׁר נִחֲלוּ אוֹתָם אֶלְעָזָר הַכֹּהֵן
וִיהוֹשֻׁעַ בִּן נוּן וְרָאשֵׁי אֲבוֹת הַמַּטּוֹת לִבְנֵי יִשְׂרָאֵל.

2 THEIR INHERITANCE IS DONE WITH A LOTTERY, AS HASHEM COMMANDED THROUGH MOSHE, FOR THE NINE AND ONE HALF-TRIBES. 3. FOR THE PORTION OF THE OTHER TWO AND A HALF TRIBES HAD BEEN ASSIGNED TO THEM BY MOSHE, ON THE OTHER SIDE OF THE YARDEN, HE DID NOT ASSIGN ANY PORTION FOR THE LEVIIM. 4 FOR THE CHILDREN OF YOSEPH WERE TWO TRIBES, MENASHE AND EPHRAIM AND THEY GAVE NO PORTION TO THE LEVIIM IN THE LAND, EXCEPT CITIES TO LIVE IN, WITH THE PASTURES FOR THEIR CATTLE AND FLOCKS. 5 AS HASHEM COMMANDED MOSHE, SO THE CHILDREN OF YISRAEL DID, AND THEY DIVIDED THE LAND.

6 THE CHILDREN OF YEHUDA AND KALEV SON OF YEPHUNNEH THE KENIZZIE APPROACHED YEHOSHUA IN GILGAL AND SAID TO HIM,

YOU KNOW WHAT INSTRUCTIONS HASHEM GAVE AT KADESH-BARNEA TO MOSHE THE MAN OF G-D CONCERNING YOU AND ME.
7 I WAS FORTY YEARS OLD WHEN MOSHE THE SERVANT OF HASHEM SENT ME FROM KADESH-BARNEA TO SPY OUT THE LAND - -

ב בְּגוֹרַל נַחֲלָתָם כַּאֲשֶׁר צִוָּה ה' בְּיַד מֹשֶׁה לְתִשְׁעַת הַמַּטּוֹת וַחֲצִי הַמַּטֶּה. **ג**
כִּי נָתַן מֹשֶׁה נַחֲלַת שְׁנֵי הַמַּטּוֹת וַחֲצִי הַמַּטֶּה מֵעֵבֶר לַיַּרְדֵּן וְלַלְוִיִּם לֹא נָתַן
נַחֲלָה בְּתוֹכָם. **ד** כִּי הָיוּ בְנֵי יוֹסֵף שְׁנֵי מַטּוֹת מְנַשֶּׁה וְאֶפְרָיִם וְלֹא נָתְנוּ חֵלֶק
לַלְוִיִּם בָּאָרֶץ כִּי אִם עָרִים לָשֶׁבֶת וּמִגְרְשֵׁיהֶם לְמִקְנֵיהֶם וּלְקִנְיָנָם. **ה** כַּאֲשֶׁר
צִוָּה ה' אֶת מֹשֶׁה כֵּן עָשׂוּ בְּנֵי יִשְׂרָאֵל וַיַּחְלְקוּ אֶת הָאָרֶץ. **ו** וַיִּגְּשׁוּ בְנֵי יְהוּדָה אֶל
יְהוֹשֻׁעַ בַּגִּלְגָּל וַיֹּאמֶר אֵלָיו כָּלֵב בֶּן יְפֻנֶּה הַקְּנִזִּי אַתָּה יָדַעְתָּ אֶת הַדָּבָר אֲשֶׁר דִּבֶּר
ה' אֶל מֹשֶׁה אִישׁ הָאֱלֹקִים עַל אֹדוֹתַי וְעַל אֹדוֹתֶיךָ בְּקָדֵשׁ בַּרְנֵעַ. **ז** בֶּן אַרְבָּעִים
שָׁנָה אָנֹכִי בִּשְׁלֹחַ מֹשֶׁה עֶבֶד ה' אֹתִי מִקָּדֵשׁ בַּרְנֵעַ לְרַגֵּל אֶת הָאָרֶץ - -

WE BOTH KNEW THERE WOULD BE TROUBLE WITH THE OTHER TEN.
THAT'S WHEN MOSHE CHANGED YOUR NAME FROM HOSHEA TO YEHOSHUA AND PRAYED ESPECIALLY FOR YOU.
I LITERALLY HAD TO GO TO CHEVRON TO THE CAVE OF MACHPELA BY MYSELF WHERE OUR FORE-FATHERS ARE BURIED. I PRAYED TO HASHEM FOR HELP THAT I SHOULDN'T BE ENTICED BY THE WICKEDNESS OF THE OTHERS...
YOU REMEMBER HOW WE ENTERED A CITY AND THE NOBLEMEN WERE STRICKEN WITH PESTILENCE AND THE VILLAGERS WERE BUSY BURYING THEIR DEAD.
WE WERE SPIES SENT INTO ENEMY TERRITORY AND NO ONE EVEN NOTICED US. NO ONE WAS SUSPICIOUS AND NO ONE ASKED ANY QUESTIONS......
YET, INSTEAD OF BEING THANKFUL TO HASHEM, THOSE INGRATES SLANDERED THE LAND BY STATING "THE LAND EATS UP ITS INHABITANTS."

- - AND I BROUGHT HIM BACK WORD AS IT WAS IN MY HEART.
WHAT I WAS REALLY DOING WAS TRYING TO GAIN CONTROL OF THE MURMURING CROWD, I PRETENDED TO BE IN FAVOR OF THE REBELLION BY SAYING
IS THIS THE ONLY THING THE SON OF AMRAM HAS DONE TO US? (BAMIDBAR 13:30) ANYONE LISTENING MIGHT HAVE THOUGHT I INTENDED TO BELITTLE MOSHE OUR TEACHER AND BE ON THEIR SIDE.
AND THEN, WHEN IT GOT ABSOLUTELY QUIET, I SAID,
DIDN'T HE SPLIT THE SEA FOR US, BRING DOWN THE MANN FOR US AND CAUSE THE QUAIL TO FLY DOWN FOR US TO EAT? WITH THE LOOK ON THEIR FACES, I THOUGHT THEY WERE GOING TO STONE ME...
NEVERTHELESS, I COULD NOT PUT DOWN THE REVOLT...
8 MY BROTHERS THAT WENT UP WITH ME MADE THE HEART OF THE PEOPLE MELT, BUT I COMPLETELY FOLLOWED HASHEM MY G-D.

– – וָאָשֵׁב אֹתוֹ דָּבָר כַּאֲשֶׁר עִם לְבָבִי. ח וְאַחַי אֲשֶׁר עָלוּ עִמִּי הִמְסִיו אֶת לֵב הָעָם וְאָנֹכִי מִלֵּאתִי אַחֲרֵי ה' אֱלֹקָי.

9 AND MOSHE SWORE ON THAT DAY, SAYING, "SURELY THE LAND WHERE YOUR FOOT HAS TRODDEN SHALL BE AN INHERITANCE FOR YOU AND FOR YOUR CHILDREN FOREVER, BECAUSE YOU HAVE FULLY FOLLOWED HASHEM MY G-D.
THE LAND HE WAS REFERRING TO IS CHEVRON.
10 AND NOW HASHEM HAS KEPT ME ALIVE AS HE PROMISED. IT IS FORTY-FIVE YEARS SINCE HASHEM MADE THIS PROMISE TO MOSHE, WHEN YISRAEL WAS JOURNEYING THROUGH THE WILDERNESS, AND HERE I AM TODAY, EIGHTY-FIVE YEARS OLD. 11 YET I AM AS STRONG TODAY AS THE DAY MOSHE SENT ME; MY STRENGTH IS THE SAME NOW AS IT WAS THEN FOR BATTLE AND FOR ALL ACTIVITIES.
12 NOW THEREFORE, GIVE ME THIS MOUNTAIN,
CHEVRON
OF WHICH HASHEM SPOKE ON THAT DAY;
THE DAY WE WENT OUT TO SPY THE LAND.
FOR YOU HEARD ON THAT DAY HOW THE ANAKIM WERE THERE,
AND THAT THESE GIANTS CAN BE EXTREMELY TERRIFYING.
AND THAT THEIR CITIES WERE GREATLY FORTIFIED
AND YOU WILL ASK, "WHO HAS THE POWER TO WAGE WAR AGAINST THEM?"
IF ONLY HASHEM WILL BE WITH ME, AND I WILL DRIVE THEM OUT, AS HASHEM PROMISED.

ט וַיִּשָּׁבַע מֹשֶׁה בַּיּוֹם הַהוּא לֵאמֹר אִם לֹא הָאָרֶץ אֲשֶׁר דָּרְכָה רַגְלְךָ בָּהּ לְךָ תִהְיֶה
לְנַחֲלָה וּלְבָנֶיךָ עַד עוֹלָם כִּי מִלֵּאתָ אַחֲרֵי ה' אֱלקי. **י** וְעַתָּה הִנֵּה הֶחֱיָה ה' אוֹתִי
כַּאֲשֶׁר דִּבֵּר זֶה אַרְבָּעִים וְחָמֵשׁ שָׁנָה מֵאָז דִּבֶּר ה' אֶת הַדָּבָר הַזֶּה אֶל מֹשֶׁה אֲשֶׁר הָלַךְ
יִשְׂרָאֵל בַּמִּדְבָּר וְעַתָּה הִנֵּה אָנֹכִי הַיּוֹם בֶּן חָמֵשׁ וּשְׁמוֹנִים שָׁנָה. **יא** עוֹדֶנִּי הַיּוֹם חָזָק
כַּאֲשֶׁר בְּיוֹם שְׁלֹחַ אוֹתִי מֹשֶׁה כְּכֹחִי אָז וּכְכֹחִי עָתָּה לַמִּלְחָמָה וְלָצֵאת וְלָבוֹא. **יב**
וְעַתָּה תְּנָה לִּי אֶת הָהָר הַזֶּה אֲשֶׁר דִּבֶּר ה' בַּיּוֹם הַהוּא כִּי אַתָּה שָׁמַעְתָּ בַיּוֹם הַהוּא
כִּי עֲנָקִים שָׁם וְעָרִים גְּדֹלוֹת בְּצֻרוֹת אוּלַי ה' אוֹתִי וְהוֹרַשְׁתִּים כַּאֲשֶׁר דִּבֶּר ה'.

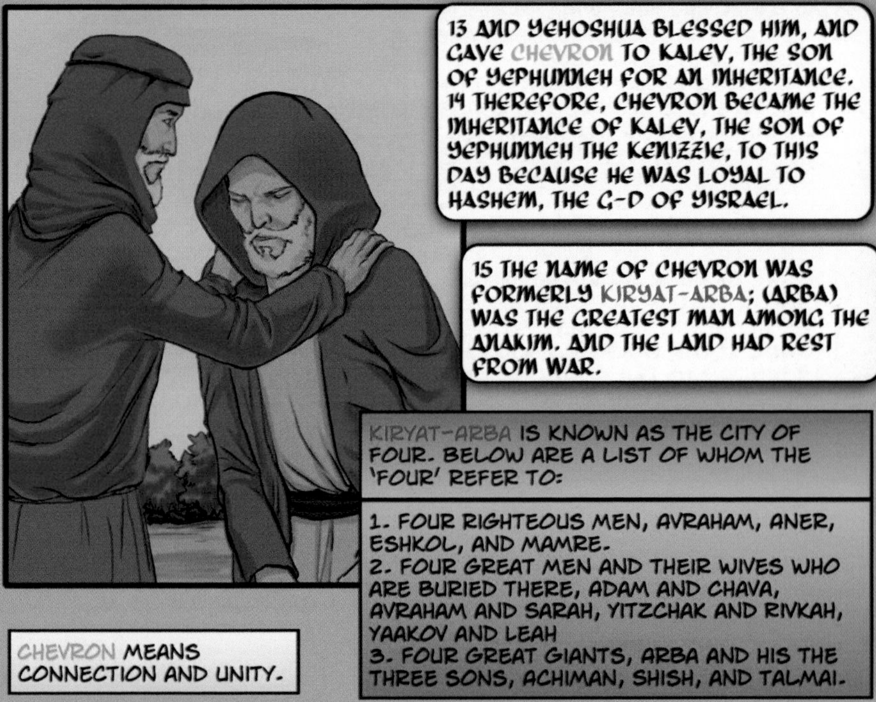
13 AND YEHOSHUA BLESSED HIM, AND GAVE CHEVRON TO KALEV, THE SON OF YEPHUNNEH FOR AN INHERITANCE. 14 THEREFORE, CHEVRON BECAME THE INHERITANCE OF KALEV, THE SON OF YEPHUNNEH THE KENIZZIE, TO THIS DAY BECAUSE HE WAS LOYAL TO HASHEM, THE G-D OF YISRAEL.
15 THE NAME OF CHEVRON WAS FORMERLY KIRYAT-ARBA; (ARBA) WAS THE GREATEST MAN AMONG THE ANAKIM. AND THE LAND HAD REST FROM WAR.
KIRYAT-ARBA IS KNOWN AS THE CITY OF FOUR. BELOW ARE A LIST OF WHOM THE 'FOUR' REFER TO:
1. FOUR RIGHTEOUS MEN, AVRAHAM, ANER, ESHKOL, AND MAMRE.
2. FOUR GREAT MEN AND THEIR WIVES WHO ARE BURIED THERE, ADAM AND CHAVA, AVRAHAM AND SARAH, YITZCHAK AND RIVKAH, YAAKOV AND LEAH
3. FOUR GREAT GIANTS, ARBA AND HIS THE THREE SONS, ACHIMAN, SHISH, AND TALMAI.
CHEVRON MEANS CONNECTION AND UNITY.

THEY ARE CONSTANTLY TALKING ABOUT US GIANTS AND OUR CONNECTION TO KIRYAT-ARBA. FATHER, ENOUGH IS ENOUGH, WILL THEY EVER STOP?!
I DON'T THINK SO TALMAI. I HAVE A FEELING THIS IS GOING TO BE A POINT OF INTEREST FOR A LONG TIME!

יג וַיְבָרְכֵהוּ יְהוֹשֻׁעַ וַיִּתֵּן אֶת חֶבְרוֹן לְכָלֵב בֶּן יְפֻנֶּה לְנַחֲלָה. **יד** עַל כֵּן הָיְתָה חֶבְרוֹן
לְכָלֵב בֶּן יְפֻנֶּה הַקְּנִזִּי לְנַחֲלָה עַד הַיּוֹם הַזֶּה יַעַן אֲשֶׁר מִלֵּא אַחֲרֵי ה' אֱלֹקֵי יִשְׂרָאֵל. **טו**
וְשֵׁם חֶבְרוֹן לְפָנִים קִרְיַת אַרְבַּע הָאָדָם הַגָּדוֹל בָּעֲנָקִים הוּא וְהָאָרֶץ שָׁקְטָה מִמִּלְחָמָה.

1 THE PORTION THAT FELL BY THE LOTTERY TO THE VARIOUS FAMILIES OF THE TRIBE OF YEHUDA LAY FARTHEST SOUTH DOWN TO THE BORDER OF EDOM, WHICH IS IN THE WILDERNESS OF TZIN. 2 THEIR SOUTHERN BOUNDARY BEGAN FROM THE TIP OF THE DEAD SEA FROM THE BAY THAT PROJECTS SOUTHWARD. 3 IT PROCEEDED TO THE SOUTH OF MAALEH AKRABIM, AND PASSED ON TO TZIN, ASCENDED TO THE SOUTH OF KADESH BARNEA, PASSED ON TO CHETZRON, ASCENDED TO IADAR , AND TURNED ABOUT TO KARKA.

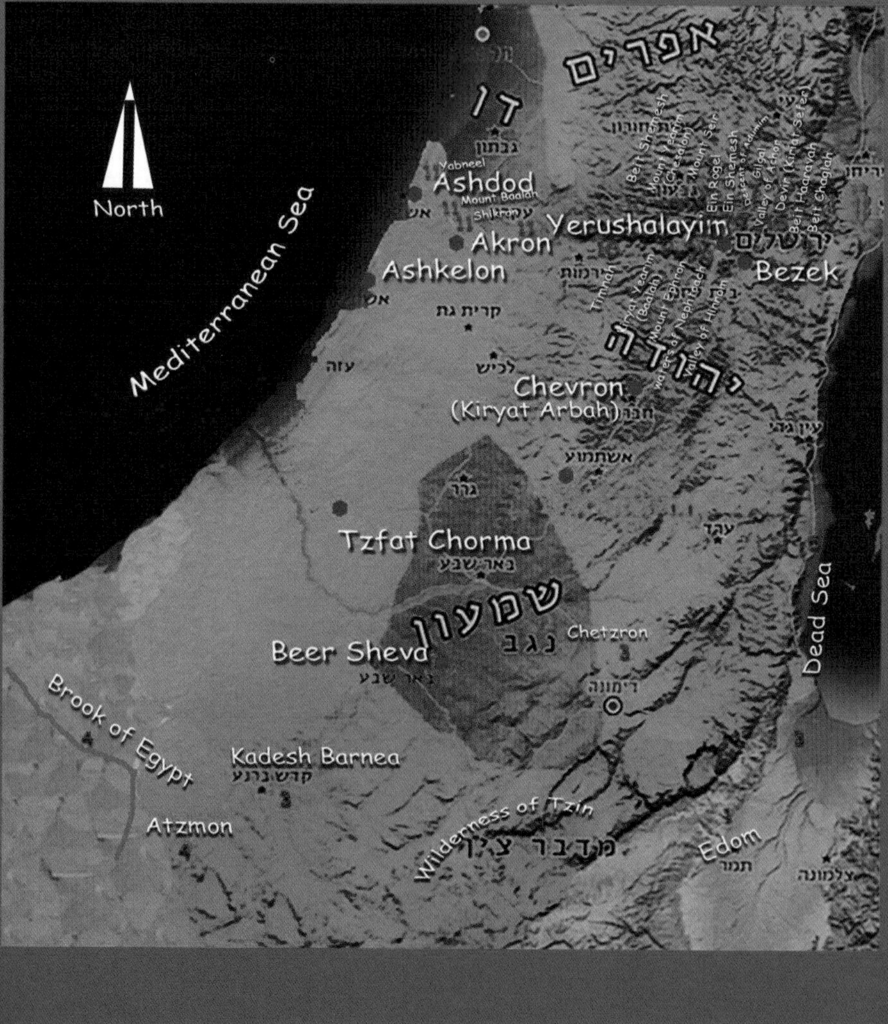

א וַיְהִי הַגּוֹרָל לְמַטֵּה בְנֵי יְהוּדָה לְמִשְׁפְּחֹתָם אֶל גְּבוּל אֱדוֹם מִדְבַּר צִן נֶגְבָּה מִקְצֵה תֵימָן. ב וַיְהִי לָהֶם גְּבוּל נֶגֶב מִקְצֵה יָם הַמֶּלַח מִן הַלָּשֹׁן הַפֹּנֶה נֶגְבָּה. ג וְיָצָא אֶל מִנֶּגֶב לְמַעֲלֵה עַקְרַבִּים וְעָבַר צִנָה וְעָלָה מִנֶּגֶב לְקָדֵשׁ בַּרְנֵעַ וְעָבַר חֶצְרוֹן וְעָלָה אַדָּרָה וְנָסַב הַקַּרְקָעָה.

4 FROM THERE YEHUDA'S BOUNDARIES PASSED ON TO ATZMON AND PROCEEDED TO THE RIVER OF EGYPT; AND THE BOUNDARY RAN TO THE SEA. THAT SHALL BE YOUR SOUTHERN BOUNDARY. 5 THE BOUNDARY ON THE EAST WAS THE DEAD SEA UP TO THE END OF THE YARDEN, ON THE NORTHERN SIDE, THE BOUNDARY BEGAN AT THE START OF THE SEA TO THE END OF THE YARDEN. 6 AND THE BORDER WENT UP TO BEIT CHAGLAH AND PASSED ALONG BY THE NORTH OF BEIT HAARAVAH AND THE BORDER WENT UP TO EVEN BOHAIM, SON OF (BEN) REUVEN. 7 AND THE BORDER WENT UP TO DEVIR FROM THE VALLEY OF ACHOR AND WENT NORTHWARD TO GILGAL FACING MAALEH ADUMIM WHICH IS ON THE SOUTH OF THE RIVER. FROM THERE THE BOUNDARY CONTINUED TO THE WATERS OF EIN SHEMESH AND RAN ON TO EIN ROGEL.

ACCORDING TO SOME, EVEN WAS THE NAME OF THE CITY AND BOHAIN SON OF REUVEN WAS THE RULER'S NAME. OTHERS SAY, THE CITY NAME WAS EVEN BOHAIN AND THE LEADER'S NAME WAS BEN REUVEN.

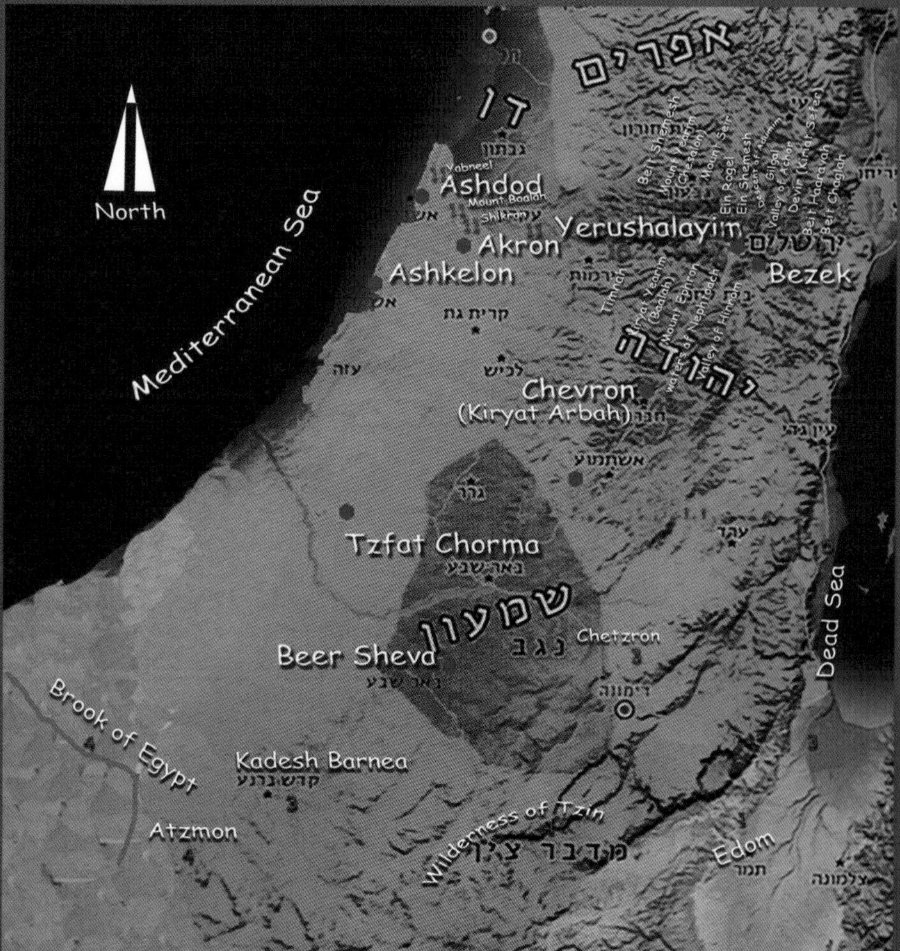

ד וְעָבַר עַצְמוֹנָה וְיָצָא נַחַל מִצְרַיִם והיה (וְהָיוּ) תֹּצְאוֹת הַגְּבוּל יָמָּה זֶה יִהְיֶה לָכֶם גְּבוּל
נֶגֶב. ה וּגְבוּל קֵדְמָה יָם הַמֶּלַח עַד קְצֵה הַיַּרְדֵּן וּגְבוּל לִפְאַת צָפוֹנָה מִלְּשׁוֹן הַיָּם מִקְצֵה
הַיַּרְדֵּן. ו וְעָלָה הַגְּבוּל בֵּית חָגְלָה וְעָבַר מִצְּפוֹן לְבֵית הָעֲרָבָה וְעָלָה הַגְּבוּל אֶבֶן בֹּהַן בֶּן
רְאוּבֵן. ז וְעָלָה הַגְּבוּל דְּבִרָה מֵעֵמֶק עָכוֹר וְצָפוֹנָה פֹּנֶה אֶל הַגִּלְגָּל אֲשֶׁר נֹכַח לְמַעֲלֵה
אֲדֻמִּים אֲשֶׁר מִנֶּגֶב לַנָּחַל וְעָבַר הַגְּבוּל אֶל מֵי עֵין שֶׁמֶשׁ וְהָיוּ תֹצְאֹתָיו אֶל עֵין רֹגֵל.

8 THEN THE BOUNDARY WENT UP TO THE VALLEY OF BEN-HINNOM,
ALONG THE SOUTHERN SIDE OF YEVUSITE- THAT IS, YERUSHALAYIM.
THE BOUNDARY THEN WENT UP THE HILL ON THE SIDE OF THE VALLEY OF
HINNOM ON THE WEST, AT THE NORTHERN END OF THE VALLEY OF
REPHAIM. 9 FROM THAT HILLTOP, THE BOUNDARY CURVED TO THE
FOUNTAIN OF THE MEI NEPHTOACH AND RAN ON TO THE CITIES OF MOUNT
EPHRON; THEN THE BOUNDARY CURVED TO BAALAH- THAT IS, KIRYAT
YEARIM. 10 FROM BAALAH THE BOUNDARY TURNED WESTWARD TO MOUNT
SEIR, PASSED NORTH OF THE SLOPE OF MOUNT YEARIM- THAT IS
CHESALON- DESCENDED TO BEIT SHEMESH, AND PASSED ON TO TIMNAH.

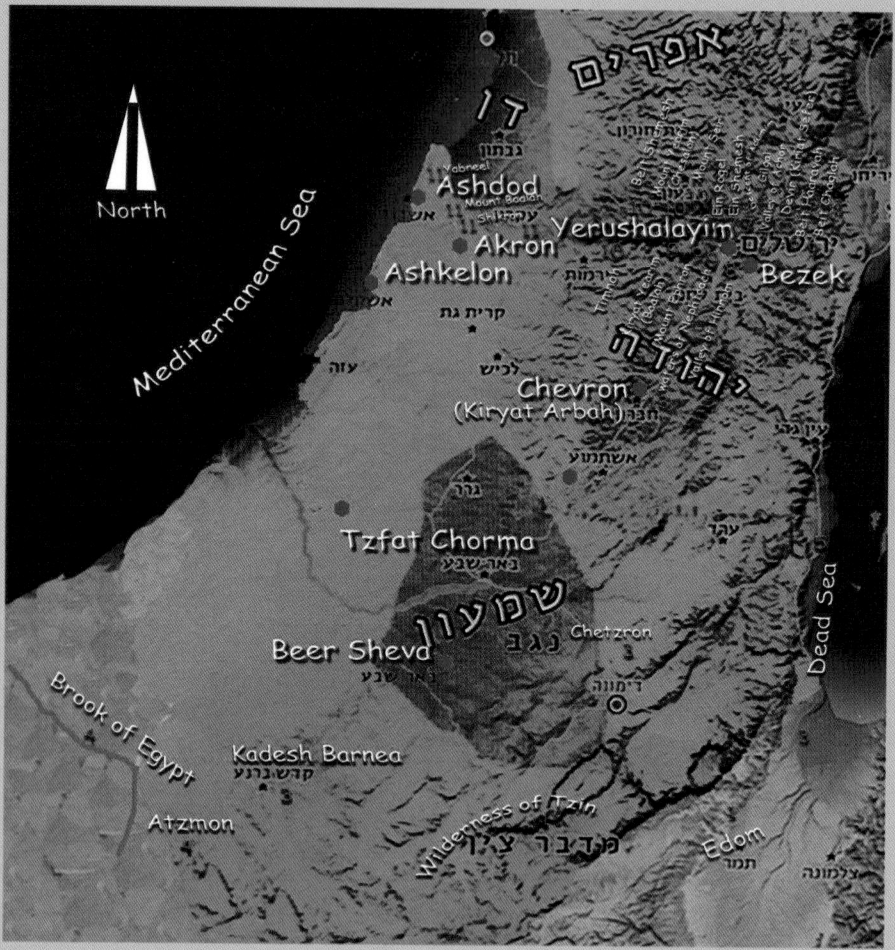

ח וְעָלָה הַגְּבוּל גֵּי בֶן הִנֹּם אֶל כֶּתֶף הַיְבוּסִי מִנֶּגֶב הִיא יְרוּשָׁלָם וְעָלָה הַגְּבוּל אֶל
רֹאשׁ הָהָר אֲשֶׁר עַל פְּנֵי גֵי הִנֹּם יָמָּה אֲשֶׁר בִּקְצֵה עֵמֶק רְפָאִים צָפוֹנָה. **ט** וְתָאַר
הַגְּבוּל מֵרֹאשׁ הָהָר אֶל מַעְיַן מֵי נֶפְתּוֹחַ וְיָצָא אֶל עָרֵי הַר עֶפְרוֹן וְתָאַר הַגְּבוּל
בַּעֲלָה הִיא קִרְיַת יְעָרִים. **י** וְנָסַב הַגְּבוּל מִבַּעֲלָה יָמָּה אֶל הַר שֵׂעִיר וְעָבַר אֶל כֶּתֶף
הַר יְעָרִים מִצָּפוֹנָה הִיא כְסָלוֹן וְיָרַד בֵּית שֶׁמֶשׁ וְעָבַר תִּמְנָה.

11 THE BOUNDARY THEN PROCEEDED TO THE NORTHERN SIDE OF AKRON; THE BOUNDARY CURVED TO SHIKRON, PASSED ON TO MOUNT BAALAH, AND THEN PROCEEDED TO YABNEEL; AND THE BOUNDARY WENT ON TO THE SEA. 12 AND THE WESTERN BOUNDARY WAS ON THE EDGE OF THE MEDITERRANEAN SEA. THOSE WERE THE BOUNDARIES OF THE VARIOUS FAMILIES OF THE CHILDREN OF YEHUDAH ON ALL SIDES. 13 IN ACCORDANCE WITH THE COMMAND OF HASHEM TO YEHOSHUA, KALEV SON OF YEPHUNEH WAS GIVEN A PORTION AMONG THE CHILDREN OF YEHUDAH, NAMELY KIRYAT-ARBA- WHICH IS CHEVRON. ARBA WAS THE FATHER OF ANAK.

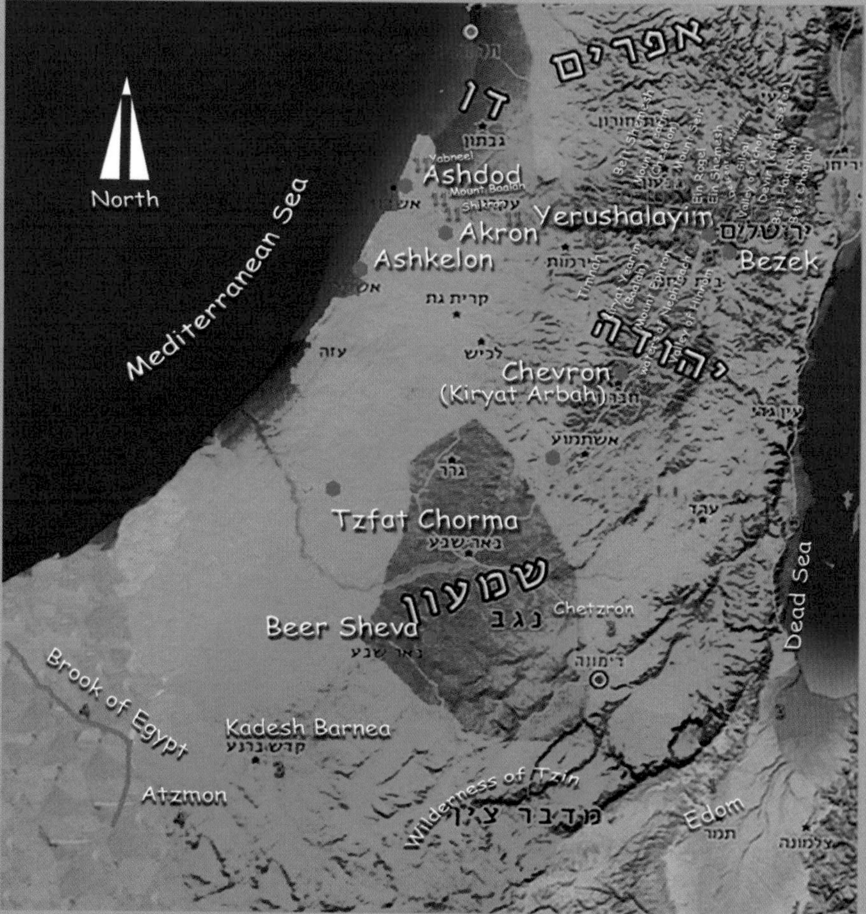

יא וְיָצָא הַגְּבוּל אֶל כֶּתֶף עֶקְרוֹן צָפוֹנָה וְתָאַר הַגְּבוּל שִׁכְּרוֹנָה וְעָבַר הַר הַבַּעֲלָה
וְיָצָא יַבְנְאֵל וְהָיוּ תֹּצְאוֹת הַגְּבוּל יָמָּה. **יב** וּגְבוּל יָם הַיָּמָּה הַגָּדוֹל וּגְבוּל זֶה גְּבוּל
בְּנֵי יְהוּדָה סָבִיב לְמִשְׁפְּחֹתָם. **יג** וּלְכָלֵב בֶּן יְפֻנֶּה נָתַן חֵלֶק בְּתוֹךְ בְּנֵי יְהוּדָה אֶל
פִּי ה' לִיהוֹשֻׁעַ אֶת קִרְיַת אַרְבַּע אֲבִי הָעֲנָק הִיא חֶבְרוֹן.

14 CONSEQUENTLY, KALEV DROVE OUT THE THREE SONS OF ANAK (THE GIANT), SHESHAI AND ACHIMAN AND TALMAI THE CHILDREN OF ANAK.

THIS *CAN'T* BE HAPPENING, OUR DYNASTY WHICH LASTED SO LONG, WILL SOON BE GONE FOREVER...

יד וַיֹּרֶשׁ מִשָּׁם כָּלֵב אֶת שְׁלוֹשָׁה בְּנֵי הָעֲנָק אֶת שֵׁשַׁי וְאֶת אֲחִימַן וְאֶת תַּלְמַי יְלִידֵי הָעֲנָק.

15 FROM THERE HE MARCHED AGAINST THE INHABITANTS OF DEVIR- THE NAME OF DEVIR WAS FORMERLY KIRYAT SEFER,

16 AND KALEV SAID,
I WILL GIVE MY DAUGHTER ACHSAH IN MARRIAGE TO THE MAN WHO ATTACKS AND CAPTURES KIRYAT SEFER.

17 AND OTHNIEL THE SON OF KENAZ, THE BROTHER OF KALEV CAPTURED IT AND HE GAVE HIM ACHSAH HIS DAUGHTER AS A WIFE.

FOUR PEOPLE MADE ***CONDITIONAL*** PROPOSITIONS WITH HASHEM. ELIEZER, KALEV, SHAUL, AND YIFTACH. THE FIRST THREE WERE ***ANSWERED*** JOYOUSLY (THE OUTCOME COULD EASILY HAVE BEEN SOMEONE WHO WAS UNFIT FOR MARRIAGE.) YIFTACH HOWEVER, WAS ANSWERED ***TRAGICALLY,*** THAT ENDED WITH THE LOSS OF HIS DAUGHTER.

טו וַיַּעַל מִשָּׁם אֶל יֹשְׁבֵי דְּבִר וְשֵׁם דְּבִר לְפָנִים קִרְיַת סֵפֶר. **טז** וַיֹּאמֶר
כָּלֵב אֲשֶׁר יַכֶּה אֶת קִרְיַת סֵפֶר וּלְכָדָהּ וְנָתַתִּי לוֹ אֶת עַכְסָה בִתִּי לְאִשָּׁה.
יז וַיִּלְכְּדָהּ עָתְנִיאֵל בֶּן קְנַז אֲחִי כָלֵב וַיִּתֶּן לוֹ אֶת עַכְסָה בִתּוֹ לְאִשָּׁה.

SOMETIME LATER...
I HATE TO DISTURB HIM, BUT I HAVE NO OTHER CHOICE...
NONE OF US WILL BE ABLE TO SURVIVE!
PLEASE ALLOW ME TO SPEAK WITH MY FATHER. WE NEED BETTER LAND.
THEN YOU WILL BE ABLE TO IMMERSE YOURSELF IN TORAH WITHOUT ANY DISTRACTION...!
GO WITH MY BLESSING...
18 AND IT CAME TO PASS WHEN SHE (ASCHA) CAME TO HIM (OTHNIEL), SHE PERSUADED HIM TO (ALLOW HER TO) ASK HER FATHER FOR A FIELD. - -
יח וַיְהִי בְּבוֹאָהּ וַתְּסִיתֵהוּ לִשְׁאוֹל מֵאֵת אָבִיהָ שָׂדֶה - -

ACHSAH LEFT AND WENT TO SPEAK WITH HER FATHER.
- -AND SHE SLID OFF HER DONKEY,
KLOPP KLOPP
IT'S WONDERFUL TO SEE YOU. I KNOW YOU TRAVELLED A GREAT DISTANCE TO SPEAK WITH ME... ON A DONKEY NO LESS!
YES, JUST AS A DONKEY BRAYS WHEN THERE IS NO FOOD IN THE TROUGH...
SO TOO, A WOMAN CRIES OUT WHEN THERE IS NO FOOD...
AND KALEV SAID TO HER
WHAT IS THE MATTER?
19 AND SHE SAID
GIVE ME A BRACHA (LAND THAT PROSPERS).
YOU HAVE GIVEN ME NEGEV (ARID) LAND
EVEN THOUGH MY HUSBAND IS FULL OF TORAH, THE HOUSE IS EMPTY OF ANY EARTHLY GOOD.
GIVE ME SPRINGS OF WATER
AND HE GAVE HER THE UPPER AND LOWER SPRINGS.
– – וַתִּצְנַח מֵעַל הַחֲמוֹר וַיֹּאמֶר לָהּ כָּלֵב מַה לָּךְ. יט וַתֹּאמֶר תְּנָה לִי בְרָכָה כִּי
אֶרֶץ הַנֶּגֶב נְתַתָּנִי וְנָתַתָּה לִי גֻּלֹּת מָיִם וַיִּתֶּן לָהּ אֵת גֻּלֹּת עִלִּיּוֹת וְאֵת גֻּלֹּת תַּחְתִּיּוֹת.

20 THIS IS THE INHERITANCE OF THE TRIBE OF THE CHILDREN OF YEHUDAH ACCORDING TO THEIR FAMILIES. 21 AND THE CITIES AT THE FAR END OF THE TRIBE OF THE CHILDREN OF YEHUDAH NEAR THE BORDER OF EDOM IN THE SOUTH WERE KABZEEL AND EDER AND YAGUR. 22 AND KINAH AND DIMONA AND ADADAH 23 AND KEDESH AND CHAZOR AND ITNAN 24 TZIPH AND TELEM AND BEALOT. 25 AND CHATZOR AND HADATTAH AND KERIOT AND CHETZRON WHICH IS CHATZOR 26 AMAM AND SHEMA AND MOLADA 27 AND CHATZAR GADDAH AND CHESHMON AND BEIT PELET 28 AND CHATZAR SHUAL AND BEER SHEVA AND BIZIOTIAH 29 BAALAH AND IYIM AND ETZEM 30 AND ELTOLAD AND CHESIL AND CHORMA 31 AND TZIKLAG AND MADMANNAH AND SANSANNAH 32 AND LEBAOT AND SHILCHIM AND AIN AND RIMMON, THE TOTAL AMOUNT OF CITIES ARE TWENTY-NINE WITH THEIR TOWNS.

Yerushalayim

Akron

Ashkelon

Bezek

ירושלים

ירמות

בית לחם

יהודה

Chevron

חברון

עין גדי

(er)

VERSE 32 STATES THERE WERE TWENTY-NINE CITIES TOTAL. HOWEVER, IF YOU COUNT THEM INDIVIDUALLY YOU FIND *THIRTY-EIGHT.* THE EXTRA NINE WERE TAKEN FROM THE TRIBE OF YEHUDAH AND GIVEN TO THE TRIBE OF SHIMON.

YAAKOV FOUND IT NECESSARY TO DIVIDE SHIMON AND LEVY AS HE STATED, " CURSED WAS THE TOWN OF SHECHEM WHERE THEY (SHIMON AND LEVY) ENTERED TO DESTROY IT IN THEIR VIOLENT WRATH (AGAINST ITS PEOPLE), AND WHERE THEY ALSO (TRIED TO KILL THEIR BROTHER); FOR THEIR HATRED OF YOSEF WAS RELENTLESS. IF THEY LIVE TOGETHER, NO KING NOR RULER MAY STAND *AGAINST* THEM. THEREFORE I WILL DIVIDE THE INHERITANCE OF SHIMON... AND THE TRIBE OF LEVI, I WILL DISPERSE AMONG ALL THE TRIBES OF YISRAEL".

BEIT PELET
CHORMA
MADMANNAH
SANSANNAH
RIMMON

שמעון

נגב

Beer Sheva

באר

28

דימונה

CHATZAR GADDAH
CHESHMON
CHATZAR SHUAL
BAALAH
IYIM
ETZEM
ELTOLAD
SHILCHIM
AIN

21 KABZEEL
21 YAGUR
22 KINAH
22 DIMONA
23 KEDESH
23, 25 CHATZOR
25 ITNAN
24 TZIPH
24 TELEM
24 BEALOT
25 CHETZRON
26 AMAM
26 SHEMA
26 MOLADA

קהשינרג

Seir

סיר

מדבר ציך

צלמון

Araba Sea

Hebrew text:

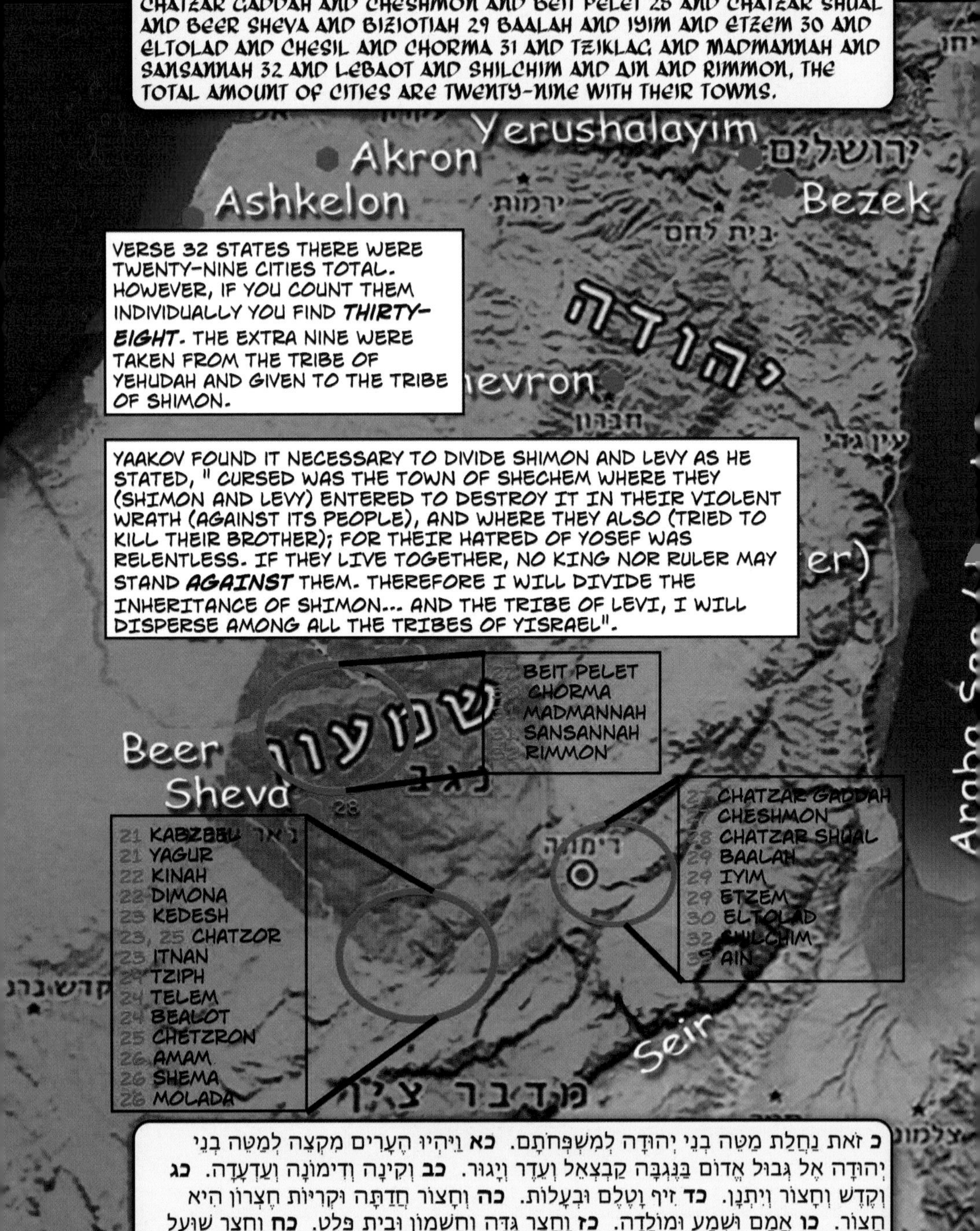

כ זֹאת נַחֲלַת מַטֵּה בְנֵי יְהוּדָה לְמִשְׁפְּחֹתָם. כא וַיִּהְיוּ הֶעָרִים מִקְצֵה לְמַטֵּה בְנֵי יְהוּדָה אֶל גְּבוּל אֱדוֹם בַּנֶּגְבָּה קַבְצְאֵל וְעֵדֶר וְיָגוּר. כב וְקִינָה וְדִימוֹנָה וְעַדְעָדָה. כג וְקֶדֶשׁ וְחָצוֹר וְיִתְנָן. כד זִיף וָטֶלֶם וּבְעָלוֹת. כה וְחָצוֹר חֲדַתָּה וּקְרִיּוֹת חֶצְרוֹן הִיא חָצוֹר. כו אֲמָם וּשְׁמַע וּמוֹלָדָה. כז וַחֲצַר גַּדָּה וְחֶשְׁמוֹן וּבֵית פָּלֶט. כח וַחֲצַר שׁוּעָל וּבְאֵר שֶׁבַע וּבִזְיוֹתְיָה. כט בַּעֲלָה וְעִיִּים וָעָצֶם. ל וְאֶלְתּוֹלַד וּכְסִיל וְחָרְמָה. לא וְצִקְלַג וּמַדְמַנָּה וְסַנְסַנָּה. לב וּלְבָאוֹת וְשִׁלְחִים וְעַיִן וְרִמּוֹן כָּל עָרִים עֶשְׂרִים וָתֵשַׁע וְחַצְרֵיהֶן.

33 IN THE LOWLAND, ESHTAOL AND TZORAH AND ASHNAH 34 AND TZANOACH AND EN GANNIM TAPUACH AND ENAM 35 YARMUT AND ADULLAM SOCHO AND AZEKAH 36 AND SHAARAIM AND ADITAIM AND GEDERAH WITH GEDEROTAIM. FOURTEEN CITIES WITH THEIR VILLAGES. 37 TZENAN AND CHADASHAH AND MIGDAL GAD 38 AND DILAN AND MITZEPH AND YOKTEEL 39 LACHISH AND BOTZAKAT AND EGLON 40 AND CHABBON AND LACHMAS AND CHITLISH 41 AND GEDEROT BEIT DAGON AND NAAMAH AND MAKKEDAH SIXTEEN CITIES WITH THEIR VILLAGES.

Yerushalayim

Akron

Ashkelon

Bezek

33 TZORAH
33 ESHTAOL
34 TZANOACH
35 YARMUT
35 ADULLAM SOCHO
35 AZEKAH

33 ASHNAH
34 ENGANNIM
34 TAPUAH
34 ENAM
36 SHAARAIM
36 GEDERAH
36 GEDEROTAIM

Chevron

37 TZENAN
37 CHADASHAH
37 MIGDAL GAD
38 DILAN
38 MITZPEH
38 YOKTEEL
39 LACHISH
39 BOTZAKAT
39 EGLON

40 CHABBON
40 LACHMAS
40 CHITLISH
40 GEDEROT
41 BEIT DAGON
41 NAAMAH
41 MAKKEDAH

Dvir (Kiryat Sefer)

Tzfat Chorma

שמעון

Beer Sheva

נגב

Araba Sea / Dead Sea

Seir

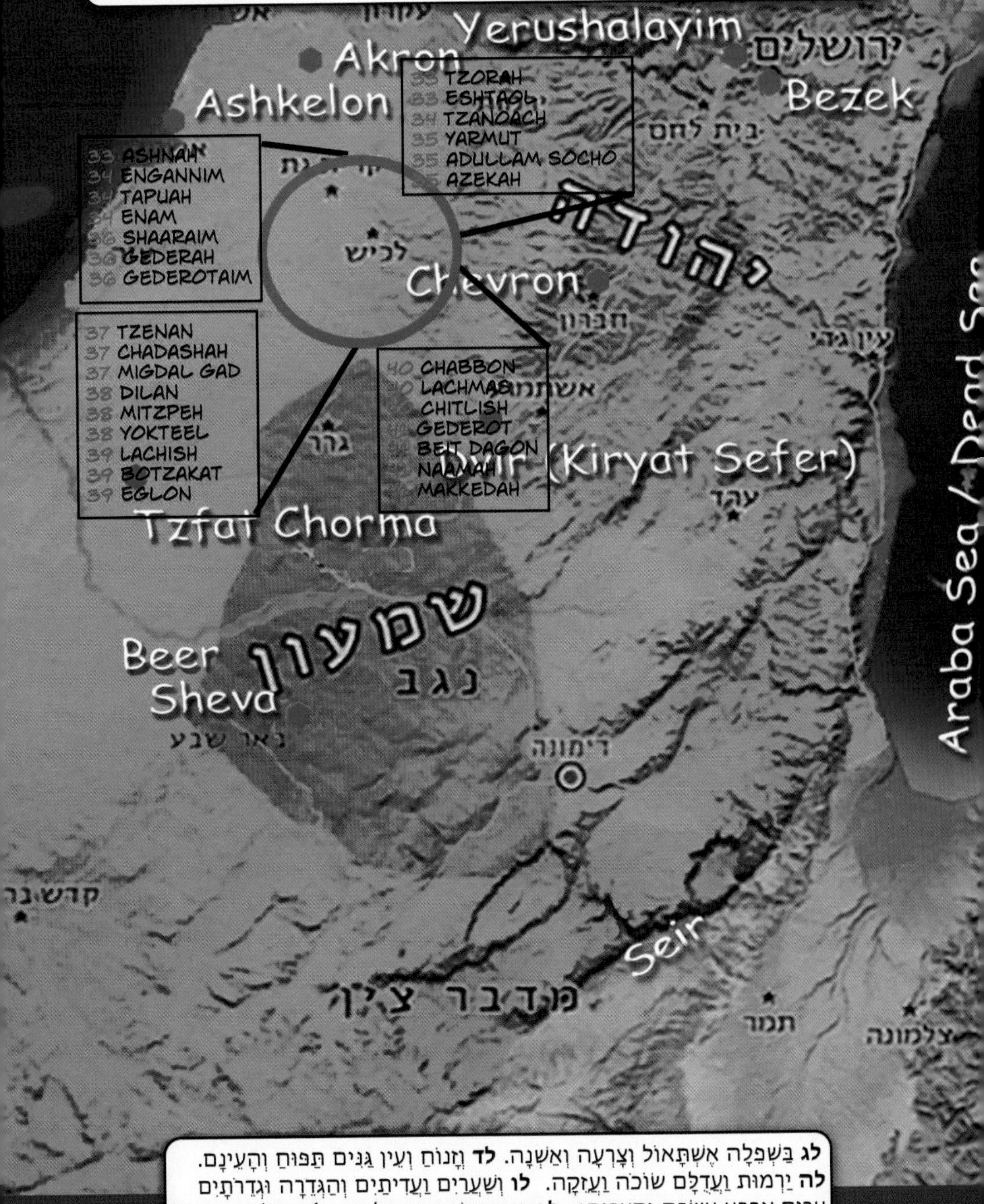

לג בַּשְּׁפֵלָה אֶשְׁתָּאוֹל וְצָרְעָה וְאַשְׁנָה. לד וְזָנוֹחַ וְעֵין גַּנִּים תַּפּוּחַ וְהָעֵינָם. לה יַרְמוּת וַעֲדֻלָּם שׂוֹכֹה וַעֲזֵקָה. לו וְשַׁעֲרַיִם וַעֲדִיתַיִם וְהַגְּדֵרָה וּגְדֵרֹתָיִם עָרִים אַרְבַּע עֶשְׂרֵה וְחַצְרֵיהֶן. לז צְנָן וַחֲדָשָׁה וּמִגְדַּל גָּד. לח וְדִלְעָן וְהַמִּצְפֶּה וְיָקְתְאֵל. לט לָכִישׁ וּבָצְקַת וְעֶגְלוֹן. מ וְכַבּוֹן וְלַחְמָס וְכִתְלִישׁ. מא וּגְדֵרוֹת בֵּית דָּגוֹן וְנַעֲמָה וּמַקֵּדָה עָרִים שֵׁשׁ עֶשְׂרֵה וְחַצְרֵיהֶן

42 LIVNAH AND ETER AND ASHAN 43 AND YIPHTACH AND ASHNAH AND NETZIV 44 AND KEILAH AND ACHZIV AND MARESHA, NINE CITIES WITH THEIR VILLAGES. 45 EKRON WITH ITS TOWNS AND ITS VILLAGES 46 FROM AKRON ALL THE WAY TO THE SEA ALL THAT WERE IN THE VICINITY OF ASHDOD WITH THEIR VILLAGES. 47 ASHDOD ITS TOWNS AND ITS VILLAGES AZZA ITS TOWNS AND ITS VILLAGES UNTIL THE RIVER OF EGYPT TO THE BORDER OF THE MEDITERRANEAN SEA. 48 AND IN THE HILL COUNTRY SHAMIR AND YATTIR AND SOCHO 49 AND DANNAH AND KIRYAT SANNAH WHICH IS DVIR 50 AND ANAV AND ESHTEMOH AND ANIM 51 AND GOSHEN AND CHOLON AND GILOH, ELEVEN CITIES WITH THEIR VILLAGES. 52 ARAV AND RUMA AND ESHAN 53 AND YANUM (YEVANIM) AND BEIT TAPPUAH AND APHEKAH 54 AND CHUMTAH AND KIRYAT ARBA, WHICH IS CHEVRON AND TZIOR, NINE CITIES WITH THEIR VILLAGES.

Yerushalayim
ירושלים
Akron
Ashkelon
Bezek
ירמות
בית לחם
קרית גת
לכיש
יהודה
42 LIVNAH
42 ETER
42 ASHAN
43 YIPHTACH
43 ASHNAH
43 NETZIV
44 KEILAH
44 ACHZIV
44 MARESHA,
45, 46 EKRON
46, 47 ASHDOD
47 AZZA
48 SHAMIR
48 YATTIR
48 SOCHO
49 DANNAH
49 KIRYAT SANNAH
50 ANAV
50 ESHTEMOH
50 ANIM
GOSHEN
CHOLON
GILOH
ARAV
RUMA
ESHAN
YANUM
BEIT TAPPUAH
APHEKAH
CHUMTAH
KIRYAT ARBA,
(CHEVRON)
54 TZIOR
Chevron
עין גדי
Dvir (Kiryat Sefer)
Tzfat Chorma
שמעון
Beer Sheva
נגב
באר שבע
דימונה
קדש ברנע
Seir

מב לִבְנָה וָעֶתֶר וְעָשָׁן. **מג** וְיִפְתָּח וְאַשְׁנָה וּנְצִיב. **מד** וּקְעִילָה וְאַכְזִיב וּמָרֵאשָׁה עָרִים תֵּשַׁע וְחַצְרֵיהֶן. **מה** עֶקְרוֹן וּבְנֹתֶיהָ וַחֲצֵרֶיהָ. **מו** מֵעֶקְרוֹן וָיָמָּה כֹּל אֲשֶׁר עַל יַד אַשְׁדּוֹד וְחַצְרֵיהֶן. **מז** אַשְׁדּוֹד בְּנוֹתֶיהָ וַחֲצֵרֶיהָ עַזָּה בְּנוֹתֶיהָ וַחֲצֵרֶיהָ עַד נַחַל מִצְרָיִם וְהַיָּם הגבול (הַגָּדוֹל) וּגְבוּל. **מח** וּבָהָר שָׁמִיר וְיַתִּיר וְשׂוֹכֹה. **מט** וְדַנָּה וְקִרְיַת סַנָּה הִיא דְבִר. **נ** וַעֲנָב וְאֶשְׁתְּמֹה וְעָנִים. **נא** וְגֹשֶׁן וְחֹלֹן וְגִלֹה עָרִים אַחַת עֶשְׂרֵה וְחַצְרֵיהֶן. **נב** אֲרַב וְרוּמָה וְאֶשְׁעָן. **נג** וינים (וְיָנוּם) וּבֵית תַּפּוּחַ וַאֲפֵקָה. **נד** וְחֻמְטָה וְקִרְיַת אַרְבַּע הִיא חֶבְרוֹן וְצִיעֹר עָרִים תֵּשַׁע וְחַצְרֵיהֶן.

55 MAON CARMEL AND ZIPH AND YUTTAH 56 AND YEZREEL AND YOKDEAM
AND ZANOACH 57 KAIN GIVAH AND TIMNAH, TEN CITIES WITH THEIR
VILLAGES. 58 CHALCHUL BEIT TZUR AND GEDOR 59 AND MAARAT AND BEIT
ANOT AND ELTEKON, SIX CITIES WITH THEIR VILLAGES. 60 KIRYAT BAAL
WHICH IS KIRYAT YEARIM AND RABBA, TWO CITIES WITH THEIR VILLAGES.
61 IN THE WILDERNESS BEIT ARAVAH MIDDIN AND SECACA 62 AND NIBSHAN
AND IR-MELACH AND EN GEDI, SIX CITIES WITH THEIR VILLAGES. 63 AND
AS FOR THE YEVUSITES THE INHABITANTS OF YERUSHALAYIM, THE
CHILDREN OF YEHUDA COULD NOT DRIVE THEM OUT BUT THE YEVUSITES
LIVED WITH THE CHILDREN OF YEHUDA IN YERUSHALAYIM UNTIL THIS DAY.

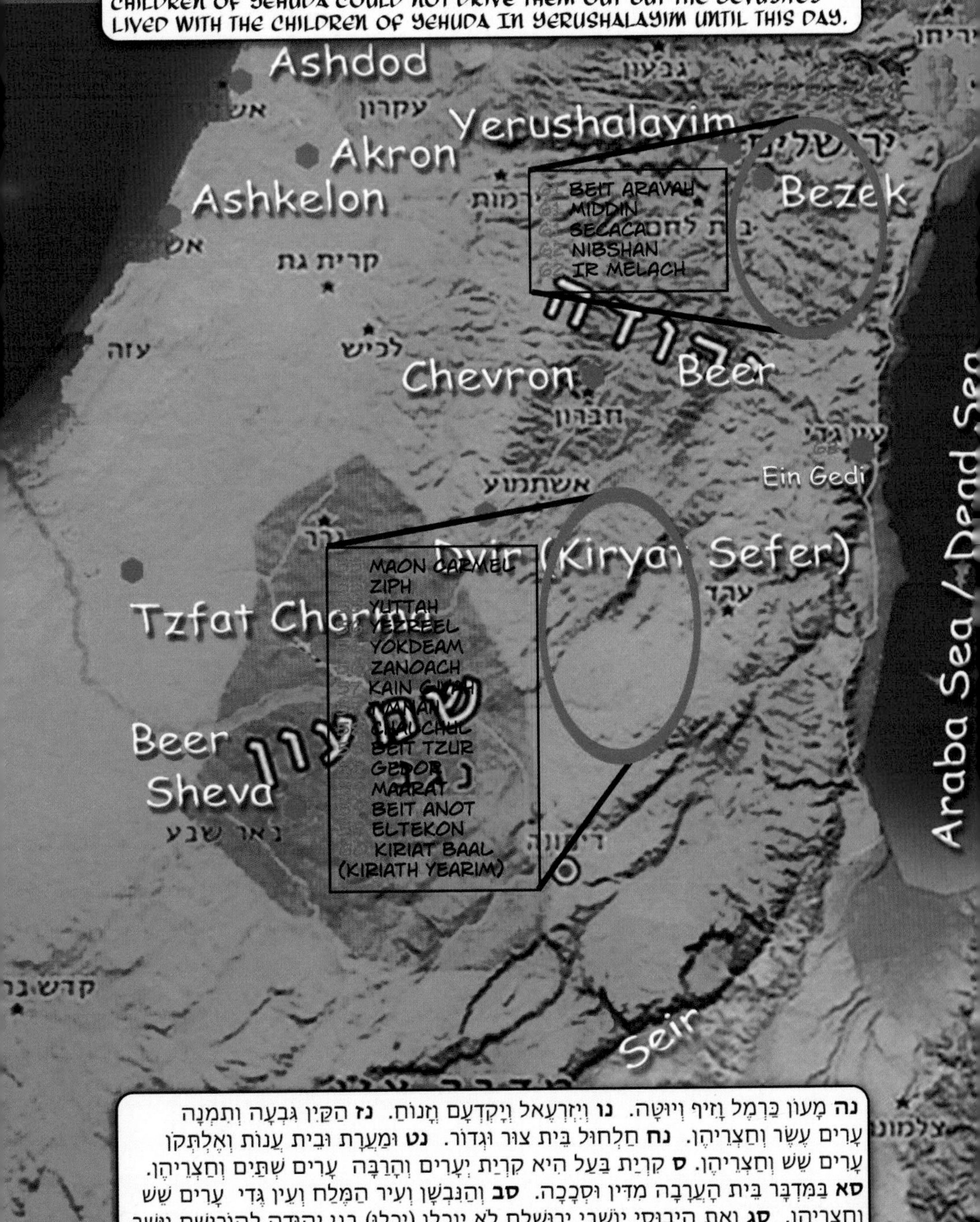
Ashdod
עקרון
Yerushalayim
Akron
Ashkelon
Bezek
BEIT ARAVAH
MIDDIN
SECACA
NIBSHAN
IR MELACH
קרית גת
עזה
לכיש
Chevron
Beer
חברון
אשתמוע
Ein Gedi
Dvir (Kiryat Sefer)
MAON CARMEL
ZIPH
YUTTAH
YEZREEL
YOKDEAM
ZANOACH
BEIT TZUR
MAARAT
BEIT ANOT
ELTEKON
KIRIAT BAAL
(KIRIATH YEARIM)
Tzfat Chorma
Beer
Sheva
באר שבע
שמעון
Seir
Araba Sea / Dead Sea

נה מָעוֹן כַּרְמֶל וָזִיף וְיוּטָּה. נו וְיִזְרְעֶאל וְיָקְדְעָם וְזָנוֹחַ. נז הַקַּיִן גִּבְעָה וְתִמְנָה
עָרִים עֶשֶׂר וְחַצְרֵיהֶן. נח חַלְחוּל בֵּית צוּר וּגְדוֹר. נט וּמַעֲרָת וּבֵית עֲנוֹת וְאֶלְתְּקֹן
עָרִים שֵׁשׁ וְחַצְרֵיהֶן. ס קִרְיַת בַּעַל הִיא קִרְיַת יְעָרִים וְהָרַבָּה עָרִים שְׁתַּיִם וְחַצְרֵיהֶן.
סא בַּמִּדְבָּר בֵּית הָעֲרָבָה מִדִּין וּסְכָכָה. סב וְהַנִּבְשָׁן וְעִיר הַמֶּלַח וְעֵין גֶּדִי עָרִים שֵׁשׁ
וְחַצְרֵיהֶן. סג וְאֶת הַיְבוּסִי יוֹשְׁבֵי יְרוּשָׁלַם לֹא יוכלו (יָכְלוּ) בְנֵי יְהוּדָה לְהוֹרִישָׁם וַיֵּשֶׁב
הַיְבוּסִי אֶת בְּנֵי יְהוּדָה בִּירוּשָׁלַם עַד הַיּוֹם הַזֶּה.

TO HELP IDENTIFY THE CITIES/REGIONS ON THE MAP, THE VERSE NUMBERS ARE REPRESENTED IN RED. THESE LOCATIONS ARE *ONLY* APPROXIMATIONS AND ARE INTENDED TO GIVE THE READER A GENERAL SENSE OF THE AREA.

YEHOSHUA CHAPTER 16
יהושע פרק טז

1 THE PORTION THAT FELL BY THE LOTTERY TO THE CHILDREN OF YOSEF
RAN FROM THE YARDEN AT YERICHO-FROM THE WATERS OF YERICHO
EAST OF THE WILDERNESS, FROM YERICHO IT ASCENDED THROUGH THE
HILL COUNTRY OF BEIT-EL. 2 FROM BEIT-EL IT RAN TO LUZ AND
PASSED ON TO THE TERRITORY OF ARCHITES TO ATAROT. 3 AND IT WENT
DOWN WESTWARD TO THE BORDER OF THE YAPHLETITES, TO THE BORDERS OF
THE LOWER BEIT-CHORON, TO GEZER AND RAN TO THE SEA. 4 AND THE
CHILDREN OF YOSEF, MENASHE AND EPHRAIM, TOOK THEIR INHERITANCE. 5
AND THE BORDER OF THE CHILDREN OF EPHRAIM ACCORDING TO THEIR
FAMILIES WAS AS FOLLOWS: THE BOUNDARY OF THEIR PORTION RAN
FROM ATROT-ADAR ON THE EAST TO UPPER BEIT-CHORON. 6 AND THE
BORDER WENT OUT WESTWARD, MICHMETAT BEING ON THE NORTH AND THE
BORDER TURNED EASTWARD TO TAANAT SHILOH, AND PASSED ALONG IT ON
THE EAST OF YANOCHA. 7 AND IT WENT DOWN FROM YANOCHA TO ATAROT,
AND TO NAARAH, AND REACHED UNTIL YERICHO, AND RAN ON TO THE YARDEN.
8 FROM TAPPUAH THE BORDER WENT WESTWARD TO THE RIVER OF KANAH;
AND RAN ON TO THE SEA. THIS IS THE INHERITANCE OF THE TRIBE OF THE
CHILDREN OF EPHRAIM ACCORDING TO THEIR FAMILIES; 9 TOGETHER WITH THE
CITIES WHICH WERE MARKED OFF FOR THE CHILDREN OF EPHRAIM WITHIN
THE TERRITORY OF THE CHILDREN OF MENASHE, ALL THE CITIES WITH THEIR
VILLAGES. 10 HOWEVER, THEY DID NOT DISPOSSESS THE CANAANIE WHO
LIVED IN GEZER, SO THE CANAANIE REMAINED LIVING WITH EPHRAIM,
AS IS STILL THE CASE. BUT AS A TAX DEBT, THEY WERE THEIR SERVANTS.

Dor
Kanah Brook
North
Michmetat
Taanat Shilo
Yanocha
Tapuach
Upper Beit Choron
אפרים
בית חורון
Lower Beit Choron
Beit El
Gezer
Yericho

א וַיֵּצֵא הַגּוֹרָל לִבְנֵי יוֹסֵף מִיַּרְדֵּן יְרִיחוֹ לְמֵי יְרִיחוֹ מִזְרָחָה הַמִּדְבָּר עֹלֶה מִירִיחוֹ בָּהָר בֵּית
אֵל. **ב** וְיָצָא מִבֵּית אֵל לוּזָה וְעָבַר אֶל גְּבוּל הָאַרְכִּי עֲטָרוֹת. **ג** וְיָרַד יָמָּה אֶל גְּבוּל הַיַּפְלֵטִי
עַד גְּבוּל בֵּית חוֹרֹן תַּחְתּוֹן וְעַד גָּזֶר וְהָיוּ תֹצְאֹתָו יָמָּה. **ד** וַיִּנְחֲלוּ בְנֵי יוֹסֵף מְנַשֶּׁה וְאֶפְרָיִם.
ה וַיְהִי גְּבוּל בְּנֵי אֶפְרַיִם לְמִשְׁפְּחֹתָם וַיְהִי גְּבוּל נַחֲלָתָם מִזְרָחָה עַטְרוֹת אַדָּר עַד בֵּית חוֹרֹן
עֶלְיוֹן. **ו** וְיָצָא הַגְּבוּל הַיָּמָּה הַמִּכְמְתָת מִצָּפוֹן וְנָסַב הַגְּבוּל מִזְרָחָה תַּאֲנַת שִׁלֹה וְעָבַר אוֹתוֹ
מִמִּזְרַח יָנוֹחָה. **ז** וְיָרַד מִיָּנוֹחָה עֲטָרוֹת וְנַעֲרָתָה וּפָגַע בִּירִיחוֹ וְיָצָא הַיַּרְדֵּן. **ח** מִתַּפּוּחַ יֵלֵךְ
הַגְּבוּל יָמָּה נַחַל קָנָה וְהָיוּ תֹצְאֹתָיו הַיָּמָּה זֹאת נַחֲלַת מַטֵּה בְנֵי אֶפְרַיִם לְמִשְׁפְּחֹתָם. **ט**
וְהֶעָרִים הַמִּבְדָּלוֹת לִבְנֵי אֶפְרַיִם בְּתוֹךְ נַחֲלַת בְּנֵי מְנַשֶּׁה כָּל הֶעָרִים וְחַצְרֵיהֶן. **י** וְלֹא הוֹרִישׁוּ
אֶת הַכְּנַעֲנִי הַיּוֹשֵׁב בְּגָזֶר וַיֵּשֶׁב הַכְּנַעֲנִי בְּקֶרֶב אֶפְרַיִם עַד הַיּוֹם הַזֶּה וַיְהִי לְמַס עֹבֵד.

YEHOSHUA CHAPTER 17
יהושע פרק יז

1 AND THIS IS THE PORTION THAT FELL BY THE LOTTERY TO THE TRIBE OF MENASHE, FOR HE WAS YOSEPH'S FIRST-BORN. SINCE MACHIR, THE FIRST-BORN OF MENASHE AND THE FATHER OF GILEAD WAS A VALIANT WARRIOR, GILEAD AND BASHAN WERE ASSIGNED TO HIM. 2 AND THE LOT WAS FOR THE REST OF THE CHILDREN OF MENASHE ACCORDING TO THEIR FAMILIES. FOR THE CHILDREN OF AVIEZER, FOR THE CHILDREN OF CHELEK, FOR THE CHILDREN OF ASRIEL, FOR THE CHILDREN OF SHECHEM, FOR THE CHILDREN OF CHEPHER AND FOR THE CHILDREN OF SHEMIDA; THESE WERE THE MALE CHILDREN OF MENASHE THE SON OF YOSEPH ACCORDING TO THEIR FAMILIES. 3 BUT TZELOPHECHAD, THE SON OF CHEPHER, WHO WAS THE SON OF GILEAD, WHO WAS THE SON OF MACHIR, WHO WAS THE SON OF MENASHE HAD NO SONS BUT ONLY DAUGHTERS. AND THESE ARE THE NAMES OF HIS DAUGHTERS, MACHLAH, NOAH, CHAGLAH, MILKAH AND TIRTZAH.

4 AND THEY APPEARED BEFORE ELAZAR, THE KOHEN AND BEFORE YEHOSHUA, THE SON OF NUN AND BEFORE THE PRINCES SAYING,

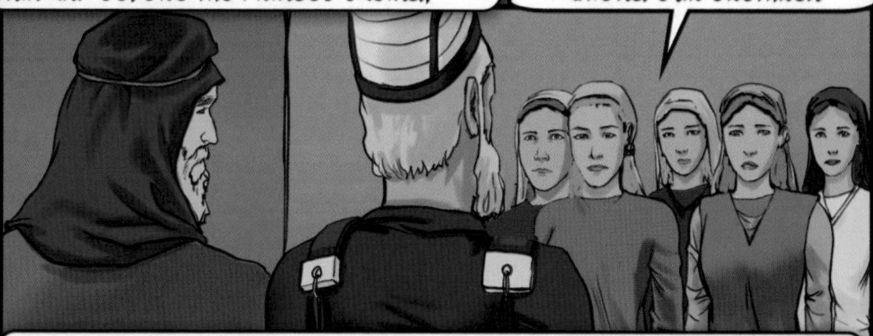
HASHEM COMMANDED MOSHE TO GIVE US AN INHERITANCE AMONG OUR BRETHREN

THEREFORE, ACCORDING TO THE COMMANDMENT OF HASHEM, HE GAVE THEM AN INHERITANCE AMONG THE BROTHERS OF THEIR FATHER. 5 TEN PORTIONS FELL TO MENASHE, APART FROM THE LANDS OF GILEAD AND BASHAN, WHICH ARE ACROSS THE YARDEN. 6 MENASHE'S DAUGHTERS INHERITED A PORTION IN THESE TOGETHER WITH HIS SONS, WHILE THE LAND OF GILEAD WAS ASSIGNED TO THE REST OF MENASHE'S DESCENDANTS.

GENERALLY, THOSE WHO LEFT EGYPT DURING THE EXODUS WERE ENTITLED TO RECEIVE A ***PORTION*** IN ERETZ YISRAEL EVEN THOUGH THEY MAY HAVE DIED IN THE DESERT AND NEVER ENTERED THE LAND. THE CHILDREN INHERITED THE LAND BASED ON THOSE WHO LEFT EGYPT. THE REASON THE DAUGHTERS OF TZELOPHECHAD INHERITED 4 PORTIONS IS AS FOLLOWS:

1. TZELOPHECHAD HIMSELF RECEIVED 2 PORTIONS BECAUSE HE WAS THE FIRSTBORN OF HIS FAMILY.
2. TZELOPHECHAD RECEIVED ANOTHER PORTION AS BEING THE ONLY LIVING HEIR TO CHEPHER HIS FATHER.
3. TZELOPHECHAD RECEIVED ONE ADDITIONAL PORTION FROM HIS BROTHER WHO DIED CHILDLESS.

א וַיְהִי הַגּוֹרָל לְמַטֵּה מְנַשֶּׁה כִּי הוּא בְּכוֹר יוֹסֵף לְמָכִיר בְּכוֹר מְנַשֶּׁה אֲבִי הַגִּלְעָד כִּי הוּא
הָיָה אִישׁ מִלְחָמָה וַיְהִי לוֹ הַגִּלְעָד וְהַבָּשָׁן. **ב** וַיְהִי לִבְנֵי מְנַשֶּׁה הַנּוֹתָרִים לְמִשְׁפְּחֹתָם
לִבְנֵי אֲבִיעֶזֶר וְלִבְנֵי חֵלֶק וְלִבְנֵי אַשְׂרִיאֵל וְלִבְנֵי שֶׁכֶם וְלִבְנֵי חֵפֶר וְלִבְנֵי שְׁמִידָע אֵלֶּה בְּנֵי
מְנַשֶּׁה בֶּן יוֹסֵף הַזְּכָרִים לְמִשְׁפְּחֹתָם. **ג** וְלִצְלָפְחָד בֶּן חֵפֶר בֶּן גִּלְעָד בֶּן מָכִיר בֶּן מְנַשֶּׁה
לֹא הָיוּ לוֹ בָּנִים כִּי אִם בָּנוֹת וְאֵלֶּה שְׁמוֹת בְּנֹתָיו מַחְלָה וְנֹעָה חָגְלָה מִלְכָּה וְתִרְצָה. **ד**
וַתִּקְרַבְנָה לִפְנֵי אֶלְעָזָר הַכֹּהֵן וְלִפְנֵי יְהוֹשֻׁעַ בִּן נוּן וְלִפְנֵי הַנְּשִׂיאִים לֵאמֹר ה' צִוָּה אֶת
מֹשֶׁה לָתֶת לָנוּ נַחֲלָה בְּתוֹךְ אַחֵינוּ וַיִּתֵּן לָהֶם אֶל פִּי ה' נַחֲלָה בְּתוֹךְ אֲחֵי אֲבִיהֶן. **ה**
וַיִּפְּלוּ חַבְלֵי מְנַשֶּׁה עֲשָׂרָה לְבַד מֵאֶרֶץ הַגִּלְעָד וְהַבָּשָׁן אֲשֶׁר מֵעֵבֶר לַיַּרְדֵּן. **ו** כִּי בְּנוֹת
מְנַשֶּׁה נָחֲלוּ נַחֲלָה בְּתוֹךְ בָּנָיו וְאֶרֶץ הַגִּלְעָד הָיְתָה לִבְנֵי מְנַשֶּׁה הַנּוֹתָרִים.

Charoshet Hagoyim
זבולון
TO HELP IDENTIFY THE LOCATIONS ON THE MAP, THE VERSE *NUMBERS* ARE REPRESENTED IN RED.
Kishon
תבור
Ein Dor
11
Megiddo
11
11 Dor
יזרעאל
Taanach
11
11,16
בית שאן
Beit Shean
Yivleam 11
מנשה
Tapuach 8
Yarden
Kanah River 9

7 AND THE BORDER OF MENASHE BEGAN FROM ASHER MICHMETA WHICH IS
NEAR SHECHEM; AND THE BORDER CONTINUED TO THE RIGHT TOWARD THE
INHABITANTS OF EIN TAPUACH. 8 THE LAND OF TAPUACH BELONGED TO
MENASHE; BUT THE PART OF TAPUACH THAT BORDERED WITH MENASHE
BELONGED TO THE CHILDREN OF EPHRAIM. 9 THEN THE BOUNDARY
DESCENDED TO THE KANAH RIVER. THOSE CITIES TO THE SOUTH OF THE
RIVER BELONGED TO EPHRAIM AS AN ENCLAVE AMONG THE CITIES OF
MENASHE. THE BOUNDARY OF MENASHE LAY NORTH OF THE RIVER AND
RAN ON TO THE SEA. 10 WHAT LAY ON THE SOUTH BELONGED TO
EPHRAIM AND WHAT LAY NORTH BELONGED TO MENASHE WITH THE SEA
AS ITS BOUNDARY. THIS AREA WAS ADJACENT TO ASHER ON THE NORTH
AND YISSACHAR ON THE EAST. 11 WITHIN YISSACHAR AND ASHER, MENASHE
POSSESSED BEIT SHEAN AND ITS TOWNS AND YIVLEAM AND ITS TOWNS
AND THE INHABITANTS OF DOR AND ITS TOWNS AND THE INHABITANTS OF EIN
DOR AND ITS TOWNS AND THE INHABITANTS OF TAANACH AND ITS TOWNS AND
THE INHABITANTS OF MEGIDDO AND ITS TOWNS, THESE CONSTITUTED THREE
REGIONS. 12 YET THE CHILDREN OF MENASHE COULD NOT DRIVE OUT THE
INHABITANTS OF THOSE CITIES; BUT THE CANAANIE WERE RESOLVED TO LIVE
IN THAT LAND. 13 AND IT CAME TO PASS WHEN THE CHILDREN OF YISRAEL
WERE VERY STRONG THAT THEY IMPOSED TAXES ON THE CANAANIE, BUT DID
NOT DRIVE THEM OUT.

ז וַיְהִי גְבוּל מְנַשֶּׁה מֵאָשֵׁר הַמִּכְמְתָת אֲשֶׁר עַל פְּנֵי שְׁכֶם וְהָלַךְ הַגְּבוּל אֶל הַיָּמִין אֶל יֹשְׁבֵי עֵין
תַּפּוּחַ. **ח** לִמְנַשֶּׁה הָיְתָה אֶרֶץ תַּפּוּחַ וְתַפּוּחַ אֶל גְּבוּל מְנַשֶּׁה לִבְנֵי אֶפְרָיִם. **ט** וְיָרַד הַגְּבוּל
נַחַל קָנָה נֶגְבָּה לַנַּחַל עָרִים הָאֵלֶּה לְאֶפְרַיִם בְּתוֹךְ עָרֵי מְנַשֶּׁה וּגְבוּל מְנַשֶּׁה מִצְּפוֹן לַנַּחַל וַיְהִי
תֹצְאֹתָיו הַיָּמָּה. **י** נֶגְבָּה לְאֶפְרַיִם וְצָפוֹנָה לִמְנַשֶּׁה וַיְהִי הַיָּם גְּבוּלוֹ; וּבְאָשֵׁר יִפְגְּעוּן מִצָּפוֹן
וּבְיִשָּׂשכָר מִמִּזְרָח. **יא** וַיְהִי לִמְנַשֶּׁה בְּיִשָּׂשכָר וּבְאָשֵׁר בֵּית שְׁאָן וּבְנוֹתֶיהָ וְיִבְלְעָם וּבְנוֹתֶיהָ
וְאֶת יֹשְׁבֵי דֹאר וּבְנוֹתֶיהָ וְיֹשְׁבֵי עֵין דֹּר וּבְנוֹתֶיהָ וְיֹשְׁבֵי תַעְנַךְ וּבְנֹתֶיהָ וְיֹשְׁבֵי מְגִדּוֹ וּבְנוֹתֶיהָ
שְׁלֹשֶׁת הַנָּפֶת. **יב** וְלֹא יָכְלוּ בְּנֵי מְנַשֶּׁה לְהוֹרִישׁ אֶת הֶעָרִים הָאֵלֶּה וַיּוֹאֶל הַכְּנַעֲנִי לָשֶׁבֶת
בָּאָרֶץ הַזֹּאת. **יג** וַיְהִי כִּי חָזְקוּ בְּנֵי יִשְׂרָאֵל וַיִּתְּנוּ אֶת הַכְּנַעֲנִי לָמַס וְהוֹרֵשׁ לֹא הוֹרִישׁוֹ.

14 AND THE CHILDREN OF YOSEPH SPOKE TO YEHOSHUA SAYING:
WHY HAVE YOU ASSIGNED AS OUR PORTION A SINGLE ALLOTMENT AND A SINGLE DISTRICT, SEEING THAT WE ARE A HUGE AMOUNT OF PEOPLE WHOM HASHEM HAS BLESSED?
IT IS TRUE THAT THE **COMBINED** TERRITORIES HAVE THE AREA OF TWO TRIBES, BUT HALF THE LAND IS USELESS!
SECONDLY, OUR **POPULATION** AS INCREASED BY MORE THAN 20,000 SINCE WE LEFT EGYPT.
יד וַיְדַבְּרוּ בְּנֵי יוֹסֵף אֶת יְהוֹשֻׁעַ לֵאמֹר מַדּוּעַ נָתַתָּה לִּי נַחֲלָה גּוֹרָל אֶחָד
וְחֶבֶל אֶחָד וַאֲנִי עַם רָב עַד אֲשֶׁר עַד כֹּה בֵּרְכַנִי ה'.

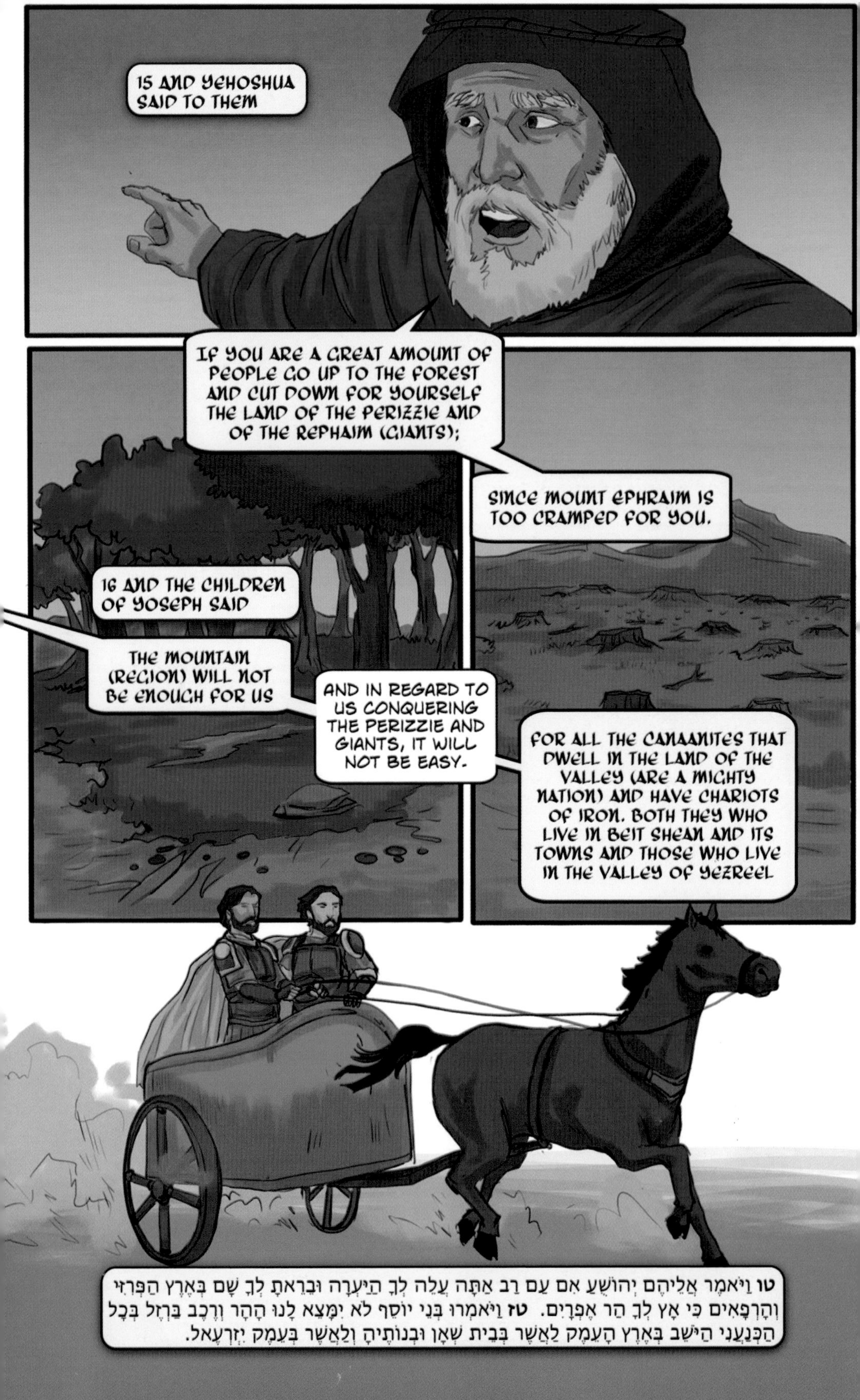
15 AND YEHOSHUA SAID TO THEM
IF YOU ARE A GREAT AMOUNT OF PEOPLE GO UP TO THE FOREST AND CUT DOWN FOR YOURSELF THE LAND OF THE PERIZZIE AND OF THE REPHAIM (GIANTS);
SINCE MOUNT EPHRAIM IS TOO CRAMPED FOR YOU.
16 AND THE CHILDREN OF YOSEPH SAID
THE MOUNTAIN (REGION) WILL NOT BE ENOUGH FOR US
AND IN REGARD TO US CONQUERING THE PERIZZIE AND GIANTS, IT WILL NOT BE EASY.
FOR ALL THE CANAANITES THAT DWELL IN THE LAND OF THE VALLEY (ARE A MIGHTY NATION) AND HAVE CHARIOTS OF IRON. BOTH THEY WHO LIVE IN BEIT SHEAN AND ITS TOWNS AND THOSE WHO LIVE IN THE VALLEY OF YEZREEL
טו וַיֹּאמֶר אֲלֵיהֶם יְהוֹשֻׁעַ אִם עַם רַב אַתָּה עֲלֵה לְךָ הַיַּעְרָה וּבֵרֵאתָ לְךָ שָׁם בְּאֶרֶץ הַפְּרִזִּי
וְהָרְפָאִים כִּי אָץ לְךָ הַר אֶפְרָיִם. **טז** וַיֹּאמְרוּ בְּנֵי יוֹסֵף לֹא יִמָּצֵא לָנוּ הָהָר וְרֶכֶב בַּרְזֶל בְּכָל
הַכְּנַעֲנִי הַיֹּשֵׁב בְּאֶרֶץ הָעֵמֶק לַאֲשֶׁר בְּבֵית שְׁאָן וּבְנוֹתֶיהָ וְלַאֲשֶׁר בְּעֵמֶק יִזְרְעֶאל.

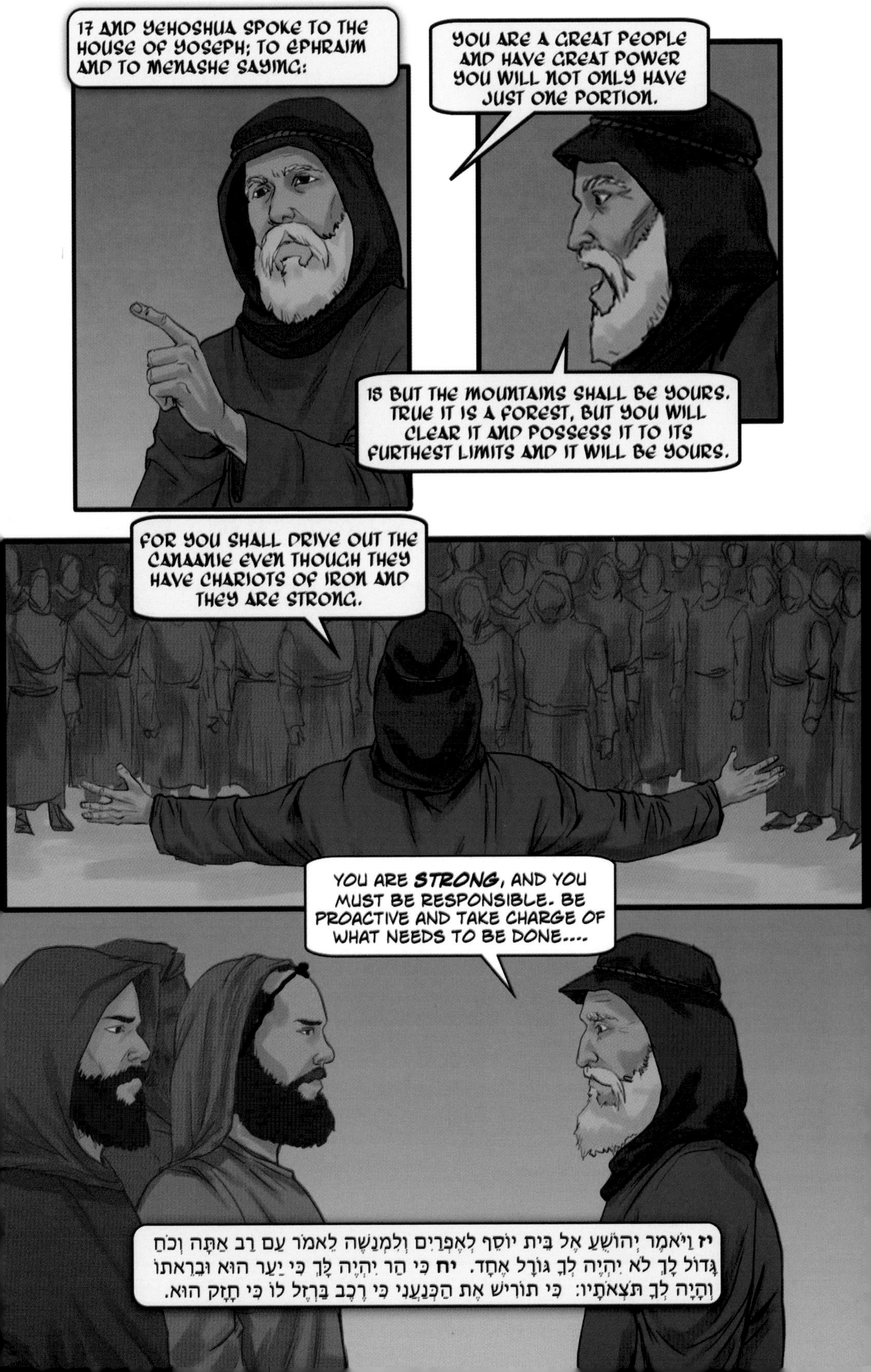

17 AND YEHOSHUA SPOKE TO THE HOUSE OF YOSEPH; TO EPHRAIM AND TO MENASHE SAYING:
YOU ARE A GREAT PEOPLE AND HAVE GREAT POWER YOU WILL NOT ONLY HAVE JUST ONE PORTION.
18 BUT THE MOUNTAINS SHALL BE YOURS. TRUE IT IS A FOREST, BUT YOU WILL CLEAR IT AND POSSESS IT TO ITS FURTHEST LIMITS AND IT WILL BE YOURS.
FOR YOU SHALL DRIVE OUT THE CANAANIE EVEN THOUGH THEY HAVE CHARIOTS OF IRON AND THEY ARE STRONG.
YOU ARE **STRONG**, AND YOU MUST BE RESPONSIBLE. BE PROACTIVE AND TAKE CHARGE OF WHAT NEEDS TO BE DONE....
יז וַיֹּאמֶר יְהוֹשֻׁעַ אֶל בֵּית יוֹסֵף לְאֶפְרַיִם וְלִמְנַשֶּׁה לֵאמֹר עַם רַב אַתָּה וְכֹחַ
גָּדוֹל לָךְ לֹא יִהְיֶה לְךָ גּוֹרָל אֶחָד. **יח** כִּי הַר יִהְיֶה לָּךְ כִּי יַעַר הוּא וּבֵרֵאתוֹ
וְהָיָה לְךָ תֹּצְאֹתָיו: כִּי תוֹרִישׁ אֶת הַכְּנַעֲנִי כִּי רֶכֶב בַּרְזֶל לוֹ כִּי חָזָק הוּא.

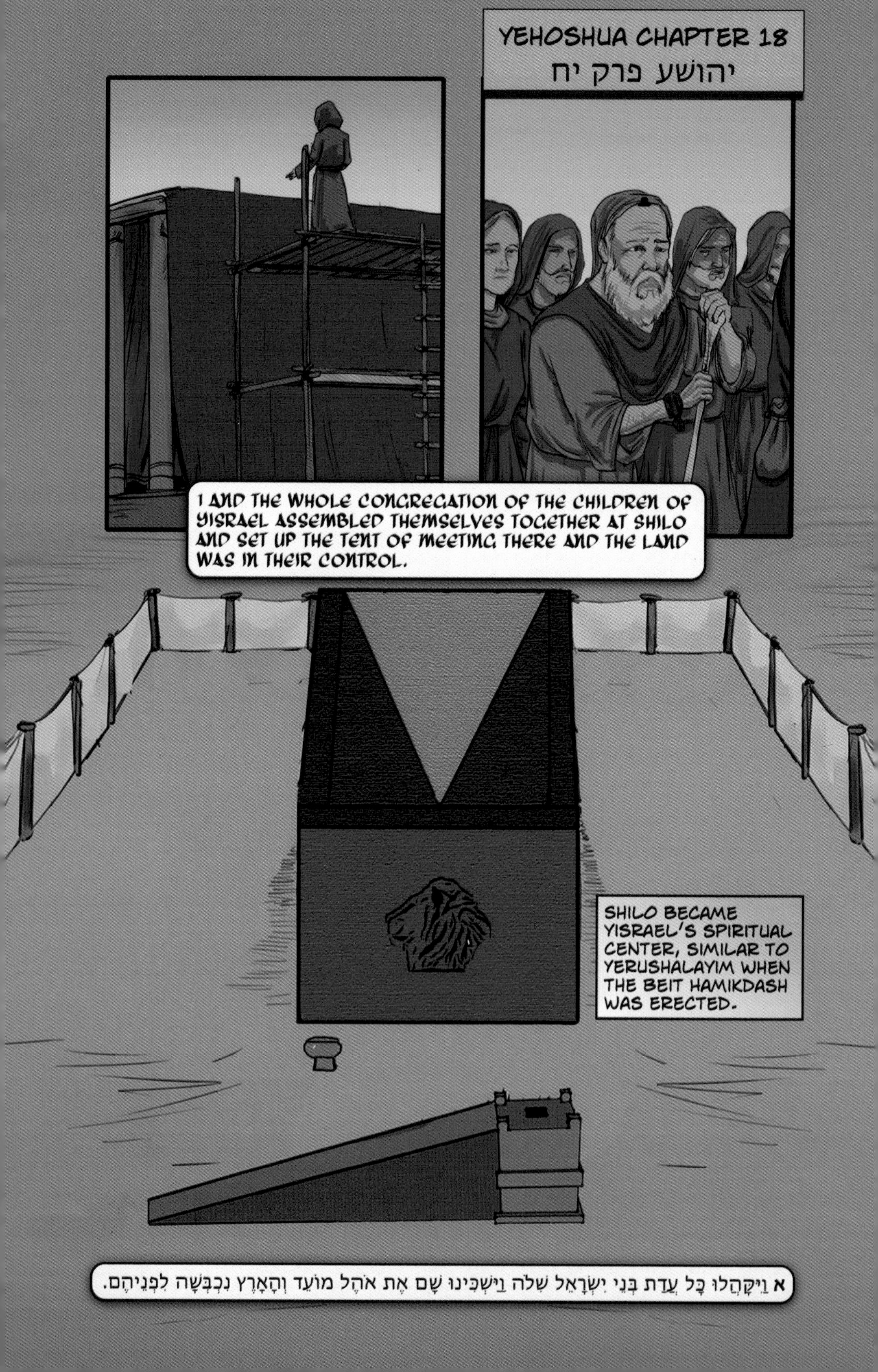
YEHOSHUA CHAPTER 18
יהושע פרק יח
1 AND THE WHOLE CONGREGATION OF THE CHILDREN OF YISRAEL ASSEMBLED THEMSELVES TOGETHER AT SHILO AND SET UP THE TENT OF MEETING THERE AND THE LAND WAS IN THEIR CONTROL.
SHILO BECAME YISRAEL'S SPIRITUAL CENTER, SIMILAR TO YERUSHALAYIM WHEN THE BEIT HAMIKDASH WAS ERECTED.
א וַיִּקָּהֲלוּ כָּל עֲדַת בְּנֵי יִשְׂרָאֵל שִׁלֹה וַיַּשְׁכִּינוּ שָׁם אֶת אֹהֶל מוֹעֵד וְהָאָרֶץ נִכְבְּשָׁה לִפְנֵיהֶם.

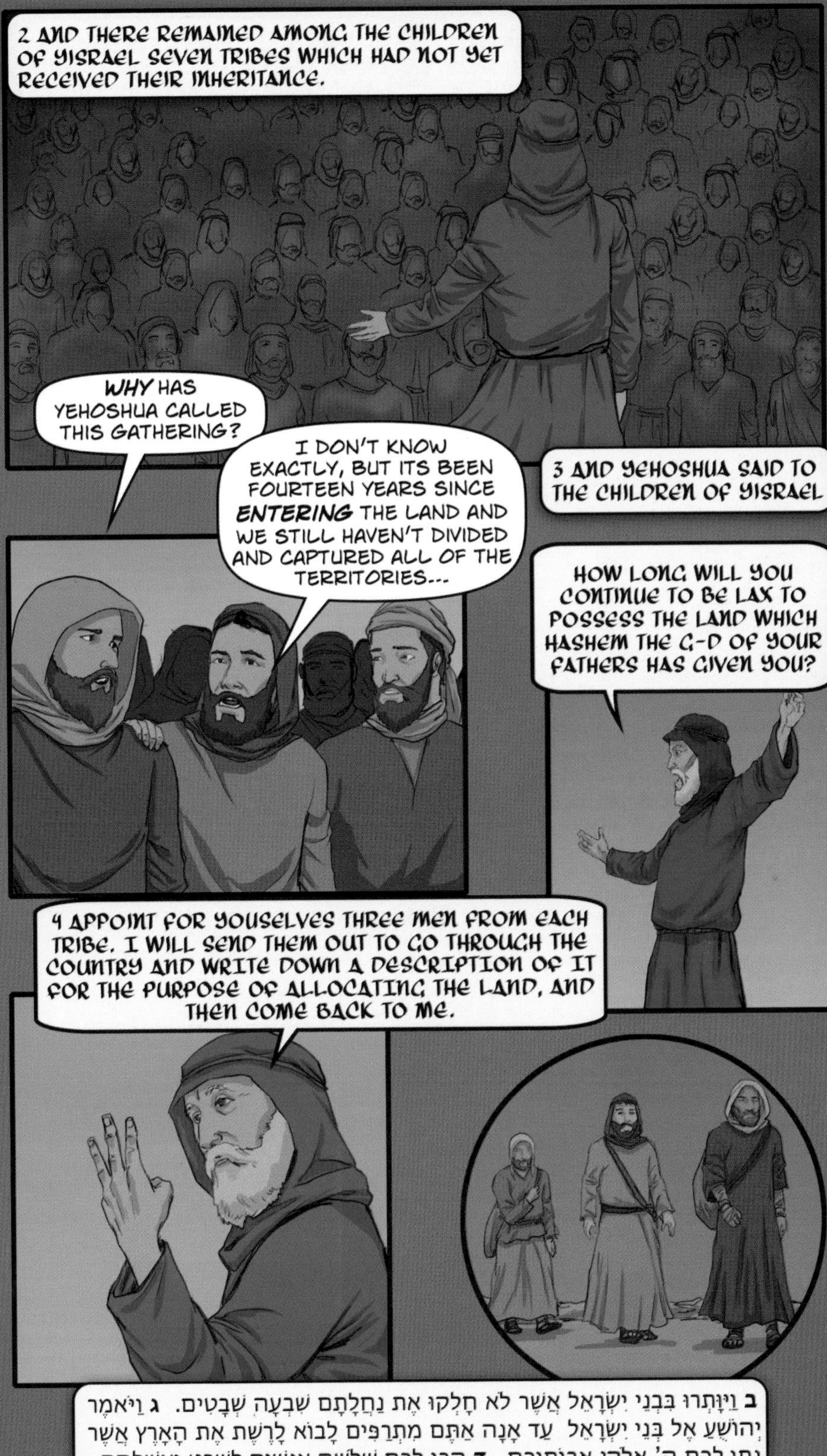

ב וַיִּוָּתְרוּ בִּבְנֵי יִשְׂרָאֵל אֲשֶׁר לֹא חָלְקוּ אֶת נַחֲלָתָם שִׁבְעָה שְׁבָטִים. **ג** וַיֹּאמֶר
יְהוֹשֻׁעַ אֶל בְּנֵי יִשְׂרָאֵל עַד אָנָה אַתֶּם מִתְרַפִּים לָבוֹא לָרֶשֶׁת אֶת הָאָרֶץ אֲשֶׁר
נָתַן לָכֶם ה' אֱלֹקֵי אֲבוֹתֵיכֶם. **ד** הָבוּ לָכֶם שְׁלֹשָׁה אֲנָשִׁים לַשָּׁבֶט וְאֶשְׁלָחֵם
וְיָקֻמוּ וְיִתְהַלְּכוּ בָאָרֶץ וְיִכְתְּבוּ אוֹתָהּ לְפִי נַחֲלָתָם וְיָבֹאוּ אֵלָי.

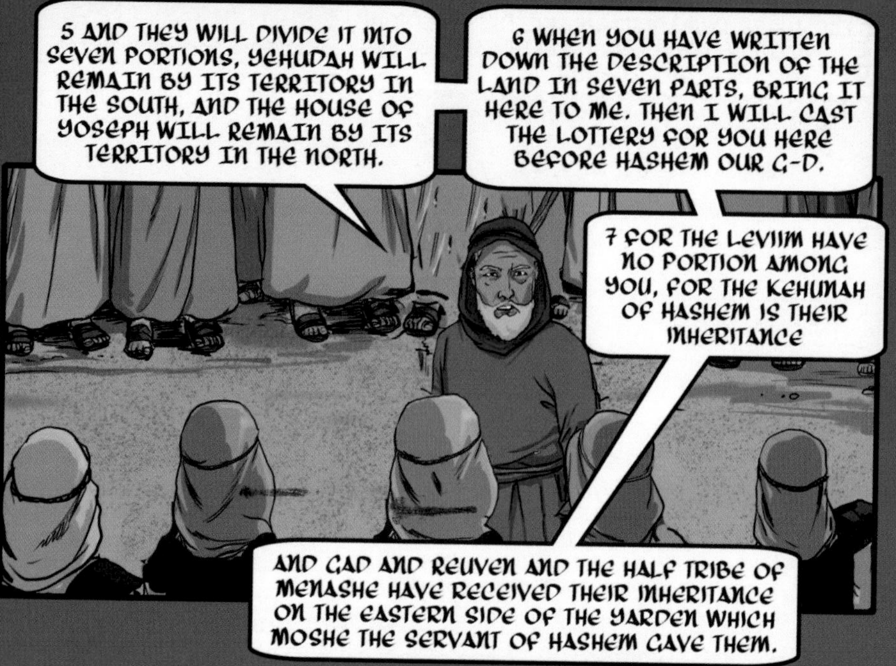
5 AND THEY WILL DIVIDE IT INTO SEVEN PORTIONS, YEHUDAH WILL REMAIN BY ITS TERRITORY IN THE SOUTH, AND THE HOUSE OF YOSEPH WILL REMAIN BY ITS TERRITORY IN THE NORTH.
6 WHEN YOU HAVE WRITTEN DOWN THE DESCRIPTION OF THE LAND IN SEVEN PARTS, BRING IT HERE TO ME. THEN I WILL CAST THE LOTTERY FOR YOU HERE BEFORE HASHEM OUR G-D.
7 FOR THE LEVIIM HAVE NO PORTION AMONG YOU, FOR THE KEHUNAH OF HASHEM IS THEIR INHERITANCE
AND GAD AND REUVEN AND THE HALF TRIBE OF MENASHE HAVE RECEIVED THEIR INHERITANCE ON THE EASTERN SIDE OF THE YARDEN WHICH MOSHE THE SERVANT OF HASHEM GAVE THEM.

8 AND THE MEN SET OUT ON THEIR JOURNEY AND YEHOSHUA INSTRUCTED THE MEN WHO WERE LEAVING TO WRITE DOWN A DESCRIPTION OF THE LAND, SAYING:
GO AND WALK THROUGH THE LAND AND DESCRIBE IT AND COME BACK TO ME AND I WILL CAST LOTS FOR YOU HERE BEFORE HASHEM IN SHILO.
COME MEN, WE HAVE A VERY *IMPORTANT* MISSION TO CARRY OUT.

ה וְהִתְחַלְּקוּ אֹתָהּ לְשִׁבְעָה חֲלָקִים יְהוּדָה יַעֲמֹד עַל גְּבוּלוֹ מִנֶּגֶב וּבֵית יוֹסֵף יַעַמְדוּ עַל
גְּבוּלָם מִצָּפוֹן. **ו** וְאַתֶּם תִּכְתְּבוּ אֶת הָאָרֶץ שִׁבְעָה חֲלָקִים וַהֲבֵאתֶם אֵלַי הֵנָּה וְיָרִיתִי
לָכֶם גּוֹרָל פֹּה לִפְנֵי ה' אֱלֹקֵינוּ. **ז** כִּי אֵין חֵלֶק לַלְוִיִּם בְּקִרְבְּכֶם כִּי כְהֻנַּת ה' נַחֲלָתוֹ וְגָד
וּרְאוּבֵן וַחֲצִי שֵׁבֶט הַמְנַשֶּׁה לָקְחוּ נַחֲלָתָם מֵעֵבֶר לַיַּרְדֵּן מִזְרָחָה אֲשֶׁר נָתַן לָהֶם מֹשֶׁה
עֶבֶד ה'. **ח** וַיָּקֻמוּ הָאֲנָשִׁים וַיֵּלֵכוּ וַיְצַו יְהוֹשֻׁעַ אֶת הַהֹלְכִים לִכְתֹּב אֶת הָאָרֶץ לֵאמֹר לְכוּ
וְהִתְהַלְּכוּ בָאָרֶץ וְכִתְבוּ אוֹתָהּ וְשׁוּבוּ אֵלַי וּפֹה אַשְׁלִיךְ לָכֶם גּוֹרָל לִפְנֵי ה' בְּשִׁלֹה.

WE KNOW THE AREA WHICH IS TO BE GIVEN TO OUR TRIBE. BUT YEHOSHUA WANTS US TO SUB-DIVIDE IT INTO PLOTS SO THE ELDERS CAN EASILY DISTRIBUTE THE LAND TO ALL PERTINENT FAMILY MEMBERS.
SOUNDS GOOD...
WE ALSO HAVE TO KEEP IN MIND THAT ALL THIS AREA HAS TO BE PORTIONED OUT EQUITABLY.
THAT IS, SOMEONE MAY GET A SMALLER PORTION OF ACTUAL LAND IF THAT PARTICULAR FIELD IS BETTER FOR FARMING, ETC.
WE GET IT! REMAIN IMPARTIAL AND BE FAIR...
9 AND THE MEN WENT AND TRAVELED THROUGH THE LAND AND THEY DESCRIBED IT IN A DOCUMENT, CITY BY CITY, IN SEVEN PARTS, AND THEY RETURNED TO YEHOSHUA IN THE CAMP AT SHILO.
ט וַיֵּלְכוּ הָאֲנָשִׁים וַיַּעַבְרוּ בָאָרֶץ וַיִּכְתְּבוּהָ לֶעָרִים לְשִׁבְעָה חֲלָקִים עַל סֵפֶר וַיָּבֹאוּ אֶל יְהוֹשֻׁעַ אֶל הַמַּחֲנֶה שִׁלֹה.

SOMETIME LATER AT SHILO...
THIS IS REALLY EXCITING. WE ARE ALL GATHERED HERE TO WITNESS THE DIVISION OF THE LAND FOR THE REMAINING SEVEN TRIBES.
I KNOW, I MISSED THE LAST GATHERING WHEN THEY DREW LOTS FOR YEHUDAH, EPHRAIM AND THE OTHER HALF TRIBE OF MENASHE. HOW DOES THIS WORK?
IT IS HARD FOR ME TO EXPLAIN YOU WILL JUST HAVE TO WATCH AND SEE...

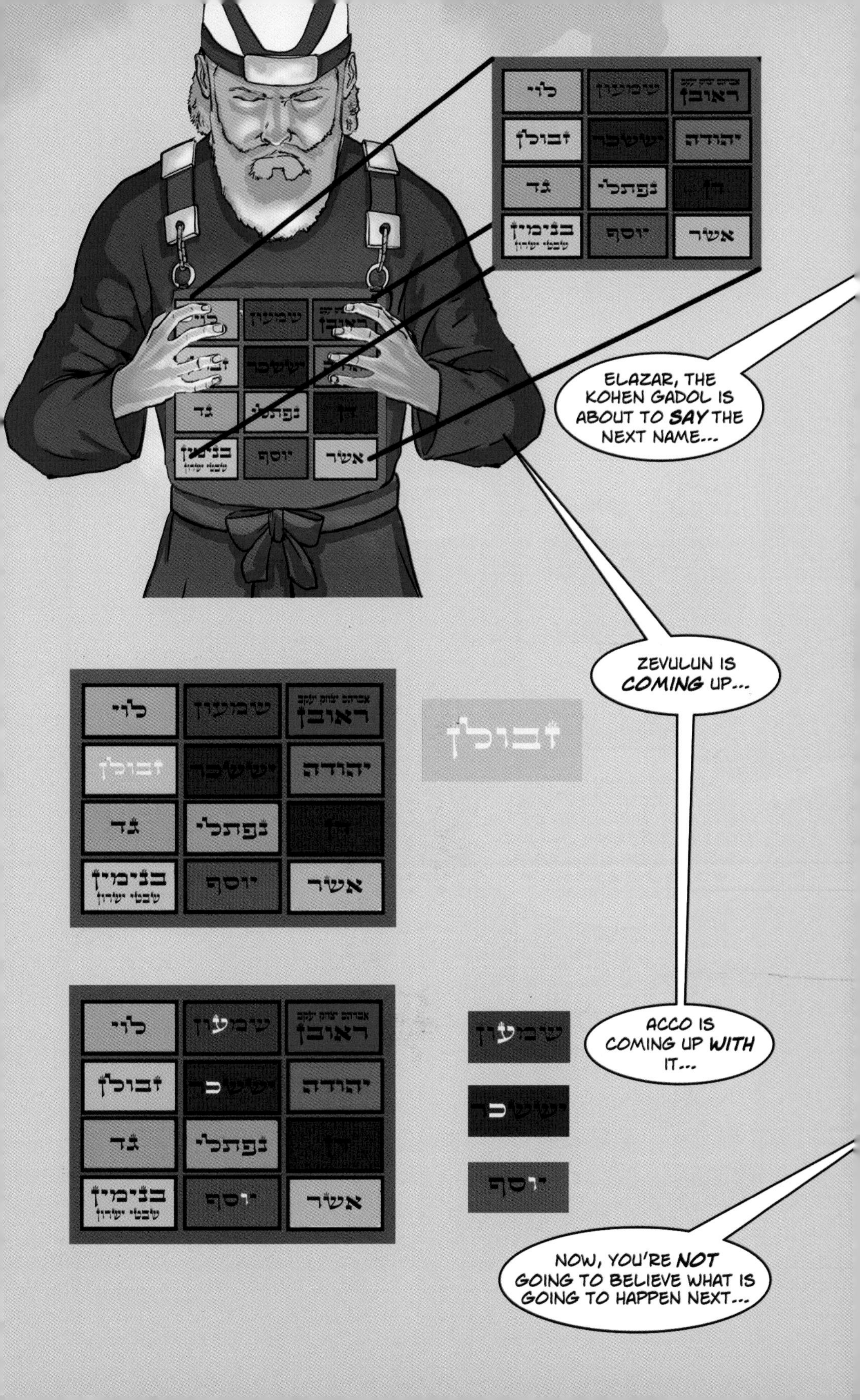
ELAZAR, THE KOHEN GADOL IS ABOUT TO *SAY* THE NEXT NAME...
ZEVULUN IS *COMING* UP...
זבולן
ACCO IS COMING UP *WITH* IT...
שמעון
יששכר
יוסף
NOW, YOU'RE *NOT* GOING TO BELIEVE WHAT IS GOING TO HAPPEN NEXT...

HE THEN **REACHES** FOR THE CONTAINER THAT HAS ALL THE NAMES OF THE TRIBES WRITTEN ON INDIVIDUAL PAPERS. SHAKES IT UP THOROUGHLY AND PULLS OUT A PIECE OF PAPER...
IT READS ***ZEVULUN!***
HE THEN GOES TO THE SECOND CONTAINER WHICH HAS ALL OF THE NAMES OF THE ***DIVIDED*** PORTIONS OF LAND. SHAKES IT UP WELL AGAIN PULLS OUT A PIECE OF PAPER AND IT READS...
ACCO.

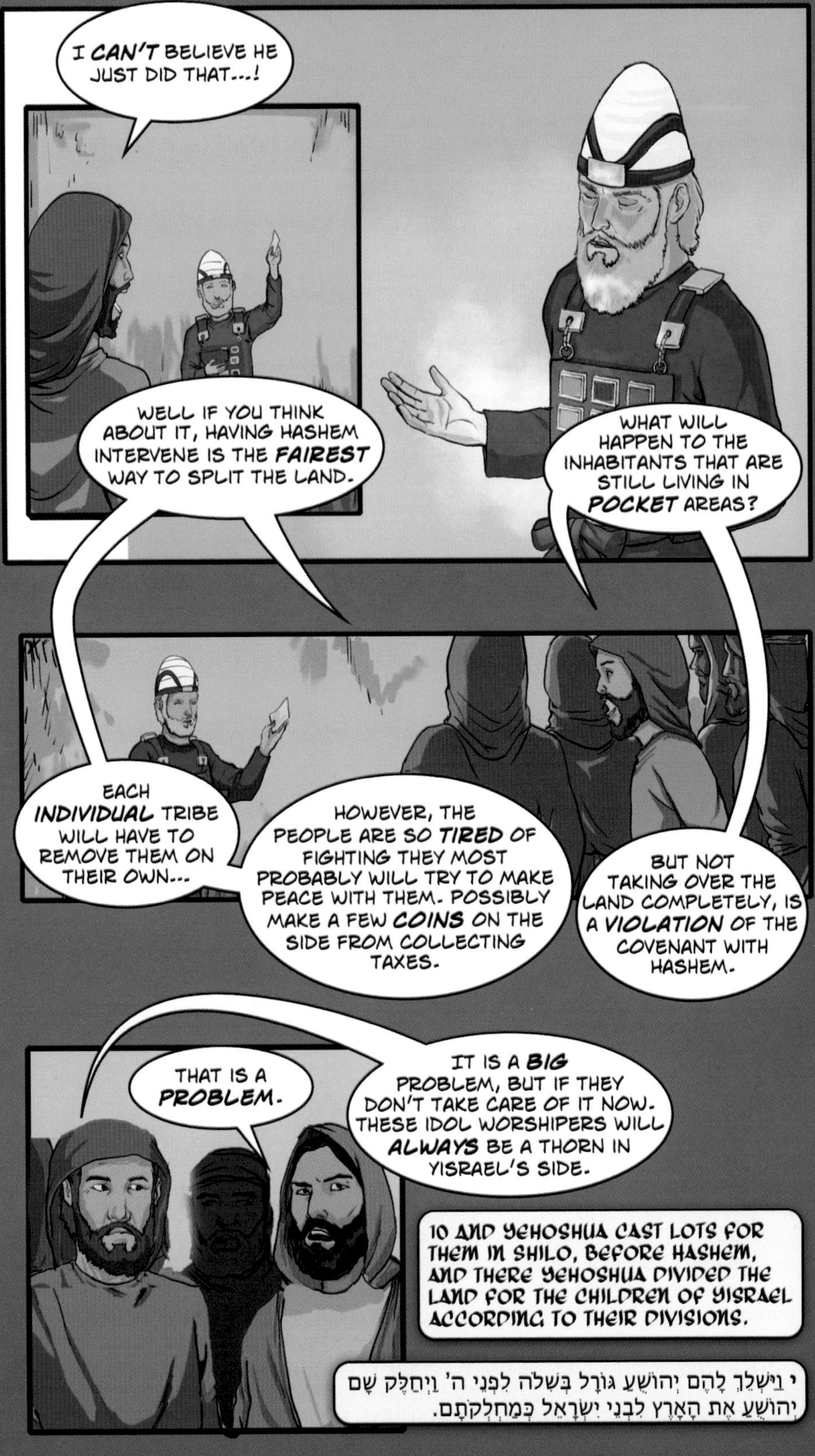
I CAN'T BELIEVE HE JUST DID THAT...!
WELL IF YOU THINK ABOUT IT, HAVING HASHEM INTERVENE IS THE FAIREST WAY TO SPLIT THE LAND.
WHAT WILL HAPPEN TO THE INHABITANTS THAT ARE STILL LIVING IN POCKET AREAS?
EACH INDIVIDUAL TRIBE WILL HAVE TO REMOVE THEM ON THEIR OWN...
HOWEVER, THE PEOPLE ARE SO TIRED OF FIGHTING THEY MOST PROBABLY WILL TRY TO MAKE PEACE WITH THEM. POSSIBLY MAKE A FEW COINS ON THE SIDE FROM COLLECTING TAXES.
BUT NOT TAKING OVER THE LAND COMPLETELY, IS A VIOLATION OF THE COVENANT WITH HASHEM.
THAT IS A PROBLEM.
IT IS A BIG PROBLEM, BUT IF THEY DON'T TAKE CARE OF IT NOW. THESE IDOL WORSHIPERS WILL ALWAYS BE A THORN IN YISRAEL'S SIDE.
10 AND YEHOSHUA CAST LOTS FOR THEM IN SHILO, BEFORE HASHEM, AND THERE YEHOSHUA DIVIDED THE LAND FOR THE CHILDREN OF YISRAEL ACCORDING TO THEIR DIVISIONS.
י וַיַּשְׁלֵךְ לָהֶם יְהוֹשֻׁעַ גּוֹרָל בְּשִׁלֹה לִפְנֵי ה' וַיְחַלֶּק שָׁם יְהוֹשֻׁעַ אֶת הָאָרֶץ לִבְנֵי יִשְׂרָאֵל כְּמַחְלְקֹתָם.

TO HELP IDENTIFY THE LOCATIONS ON THE MAP, THE VERSE NUMBERS ARE REPRESENTED IN RED.

YEHOSHUA CHAPTER 19
יהושע פרק יט

1 AND THE SECOND LOT FELL TO SHIMON, FOR THE TRIBE OF THE CHILDREN OF SHIMON ACCORDING TO THEIR FAMILIES; AND THEIR INHERITANCE WAS WITHIN (INSIDE) THE PORTION OF THE CHILDREN OF YEHUDAH. 2 AND THEY HAD FOR THEIR INHERITANCE BEER-SHEVA (AKA SHEVA), AND MOLADAH; 3 AND CHATZAR-SHUAL, AND VALAH, AND ATZEM; 4 AND ELTOLAD, AND BETUL, AND CHARMAH; 5 AND TZIKLAG, AND BEIT-MARCAVOT, AND CHATZAR-SUSAH; 6 AND BEIT-LEVAOT, AND SHARUCHEN; THIRTEEN CITIES WITH THEIR VILLAGES: 7 AYIN, RIMON, AND ETER, AND ASHAN; FOUR CITIES WITH THEIR VILLAGES; 8 AND ALL THE VILLAGES THAT WERE IN THE VICINITY OF THESE CITIES TO BAALAT-BEER, AS FAR AS RAMAT NEGEV. THIS IS THE INHERITANCE OF THE TRIBE OF THE CHILDREN OF SHIMON ACCORDING TO THEIR FAMILIES. 9 THE PORTION OF SHIMON WAS PART OF THE TERRITORY OF YEHUDAH; SINCE THE PORTION OF YEHUDAH WAS LARGER THAN THEY NEEDED, SHIMON RECEIVED A PORTION INSIDE YEHUDAH'S PORTION.

SHIMON, BEING ***TOTALLY*** SURROUNDED BY YEHUDAH, IS DUE TO MOSHE NOT BLESSING THE TRIBE OF SHIMON AT THE TIME OF HIS DEATH. THE REASON IS BECAUSE OF THE INCIDENT WITH ZIMRI, SON OF SALU, FROM THE TRIBE OF SHIMON (BAMIDBAR 25:14).

ALTERNATIVELY, THIS MAY BE THE ***OUTCOME*** OF THE CURSE OF YAAKOV THAT HE GAVE TO SHIMON. (BREISHIT 49:5-7). THIS CAN BE COMPARED TO A ***PARABLE*** OF AN OX WHO BECAME WILD. WHAT DID THEY DO? A LION (WHICH IS COMPARED TO YEHUDAH) WAS TIED UP NEAR THE TROUGH OF THE OX (WHICH IS COMPARED TO SHIMON). WHENEVER THE OX LOOKED AT THE LION, THE OX LOST ITS STRENGTH.

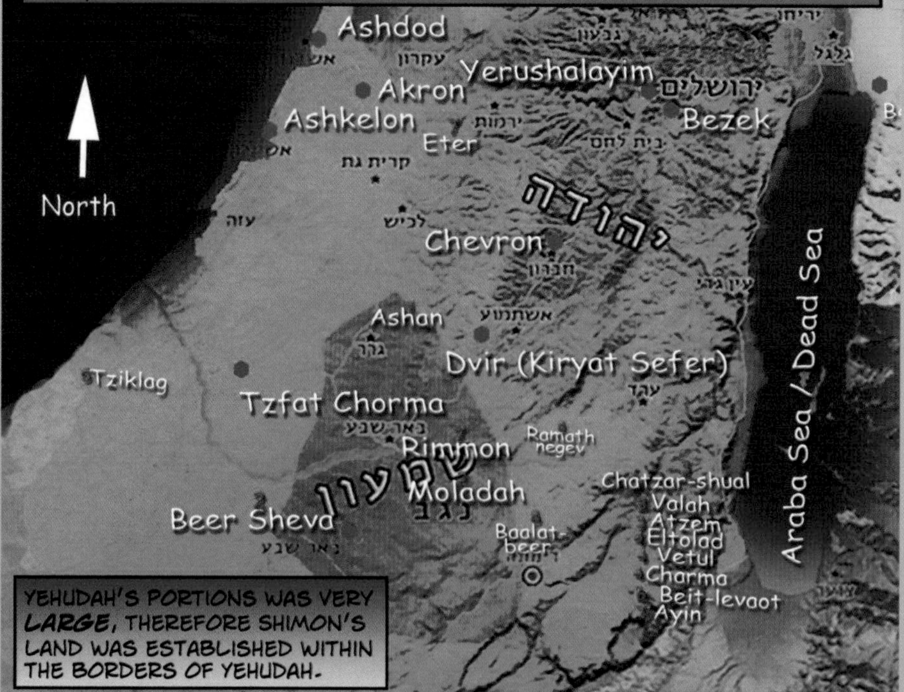

YEHUDAH'S PORTIONS WAS VERY ***LARGE***, THEREFORE SHIMON'S LAND WAS ESTABLISHED WITHIN THE BORDERS OF YEHUDAH.

א וַיֵּצֵא הַגּוֹרָל הַשֵּׁנִי לְשִׁמְעוֹן לְמַטֵּה בְנֵי שִׁמְעוֹן לְמִשְׁפְּחוֹתָם וַיְהִי נַחֲלָתָם בְּתוֹךְ נַחֲלַת בְּנֵי
יְהוּדָה. **ב** וַיְהִי לָהֶם בְּנַחֲלָתָם בְּאֵר שֶׁבַע וְשֶׁבַע וּמוֹלָדָה. **ג** וַחֲצַר שׁוּעָל וּבָלָה וָעָצֶם. **ד** וְאֶלְתּוֹלַד
וּבְתוּל וְחָרְמָה. **ה** וְצִקְלַג וּבֵית הַמַּרְכָּבוֹת וַחֲצַר סוּסָה. **ו** וּבֵית לְבָאוֹת וְשָׁרוּחֶן עָרִים שְׁלֹשׁ
עֶשְׂרֵה וְחַצְרֵיהֶן. **ז** עַיִן רִמּוֹן, וָעֶתֶר וְעָשָׁן עָרִים אַרְבַּע וְחַצְרֵיהֶן. **ח** וְכָל הַחֲצֵרִים אֲשֶׁר סְבִיבוֹת
הֶעָרִים הָאֵלֶּה עַד בַּעֲלַת בְּאֵר רָאמַת נֶגֶב זֹאת נַחֲלַת מַטֵּה בְנֵי שִׁמְעוֹן לְמִשְׁפְּחֹתָם. **ט** מֵחֶבֶל בְּנֵי
יְהוּדָה נַחֲלַת בְּנֵי שִׁמְעוֹן כִּי הָיָה חֵלֶק בְּנֵי יְהוּדָה רַב מֵהֶם וַיִּנְחֲלוּ בְנֵי שִׁמְעוֹן בְּתוֹךְ נַחֲלָתָם.

10 AND THE THIRD LOTTERY EMERGED FOR THE CHILDREN OF ZEVULUM ACCORDING TO THEIR FAMILIES; AND THE BORDER OF THEIR INHERITANCE WAS UNTIL SARID. 11 AND THEIR BORDER WENT UP WESTWARD TO MARALAH, AND REACHED TO DABASHET; AND IT REACHED TO THE RIVER THAT IS ALONGSIDE YAKNEAM. 12 AND IT ALSO RAN FROM SARID ALONG THE EASTERN SIDE, WHERE THE SUN RISES, PAST THE TERRITORY OF KISLOT-TABOR AND ON TO DAVRAT AND ASCENDED TO YAPHIA. 13 AND FROM THERE IT PASSED ALONG EASTWARD TO GAT-CHEPHER, TO ITAH-KATZIM; AND IT WENT OUT AT RIMON CURVING TO NEAH. 14 AND THE BORDER TURNED TO THE NORTH TO CHANATON; ITS EXTREME LIMITS WERE THE VALLEY OF YIPHTACH-EL; 15 AND KATATH, AND NAHALAL, AND SHIMRON, AND YIDALAH, AND BEIT-LACHEM; TWELVE CITIES WITH THEIR VILLAGES. 16 THIS IS THE INHERITANCE OF THE CHILDREN OF ZEVULUN ACCORDING TO THEIR FAMILIES, THESE CITIES WITH THEIR VILLAGES.

י וַיַּעַל הַגּוֹרָל הַשְּׁלִישִׁי לִבְנֵי זְבוּלֻן לְמִשְׁפְּחֹתָם וַיְהִי גְּבוּל נַחֲלָתָם עַד שָׂרִיד. **יא** וְעָלָה
גְבוּלָם לַיָּמָּה וּמַרְעֲלָה וּפָגַע בְּדַבָּשֶׁת וּפָגַע אֶל הַנַּחַל אֲשֶׁר עַל פְּנֵי יָקְנְעָם. **יב** וְשָׁב מִשָּׂרִיד
קֵדְמָה מִזְרַח הַשֶּׁמֶשׁ עַל גְּבוּל כִּסְלֹת תָּבֹר וְיָצָא אֶל הַדָּבְרַת וְעָלָה יָפִיעַ. **יג** וּמִשָּׁם עָבַר
קֵדְמָה מִזְרָחָה גִּתָּה חֵפֶר עִתָּה קָצִין וְיָצָא רִמּוֹן הַמְּתֹאָר הַנֵּעָה. **יד** וְנָסַב אֹתוֹ הַגְּבוּל מִצְּפוֹן
חַנָּתֹן וְהָיוּ תֹּצְאֹתָיו גֵּי יִפְתַּח אֵל. **טו** וְקַטָּת וְנַהֲלָל וְשִׁמְרוֹן וְיִדְאֲלָה וּבֵית לָחֶם: עָרִים שְׁתֵּים
עֶשְׂרֵה וְחַצְרֵיהֶן. **טז** זֹאת נַחֲלַת בְּנֵי זְבוּלֻן לְמִשְׁפְּחוֹתָם הֶעָרִים הָאֵלֶּה וְחַצְרֵיהֶן.

17 THE FOURTH LOTTERY EMERGED FOR YISSACHAR, AND FOR THE CHILDREN OF YISSACHAR ACCORDING TO THEIR FAMILIES. 18 AND THEIR BORDER WAS YEZREEL, AND KESULOT, AND SHUNEM; 19 AND CHAPHARAYIM, AND SHION, AND ANACHARAT; 20 AND RABIT, AND KISHYON, AND AVETZ; 21 AND REMET, AND EIN-GANIM, AND EIN-CHADAH, AND BEIT-PATZETZ; 22 AND THE BORDER REACHED TO TAVOR, AND SHACHATZIMAH, AND BEIT-SHEMESH; AND THEIR BOUNDARY RAN TO THE YARDEN; SIXTEEN CITIES WITH THEIR VILLAGES. 23 THIS IS THE INHERITANCE OF THE TRIBE OF THE CHILDREN OF YISSACHAR ACCORDING TO THEIR FAMILIES, THE CITIES WITH THEIR VILLAGES.

CHAPHARAYIM IS ONE OF THE CITIES WHICH ***SUPPLIED*** THE FINE FLOUR FOR THE OFFERINGS IN THE BEIT HAMIKDOSH.

כנרת
Kinneret
זבול
Ein-ganim
Beit-shemesh
Ein-chadah
Tavor
Shion
Kishyon
Rabit
Avetz
Shunem
Beit-patzetz
Anacharat
Chapharayim
Yezreel
בית שאן

SHACHATZIMAH COULD BE A HABITAT FOR LIONS, ORIGINATING FROM THE WORD ***SHACHATZ***, WHICH IS TRANSLATED TO MEAN A LION IN IYOV 28:8. THERE ARE SIX OTHER WORDS TO DESCRIBE A LION; 1) ***ARI***, BREISHEET 49:9; 2) ***KEFIR***, SHOFTIM 14:5; 3) ***LEVIAH***, BREISHEET 49:9; 4) ***LAISH***, YESHAYAHU 30:6; 5) ***SHACHAL***, TEHILIM 61:13; 6) ***GUR***, BREISHEET 49:9).

יז לְיִשָּׂשכָר יָצָא הַגּוֹרָל הָרְבִיעִי לִבְנֵי יִשָּׂשכָר לְמִשְׁפְּחוֹתָם. **יח** וַיְהִי גְּבוּלָם
יִזְרְעֶאלָה וְהַכְּסוּלֹת וְשׁוּנֵם. **יט** וַחֲפָרַיִם וְשִׁיאֹן וַאֲנָחֲרַת. **כ** וְהָרַבִּית וְקִשְׁיוֹן
וָאָבֶץ. **כא** וְרֶמֶת וְעֵין גַּנִּים וְעֵין חַדָּה וּבֵית פַּצֵּץ. **כב** וּפָגַע הַגְּבוּל בְּתָבוֹר
ושחצומה (וְשַׁחֲצִימָה) וּבֵית שֶׁמֶשׁ וְהָיוּ תֹּצְאוֹת גְּבוּלָם הַיַּרְדֵּן עָרִים שֵׁשׁ עֶשְׂרֵה
וְחַצְרֵיהֶן. **כג** זֹאת נַחֲלַת מַטֵּה בְנֵי יִשָּׂשכָר לְמִשְׁפְּחֹתָם הֶעָרִים וְחַצְרֵיהֶן.

24 AND THE FIFTH LOTTERY EMERGED FOR THE TRIBE OF THE CHILDREN OF
ASHER ACCORDING TO THEIR FAMILIES. 25 AND THEIR BORDER WAS
CHELKAT, AND CHALI, AND VETEN, AND ACHSHAPH; 26 AND ALAMELECH, AND
AMAD, AND MISHAL; AND IT REACHED TO CARMEL WESTWARD, AND TO
SHICHOR-LIVNAT. 27 AND IT RAN ALONG THE EAST SIDE TO BEIT-DAGON, AND
REACHED TO ZEVULUN AND TO THE VALLEY OF YIPHTACH-EL NORTHWARD AT
BEIT-EMEK AND NEIEL; THEN IT RAN TO KAVUL ON THE NORTH, 28 AND
EVRON, AND RECHOV, AND CHAMON, AND KANAH, UP TO GREAT TZIDON. 29
AND THE BORDER TURNED TO RAMAH, AND TO THE FORTIFIED CITY OF TZOR;
AND THE BORDER TURNED TO CHOSAH; IT RAN ON WESTWARD TO MECHEVEL-ACHZIV; 30 UMAH AND APHEK, AND RECHOV; TWENTY TWO CITIES WITH THEIR
VILLAGES. 31 THIS IS THE INHERITANCE OF THE TRIBE OF THE CHILDREN OF
ASHER ACCORDING TO THEIR FAMILIES, THESE CITIES WITH THEIR VILLAGES.

כד וַיֵּצֵא הַגּוֹרָל הַחֲמִישִׁי לְמַטֵּה בְנֵי אָשֵׁר לְמִשְׁפְּחוֹתָם. **כה** וַיְהִי גְּבוּלָם חֶלְקַת וַחֲלִי וָבֶטֶן
וְאַכְשָׁף. **כו** וְאַלַמֶּלֶךְ וְעַמְעָד וּמִשְׁאָל וּפָגַע בְּכַרְמֶל הַיָּמָּה וּבְשִׁיחוֹר לִבְנָת. **כז** וְשָׁב מִזְרַח
הַשֶּׁמֶשׁ בֵּית דָּגֹן וּפָגַע בִּזְבֻלוּן וּבְגֵי יִפְתַּח אֵל צָפוֹנָה בֵּית הָעֵמֶק וּנְעִיאֵל וְיָצָא אֶל כָּבוּל
מִשְּׂמֹאל. **כח** וְעֶבְרֹן וּרְחֹב וְחַמּוֹן וְקָנָה עַד צִידוֹן רַבָּה. **כט** וְשָׁב הַגְּבוּל הָרָמָה וְעַד עִיר מִבְצַר
צֹר וְשָׁב הַגְּבוּל חֹסָה ויהיו (וְהָיוּ) תֹצְאֹתָיו הַיָּמָּה מֵחֶבֶל אַכְזִיבָה. **ל** וְעֻמָה וַאֲפֵק וּרְחֹב עָרִים
עֶשְׂרִים וּשְׁתַּיִם וְחַצְרֵיהֶן. **לא** זֹאת נַחֲלַת מַטֵּה בְנֵי אָשֵׁר לְמִשְׁפְּחֹתָם הֶעָרִים הָאֵלֶּה וְחַצְרֵיהֶן.

32 THE SIXTH LOTTERY EMERGED FOR THE CHILDREN OF NAPHTALI, AND FOR THE CHILDREN OF NAPHTALI ACCORDING TO THEIR FAMILIES. 33 AND THEIR BORDER WAS FROM CHELEPH, FROM ELON-BEZTAANANIM, AND ADAMI-NEKEV, AND YAVNEEL, UNTIL LAKUM; AND IT ENDED UP AT THE YARDEN. 34 AND THE BORDER TURNED WESTWARD TO AZNOT-TAVOR, AND WENT OUT FROM THERE TO CHUKOK; AND IT REACHED TO ZEVULUN ON THE SOUTH, AND REACHED TO ASHER ON THE WEST, AND TO YEHUDAH AT THE YARDEN TOWARD THE EAST. 35 AND THE FORTIFIED CITIES WERE TZIDIM, TZER, AND CHAMATH, AND RAKAT, AND KINERET; 36 AND ADAMAH, AND RAMAH, AND CHATZOR; 37 AND KEDESH, AND EDREI, AND EN-CHATZOR; 38 AND YIRON, AND MIGDAL-EL, AND CHAREM, AND BEIT-ANAT, AND BEIT-SHEMESH; NINETEEN CITIES WITH THEIR VILLAGES. 39 THIS IS THE INHERITANCE OF THE TRIBE OF THE CHILDREN OF NAPHTALI ACCORDING TO THEIR FAMILIES, THE CITIES WITH THEIR VILLAGES.

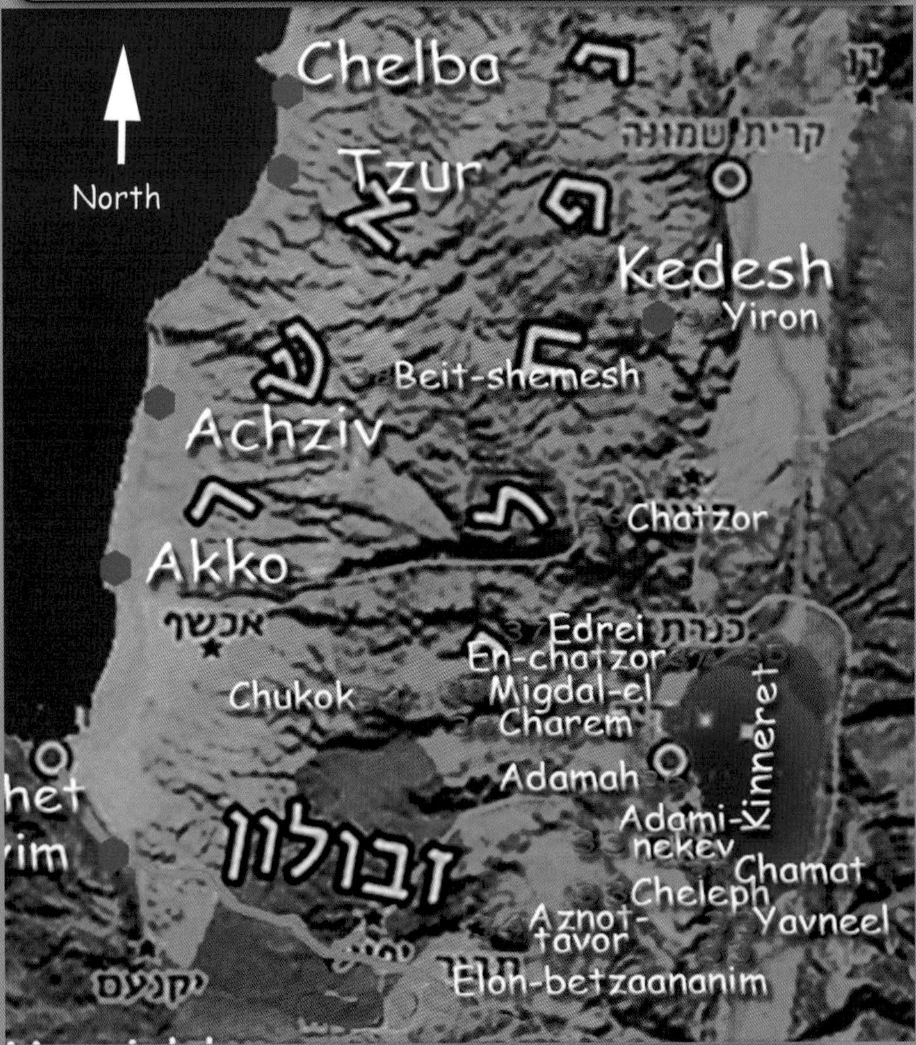

לב לִבְנֵי נַפְתָּלִי יָצָא הַגּוֹרָל הַשִּׁשִּׁי לִבְנֵי נַפְתָּלִי לְמִשְׁפְּחֹתָם. **לג** וַיְהִי גְבוּלָם
מֵחֵלֶף מֵאֵלוֹן בְּצַעֲנַנִּים וַאֲדָמִי הַנֶּקֶב וְיַבְנְאֵל עַד לַקּוּם וַיְהִי תֹצְאֹתָיו הַיַּרְדֵּן.
לד וְשָׁב הַגְּבוּל יָמָּה אַזְנוֹת תָּבוֹר וְיָצָא מִשָּׁם חוּקֹקָה וּפָגַע בִּזְבֻלוּן מִנֶּגֶב
וּבְאָשֵׁר פָּגַע מִיָּם וּבִיהוּדָה הַיַּרְדֵּן מִזְרַח הַשָּׁמֶשׁ. **לה** וְעָרֵי מִבְצָר הַצִּדִּים צֵר
וְחַמַּת רַקַּת וְכִנָּרֶת. **לו** וַאֲדָמָה וְהָרָמָה וְחָצוֹר. **לז** וְקֶדֶשׁ וְאֶדְרֶעִי וְעֵין
חָצוֹר. **לח** וְיִרְאוֹן וּמִגְדַּל אֵל חֳרֵם וּבֵית עֲנָת וּבֵית שָׁמֶשׁ עָרִים תְּשַׁע עֶשְׂרֵה
וְחַצְרֵיהֶן. **לט** זֹאת נַחֲלַת מַטֵּה בְנֵי נַפְתָּלִי לְמִשְׁפְּחֹתָם הֶעָרִים וְחַצְרֵיהֶן.

40 THE SEVENTH LOTTERY EMERGED FOR THE TRIBE OF THE CHILDREN OF DAN ACCORDING TO THEIR FAMILIES. 41 AND THE BORDER OF THEIR INHERITANCE WAS TZARAH, AND ESHTAOL, AND IR-SHAMESH; 42 AND SHAALABIN, AND AYALON, AND YITLAH; 43 AND ELON, AND TIMNAH, AND EKRON; 44 AND ELTEKEH, AND GIBTON, AND VAALATH; 45 AND YEHUD, AND BNEI-BERAK, AND GAT-RIMON; 46 AND MEI-YARKON, AND RAKON, WITH THE BORDER NEAR YAFO. 47 BUT THE TERRITORY OF THE CHILDREN OF DAN SLIPPED FROM THEIR GRASP. SO THE CHILDREN OF DAN WENT UP AND MADE WAR ON LESHEM. THEY CAPTURED IT AND KILLED THEM ALL; TOOK THEIR POSSESSIONS AND SETTLED THERE. AND THEY CHANGED THE NAME OF LESHEM TO DAN AFTER THEIR ANCESTOR DAN. 48 THIS IS THE INHERITANCE OF THE TRIBE OF THE CHILDREN OF DAN ACCORDING TO THEIR FAMILIES, THESE CITIES WITH THEIR VILLAGES.

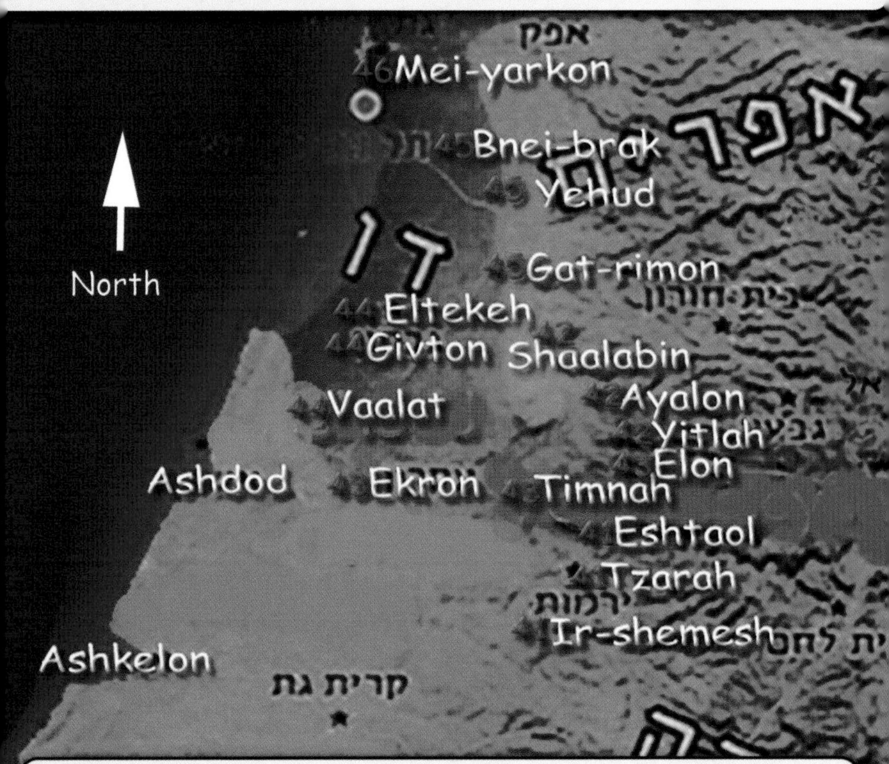

49 WHEN THEY FINISHED ALLOTTING THE LAND BY ITS BOUNDARIES, THE CHILDREN OF YISRAEL GAVE A PORTION IN THEIR MIDST TO YEHOSHUA THE SON OF NUN. 50 ACCORDING TO THE COMMANDMENT OF HASHEM THEY GAVE HIM THE CITY WHICH HE ASKED, FOR EVEN TIMNAT-SERACH IN THE HILL-COUNTRY OF EPHRAIM; AND HE BUILT THE CITY, AND LIVED THERE. 51 THESE ARE THE INHERITANCES, WHICH ELAZAR THE KOHEN, AND YEHOSHUA THE SON OF NUN, AND THE HEADS OF THE FATHERS' HOUSES OF THE TRIBES OF THE CHILDREN OF YISRAEL, DISTRIBUTED FOR INHERITANCE BY LOT BEFORE HASHEM AT SHILO, AT THE DOOR OF THE TENT OF MEETING. AND THEY COMPLETED THE DIVIDING OF THE LAND.

מ לְמַטֵּה בְנֵי דָן לְמִשְׁפְּחֹתָם יָצָא הַגּוֹרָל הַשְּׁבִיעִי. **מא** וַיְהִי גְּבוּל נַחֲלָתָם צָרְעָה וְאֶשְׁתָּאוֹל
וְעִיר שָׁמֶשׁ. **מב** וְשַׁעֲלַבִּין וְאַיָּלוֹן וְיִתְלָה. **מג** וְאֵילוֹן וְתִמְנָתָה וְעֶקְרוֹן. **מד** וְאֶלְתְּקֵה וְגִבְּתוֹן
וּבַעֲלָת. **מה** וִיהֻד וּבְנֵי בְרַק וְגַת רִמּוֹן. **מו** וּמֵי הַיַּרְקוֹן וְהָרַקּוֹן עִם הַגְּבוּל מוּל יָפוֹ. **מז** וַיֵּצֵא
גְּבוּל בְּנֵי דָן מֵהֶם וַיַּעֲלוּ בְנֵי דָן וַיִּלָּחֲמוּ עִם לֶשֶׁם וַיִּלְכְּדוּ אוֹתָהּ וַיַּכּוּ אוֹתָהּ לְפִי חֶרֶב וַיִּרְשׁוּ
אוֹתָהּ וַיֵּשְׁבוּ בָהּ וַיִּקְרְאוּ לְלֶשֶׁם דָּן כְּשֵׁם דָּן אֲבִיהֶם. **מח** זֹאת נַחֲלַת מַטֵּה בְנֵי דָן לְמִשְׁפְּחֹתָם
הֶעָרִים הָאֵלֶּה וְחַצְרֵיהֶן. **מט** וַיְכַלּוּ לִנְחֹל אֶת הָאָרֶץ לִגְבוּלֹתֶיהָ וַיִּתְּנוּ בְנֵי יִשְׂרָאֵל נַחֲלָה
לִיהוֹשֻׁעַ בִּן נוּן בְּתוֹכָם. **נ** עַל פִּי ה' נָתְנוּ לוֹ אֶת הָעִיר אֲשֶׁר שָׁאָל אֶת תִּמְנַת סֶרַח בְּהַר אֶפְרָיִם
וַיִּבְנֶה אֶת הָעִיר וַיֵּשֶׁב בָּהּ. **נא** אֵלֶּה הַנְּחָלֹת אֲשֶׁר נִחֲלוּ אֶלְעָזָר הַכֹּהֵן וִיהוֹשֻׁעַ בִּן נוּן וְרָאשֵׁי
הָאָבוֹת לְמַטּוֹת בְּנֵי יִשְׂרָאֵל בְּגוֹרָל בְּשִׁלֹה לִפְנֵי ה' פֶּתַח אֹהֶל מוֹעֵד וַיְכַלּוּ מֵחַלֵּק אֶת הָאָרֶץ.

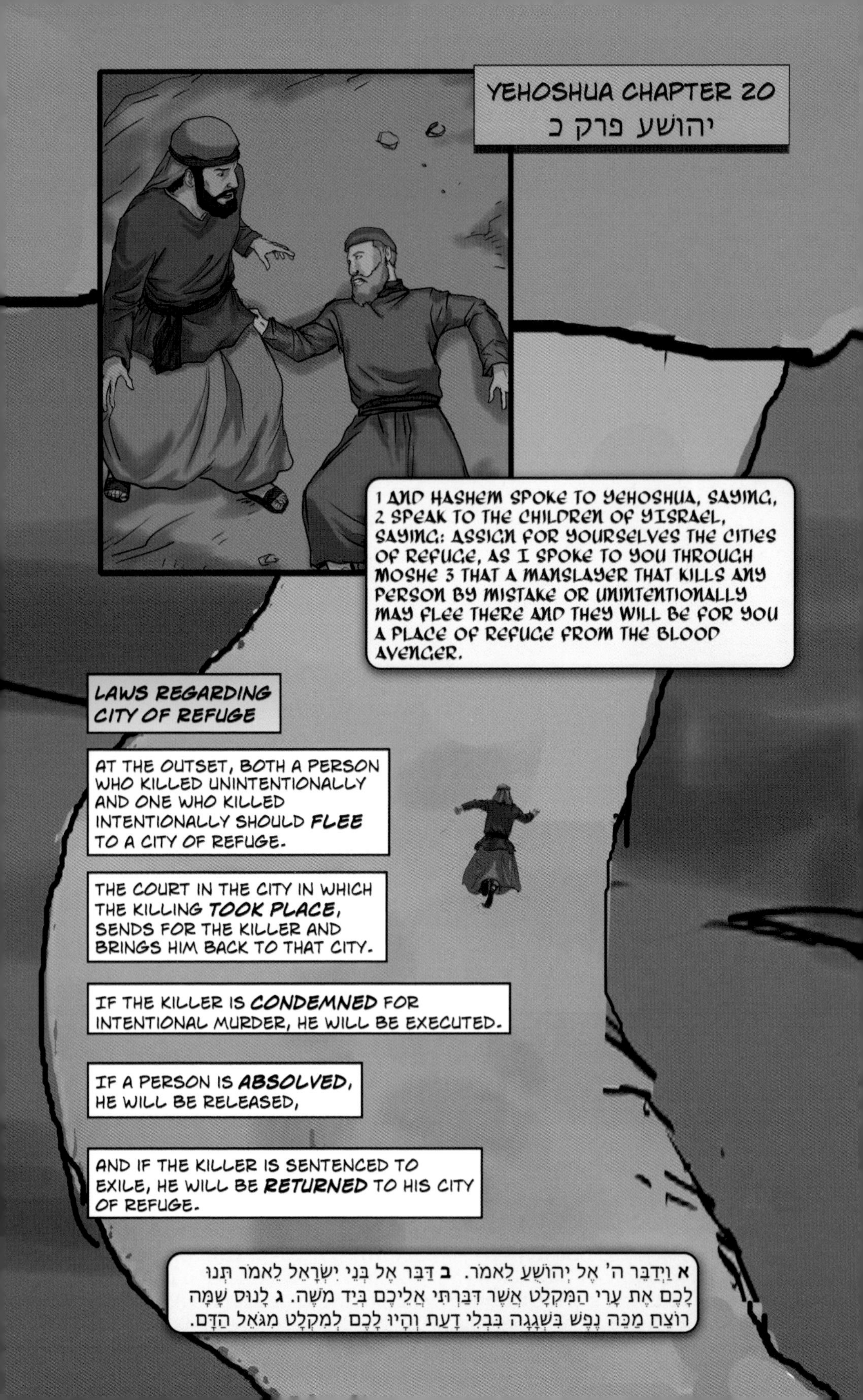
YEHOSHUA CHAPTER 20
יהושע פרק כ
1 AND HASHEM SPOKE TO YEHOSHUA, SAYING, 2 SPEAK TO THE CHILDREN OF YISRAEL, SAYING: ASSIGN FOR YOURSELVES THE CITIES OF REFUGE, AS I SPOKE TO YOU THROUGH MOSHE 3 THAT A MANSLAYER THAT KILLS ANY PERSON BY MISTAKE OR UNINTENTIONALLY MAY FLEE THERE AND THEY WILL BE FOR YOU A PLACE OF REFUGE FROM THE BLOOD AVENGER.
LAWS REGARDING CITY OF REFUGE
AT THE OUTSET, BOTH A PERSON WHO KILLED UNINTENTIONALLY AND ONE WHO KILLED INTENTIONALLY SHOULD ***FLEE*** TO A CITY OF REFUGE.
THE COURT IN THE CITY IN WHICH THE KILLING ***TOOK PLACE***, SENDS FOR THE KILLER AND BRINGS HIM BACK TO THAT CITY.
IF THE KILLER IS ***CONDEMNED*** FOR INTENTIONAL MURDER, HE WILL BE EXECUTED.
IF A PERSON IS ***ABSOLVED***, HE WILL BE RELEASED,
AND IF THE KILLER IS SENTENCED TO EXILE, HE WILL BE ***RETURNED*** TO HIS CITY OF REFUGE.
א וַיְדַבֵּר ה' אֶל יְהוֹשֻׁעַ לֵאמֹר. **ב** דַּבֵּר אֶל בְּנֵי יִשְׂרָאֵל לֵאמֹר תְּנוּ
לָכֶם אֶת עָרֵי הַמִּקְלָט אֲשֶׁר דִּבַּרְתִּי אֲלֵיכֶם בְּיַד מֹשֶׁה. **ג** לָנוּס שָׁמָּה
רוֹצֵחַ מַכֵּה נֶפֶשׁ בִּשְׁגָגָה בִּבְלִי דָעַת וְהָיוּ לָכֶם לְמִקְלָט מִגֹּאֵל הַדָּם.

YOU HAVE BEEN FOUND GUILTY OF KILLING SOMEONE ACCIDENTALLY. AS AN ATONEMENT FOR YOUR CRIME, YOU ARE TO BE ESCORTED BY THESE TWO DISTINGUISHED GENTLEMEN TO THE CITY OF REFUGE...
THERE HE IS! THAT IS THE PERSON THAT KILLED MY BROTHER.
LET'S GO AFTER HIM AND GIVE HIM HIS DUE JUSTICE!!!

HAND HIM OVER RABBI. IT IS MY RIGHT TO TAKE VENGEANCE...
WE WILL DO NO SUCH THING. THIS MAN IS OUR RESPONSIBILITY. IT HAS BEEN DECIDED BY BEIT DIN THAT HE KILLED YOUR BROTHER ACCIDENTALLY.
HE DESERVES TO DIE...
NOT IN OUR OPINION. BE WARNED, SHOULD ANYTHING HAPPEN TO THIS MAN WHILE WE ESCORT HIM TO THE CITY OF REFUGE, YOU WILL BE BROUGHT TO BEIT DIN FOR THE CRIME OF MURDER...
FURTHERMORE, ONCE HE ARRIVES AT THE CITY, HE IS NOT TO BE HARMED WHILE HE IS WITHIN ITS BORDERS.
HE HAS BEEN INSTRUCTED THAT HE CAN NEVER LEAVE UNTIL THE DEATH OF THE KOHEN GADOL. SHOULD HE EXIT THE CITY FOR ANY REASON PRIOR TO THIS CONDITION, THEN YOU AS A BLOOD AVENGER WILL HAVE EVERY RIGHT TO KILL HIM.
YOU HEAR THAT FRIEND, YOU BETTER NOT PUT ONE TOE OUT OF THAT CITY. BECAUSE IF YOU DO, I WILL KILL YOU LIKE YOU KILLED MY BROTHER...

HERE ARE THREE CATEGORIES OF UNINTENTIONAL KILLERS:
1. A PERSON WHO KILLS UNINTENTIONALLY WITHOUT ANY KNOWLEDGE THAT THIS WILL BE THE CONSEQUENCE OF HIS ACTIONS. THIS PERSON WILL HAVE THE OPPORTUNITY TO GO INTO EXILE.
YAAKOV, YOU'RE TAKING DOWN A WALL, AREN'T YOU AFRAID SOMEONE ON THE OTHER SIDE WILL WALK BY AND HAVE A STONE CHAS V'SHALOM FALL ON THEIR HEAD?
DON'T WORRY LEAH, I'VE TAKEN ALL THE NECESSARY PRECAUTIONS.
I BLOCKED OFF THE PATH FROM BOTH SIDES, AND I PLACED WARNING SIGNS CAUTIONING ALL WHO COME CLOSE.
THIS IS A GREAT SHORTCUT. ALL I HAVE TO DO IS GO AROUND THIS WALL.
I SEE THE WARNING SIGNS, BUT I DON'T HEAR ANY CONSTRUCTION GOING ON. I WILL BE EXTRA CAREFUL...
UH OH...

HELP!!!
WHY WAS HE THERE? I TOOK ALL OF THE NECESSARY PRECAUTIONS...
LEAH, GO GET HELP!
CHAIM, ANY WORD ON WHAT HAPPENED WITH THE MAN?
THE DOCTOR'S SAID THERE WAS NOTHING THEY COULD DO. THEY SAID HE DIED INSTANTLY FROM ONE OF THE BOULDERS HITTING HIM ON THE HEAD.
I'M SORRY TO HEAR THAT. I NEVER INTENDED TO HURT ANYONE. I NOW HAVE TO GO TO THE CITY OF REFUGE AND WAIT THERE UNTIL BEIT DIN ESCORTS ME BACK HERE TO STAND TRIAL.
SOMETIME LATER, BACK IN THE CITY WHERE THE ACCIDENT OCCURRED...
LEAH, THE BEIT DIN CONVENED AND FOUND ME GUILTY OF KILLING SOMEONE UNINTENTIONALLY. THEIR REASONING WAS THAT, EVEN THOUGH I THOUGHT I TOOK "ALL" THE NECESSARY PRECAUTIONS, I SHOULD HAVE STATIONED A WATCHMAN AT THE ENTRANCE TO THE PATH.
I AM TO GO AT ONCE TO THE CITY OF REFUGE AND REMAIN THERE UNTIL THE KOHEN GADOL DIES. THERE ARE ESCORTS WAITING FOR ME AS WE SPEAK.

2. A PERSON WHO KILLS UNINTENTIONALLY BUT THE ACTION RESEMBLES SOMEONE WHO ACTED DELIBERATELY. (I.E. WHERE THERE WAS NEGLIGENCE OR THERE WAS RECKLESS BEHAVIOR.)
SUCH A PERSON IS NOT SENTENCED TO EXILE, BECAUSE HIS SIN IS VERY SEVERE AND EXILE CANNOT BRING HIM ATONEMENT, NOR DO THE CITIES OF REFUGE SERVE AS A SAFE HAVEN FOR HIM.
YOU KNOW THAT WALL YOUR TAKING DOWN IS RIGHT ON THE MAIN THOROUGHFARE. PEOPLE WALK ON THAT PATH ALL THE TIME. AREN'T YOU AFRAID SOMEONE MIGHT GET HURT BY A FLYING STONE?
I KNOW, BUT I AM ONLY BREAKING A LITTLE BIT, ENOUGH FOR A SMALL WINDOW. IT WILL TAKE ME NO TIME AT ALL...
BESIDES, I JUST CHECKED AND NO ONE IS COMING.
WHAT A LOVELY DAY FOR A STROLL.
AFTER THE MANSLAYER'S RETURN FROM CITY OF REFUGE, THE BEIT DIN CONVENED AND FOUND THIS INCIDENT TO BE COMPLETELY HIS FAULT. THE MANSLAYER SHOULD HAVE TAKEN THE NECESSARY PRECAUTIONS AND BECAUSE OF HIS RECKLESSNESS, SOMEONE IS DEAD.
FURTHERMORE, HE DOES NOT HAVE THE OPTION OF GOING TO A CITY OF REFUGE. HE WILL HAVE TO LIVE HIS ENTIRE LIFE LOOKING OVER HIS SHOULDER, WONDERING IF A BLOOD RELATIVE WILL TAKE HIS LIFE...

3. A PERSON WHO KILLS UNINTENTIONALLY WHOSE ACTS RESEMBLE THOSE CAUSED BY FORCES BEYOND HIS CONTROL. SUCH A PERSON IS NOT LIABLE TO BE EXILED, AND IF HE IS KILLED BY THE BLOOD AVENGER, THE BLOOD AVENGER WILL BE EXECUTED FOR MURDER.
PLEASE BE CAREFUL, I DON'T WANT ANYONE GETTING HURT...
WHO CAN GET HURT, THIS IS PRIVATE PROPERTY AND IT'S ONLY YOU AND I LIVING HERE.
ALL THE ENTRANCES ARE LOCKED AND I PLACED WARNING SIGNS THAT STATE "DANGER KEEP OUT!" THERE IS NOTHING MORE THAT I CAN DO TO SECURE THIS AREA.
I'VE NEVER USED THIS SHORTCUT BEFORE... I KNOW IT'S PRIVATE PROPERTY, BUT SINCE THEY ARE DOING CONSTRUCTION HERE, THE OWNER WON'T MIND. I WILL FIND A WAY TO PASS THROUGH HERE VERY QUICKLY AND UNNOTICED.
AFTER THE MANSLAYER'S RETURN FROM CITY OF REFUGE, THE BEIT DIN CONVENED AND FOUND HIM BLAMELESS ON ALL COUNTS.

THE **MOTHER** OF THE KOHEN GADOL WOULD PROVIDE FOOD AND CLOTHING FOR THOSE WHO ARE IN THE CITIES OF REFUGE, SO THEY WILL NOT PRAY FOR THEIR SON TO DIE.

RACHEL, YOU MADE SURE TO **PACK** THAT SPECIAL BRISKET I PREPARED.

[TH]E KOHEN GADOL IS **NOT** [CO]NSIDERED BLAMELESS [WH]EN PEOPLE ARE KILLED INTENTIONALLY, BECAUSE [HE] SHOULD HAVE **PRAYED** [TH]AT SUCH ACCIDENTS NOT [TA]KE PLACE.

YES MAMA, EVERYTHING GOT LOADED. I KNOW YOU WANT THE NEW RESIDENT AT THE CITY OF REFUGE TO FEEL AS **COMFORTABLE** AS POSSIBLE...

AND HE MUST RUN TO ONE OF THOSE CITIES, PRESENT HIMSELF AT THE [EN]TRANCE OF THE CITY GATES, AND PLEAD HIS CASE BEFORE THE [EL]DERS OF THAT CITY, AND THEY WILL ADMIT HIM INTO THE CITY AND [GI]VE HIM A PLACE TO LIVE AMONG THEM. 5 SHOULD THE BLOOD [A]VENGER PURSUE HIM, THEY CANNOT HAND THE KILLER OVER TO HIM, [SI]NCE HE KILLED THE OTHER PERSON UNINTENTIONALLY AND WAS NOT [HI]S ENEMY IN THE PAST. 6 HE WILL LIVE IN THAT CITY UNTIL HE CAN [ST]AND TRIAL BEFORE THE ASSEMBLY, (AND REMAIN THERE) UNTIL THE [D]EATH OF THE KOHEN GADOL WHO IS IN OFFICE AT THAT TIME. AFTER [TH]AT, THE KILLER MAY RETURN TO HIS HOMETOWN, FROM THE TOWN THAT [H]E ORIGINALLY FLED FROM.'

HOME SWEET HOME...

[Y]AKOV, IT'S REALLY [G]OOD TO SEE YOU BACK.

GOOD TO SEE YOU TOO, I'VE BEEN AWAY FOR A REALLY LONG TIME... I REALLY **MISSED** THIS PLACE.

EVERYTHING SEEMS SO DIFFERENT. ALL THE **YOUNG** PEOPLE HAVE GROWN UP...

ד וְנָס אֶל אַחַת מֵהֶעָרִים הָאֵלֶּה וְעָמַד פֶּתַח שַׁעַר הָעִיר וְדִבֶּר בְּאָזְנֵי זִקְנֵי הָעִיר הַהִיא אֶת דְּבָרָיו וְאָסְפוּ אֹתוֹ הָעִירָה אֲלֵיהֶם וְנָתְנוּ לוֹ מָקוֹם וְיָשַׁב עִמָּם. ה וְכִי יִרְדֹּף גֹּאֵל הַדָּם אַחֲרָיו וְלֹא יַסְגִּרוּ אֶת הָרֹצֵחַ בְּיָדוֹ כִּי בִּבְלִי דַעַת הִכָּה אֶת רֵעֵהוּ וְלֹא שֹׂנֵא הוּא לוֹ מִתְּמוֹל שִׁלְשׁוֹם. ו וְיָשַׁב בָּעִיר הַהִיא עַד עָמְדוֹ לִפְנֵי הָעֵדָה לַמִּשְׁפָּט עַד מוֹת הַכֹּהֵן הַגָּדוֹל אֲשֶׁר יִהְיֶה בַּיָּמִים הָהֵם אָז יָשׁוּב הָרוֹצֵחַ וּבָא אֶל עִירוֹ וְאֶל בֵּיתוֹ אֶל הָעִיר אֲשֶׁר נָס מִשָּׁם.

THE JEWISH COURT IS ***OBLIGATED*** TO CONSTRUCT ROADS LEADING TO THE CITIES OF REFUGE. THEY SHOULD BE BUILT PROPERLY AND MAINTAINED. ANY STUMBLING BLOCK AND OBSTACLE SHOULD BE REMOVED FROM THE ROADS.

THE WIDTH OF THE ROAD TO THE CITY OF REFUGE SHOULD NOT BE LESS THAN 32 CUBITS (APPROXIMATELY 50 FEET). SIGNS STATING "REFUGE, REFUGE," SHOULD BE WRITTEN AT INTERSECTIONS, SO THAT THE UNINTENTIONAL KILLERS KNOW IN WHAT DIRECTION TO GO.

EVERY YEAR, ON THE FIFTEENTH OF ADAR, THE COURT WOULD SEND OUT EMISSARIES TO ***INSPECT*** THE ROADS LEADING TO THE CITIES OF REFUGE. WHEREVER THEY FOUND FLAWS, THEY WOULD HAVE THEM REPAIRED. IF A COURT PROCRASTINATED REGARDING THIS MATTER, IT IS CONSIDERED AS IF THEY HAVE SHED BLOOD.

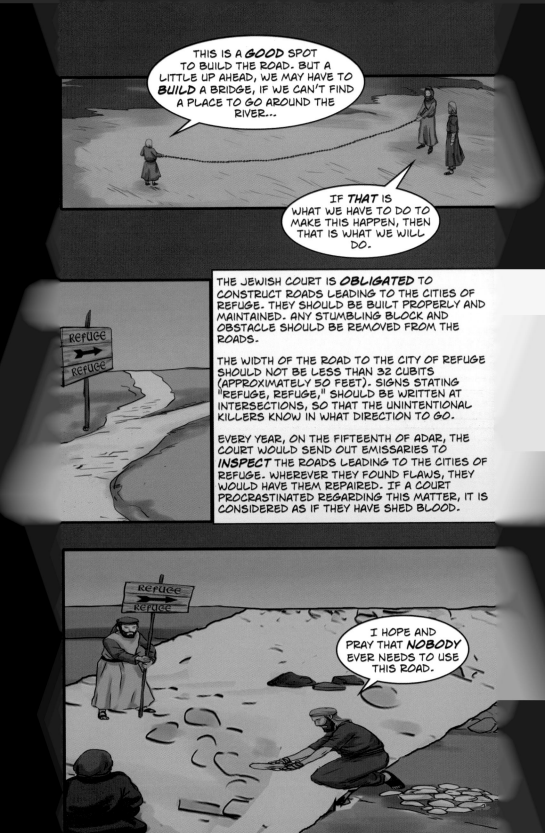

7 AND THEY SET APART KEDESH IN GALILEE IN THE HILL-COUNTRY OF NAPHTALI, AND SHECHEM IN THE HILL-COUNTRY OF EPHRAIM, AND KIRIAT-ARBA, WHICH IS CHEVRON, IN THE HILL-COUNTRY OF YEHUDAH. 8 AND ACROSS THE YARDEN AT YERICHO EASTWARD, THEY ASSIGNED BEZER IN THE WILDERNESS, IN THE PLATEAU FROM THE TRIBE OF REUVEN, AND RAMOT IN GILEAD FROM THE TRIBE OF GAD, AND GOLAN IN BASHAN FROM THE TRIBE OF MENASHE. 9 THESE WERE THE APPOINTED CITIES FOR ALL THE CHILDREN OF YISRAEL, AND FOR THE FOREIGNERS WHO LIVE AMONG THEM, THAT ANYONE WHO UNINTENTIONALLY KILLS A PERSON MAY FLEE THERE, AND NOT DIE BY THE HAND OF THE BLOOD AVENGER BEFORE STANDING TRIAL BY THE ASSEMBLY.
TO HELP IDENTIFY THE LOCATIONS ON THE MAP, THE VERSE NUMBERS ARE REPRESENTED IN RED.
Mount Chermon
Tzidon
Geshure
8
Golan
Kinneret
Ashtarot
Edrei
זבולן
Megiddo
Dor
Taanach
Beit Shean
מנשה
Gilead
Salcha
8
Ramot-Gilead
North
מנשה
Yarden
Yaabok
Shechem
אפרים
גד
דן
עמון
Ashdod
Cheshbon
Ammon
8
Betzer
Akron
Yerushalayim
Ashkelon
Bezek
Beit Hayesimot
ראובן
יהודה
Chevron
Sichon
Aroer ?
Arnon
Dvir (Kiryat Sefer)
Tzfat Chorma
Araba Sea / Dead Sea
מואב
שמעון
Beer Sheva
נגב
ז וַיַּקְדִּשׁוּ אֶת קֶדֶשׁ בַּגָּלִיל בְּהַר נַפְתָּלִי וְאֶת שְׁכֶם בְּהַר אֶפְרָיִם וְאֶת קִרְיַת אַרְבַּע
הִיא חֶבְרוֹן בְּהַר יְהוּדָה. ח וּמֵעֵבֶר לְיַרְדֵּן יְרִיחוֹ מִזְרָחָה נָתְנוּ אֶת בֶּצֶר בַּמִּדְבָּר
בַּמִּישֹׁר מִמַּטֵּה רְאוּבֵן וְאֶת רָאמֹת בַּגִּלְעָד מִמַּטֵּה גָד וְאֶת גלון (גּוֹלָן) בַּבָּשָׁן מִמַּטֵּה
מְנַשֶּׁה. ט אֵלֶּה הָיוּ עָרֵי הַמּוּעָדָה לְכֹל בְּנֵי יִשְׂרָאֵל וְלַגֵּר הַגָּר בְּתוֹכָם לָנוּס שָׁמָּה
כָּל מַכֵּה נֶפֶשׁ בִּשְׁגָגָה וְלֹא יָמוּת בְּיַד גֹּאֵל הַדָּם עַד עָמְדוֹ לִפְנֵי הָעֵדָה.

1 THE HEADS OF THE FATHERS HOUSES OF THE LEVIIM CAME NEAR TO ELAZAR, THE KOHEN, AND TO YEHOSHUA, THE SON OF NUN, AND TO THE HEADS OF THE FATHERS HOUSES OF THE TRIBES OF THE CHILDREN OF YISRAEL. 2 AND THEY SPOKE TO THEM AT SHILOH, IN THE LAND OF CANAAN, SAYING,

HASHEM COMMANDED THROUGH MOSHE TO GIVE US CITIES TO DWELL IN, WITH OPEN LAND FOR OUR CATTLE.

3 AND THE CHILDREN OF YISRAEL, IN ACCORDANCE WITH THE COMMAND OF HASHEM, ASSIGNED TO THE LEVIIM, OUT OF THEIR OWN PORTIONS, THE FOLLOWING TOWNS WITH THEIR PASTURES. 4 AND THE LOTTERY FELL TO THE FAMILIES OF THE KOHATIES; AND THE CHILDREN OF AHARON HAKOHEN, WHO WERE OF THE LEVIIM, THERE FELL THE LOTTERY, THIRTEEN CITIES FROM THE TRIBE OF YEHUDAH, THE TRIBE OF SHIMON, AND THE TRIBE OF BINYAMIN. 5 AND THE REST OF THE CHILDREN OF KOHAT FELL BY THE LOTTERY, TEN CITIES FROM THE FAMILIES OF THE TRIBE OF EPHRAIM, THE TRIBE OF DAN, AND THE HALF-TRIBE OF MENASHE. 6 AND TO THE CHILDREN OF GERSHON FELL BY THE LOTTERY THIRTEEN CITIES FROM THE FAMILIES OF THE TRIBE OF YISSACHAR, THE TRIBE OF ASHER, NAPHTALI AND THE HALF-TRIBE OF MENASHE IN BASHAN. 7 THE CHILDREN OF MERARI ACCORDING TO THEIR FAMILIES HAD TWELVE CITIES, FROM THE TRIBE OF REUVEN, THE TRIBE OF GAD, AND FROM THE TRIBE OF ZEVULUM.

THE LEVIIM WERE ***SINGLED*** OUT TO SERVE HASHEM AND PERFORM SERVICES TO HIM, TO TEACH HIS UPRIGHT WAYS AND JUST LAWS TO THE MASSES. THEY WERE SEPARATED FROM WORLDLY AFFAIRS: THEY FOUGHT NO BATTLES, THEY INHERITED NO LAND, AND THEY EARNED NOTHING BY MEANS OF THEIR PHYSICAL ACTIVITIES. THEY ARE INDEED THE ARMY OF HASHEM.

THE ***DIVISION*** OF LAND FOR THE TRIBE OF LEVI WAS DIVIDED INTO 4 PORTIONS PARALLEL TO THE LEVEL OF HOLINESS OF EACH LEVITE FAMILY REGARDING THEIR SERVICE OF THE MISHKAN.

THE CHILDREN OF AHARON HAKOHEN WERE THE CLOSET TO THE MISHKAN AND MIKDASH THEY RECEIVED LAND BY YEHUDA, SHIMON, AND BINYAMIN CLOSEST TO THE MIKDASH.

CHILDREN OF KOHAT WERE NEXT AS THEY WERE ALSO VERY CLOSE TO THE MISHKAN AND MIKDASH, AS THEY CARRIED THE ARON, SHULCHAN AND THE VESSELS AND INSTRUMENTS OF THE MIKDASH. THEY RECEIVED LAND BY YOSEF'S PORTION (DAN) CLOSEST TO BINYAMIN.

THE CHILDREN OF GERSHON CARRIED THE TENT, THE COVERINGS, THE DRAPING'S AND ALL THE ITEMS SURROUNDING THE HOLIEST VESSELS. THEY RECEIVED LAND BY YISASCHAR AND ASHER THAT WERE CLOSEST TO YOSEF.

THE CHILDREN OF MERARI WERE THE LAST, AS THEY CARRIED THE WOODEN PLANKS, THE POLES. SOCKETS ETC. THEY RECEIVED LAND BY REUVAN/GAD WHO LIVED AT THE FURTHEST PART OF YISRAEL BY THE YARDEN.

8 AND THE CHILDREN OF YISRAEL ASSIGNED THOSE CITIES WITH THE PASTURES, BY THE LOTTERY TO THE LEVIIM, AS HASHEM HAD COMMANDED THROUGH MOSHE. 9 FROM THE TRIBE OF YEHUDA, AND FROM THE TRIBE OF SHIMON WERE ASSIGNED THE FOLLOWING CITIES WHICH WERE LISTED BY NAME. 10 AND THEY WENT TO THE DESCENDENTS OF AHARON AMONG THE FAMILIES OF KOHAT, THE CHILDREN OF LEVI, FOR THE FIRST LOT HAD FALLEN TO THEM.

א וַיִּגְּשׁוּ רָאשֵׁי אֲבוֹת הַלְוִיִּם אֶל אֶלְעָזָר הַכֹּהֵן וְאֶל יְהוֹשֻׁעַ בִּן נוּן וְאֶל רָאשֵׁי אֲבוֹת הַמַּטּוֹת לִבְנֵי יִשְׂרָאֵל.
ב וַיְדַבְּרוּ אֲלֵיהֶם בְּשִׁלֹה בְּאֶרֶץ כְּנַעַן לֵאמֹר ה' צִוָּה בְיַד מֹשֶׁה לָתֶת לָנוּ עָרִים לָשָׁבֶת וּמִגְרְשֵׁיהֶן לִבְהֶמְתֵּנוּ.
ג וַיִּתְּנוּ בְנֵי יִשְׂרָאֵל לַלְוִיִּם מִנַּחֲלָתָם אֶל פִּי ה' אֶת הֶעָרִים הָאֵלֶּה וְאֶת מִגְרְשֵׁיהֶן. **ד** וַיֵּצֵא הַגּוֹרָל
לְמִשְׁפְּחֹת הַקְּהָתִי וַיְהִי לִבְנֵי אַהֲרֹן הַכֹּהֵן מִן הַלְוִיִּם מִמַּטֵּה יְהוּדָה וּמִמַּטֵּה הַשִּׁמְעֹנִי וּמִמַּטֵּה בִנְיָמִן
בַּגּוֹרָל עָרִים שְׁלֹשׁ עֶשְׂרֵה. **ה** וְלִבְנֵי קְהָת הַנּוֹתָרִים מִמִּשְׁפְּחֹת מַטֵּה אֶפְרַיִם וּמִמַּטֵּה דָן וּמֵחֲצִי מַטֵּה
מְנַשֶּׁה בַּגּוֹרָל עָרִים עָשֶׂר. **ו** וְלִבְנֵי גֵרְשׁוֹן מִמִּשְׁפְּחוֹת מַטֵּה יִשָּׂשכָר וּמִמַּטֵּה אָשֵׁר וּמִמַּטֵּה נַפְתָּלִי וּמֵחֲצִי
מַטֵּה מְנַשֶּׁה בַבָּשָׁן בַּגּוֹרָל עָרִים שְׁלֹשׁ עֶשְׂרֵה. **ז** לִבְנֵי מְרָרִי לְמִשְׁפְּחֹתָם מִמַּטֵּה רְאוּבֵן וּמִמַּטֵּה גָד וּמִמַּטֵּה
זְבוּלֻן עָרִים שְׁתֵּים עֶשְׂרֵה. **ח** וַיִּתְּנוּ בְנֵי יִשְׂרָאֵל לַלְוִיִּם אֶת הֶעָרִים הָאֵלֶּה וְאֶת מִגְרְשֵׁיהֶן כַּאֲשֶׁר צִוָּה ה'
בְּיַד מֹשֶׁה בַּגּוֹרָל. ט וַיִּתְּנוּ מִמַּטֵּה בְּנֵי יְהוּדָה וּמִמַּטֵּה בְּנֵי שִׁמְעוֹן אֵת הֶעָרִים הָאֵלֶּה אֲשֶׁר יִקְרָא אֶתְהֶן
בְּשֵׁם. **י** וַיְהִי לִבְנֵי אַהֲרֹן מִמִּשְׁפְּחוֹת הַקְּהָתִי מִבְּנֵי לֵוִי כִּי לָהֶם הָיָה הַגּוֹרָל רִאישֹׁנָה.

11 AND THEY GAVE THEM KIRYAT ARBA, (ARBA WAS) THE FATHER OF ANAK WHICH IS CHEVRON IN THE HILL COUNTRY OF YEHUDA, TOGETHER WITH THE PASTURES AROUND IT. 12 THEY GAVE THE FIELDS OF THE VILLAGES OF THE TOWN TO KALEV THE SON OF YEPHUNEH AS HIS POSSESSION. 13 AND TO THE CHILDREN OF AHARON THE KOHEN THEY GAVE CHEVRON TOGETHER WITH THE PASTURES AROUND IT, THE CITY OF REFUGE FOR THE MANSLAYER, AND LIBNAH TOGETHER WITH THE PASTURES AROUND IT. 14 AND YATIR TOGETHER WITH THE PASTURES AROUND IT, AND ESHTEMOA TOGETHER WITH THE PASTURES AROUND IT. 15 AND CHOLON TOGETHER WITH THE PASTURES AROUND IT, AND DEVIR TOGETHER WITH THE PASTURES AROUND IT. 16 AND AYIM TOGETHER WITH THE PASTURES AROUND IT, AND YUTAH TOGETHER WITH THE PASTURES AROUND IT AND BEIT SHEMESH TOGETHER WITH THE PASTURES AROUND IT; NINE CITIES FROM THOSE TWO TRIBES. 17 AND FROM THE TRIBE OF BINYAMIN, GIVEON TOGETHER WITH THE PASTURES AROUND IT, GEVA TOGETHER WITH THE PASTURES AROUND IT. 18 ANATOT TOGETHER WITH THE PASTURES AROUND IT, AND ALMON TOGETHER WITH THE PASTURES AROUND IT; FOUR CITIES. 19 ALL THE CITIES OF THE CHILDREN OF AHARON, THE KOHANIM, WERE THIRTEEN CITIES TOGETHER WITH THE PASTURES AROUND IT. 20 AS FOR THE OTHER FAMILIES OF KOHAT, THE REMAINING LEVIIM THAT DESCENDED FROM KOHAT, THE CITIES FROM THEIR LOTTERY WERE FROM THE TRIBE OF EPHRAIM. 21 AND THEY GAVE THEM SHECHEM TOGETHER WITH THE PASTURES AROUND IT IN THE HILL COUNTRY OF EPHRAIM, THE CITY OF REFUGE FOR THE MANSLAYER, AND GEZER TOGETHER WITH THE PASTURES AROUND IT. 22 KIVTZAYIM TOGETHER WITH THE PASTURES AROUND IT, AND BEIT-CHORON TOGETHER WITH THE PASTURES AROUND IT; FOUR CITIES. 23 AND FROM THE TRIBE OF DAN, ELTEKE TOGETHER WITH THE PASTURES AROUND IT, GIBTON TOGETHER WITH THE PASTURES AROUND IT. 24 AYALON TOGETHER WITH THE PASTURES AROUND IT, GAT RIMON TOGETHER WITH THE PASTURES AROUND IT, FOUR CITIES. 25 AND FROM THE HALF-TRIBE OF MENASHE, TAANACH TOGETHER WITH THE PASTURES AROUND IT, AND GAT RIMON TOGETHER WITH THE PASTURES AROUND IT, TWO CITIES. 26 ALL THE CITIES FOR THE REMAINING FAMILIES OF KOHAT TOTALLED TEN WITH THEIR PASTURES.

יא וַיִּתְּנוּ לָהֶם אֶת קִרְיַת אַרְבַּע אֲבִי הָעֲנוֹק הִיא חֶבְרוֹן בְּהַר יְהוּדָה וְאֶת מִגְרָשֶׁהָ סְבִיבֹתֶיהָ. **יב** וְאֶת
שְׂדֵה הָעִיר וְאֶת חֲצֵרֶיהָ נָתְנוּ לְכָלֵב בֶּן יְפֻנֶּה בַּאֲחֻזָּתוֹ. **יג** וְלִבְנֵי אַהֲרֹן הַכֹּהֵן נָתְנוּ אֶת עִיר מִקְלַט הָרֹצֵחַ
אֶת חֶבְרוֹן וְאֶת מִגְרָשֶׁהָ וְאֶת לִבְנָה וְאֶת מִגְרָשֶׁהָ. **יד** וְאֶת יַתִּר וְאֶת מִגְרָשֶׁהָ וְאֶת אֶשְׁתְּמֹעַ וְאֶת מִגְרָשֶׁהָ.
טו וְאֶת חֹלֹן וְאֶת מִגְרָשֶׁהָ וְאֶת דְּבִר וְאֶת מִגְרָשֶׁהָ. **טז** וְאֶת עַיִן וְאֶת מִגְרָשֶׁהָ וְאֶת יֻטָּה וְאֶת מִגְרָשֶׁהָ אֶת
בֵּית שֶׁמֶשׁ וְאֶת מִגְרָשֶׁהָ עָרִים תֵּשַׁע מֵאֵת שְׁנֵי הַשְּׁבָטִים הָאֵלֶּה. **יז** וּמִמַּטֵּה בִנְיָמִין אֶת גִּבְעוֹן וְאֶת
מִגְרָשֶׁהָ אֶת גֶּבַע וְאֶת מִגְרָשֶׁהָ. **יח** אֶת עֲנָתוֹת וְאֶת מִגְרָשֶׁהָ וְאֶת עַלְמוֹן וְאֶת מִגְרָשֶׁהָ עָרִים אַרְבַּע. **יט**
כָּל עָרֵי בְנֵי אַהֲרֹן הַכֹּהֲנִים שְׁלֹשׁ עֶשְׂרֵה עָרִים וּמִגְרְשֵׁיהֶן. **כ** וּלְמִשְׁפְּחוֹת בְּנֵי קְהָת הַלְוִיִּם הַנּוֹתָרִים מִבְּנֵי
קְהָת וַיְהִי עָרֵי גוֹרָלָם מִמַּטֵּה אֶפְרָיִם. **כא** וַיִּתְּנוּ לָהֶם אֶת עִיר מִקְלַט הָרֹצֵחַ אֶת שְׁכֶם וְאֶת מִגְרָשֶׁהָ בְּהַר
אֶפְרָיִם וְאֶת גֶּזֶר וְאֶת מִגְרָשֶׁהָ. **כב** וְאֶת קִבְצַיִם וְאֶת מִגְרָשֶׁהָ וְאֶת בֵּית חוֹרֹן וְאֶת מִגְרָשֶׁהָ עָרִים אַרְבַּע.
כג וּמִמַּטֵּה דָן אֶת אֶלְתְּקֵא וְאֶת מִגְרָשֶׁהָ אֶת גִּבְּתוֹן וְאֶת מִגְרָשֶׁהָ. **כד** אֶת אַיָּלוֹן וְאֶת מִגְרָשֶׁהָ אֶת גַּת רִמּוֹן
וְאֶת מִגְרָשֶׁהָ עָרִים אַרְבַּע. **כה** וּמִמַּחֲצִית מַטֵּה מְנַשֶּׁה אֶת תַּעְנַךְ וְאֶת מִגְרָשֶׁהָ וְאֶת גַּת רִמּוֹן וְאֶת
מִגְרָשֶׁהָ עָרִים שְׁתָּיִם. **כו** כָּל עָרִים עֶשֶׂר וּמִגְרְשֵׁיהֶן לְמִשְׁפְּחוֹת בְּנֵי קְהָת הַנּוֹתָרִים.

27 AND TO THE CHILDREN OF GERSHON, OF THE FAMILIES OF THE LEVIIM,
FROM THE HALF-TRIBE OF MENASHE THEY GAVE GOLAN IN BASHAN
TOGETHER WITH THE PASTURES AROUND IT, AS THE CITY OF REFUGE FOR THE
MANSLAYER; AND BEESHTERAH TOGETHER WITH THE PASTURES AROUND IT,
TWO CITIES. 28 AND FROM THE TRIBE OF YISSACHAR, KISHYON TOGETHER
WITH THE PASTURES AROUND IT, DAVRAT TOGETHER WITH THE PASTURES
AROUND IT, 29 YARMUT TOGETHER WITH THE PASTURES AROUND IT, EN GANIM
TOGETHER WITH THE PASTURES AROUND IT, FOUR CITIES. 30 AND FROM THE
TRIBE OF ASHER, MISHAL TOGETHER WITH THE PASTURES AROUND IT, AVDON
TOGETHER WITH THE PASTURES AROUND IT, 31 CHELKAT TOGETHER WITH THE
PASTURES AROUND IT, AND RECHOV TOGETHER WITH THE PASTURES AROUND
IT, FOUR CITIES. 32 AND FROM THE TRIBE OF NAPHTALI, KEDESH IN GALILEE
TOGETHER WITH THE PASTURES AROUND IT, AS THE CITY OF REFUGE FOR THE
MANSLAYER, AND CHAMOT DOR TOGETHER WITH THE PASTURES AROUND IT,
AND KARTAN TOGETHER WITH THE PASTURES AROUND IT, THREE CITIES. 33 ALL
THE CITIES OF THE GERSHONIE ACCORDING TO THEIR FAMILIES WERE
THIRTEEN CITIES TOGETHER WITH THE PASTURES AROUND IT. 34 AND TO THE
FAMILIES OF THE CHILDREN OF MERARI, THE REST OF THE LEVIIM, FROM THE
TRIBE OF ZEVULUN, YAKNEAM TOGETHER WITH THE PASTURES AROUND IT,
AND KARTAH TOGETHER WITH THE PASTURES AROUND IT. 35 DIMNAH
TOGETHER WITH THE PASTURES AROUND IT, NAHALAL TOGETHER WITH THE
PASTURES AROUND IT, FOUR CITIES. 36 AND FROM THE TRIBE OF GAD,
RAMOT IN GILEAD TOGETHER WITH THE PASTURES AROUND IT, AS THE CITY OF
REFUGE FOR THE MANSLAYER, AND MACHANAIM TOGETHER WITH THE
PASTURES AROUND IT. 37 CHESHBON TOGETHER WITH THE PASTURES AROUND
IT, YAZER TOGETHER WITH THE PASTURES AROUND IT, FOUR CITIES IN ALL. 38
ALL THESE WERE THE CITIES OF THE CHILDREN OF MERARI ACCORDING TO
THEIR FAMILIES, THE REST OF THE FAMILIES OF THE LEVIIM; AND THEIR
PORTION WAS TWELVE CITIES. 39 THE CITIES OF THE LEVIIM WITHIN THE
TERRITORY OF THE CHILDREN OF YISRAEL TOTALED FORTY-EIGHT CITIES AND
THEIR PASTURELANDS. 40 THESE CITIES, EVERY ONE TOGETHER WITH THE
PASTURES AROUND IT, SO IT WILL BE WITH ALL THESE CITIES. 41 SO HASHEM
GAVE TO YISRAEL ALL THE LAND WHICH HE SWORE TO GIVE TO THEIR
FATHERS; AND THEY POSSESSED IT, AND LIVED IN IT. 42 AND HASHEM GAVE
THEM REST (FROM THEIR ENEMIES) ON ALL SIDES, JUST AS HE SWORE TO
THEIR FATHERS, NOT ONE OF THEIR ENEMIES STOOD UP AGAINST THEM,
FOR HASHEM HAD GIVEN ALL OF THEIR ENEMIES INTO THEIR HANDS 43
NOT ONE OF THE GOOD THINGS THAT HASHEM HAD PROMISED TO THE
CHILDREN OF YISRAEL WAS LACKING, EVERYTHING WAS FULFILLED.

כז וְלִבְנֵי גֵרְשׁוֹן מִמִּשְׁפְּחֹת הַלְוִיִּם מֵחֲצִי מַטֵּה מְנַשֶּׁה אֶת עִיר מִקְלַט הָרֹצֵחַ אֶת גלון (גּוֹלָן)
בַּבָּשָׁן וְאֶת מִגְרָשֶׁהָ וְאֶת בְּעֶשְׁתְּרָה וְאֶת מִגְרָשֶׁהָ עָרִים שְׁתָּיִם. **כח** וּמִמַּטֵּה יִשָּׂשכָר אֶת
קִשְׁיוֹן וְאֶת מִגְרָשֶׁהָ אֶת דָּבְרַת וְאֶת מִגְרָשֶׁהָ. **כט** אֶת יַרְמוּת וְאֶת מִגְרָשֶׁהָ אֶת עֵין גַּנִּים וְאֶת
מִגְרָשֶׁהָ עָרִים אַרְבַּע. **ל** וּמִמַּטֵּה אָשֵׁר אֶת מִשְׁאָל וְאֶת מִגְרָשֶׁהָ אֶת עַבְדּוֹן וְאֶת מִגְרָשֶׁהָ.
לא אֶת חֶלְקַת וְאֶת מִגְרָשֶׁהָ וְאֶת רְחֹב וְאֶת מִגְרָשֶׁהָ עָרִים אַרְבַּע. **לב** וּמִמַּטֵּה נַפְתָּלִי אֶת
עִיר מִקְלַט הָרֹצֵחַ אֶת קֶדֶשׁ בַּגָּלִיל וְאֶת מִגְרָשֶׁהָ וְאֶת חַמֹּת דֹּאר וְאֶת מִגְרָשֶׁהָ וְאֶת קַרְתָּן
וְאֶת מִגְרָשֶׁהָ עָרִים שָׁלֹשׁ. **לג** כָּל עָרֵי הַגֵּרְשֻׁנִּי לְמִשְׁפְּחֹתָם שְׁלֹשׁ עֶשְׂרֵה עִיר וּמִגְרְשֵׁיהֶן.
לד וּלְמִשְׁפְּחוֹת בְּנֵי מְרָרִי הַלְוִיִּם הַנּוֹתָרִים מֵאֵת מַטֵּה זְבוּלֻן אֶת יָקְנְעָם וְאֶת מִגְרָשֶׁהָ אֶת
קַרְתָּה וְאֶת מִגְרָשֶׁהָ. **לה** אֶת דִּמְנָה וְאֶת מִגְרָשֶׁהָ אֶת נַהֲלָל וְאֶת מִגְרָשֶׁהָ עָרִים אַרְבַּע. **לו**
וּמִמַּטֵּה גָד אֶת עִיר מִקְלַט הָרֹצֵחַ אֶת רָמֹת בַּגִּלְעָד וְאֶת מִגְרָשֶׁהָ וְאֶת מַחֲנַיִם וְאֶת מִגְרָשֶׁהָ.
לז אֶת חֶשְׁבּוֹן וְאֶת מִגְרָשֶׁהָ אֶת יַעְזֵר וְאֶת מִגְרָשֶׁהָ כָּל עָרִים אַרְבַּע. **לח** כָּל הֶעָרִים לִבְנֵי
מְרָרִי לְמִשְׁפְּחֹתָם הַנּוֹתָרִים מִמִּשְׁפְּחוֹת הַלְוִיִּם וַיְהִי גּוֹרָלָם עָרִים שְׁתֵּים עֶשְׂרֵה. **לט** כֹּל עָרֵי
הַלְוִיִּם בְּתוֹךְ אֲחֻזַּת בְּנֵי יִשְׂרָאֵל עָרִים אַרְבָּעִים וּשְׁמֹנֶה וּמִגְרְשֵׁיהֶן. **מ** תִּהְיֶינָה הֶעָרִים
הָאֵלֶּה עִיר עִיר וּמִגְרָשֶׁיהָ סְבִיבֹתֶיהָ כֵּן לְכָל הֶעָרִים הָאֵלֶּה. **מא** וַיִּתֵּן ה' לְיִשְׂרָאֵל אֶת כָּל
הָאָרֶץ אֲשֶׁר נִשְׁבַּע לָתֵת לַאֲבוֹתָם וַיִּרָשׁוּהָ וַיֵּשְׁבוּ בָהּ. **מב** וַיָּנַח ה' לָהֶם מִסָּבִיב כְּכֹל אֲשֶׁר
נִשְׁבַּע לַאֲבוֹתָם וְלֹא עָמַד אִישׁ בִּפְנֵיהֶם מִכָּל אֹיְבֵיהֶם אֵת כָּל אֹיְבֵיהֶם נָתַן ה' בְּיָדָם. **מג**
לֹא נָפַל דָּבָר מִכֹּל הַדָּבָר הַטּוֹב אֲשֶׁר דִּבֶּר ה' אֶל בֵּית יִשְׂרָאֵל הַכֹּל בָּא.

North
Mount Chermon
Tzidon
Maacha
Beit Anat
Chelba
Beit Shemesh (North
Tzur
Kedesh
Avdon
Achziv
Chelkat
Bashan
Akko
Rechov
Mishal
Geshure
Nahalal
Kartan
Kinneret
Golan
27
Ashtarot
Charoshet
Hagoyim
זבולון
Davrat
Ein-Ganim
Kishyon
Yarmut
Edrei
Yakneam
Megiddo
Dor
Taanach
Beit Shean
מנשה
Gilead
Salcha
Ramot-Gilead
מנשה
Yarden
Yaabok
גד
אפרים
דן
Machayim
Yazer
עמון
Gat-Rimon
Ayalon
Ashdod
Cheshbon
Ammon
Yerushalayim
ירושלים
Bezek
Beit Hayesimot
Ashkelon
ראובן
יהודה
Chevron
Sichon
Aroer ?
Arnon
Dvir (Kiryat Sefer)
Tzfat Chorma
מואב
שמעון
Beer Sheva
נגב
Araba Sea / Dead Sea
מדבר צין

YEHOSHUA CHAPTER 22
יהושע פרק כב

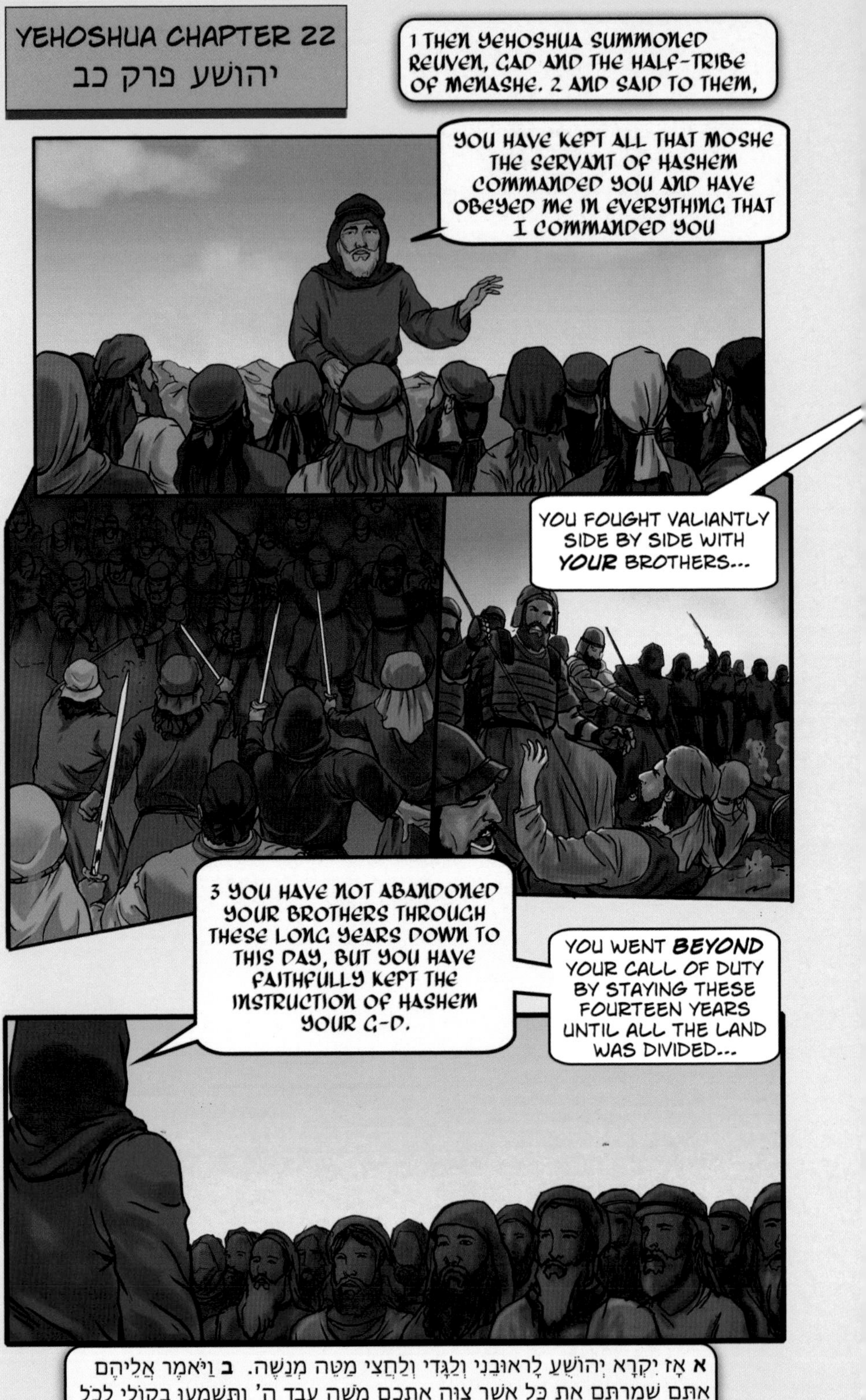

א אָז יִקְרָא יְהוֹשֻׁעַ לָראוּבֵנִי וְלַגָּדִי וְלַחֲצִי מַטֵּה מְנַשֶּׁה. **ב** וַיֹּאמֶר אֲלֵיהֶם
אַתֶּם שְׁמַרְתֶּם אֵת כָּל אֲשֶׁר צִוָּה אֶתְכֶם מֹשֶׁה עֶבֶד ה' וַתִּשְׁמְעוּ בְקוֹלִי לְכֹל
אֲשֶׁר צִוִּיתִי אֶתְכֶם. **ג** לֹא עֲזַבְתֶּם אֶת אֲחֵיכֶם זֶה יָמִים רַבִּים עַד הַיּוֹם הַזֶּה
וּשְׁמַרְתֶּם אֶת מִשְׁמֶרֶת מִצְוַת ה' אֱלֹקֵיכֶם.

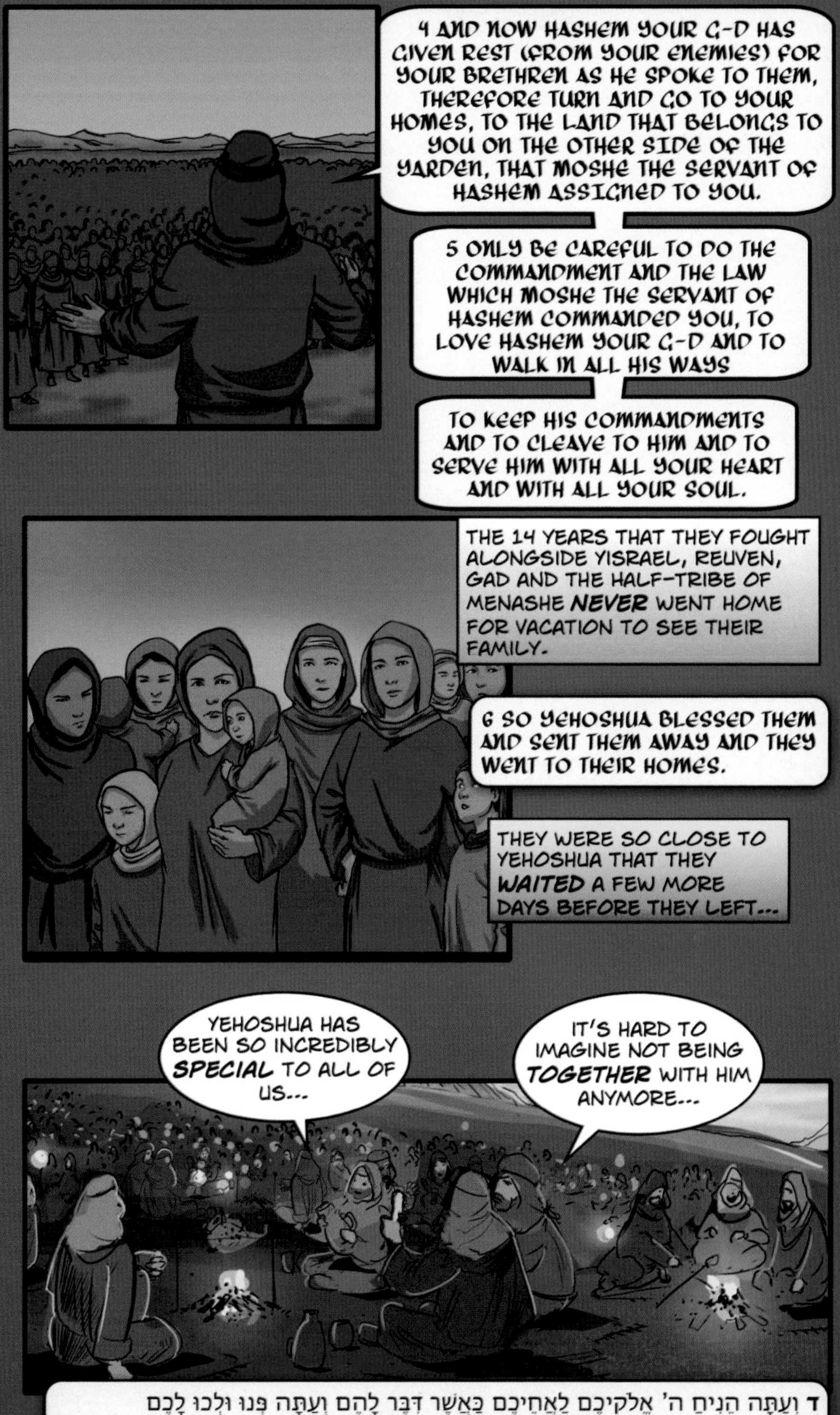
4 AND NOW HASHEM YOUR G-D HAS GIVEN REST (FROM YOUR ENEMIES) FOR YOUR BRETHREN AS HE SPOKE TO THEM, THEREFORE TURN AND GO TO YOUR HOMES, TO THE LAND THAT BELONGS TO YOU ON THE OTHER SIDE OF THE YARDEN, THAT MOSHE THE SERVANT OF HASHEM ASSIGNED TO YOU.
5 ONLY BE CAREFUL TO DO THE COMMANDMENT AND THE LAW WHICH MOSHE THE SERVANT OF HASHEM COMMANDED YOU, TO LOVE HASHEM YOUR G-D AND TO WALK IN ALL HIS WAYS
TO KEEP HIS COMMANDMENTS AND TO CLEAVE TO HIM AND TO SERVE HIM WITH ALL YOUR HEART AND WITH ALL YOUR SOUL.
THE 14 YEARS THAT THEY FOUGHT ALONGSIDE YISRAEL, REUVEN, GAD AND THE HALF-TRIBE OF MENASHE **NEVER** WENT HOME FOR VACATION TO SEE THEIR FAMILY.
6 SO YEHOSHUA BLESSED THEM AND SENT THEM AWAY AND THEY WENT TO THEIR HOMES.
THEY WERE SO CLOSE TO YEHOSHUA THAT THEY **WAITED** A FEW MORE DAYS BEFORE THEY LEFT...
YEHOSHUA HAS BEEN SO INCREDIBLY **SPECIAL** TO ALL OF US...
IT'S HARD TO IMAGINE NOT BEING **TOGETHER** WITH HIM ANYMORE...

ד וְעַתָּה הֵנִיחַ ה' אֱלֹקיכֶם לַאֲחֵיכֶם כַּאֲשֶׁר דִּבֶּר לָהֶם וְעַתָּה פְּנוּ וּלְכוּ לָכֶם
לְאָהֳלֵיכֶם אֶל אֶרֶץ אֲחֻזַּתְכֶם אֲשֶׁר נָתַן לָכֶם מֹשֶׁה עֶבֶד ה' בְּעֵבֶר הַיַּרְדֵּן. **ה** רַק שִׁמְרוּ
מְאֹד לַעֲשׂוֹת אֶת הַמִּצְוָה וְאֶת הַתּוֹרָה אֲשֶׁר צִוָּה אֶתְכֶם מֹשֶׁה עֶבֶד ה' לְאַהֲבָה אֶת
ה' אֱלֹקיכֶם וְלָלֶכֶת בְּכָל דְּרָכָיו וְלִשְׁמֹר מִצְוֹתָיו וּלְדָבְקָה בוֹ וּלְעָבְדוֹ בְּכָל לְבַבְכֶם וּבְכָל
נַפְשְׁכֶם. **ו** וַיְבָרְכֵם יְהוֹשֻׁעַ וַיְשַׁלְּחֵם וַיֵּלְכוּ אֶל אָהֳלֵיהֶם.

YEHOSHUA FELT VERY CLOSE AS WELL. SO MUCH SO THAT HE **ESCORTED** THEM ALL THE WAY TO THE YARDEN.

WE **CAN'T** ALLOW YEHOSHUA TO LEAVE UNACCOMPANIED.
I AGREE, I WILL **ESCORT** HIM.

I WILL **ESCORT** HIM...
NO, I WILL **ESCORT** HIM...
I WILL ESCORT HIM...

ULTIMATELY, EVERYONE FROM REUVEN, GAD AND THE HALF-TRIBE OF MENASHE **RETURNED** WITH YEHOSHUA TO SHILO TO BID THEIR FINAL FAREWELL AND TO RECEIVE ONE ADDITIONAL BLESSING.
7 NOW TO THE HALF-TRIBE OF MENASHE MOSHE HAD GIVEN INHERITANCE IN BASHAN BUT TO THE OTHER HALF, YEHOSHUA ASSIGNED (TERRITORY) ON THE WEST SIDE OF THE YARDEN WITH THEIR BROTHERS. FURTHERMORE WHEN YEHOSHUA SENT THEM AWAY TO THEIR HOMES HE BLESSED THEM
8 AND SPOKE TO THEM SAYING
RETURN TO YOUR HOMES WITH GREAT WEALTH, WITH TREMENDOUS AMOUNT OF LIVESTOCK, WITH SILVER AND GOLD, WITH COPPER AND IRON, WITH A HUGE QUANTITY OF CLOTHING, AND DIVIDE THE SPOIL OF YOUR ENEMIES WITH YOUR BROTHERS.
9 SO THE CHILDREN OF REUVEN AND GAD AND HALF-TRIBE OF MENASHE LEFT THE CHILDREN OF YISRAEL AT SHILOH, IN THE LAND OF CANAAN AND MADE THEIR WAY BACK TO THE LAND OF GILEAD, TO THE LAND THAT BELONGS TO THEM, WHICH THEY ACQUIRED BY THE COMMAND OF HASHEM THROUGH MOSHE.
DURING THE 14 YEARS OF SEPARATION, BOTH THE FATHERS AND SONS VOWED **NOT** TO CUT THEIR HAIR UNTIL THEY WERE REUNITED...

ז וְלַחֲצִי שֵׁבֶט הַמְנַשֶּׁה נָתַן מֹשֶׁה בַּבָּשָׁן וּלְחֶצְיוֹ נָתַן יְהוֹשֻׁעַ עִם אֲחֵיהֶם מעבר
(בְּעֵבֶר) הַיַּרְדֵּן יָמָּה וְגַם כִּי שִׁלְּחָם יְהוֹשֻׁעַ אֶל אָהֳלֵיהֶם וַיְבָרְכֵם. **ח** וַיֹּאמֶר אֲלֵיהֶם
לֵאמֹר בִּנְכָסִים רַבִּים שׁוּבוּ אֶל אָהֳלֵיכֶם וּבְמִקְנֶה רַב מְאֹד בְּכֶסֶף וּבְזָהָב וּבִנְחֹשֶׁת
וּבְבַרְזֶל וּבִשְׂלָמוֹת הַרְבֵּה מְאֹד חִלְקוּ שְׁלַל אֹיְבֵיכֶם עִם אֲחֵיכֶם. **ט** וַיָּשֻׁבוּ וַיֵּלְכוּ בְּנֵי
רְאוּבֵן וּבְנֵי גָד וַחֲצִי שֵׁבֶט הַמְנַשֶּׁה מֵאֵת בְּנֵי יִשְׂרָאֵל מִשִּׁלֹה אֲשֶׁר בְּאֶרֶץ כְּנָעַן לָלֶכֶת
אֶל אֶרֶץ הַגִּלְעָד אֶל אֶרֶץ אֲחֻזָּתָם אֲשֶׁר נֹאחֲזוּ בָהּ עַל פִּי ה' בְּיַד מֹשֶׁה.

MEANWHILE, AFTER THEY CROSSED THE YARDEN, THE RETURNING SOLDIERS SEE FROM A DISTANCE THEIR VILLAGES ARE UNDER ATTACK...

WE HAVE TO HELP, BUT I CAN'T TELL THE DIFFERENCE BETWEEN OUR CHILDREN AND THE ENEMY.
IT'S BEEN SO LONG SINCE WE'VE SEEN OUR FAMILIES...
AND BOTH SIDES HAVE LONG HAIR AND ARE DRESSED THE SAME!

PLEASE HASHEM HELP US!!!
ANSWER US G-D OF AVRAHAM, YITZCHAK AND YAAKOV!!!
DID YOU HEAR THAT! THAT IS ONE OF OURS...
VEETUR, NAPHISH, AND NODAV FROM YISHMAEL DECIDED TO ATTACK YISRAEL WITH THE HOPE OF BANISHING THEM FROM THE LAND.
REUVEN, GAD AND THE HALF-TRIBE OF MENASHE DEFEATED THEM AND CAPTURED THEIR CATTLE, 50,000 CAMELS, 250,000 SHEEP, 2,000 DONKEYS, AND 100,000 MEN.
ATTACK!!!
WE CAME BACK JUST IN TIME...

I AM SO GRATEFUL TO BE BACK AT HOME WITH MY FAMILY.
TO SEE HOW MY CHILDREN HAVE GROWN UP, AND HOW THEY HAVE CHILDREN OF THEIR OWN.
AND FOR ALL TO ENJOY THE MANY GIFTS HASHEM HAS GIVEN US...
TO THINK HOW LOPSIDED OUR PRIORITIES WERE 14 YEARS AGO, THAT WE CARED MORE ABOUT OUR PROPERTY THAN OUR WIVES AND CHILDREN BY SAYING "WE WILL (FIRST) BUILD HERE SHEEP ENCLOSURES FOR OUR LIVESTOCK AND (AFTERWARDS WE WILL BUILD) CITIES FOR OUR CHILDREN." (BAMIDBAR 32:16)
MOSHE OUR TEACHER QUICKLY CORRECTED US BY STATING THAT YOUR FAMILY TAKES PRIORITY OVER YOUR PROPERTY AS IT STATES "(FIRST) BUILD YOURSELVES CITIES FOR YOUR CHILDREN AND (AFTERWARDS BUILD) ENCLOSURES FOR YOUR SHEEP... (BAMIDBAR 32:24)
AFTER 14 YEARS AWAY AND FULFILLING OUR DUTIES TO HASHEM AND YISRAEL, WE NOW UNDERSTAND WHAT IS REALLY IMPORTANT IN LIFE.

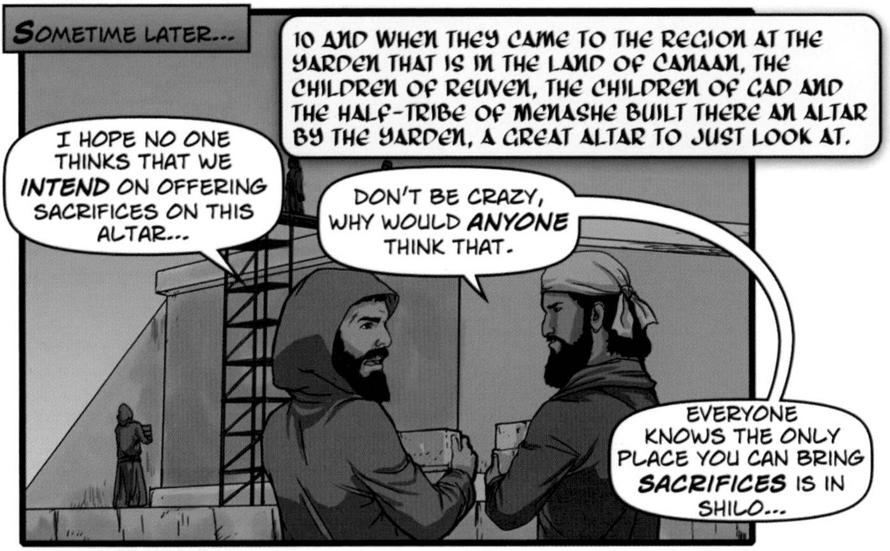
SOMETIME LATER...
10 AND WHEN THEY CAME TO THE REGION AT THE YARDEN THAT IS IN THE LAND OF CANAAN, THE CHILDREN OF REUVEN, THE CHILDREN OF GAD AND THE HALF-TRIBE OF MENASHE BUILT THERE AN ALTAR BY THE YARDEN, A GREAT ALTAR TO JUST LOOK AT.
I HOPE NO ONE THINKS THAT WE INTEND ON OFFERING SACRIFICES ON THIS ALTAR...
DON'T BE CRAZY, WHY WOULD ANYONE THINK THAT.
EVERYONE KNOWS THE ONLY PLACE YOU CAN BRING SACRIFICES IS IN SHILO...

MEANWHILE AT SHILO...
11 A REPORT REACHED THE CHILDREN OF YISRAEL SAYING,
THE CHILDREN OF REUVEN, GAD AND THE HALF-TRIBE OF MENASHE HAVE BUILT AN ALTER OPPOSITE THE LAND OF CANAAN, IN THE REGION OF THE YARDEN, ACROSS FROM THE CHILDREN OF YISRAEL.
LET ME GET THIS STRAIGHT. YOUR TELLING ME THEY BUILT A REPLICA OF THE ALTAR THAT IS CURRENTLY IN SHILO...FOR WHAT PURPOSE?
ISN'T IT OBVIOUS, THEY EITHER WANT TO BRING SACRIFICES TO HASHEM OUTSIDE OF SHILO, OR THEY WANT TO BRING SACRIFICES TO PAGAN IDOLS...

12 AND WHEN THE CHILDREN OF YISRAEL HEARD OF IT, THE WHOLE COMMUNITY OF THE CHILDREN OF YISRAEL ASSEMBLED AT SHILO TO MAKE WAR AGAINST THEM.
THIS CANNOT BE TOLERATED...
TO THINK THAT ONE OF OUR OWN COULD DO SUCH A THING!

י וַיָּבֹאוּ אֶל גְּלִילוֹת הַיַּרְדֵּן אֲשֶׁר בְּאֶרֶץ כְּנָעַן וַיִּבְנוּ בְנֵי רְאוּבֵן וּבְנֵי גָד וַחֲצִי שֵׁבֶט הַמְנַשֶּׁה שָׁם
מִזְבֵּחַ עַל-הַיַּרְדֵּן מִזְבֵּחַ גָּדוֹל לְמַרְאֶה. **יא** וַיִּשְׁמְעוּ בְנֵי יִשְׂרָאֵל לֵאמֹר הִנֵּה בָנוּ בְנֵי רְאוּבֵן
וּבְנֵי גָד וַחֲצִי שֵׁבֶט הַמְנַשֶּׁה אֶת הַמִּזְבֵּחַ אֶל מוּל אֶרֶץ כְּנַעַן אֶל גְּלִילוֹת הַיַּרְדֵּן אֶל עֵבֶר בְּנֵי
יִשְׂרָאֵל. **יב** וַיִּשְׁמְעוּ בְּנֵי יִשְׂרָאֵל וַיִּקָּהֲלוּ כָּל עֲדַת בְּנֵי יִשְׂרָאֵל שִׁלֹה לַעֲלוֹת עֲלֵיהֶם לַצָּבָא.

THIS IS VERY DISTURBING NEWS. PINCHAS, I NEED YOU TO GO WITH TEN REPRESENTATIVES FROM EACH TRIBE, AND IMPRESS UPON THEM THE SERIOUSNESS OF THEIR TRANSGRESSION...
PINCHAS WAS CHOSEN AS A SYMBOL OF PEACE, A SYMBOL OF WAR, AND FOR HIS NO NONSENSE ATTITUDE TOWARD TRANSGRESSION.
13 BUT FIRST THE CHILDREN OF YISRAEL SENT PINCHAS THE SON OF ELAZER HAKOHEN TO THE CHILDREN OF REUVEN, GAD AND THE HALF-TRIBE OF MENASHE IN THE LAND OF GILEAD. 14 AND WITH HIM TEN PRINCES, ONE PRINCE FROM A FATHERS' HOUSE FOR EACH OF THE TRIBES OF YISRAEL AND EVERYONE OF THEM WERE THE HEADS OF THEIR FATHER'S HOUSES FROM THE CONTINGENTS OF YISRAEL.
15 AND THEY CAME TO THE CHILDREN OF REUVEN AND TO THE CHILDREN OF GAD AND TO THE HALF-TRIBE OF MENASHE TO THE LAND OF GILEAD AND THEY SPOKE WITH THEM SAYING,

יג וַיִּשְׁלְחוּ בְנֵי יִשְׂרָאֵל אֶל בְּנֵי רְאוּבֵן וְאֶל בְּנֵי גָד וְאֶל חֲצִי שֵׁבֶט מְנַשֶּׁה אֶל אֶרֶץ
הַגִּלְעָד אֶת פִּינְחָס בֶּן אֶלְעָזָר הַכֹּהֵן. **יד** וַעֲשָׂרָה נְשִׂאִים עִמּוֹ נָשִׂיא אֶחָד נָשִׂיא אֶחָד
לְבֵית אָב לְכֹל מַטּוֹת יִשְׂרָאֵל וְאִישׁ רֹאשׁ בֵּית אֲבוֹתָם הֵמָּה לְאַלְפֵי יִשְׂרָאֵל. **טו** וַיָּבֹאוּ
אֶל בְּנֵי רְאוּבֵן וְאֶל בְּנֵי גָד וְאֶל חֲצִי שֵׁבֶט מְנַשֶּׁה אֶל אֶרֶץ הַגִּלְעָד וַיְדַבְּרוּ אִתָּם לֵאמֹר.

16 SO SAYS THE ENTIRE COMMUNITY OF HASHEM, WHAT TREACHERY IS THIS THAT YOU HAVE COMMITTED AGAINST THE G-D OF YISRAEL, TO TURN AWAY THIS DAY FROM FOLLOWING HASHEM IN THAT YOU HAVE BUILT AN ALTAR TO REBEL THIS DAY AGAINST HASHEM? 17 IS THE SIN OF PEOR, WHICH BROUGHT A PLAGUE UPON THE COMMUNITY OF HASHEM, SUCH A SMALL THING TO US? WE HAVE NOT CLEANSED OURSELVES FROM IT TO THIS DAY.
IN ORDER TO WEAKEN THE RELATIONSHIP WITH HASHEM, MOAV FACILITATED THE WORSHIPPING OF THE IDOL PEOR BY YISRAEL. AS A RESULT OF THIS SIN, YISRAEL WAS PUNISHED WITH A PLAGUE THAT KILLED 24,000 PEOPLE. (BAMIDBAR 25:1-9)
18 AND NOW YOU WOULD TURN AWAY FROM HASHEM? IF YOU REBEL AGAINST HASHEM TODAY, TOMORROW HE WILL BE ANGRY WITH THE WHOLE COMMUNITY OF YISRAEL
19 IF IT IS BECAUSE THE LAND THAT YOU ARE LIVING IN IS UNCLEAN, CROSS OVER TO THE LAND OF HASHEM WHERE THE MISHKAN OF HASHEM STANDS AND LIVE THERE WITH US.
BUT DO NOT REBEL AGAINST HASHEM OR REBEL AGAINST US BY BUILDING FOR YOURSELVES AN ALTAR INSTEAD OF THE ALTAR OF HASHEM OUR G-D.
20 DID NOT ACHAN, THE SON OF ZERACH COMMIT A VIOLATION REGARDING THE SANCTIFIED THINGS AND ANGER FELL ON THE ENTIRE COMMUNITY OF YISRAEL? AND HE WAS NOT THE ONLY ONE WHO DIED BECAUSE OF HIS SIN.

טז כֹּה אָמְרוּ כֹּל עֲדַת ה' מָה הַמַּעַל הַזֶּה אֲשֶׁר מְעַלְתֶּם בֵּאלֹקֵי יִשְׂרָאֵל לָשׁוּב הַיּוֹם
מֵאַחֲרֵי ה' בִּבְנוֹתְכֶם לָכֶם מִזְבֵּחַ לִמְרָדְכֶם הַיּוֹם בַּה'. **יז** הַמְעַט לָנוּ אֶת עֲוֹן פְּעוֹר אֲשֶׁר
לֹא הִטַּהַרְנוּ מִמֶּנּוּ עַד הַיּוֹם הַזֶּה וַיְהִי הַנֶּגֶף בַּעֲדַת ה'. **יח** וְאַתֶּם תָּשֻׁבוּ הַיּוֹם מֵאַחֲרֵי ה'
וְהָיָה אַתֶּם תִּמְרְדוּ הַיּוֹם בַּה' וּמָחָר אֶל כָּל עֲדַת יִשְׂרָאֵל יִקְצֹף. **יט** וְאַךְ אִם טְמֵאָה אֶרֶץ
אֲחֻזַּתְכֶם עִבְרוּ לָכֶם אֶל אֶרֶץ אֲחֻזַּת ה' אֲשֶׁר שָׁכַן שָׁם מִשְׁכַּן ה' וְהֵאָחֲזוּ בְּתוֹכֵנוּ וּבַה' אַל
תִּמְרֹדוּ וְאֹתָנוּ אַל תִּמְרֹדוּ בִּבְנֹתְכֶם לָכֶם מִזְבֵּחַ מִבַּלְעֲדֵי מִזְבַּח ה' אֱלֹקֵינוּ. **כ** הֲלוֹא עָכָן בֶּן
זֶרַח מָעַל מַעַל בַּחֵרֶם וְעַל כָּל עֲדַת יִשְׂרָאֵל הָיָה קָצֶף וְהוּא אִישׁ אֶחָד לֹא גָוַע בַּעֲוֹנוֹ.

21 THEN THE CHILDREN OF REUVEN, THE CHILDREN OF GAD AND THE HALF-TRIBE OF MENASHE ANSWERED AND SPOKE TO THE HEADS OF THE CONTINGENTS OF YISRAEL,

22 G-D G-D, HASHEM, G-D G-D HASHEM, HE KNOWS AND YISRAEL WILL ALSO KNOW, IF WE ACTED IN REBELLION OR IN TREACHERY AGAINST HASHEM, DO NOT SPARE US TODAY!

THE REASON FOR THE NAME OF HASHEM BEING REPEATED:

ONE NAME STANDS FOR THE THREE ATTRIBUTES BY WHICH THE WORLD WAS ***CREATED***, AND ONE NAME STANDS FOR THE THREE ATTRIBUTES WHEREBY THE TORAH WAS GIVEN.

OTHERS SAY, IT IS FOR THE PURPOSE OF ***PROCLAIMING*** THEIR BELIEF IN ONE G-D BOTH IN THIS WORLD AND IN THE WORLD TO COME.

23 IF WE BUILT AN ALTER TO TURN AWAY FROM HASHEM, IF IT WAS TO OFFER BURNT OFFERING OR MEAL OFFERINGS ON IT, OR TO OFFER SACRIFICES OF WELL-BEING ON IT, MAY HASHEM TAKE HIS VENGEANCE.

AND ***PUNISH*** US.

24 RATHER WE DID THIS THING ONLY OUT OF CONCERN THAT, IN THE FUTURE, YOUR CHILDREN MAY SAY TO OUR CHILDREN, "WHAT DO YOU HAVE TO DO WITH HASHEM, THE G-D OF YISRAEL.

25 FOR HASHEM HAS MADE THE YARDEN A BORDER BETWEEN US AND YOU, CHILDREN OF REUVEN, CHILDREN OF GAD, YOU HAVE NO PORTION IN HASHEM." SO YOUR CHILDREN WILL CAUSE OUR CHILDREN TO STOP FEARING (SERVING) HASHEM.

IN OTHER WORDS, WHEN THE TIME COMES TO GO TO SHILO AND ***BRING*** SACRIFICES, YOUR CHILDREN WILL SAY "WHAT BUSINESS DO YOU HAVE WITH HASHEM? YOU DO NOT LIVE IN THE LAND, YOU LIVE ON THE OTHER SIDE OF THE YARDEN..."

26 THEREFORE WE SAID, LET US BUILD FOR OURSELVES AN ALTAR NOT FOR BURNT OFFERING OR FOR OTHER SACRIFICES, 27 BUT IT SHALL BE A WITNESS BETWEEN US AND YOU AND BETWEEN OUR GENERATIONS AFTER US THAT WE MAY DO THE SERVICE OF HASHEM BEFORE HIM WITH OUR BURNT OFFERINGS, WITH OUR SACRIFICES AND WITH OUR PEACE OFFERINGS, AND THAT YOUR CHILDREN WILL NOT SAY TO OUR CHILDREN IN TIME TO COME, "YOU HAVE NO PORTION IN HASHEM."

כא וַיַּעֲנוּ בְּנֵי רְאוּבֵן וּבְנֵי גָד וַחֲצִי שֵׁבֶט הַמְנַשֶּׁה וַיְדַבְּרוּ אֶת רָאשֵׁי אַלְפֵי יִשְׂרָאֵל. **כב** אֵל אֱלֹקִים ה'
אֵל אֱלֹקִים ה' הוּא יֹדֵעַ וְיִשְׂרָאֵל הוּא יֵדָע אִם בְּמֶרֶד וְאִם בְּמַעַל בַּה 'אַל תּוֹשִׁיעֵנוּ הַיּוֹם הַזֶּה. **כג**
לִבְנוֹת לָנוּ מִזְבֵּחַ לָשׁוּב מֵאַחֲרֵי ה' וְאִם לְהַעֲלוֹת עָלָיו עוֹלָה וּמִנְחָה וְאִם לַעֲשׂוֹת עָלָיו זִבְחֵי שְׁלָמִים
ה' הוּא יְבַקֵּשׁ. **כד** וְאִם לֹא מִדְּאָגָה מִדָּבָר עָשִׂינוּ אֶת זֹאת לֵאמֹר מָחָר יֹאמְרוּ בְנֵיכֶם לְבָנֵינוּ לֵאמֹר
מַה לָּכֶם וְלַה' אֱלֹקֵי יִשְׂרָאֵל. **כה** וּגְבוּל נָתַן ה' בֵּינֵנוּ וּבֵינֵיכֶם בְּנֵי רְאוּבֵן וּבְנֵי גָד אֶת הַיַּרְדֵּן אֵין
לָכֶם חֵלֶק בַּה' וְהִשְׁבִּיתוּ בְנֵיכֶם אֶת בָּנֵינוּ לְבִלְתִּי יְרֹא אֶת ה'. **כו** וַנֹּאמֶר נַעֲשֶׂה נָּא לָנוּ לִבְנוֹת אֶת
הַמִּזְבֵּחַ לֹא לְעוֹלָה וְלֹא לְזָבַח. **כז** כִּי עֵד הוּא בֵּינֵינוּ וּבֵינֵיכֶם וּבֵין דֹּרוֹתֵינוּ אַחֲרֵינוּ לַעֲבֹד אֶת עֲבֹדַת
ה' לְפָנָיו בְּעֹלוֹתֵינוּ וּבִזְבָחֵינוּ וּבִשְׁלָמֵינוּ וְלֹא יֹאמְרוּ בְנֵיכֶם מָחָר לְבָנֵינוּ אֵין לָכֶם חֵלֶק בַּה.'

28 THEREFORE WE SAID, IT SHALL BE WHEN THEY SAY TO US OR TO OUR GENERATIONS IN THE FUTURE, THAT WE SHALL SAY, "BEHOLD THE REPLICA OF THE ALTAR OF HASHEM, WHICH OUR FATHERS DID NOT MAKE FOR BURNT OFFERING, OR FOR SACRIFICES BUT AS A WITNESS BETWEEN US AND YOU. 29 FAR BE IT FROM US THAT WE SHOULD REBEL AGAINST HASHEM AND TURN AWAY THIS DAY FROM FOLLOWING HASHEM TO BUILD AN ALTAR FOR BURNT OFFERING, FOR MEAL OFFERING OR FOR OTHER SACRIFICES, OTHER THAN THE ALTAR OF HASHEM OUR G-D THAT IS BEFORE HIS MISHKAN.

30 AND WHEN PINCHAS HAKOHEN, AND THE PRINCES OF THE COMMUNITY (WHO REPRESENTED) THE HEADS OF THE CONTINGENTS OF YISRAEL THAT WERE WITH HIM HEARD THE EXPLANATION OF THE CHILDREN OF REUVEN, THE CHILDREN OF GAD AND THE CHILDREN OF MENASHE, IT WAS GOOD IN THEIR EYES AND IT PLEASED THEM.

31 AND PINCHAS, THE SON OF ELAZAR THE KOHEN, SAID TO THE CHILDREN OF REUVEN, TO THE CHILDREN OF GAD AND TO THE CHILDREN OF MENASHE,

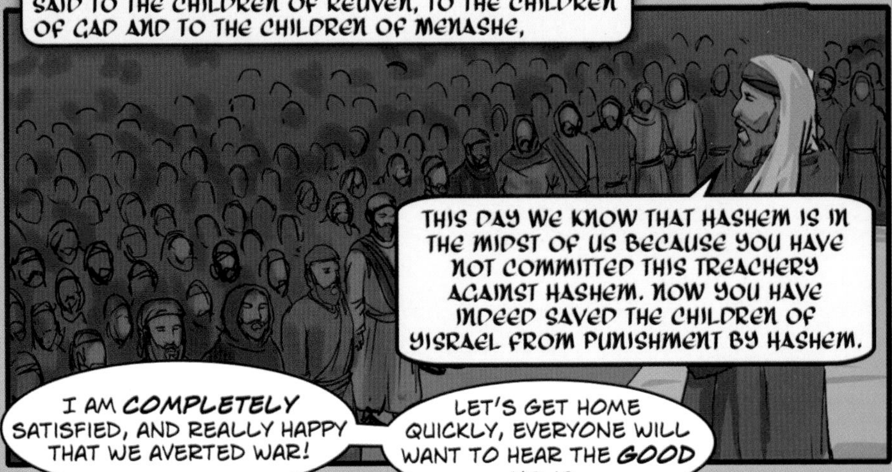
THIS DAY WE KNOW THAT HASHEM IS IN THE MIDST OF US BECAUSE YOU HAVE NOT COMMITTED THIS TREACHERY AGAINST HASHEM. NOW YOU HAVE INDEED SAVED THE CHILDREN OF YISRAEL FROM PUNISHMENT BY HASHEM.
I AM ***COMPLETELY*** SATISFIED, AND REALLY HAPPY THAT WE AVERTED WAR!
LET'S GET HOME QUICKLY, EVERYONE WILL WANT TO HEAR THE ***GOOD*** NEWS.

32 AND PINCHAS, THE SON OF ELAZAR HAKOHEN, AND THE PRINCES RETURNED FROM THE CHILDREN OF REUVEN, AND OF THE CHILDREN OF GAD IN THE LAND OF GILEAD TO THE LAND OF CANAAN TO THE CHILDREN OF YISRAEL, AND BROUGHT THEM BACK WORD.

33 AND THE CHILDREN OF YISRAEL WERE PLEASED, AND THE CHILDREN OF YISRAEL BLESSED G-D AND SPOKE NO MORE OF MAKING WAR AGAINST THEM TO DESTROY THE LAND WHERE THE CHILDREN OF REUVEN AND THE CHILDREN OF GAD LIVED. 34 AND THE CHILDREN OF REUVEN AND THE CHILDREN OF GAD CALLED THE ALTAR, 'WITNESS' FOR IT IS A WITNESS BETWEEN US (ALL OF YISRAEL) THAT HASHEM IS G-D.

כח וַנֹּאמֶר וְהָיָה כִּי יֹאמְרוּ אֵלֵינוּ וְאֶל דֹּרֹתֵינוּ מָחָר וְאָמַרְנוּ רְאוּ אֶת תַּבְנִית מִזְבַּח ה' אֲשֶׁר עָשׂוּ אֲבוֹתֵינוּ לֹא
לְעוֹלָה וְלֹא לְזֶבַח כִּי עֵד הוּא בֵּינֵינוּ וּבֵינֵיכֶם. **כט** חָלִילָה לָּנוּ מִמֶּנּוּ לִמְרֹד בַּה' וְלָשׁוּב הַיּוֹם מֵאַחֲרֵי ה' לִבְנוֹת
מִזְבֵּחַ לְעֹלָה לְמִנְחָה וּלְזָבַח מִלְּבַד מִזְבַּח ה' אֱלֹקֵינוּ אֲשֶׁר לִפְנֵי מִשְׁכָּנוֹ. **ל** וַיִּשְׁמַע פִּינְחָס הַכֹּהֵן וּנְשִׂיאֵי הָעֵדָה
וְרָאשֵׁי אַלְפֵי יִשְׂרָאֵל אֲשֶׁר אִתּוֹ אֶת הַדְּבָרִים אֲשֶׁר דִּבְּרוּ בְּנֵי רְאוּבֵן וּבְנֵי גָד וּבְנֵי מְנַשֶּׁה וַיִּיטַב בְּעֵינֵיהֶם. **לא**
וַיֹּאמֶר פִּינְחָס בֶּן אֶלְעָזָר הַכֹּהֵן אֶל בְּנֵי רְאוּבֵן וְאֶל בְּנֵי גָד וְאֶל בְּנֵי מְנַשֶּׁה הַיּוֹם יָדַעְנוּ כִּי בְתוֹכֵנוּ ה' אֲשֶׁר לֹא
מְעַלְתֶּם בַּה' הַמַּעַל הַזֶּה אָז הִצַּלְתֶּם אֶת בְּנֵי יִשְׂרָאֵל מִיַּד ה'. **לב** וַיָּשָׁב פִּינְחָס בֶּן אֶלְעָזָר הַכֹּהֵן וְהַנְּשִׂיאִים
מֵאֵת בְּנֵי רְאוּבֵן וּמֵאֵת בְּנֵי גָד מֵאֶרֶץ הַגִּלְעָד אֶל אֶרֶץ כְּנַעַן אֶל בְּנֵי יִשְׂרָאֵל וַיָּשִׁבוּ אוֹתָם דָּבָר. לג וַיִּיטַב הַדָּבָר
בְּעֵינֵי בְּנֵי יִשְׂרָאֵל וַיְבָרְכוּ אֱלֹקִים בְּנֵי יִשְׂרָאֵל וְלֹא אָמְרוּ לַעֲלוֹת עֲלֵיהֶם לַצָּבָא לְשַׁחֵת אֶת הָאָרֶץ אֲשֶׁר בְּנֵי רְאוּבֵן
וּבְנֵי גָד יֹשְׁבִים בָּהּ. **לד** וַיִּקְרְאוּ בְּנֵי רְאוּבֵן וּבְנֵי גָד לַמִּזְבֵּחַ כִּי עֵד הוּא בֵּינֹתֵינוּ כִּי ה' הָאֱלֹקִים.

YEHOSHUA CHAPTER 23
יהושע פרק כג

1 AND IT CAME TO PASS AFTER MANY DAYS WHEN HASHEM HAD GIVEN REST TO YISRAEL FROM ALL THEIR ENEMIES SURROUNDING THEM. AND YEHOSHUA WAS OLD AND ADVANCED IN HIS YEARS.
YEHOSHUA SHOULD HAVE LIVED AS LONG AS MOSHE, 120 YEARS. AS IT STATES, (HASHEM SAID) "... AS I WAS WITH MOSHE, SO I WILL BE WITH YOU..." (YEHOSHUA 1:5). YEHOSHUA THOUGHT TO HIMSELF, 'IF I KILL THE KINGS ALL AT ONCE, I WILL DIE UPON COMPLETION...' HE THEREFORE DELAYED THE WAR EFFORT. SAID THE HOLY ONE BLESSED BE HE, 'SO THIS IS WHAT YOU HAVE DONE, IS IT? I WILL SHORTEN YOUR LIFE BY 10 YEARS.'
2 YEHOSHUA CALLED FOR ALL YISRAEL, FOR THEIR ELDERS, FOR THEIR LEADERS, FOR THEIR JUDGES AND FOR THEIR OFFICERS AND SAID TO THEM,
I AM OLD AND ADVANCED IN MY YEARS. 3 AND YOU HAVE SEEN ALL THAT HASHEM YOUR G-D HAS DONE TO ALL THESE NATIONS ON YOUR BEHALF. FOR IT WAS HASHEM YOUR G-D WHO FOUGHT FOR YOU.
4 BEHOLD I HAVE ALLOTED TO YOU BY YOUR TRIBES, THE TERRITORY OF THESE NATIONS THAT STILL REMAIN, TOGETHER WITH ALL THE NATIONS THAT I HAVE DESTROYED, FROM THE YARDEN TO THE MEDITERRANEAN SEA IN THE WEST.

א וַיְהִי מִיָּמִים רַבִּים אַחֲרֵי אֲשֶׁר הֵנִיחַ ה' לְיִשְׂרָאֵל מִכָּל אֹיְבֵיהֶם מִסָּבִיב וִיהוֹשֻׁעַ זָקֵן בָּא
בַּיָּמִים. ב וַיִּקְרָא יְהוֹשֻׁעַ לְכָל יִשְׂרָאֵל לִזְקֵנָיו וּלְרָאשָׁיו וּלְשֹׁפְטָיו וּלְשֹׁטְרָיו וַיֹּאמֶר אֲלֵהֶם אֲנִי
זָקַנְתִּי בָּאתִי בַּיָּמִים. ג וְאַתֶּם רְאִיתֶם אֵת כָּל אֲשֶׁר עָשָׂה ה' אֱלֹקֵיכֶם לְכָל הַגּוֹיִם הָאֵלֶּה
מִפְּנֵיכֶם כִּי ה' אֱלֹקֵיכֶם הוּא הַנִּלְחָם לָכֶם. ד רְאוּ הִפַּלְתִּי לָכֶם אֶת הַגּוֹיִם הַנִּשְׁאָרִים
הָאֵלֶּה בְּנַחֲלָה לְשִׁבְטֵיכֶם מִן הַיַּרְדֵּן וְכָל הַגּוֹיִם אֲשֶׁר הִכְרַתִּי וְהַיָּם הַגָּדוֹל מְבוֹא הַשָּׁמֶשׁ.

5 AND HASHEM YOUR G-D WILL PUSH THEM OUT AND DRIVE THEM OUT OF YOUR SIGHT AND YOU SHALL POSSESS THEIR LAND AS HASHEM YOUR G-D SPOKE TO YOU.
6 BUT BE MOST RESOLUTE TO OBSERVE FAITHFULLY ALL THAT IS WRITTEN IN THE BOOK OF THE LAW OF MOSHE WITHOUT EVER DEVIATING FROM IT TO THE RIGHT OR TO THE LEFT.
7 AND WITHOUT INTERMINGLING WITH THESE NATIONS THAT ARE LEFT AMONG YOU, DO NOT MENTION THE NAME OF THEIR gods OR SWEAR BY THEM, DO NOT SERVE THEM OR BOW DOWN TO THEM.
8 BUT CLING TO HASHEM YOUR G-D AS YOU HAVE DONE UNTIL THIS DAY
9 HASHEM HAS DRIVEN OUT FROM YOU GREAT AND MIGHTY NATIONS, YET NO MAN HAS STOOD AGAINST YOU TO THIS DAY.
10 A SINGLE MAN OF YOU HAS CHASED A THOUSAND, FOR HASHEM YOUR G-D HIMSELF HAS BEEN FIGHTING FOR YOU, AS HE HAS PROMISED YOU.

ה וַה' אֱלֹקֵיכֶם הוּא יֶהְדֳּפֵם מִפְּנֵיכֶם וְהוֹרִישׁ אֹתָם מִלִּפְנֵיכֶם וִירִשְׁתֶּם אֶת אַרְצָם
כַּאֲשֶׁר דִּבֶּר ה' אֱלֹקֵיכֶם לָכֶם. **ו** וַחֲזַקְתֶּם מְאֹד לִשְׁמֹר וְלַעֲשׂוֹת אֵת כָּל הַכָּתוּב בְּסֵפֶר
תּוֹרַת מֹשֶׁה לְבִלְתִּי סוּר מִמֶּנּוּ יָמִין וּשְׂמֹאול. **ז** לְבִלְתִּי בֹא בַּגּוֹיִם הָאֵלֶּה הַנִּשְׁאָרִים
הָאֵלֶּה אִתְּכֶם וּבְשֵׁם אֱלֹהֵיהֶם לֹא תַזְכִּירוּ וְלֹא תַשְׁבִּיעוּ וְלֹא תַעַבְדוּם וְלֹא תִשְׁתַּחֲווּ
לָהֶם. **ח** כִּי אִם בַּה' אֱלֹקֵיכֶם תִּדְבָּקוּ כַּאֲשֶׁר עֲשִׂיתֶם עַד הַיּוֹם הַזֶּה. **ט** וַיּוֹרֶשׁ ה'
מִפְּנֵיכֶם גּוֹיִם גְּדֹלִים וַעֲצוּמִים וְאַתֶּם לֹא עָמַד אִישׁ בִּפְנֵיכֶם עַד הַיּוֹם הַזֶּה. **י** אִישׁ אֶחָד
מִכֶּם יִרְדָּף אָלֶף כִּי ה' אֱלֹקֵיכֶם הוּא הַנִּלְחָם לָכֶם כַּאֲשֶׁר דִּבֶּר לָכֶם.

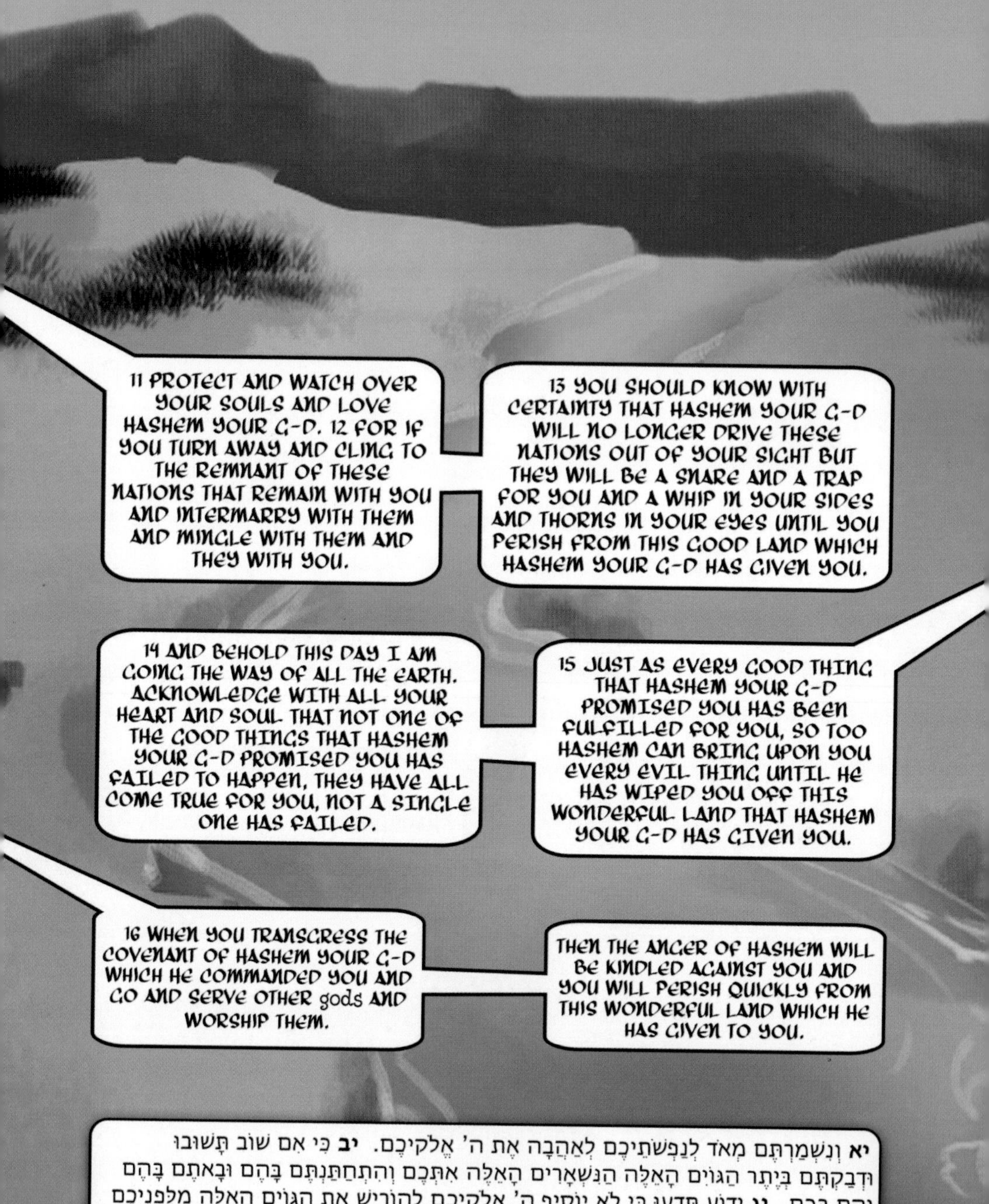
11 PROTECT AND WATCH OVER YOUR SOULS AND LOVE HASHEM YOUR G-D. 12 FOR IF YOU TURN AWAY AND CLING TO THE REMNANT OF THESE NATIONS THAT REMAIN WITH YOU AND INTERMARRY WITH THEM AND MINGLE WITH THEM AND THEY WITH YOU.
13 YOU SHOULD KNOW WITH CERTAINTY THAT HASHEM YOUR G-D WILL NO LONGER DRIVE THESE NATIONS OUT OF YOUR SIGHT BUT THEY WILL BE A SNARE AND A TRAP FOR YOU AND A WHIP IN YOUR SIDES AND THORNS IN YOUR EYES UNTIL YOU PERISH FROM THIS GOOD LAND WHICH HASHEM YOUR G-D HAS GIVEN YOU.
14 AND BEHOLD THIS DAY I AM GOING THE WAY OF ALL THE EARTH. ACKNOWLEDGE WITH ALL YOUR HEART AND SOUL THAT NOT ONE OF THE GOOD THINGS THAT HASHEM YOUR G-D PROMISED YOU HAS FAILED TO HAPPEN, THEY HAVE ALL COME TRUE FOR YOU, NOT A SINGLE ONE HAS FAILED.
15 JUST AS EVERY GOOD THING THAT HASHEM YOUR G-D PROMISED YOU HAS BEEN FULFILLED FOR YOU, SO TOO HASHEM CAN BRING UPON YOU EVERY EVIL THING UNTIL HE HAS WIPED YOU OFF THIS WONDERFUL LAND THAT HASHEM YOUR G-D HAS GIVEN YOU.
16 WHEN YOU TRANSGRESS THE COVENANT OF HASHEM YOUR G-D WHICH HE COMMANDED YOU AND GO AND SERVE OTHER gods AND WORSHIP THEM.
THEN THE ANGER OF HASHEM WILL BE KINDLED AGAINST YOU AND YOU WILL PERISH QUICKLY FROM THIS WONDERFUL LAND WHICH HE HAS GIVEN TO YOU.

יא וְנִשְׁמַרְתֶּם מְאֹד לְנַפְשֹׁתֵיכֶם לְאַהֲבָה אֶת ה' אֱלֹקיכֶם. **יב** כִּי אִם שׁוֹב תָּשׁוּבוּ
וּדְבַקְתֶּם בְּיֶתֶר הַגּוֹיִם הָאֵלֶּה הַנִּשְׁאָרִים הָאֵלֶּה אִתְּכֶם וְהִתְחַתַּנְתֶּם בָּהֶם וּבָאתֶם בָּהֶם
וְהֵם בָּכֶם. **יג** יָדוֹעַ תֵּדְעוּ כִּי לֹא יוֹסִיף ה' אֱלֹקיכֶם לְהוֹרִישׁ אֶת הַגּוֹיִם הָאֵלֶּה מִלִּפְנֵיכֶם
וְהָיוּ לָכֶם לְפַח וּלְמוֹקֵשׁ וּלְשֹׁטֵט בְּצִדֵּיכֶם וְלִצְנִנִים בְּעֵינֵיכֶם עַד אֲבָדְכֶם מֵעַל הָאֲדָמָה
הַטּוֹבָה הַזֹּאת אֲשֶׁר נָתַן לָכֶם ה' אֱלֹקיכֶם. **יד** וְהִנֵּה אָנֹכִי הוֹלֵךְ הַיּוֹם בְּדֶרֶךְ כָּל הָאָרֶץ
וִידַעְתֶּם בְּכָל לְבַבְכֶם וּבְכָל נַפְשְׁכֶם כִּי לֹא נָפַל דָּבָר אֶחָד מִכֹּל הַדְּבָרִים הַטּוֹבִים אֲשֶׁר דִּבֶּר
ה' אֱלֹקיכֶם עֲלֵיכֶם הַכֹּל בָּאוּ לָכֶם לֹא נָפַל מִמֶּנּוּ דָּבָר אֶחָד. **טו** וְהָיָה כַּאֲשֶׁר בָּא עֲלֵיכֶם
כָּל הַדָּבָר הַטּוֹב אֲשֶׁר דִּבֶּר ה' אֱלֹקיכֶם אֲלֵיכֶם כֵּן יָבִיא ה' עֲלֵיכֶם אֵת כָּל הַדָּבָר הָרָע עַד
הַשְׁמִידוֹ אוֹתְכֶם מֵעַל הָאֲדָמָה הַטּוֹבָה הַזֹּאת אֲשֶׁר נָתַן לָכֶם ה' אֱלֹקיכֶם. **טז** בְּעָבְרְכֶם
אֶת בְּרִית ה' אֱלֹקיכֶם אֲשֶׁר צִוָּה אֶתְכֶם וַהֲלַכְתֶּם וַעֲבַדְתֶּם אֱלֹהִים אֲחֵרִים וְהִשְׁתַּחֲוִיתֶם
לָהֶם וְחָרָה אַף ה' בָּכֶם וַאֲבַדְתֶּם מְהֵרָה מֵעַל הָאָרֶץ הַטּוֹבָה אֲשֶׁר נָתַן לָכֶם.

YEHOSHUA CHAPTER 24
יהושע פרק כד

1 AND YEHOSHUA GATHERED ALL THE TRIBES OF YISRAEL TO SHECHEM, AND CALLED FOR THE ELDERS OF YISRAEL, THEIR HEADS, THEIR JUDGES, AND FOR THEIR OFFICERS; AND THEY PRESENTED THEMSELVES BEFORE G-D.

2 AND YEHOSHUA SAID TO ALL THE PEOPLE,
THUS SAYS HASHEM, THE G-D OF YISRAEL, - -

AT THIS MOMENTOUS TIME WHEN YEHOSHUA GATHERS ALL OF YISRAEL, HE CHOOSES THE CITY OF SHECHEM TO DELIVER HIS ***FINAL*** MESSAGE. SHECHEM IS CLEARLY THE MOST BEFITTING LOCATION BEING THE PLACE WHERE HASHEM PROMISED TO AVRAHAM THAT HIS CHILDREN WOULD INHERIT THE LAND. (BERESHEET 12:7). NEVERTHELESS, IT WOULD BE REMISS NOT TO THINK THERE ARE MUCH MORE REASONS AS TO WHY HE CHOSE SHECHEM. BELOW IS A ***LIST OF EVENTS*** THAT TOOK PLACE IN SHECHEM THAT WILL SHED SOME LIGHT ABOUT THIS PROFOUND CITY IN ERETZ ISRAEL.

- SHECHEM IS THE FIRST CITY THAT AVRAHAM REACHED WHEN HE CAME INTO THE LAND. (BERESHEET 12:6)
- SHECHEM IS THE CITY WHERE AVRAHAM WAS PROMISED HIS CHILDREN WILL INHERIT THE LAND. (BERESHEET 12:7)
- SHECHEM IS THE FIRST CITY WHERE AVRAHAM BUILDS A MIZBAYACH (ALTAR). (BERESHEET 12:7)
- SHECHEM IS THE FIRST CANAAN CITY THAT YAAKOV RETURNS TO AFTER LIVING WITH LAVAN, AND PARTING WAYS WITH EISAV. (BERESHEET 33:18)
- YAAKOV'S FIRST PURCHASE OF LAND IN CANAAN IS SHECHEM, A FIELD BOUGHT FROM CHAMOR. HE ERECTS AN ALTAR PRAISING HASHEM BY PROCLAIMING "HASHEM IS THE G-D OF YISRAEL." (BERESHEET 33:20)
- SHECHEM IS THE CITY WHERE THE TRAGIC STORY OF DINA TOOK PLACE. (BERESHEET 34)
- SHIMON AND LEVI WIPE OUT THE ENTIRE CITY OF SHECHEM. (BERESHEET 34)
- YAAKOV BURIES THE IDOLS NEAR SHECHEM. (BERESHEET 35:4)
- YAAKOV SENDS YOSEF TO CHECK ON THE WELFARE OF HIS BROTHERS IN SHECHEM PRIOR TO BEING SOLD INTO SLAVERY. (BERESHEET 37)
- THE BROTHERS SELL YOSEF INTO SLAVERY IN SHECHEM. (BERESHEET 37)
- YAAKOV GAVE YOSEF SHECHEM AS AN INHERITANCE. (BERESHEET 48:22)
- AFTER YEHOSHUA CONQUERED AI HE ERECTED AN ALTAR AT HAR EIVAL NEXT TO SHECHEM. (YEHOSHUA 8:30-35)
- SHECHEM IS DESIGNATED AS A CITY OF REFUGE. (YEHOSHUA 20:7)
- EPHRAIM EVENTUALLY GAVE SHECHEM TO KEHAT. (YEHOSHUA 21:21)
- YEHOSHUA DELIVERS HIS FINAL WORDS TO YISRAEL IN SHECHEM. (YEHOSHUA 24:1)
- YOSEF IS BURIED IN SHECHEM. (YEHOSHUA 24:32)
- AVIMELECH SON OF GIDEON COMES FROM SHECHEM. (SHOFTIM 8:31)
- YOTAM MAKES HIS SPEECH TO THE MEN OF SHECHEM ON HAR GERIZIM. (SHOFTIM 9:7)
- THE MEN OF SHECHEM EVENTUALLY BETRAY AVIMELECH. (SHOFTIM 9:23)
- AFTER SHLOMO DIES RECHAVAM CROWNS HIMSELF KING IN SHECHEM. (MELACHIM I 12:1)
- YERAVAM FORTIFIES HIS KINGDOM IN SHECHEM. (MELACHIM I 12:25)
- MEN FROM SHECHEM MURDERED GEDALIA. (YIRMIYAHU 41:5)

א וַיֶּאֱסֹף יְהוֹשֻׁעַ אֶת כָּל שִׁבְטֵי יִשְׂרָאֵל שְׁכֶמָה וַיִּקְרָא לְזִקְנֵי יִשְׂרָאֵל וּלְרָאשָׁיו
וּלְשֹׁפְטָיו וּלְשֹׁטְרָיו וַיִּתְיַצְּבוּ לִפְנֵי הָאֱלֹקִים. **ב** וַיֹּאמֶר יְהוֹשֻׁעַ אֶל כָּל הָעָם כֹּה
אָמַר ה' אֱלֹקֵי יִשְׂרָאֵל - -

THE FOLLOWING VERSES ARE RECITED IN THE *HAGADDA* ON PESACH EVERY YEAR.
- - IN OLDEN TIMES, YOUR FATHERS-TERACH, FATHER OF AVRAHAM AND OF NACHOR-LIVED BEYOND THE EUPHRATES RIVER,
AND THEY SERVED OTHER gods
3 AND I TOOK YOUR FATHER AVRAHAM FROM BEYOND THE EUPHRATES RIVER, AND LED HIM THROUGHOUT ALL THE LAND OF CANAAN, AND MULTIPLIED HIS OFFSPRING, AND GAVE HIM YITZCHAK.
4 AND I GAVE TO YITZCHAK YAAKOV AND EISAV
AND I GAVE TO EISAV, MOUNT SEIR, TO POSSESS IT - -
WE WILL BE A **GREAT** NATION, FOR I AM EISAV THE SON OF YITZCHAK...

– – בְּעֵבֶר הַנָּהָר יָשְׁבוּ אֲבוֹתֵיכֶם מֵעוֹלָם תֶּרַח אֲבִי אַבְרָהָם וַאֲבִי נָחוֹר וַיַּעַבְדוּ
אֱלֹהִים אֲחֵרִים. **ג** וָאֶקַּח אֶת אֲבִיכֶם אֶת אַבְרָהָם מֵעֵבֶר הַנָּהָר וָאוֹלֵךְ אוֹתוֹ בְּכָל
אֶרֶץ כְּנָעַן וארב (וָאַרְבֶּה) אֶת זַרְעוֹ וָאֶתֶּן לוֹ אֶת יִצְחָק. **ד** וָאֶתֵּן לְיִצְחָק אֶת יַעֲקֹב
וְאֶת עֵשָׂו וָאֶתֵּן לְעֵשָׂו אֶת הַר שֵׂעִיר לָרֶשֶׁת אוֹתוֹ – –

- - AND YAAKOV AND HIS CHILDREN WENT DOWN INTO EGYPT.
5 I SENT MOSHE AND AHARON,
AND I PLAGUED EGYPT IN THEIR MIDST, WITH (THE WONDERS) THAT I SMASHED THEM WITH. AND AFTERWARD, I BROUGHT YOU OUT.
HOW DID WE TURN OUR BACKS ON YISRAEL AND DESPISE THEM, WHEN IT WAS YOSEPH WHO SAVED US FROM EXTINCTION OVER 200 YEARS AGO.
THE G-D OF YISRAEL HAS BROUGHT ABSOLUTE DESTRUCTION TO ALL OF EGYPT...
HE HAS PUNISHED US ALL FOR THE HORRIFIC WAY WE ENSLAVED THE NATION OF YISRAEL.
- - וְיַעֲקֹב וּבָנָיו יָרְדוּ מִצְרָיִם. ה וָאֶשְׁלַח אֶת מֹשֶׁה וְאֶת אַהֲרֹן וָאֶגֹּף אֶת
מִצְרַיִם כַּאֲשֶׁר עָשִׂיתִי בְּקִרְבּוֹ וְאַחַר הוֹצֵאתִי אֶתְכֶם.

ו וָאוֹצִיא אֶת אֲבוֹתֵיכֶם מִמִּצְרַיִם וַתָּבֹאוּ הַיָּמָּה וַיִּרְדְּפוּ מִצְרַיִם אַחֲרֵי
אֲבוֹתֵיכֶם בְּרֶכֶב וּבְפָרָשִׁים יַם סוּף.

ז וַיִּצְעֲקוּ אֶל ה' וַיָּשֶׂם מַאֲפֵל בֵּינֵיכֶם וּבֵין הַמִּצְרִים - -

LOOK BEHIND YOU, THE CLOUD IS LIFTING...
I KNOW, WE ARE ALMOST ACROSS.
I TOLD YOU THE CLOUD WOULD LIFT.
WHEN I CATCH THEM, I AM GOING TO BEAT THEM EXTRA HARD FOR MAKING US CHASE AFTER THEM...
- - AND BROUGHT THE SEA UPON THEM, AND COVERED THEM. - -
WE CAN NEVER DEFEAT THE G-D OF YISRAEL!!
WE AND OUR NATION ARE DOOMED FOREVERRR!!!
- - וַיָּבֵא עָלָיו אֶת הַיָּם וַיְכַסֵּהוּ - -

- - AND YOUR EYES SAW WHAT I DID IN EGYPT

HASHEM WASHED **ALL** THE DEAD BODIES TO SHORE, JUST SO WE KNOW THAT THE EGYPTIANS WILL NEVER BOTHER US AGAIN.

WE JUST PARTICIPATED IN THE **GREATEST** MIRACLE OF ALL TIME.

THIS STORY WILL BE TOLD FOR **GENERATIONS** TO COME...

AND YOU LIVED IN THE DESERT MANY YEARS.

5 AND I BROUGHT YOU INTO THE LAND OF THE AMORITES, THAT DWELLED BEYOND (EAST OF) THE YARDEN. AND THEY FOUGHT WITH YOU, AND I GAVE THEM INTO YOUR HAND, AND YOU POSSESSED THEIR LAND, AND I DESTROYED THEM FOR YOU.

‫- - וָאָבִיא אֶתְכֶם אֶל אֶרֶץ הָאֱמֹרִי הַיּוֹשֵׁב בְּעֵבֶר הַיַּרְדֵּן‬
‫רַבִּים. ח וָאָבִאָה (וָאָבִא) אֶתְכֶם אֶל אֶרֶץ הָאֱמֹרִי הַיּוֹשֵׁב בְּעֵבֶר הַיַּרְדֵּן‬
‫וַיִּלָּחֲמוּ אִתְּכֶם וָאֶתֵּן אוֹתָם בְּיֶדְכֶם וַתִּירְשׁוּ אֶת אַרְצָם וָאַשְׁמִידֵם מִפְּנֵיכֶם.‬

9 THEN BALAK THE SON OF TZIPPOR, KING OF MOAV, AROSE PREPARING TO FIGHT AGAINST YISRAEL. AND HE SENT AND CALLED BILAAM, THE SON OF BEOR TO CURSE YOU.
...CURSE THEM FOR ME...
HOW GOOD ARE YOUR TENTS, O' YAAKOV, YOUR DWELLING PLACES, O' YISRAEL...
...THOSE WHO BLESS YOU, ARE BLESSED, THOSE WHO CURSE YOU, ARE CURSED.
BALAK SAID TO BILAAM,
"I SUMMONED YOU, TO CURSE MY ENEMIES, AND INSTEAD YOU HAVE BLESSED THEM, THESE THREE TIMES!"... (BAMIDBAR 24:5-10)
I ALREADY INFORMED YOU BALAK, "...I CANNOT TRANSGRESS THE WORD OF HASHEM... ONLY WHAT HASHEM SPEAKS CAN I SAY..." (BAMIDBAR 24:13)
10 BUT I REFUSED TO LISTEN TO BILAAM; HE HAD TO BLESS YOU, SO I SAVED YOU FROM HIS HAND.
ט וַיָּקָם בָּלָק בֶּן צִפּוֹר מֶלֶךְ מוֹאָב וַיִּלָּחֶם בְּיִשְׂרָאֵל וַיִּשְׁלַח וַיִּקְרָא לְבִלְעָם בֶּן בְּעוֹר לְקַלֵּל אֶתְכֶם. י וְלֹא אָבִיתִי לִשְׁמֹעַ לְבִלְעָם וַיְבָרֶךְ בָּרוֹךְ אֶתְכֶם וָאַצִּל אֶתְכֶם מִיָּדוֹ.

11 AND YOU WENT ACROSS THE YARDEN,
AND CAME TO YERICHO.
AND THE MEN OF YERICHO FOUGHT AGAINST YOU, THE AMORITE, AND THE PERIZZITE, AND THE CANAANITE, AND THE CHITTITE, AND THE GIRGASHITE, THE CHIVITE, AND THE YEVUSITE; AND I DELIVERED THEM INTO YOUR HANDS.
יא וַתַּעַבְרוּ אֶת הַיַּרְדֵּן וַתָּבֹאוּ אֶל יְרִיחוֹ וַיִּלָּחֲמוּ בָכֶם בַּעֲלֵי יְרִיחוֹ הָאֱמֹרִי
וְהַפְּרִזִּי וְהַכְּנַעֲנִי וְהַחִתִּי וְהַגִּרְגָּשִׁי הַחִוִּי וְהַיְבוּסִי וָאֶתֵּן אוֹתָם בְּיֶדְכֶם.

יב וָאֶשְׁלַח לִפְנֵיכֶם אֶת הַצִּרְעָה וַתְּגָרֶשׁ אוֹתָם מִפְּנֵיכֶם שְׁנֵי מַלְכֵי הָאֱמֹרִי
לֹא בְחַרְבְּךָ וְלֹא בְקַשְׁתֶּךָ. **יג** וָאֶתֵּן לָכֶם אֶרֶץ אֲשֶׁר לֹא יָגַעְתָּ בָּהּ וְעָרִים אֲשֶׁר
לֹא בְנִיתֶם וַתֵּשְׁבוּ בָּהֶם כְּרָמִים וְזֵיתִים אֲשֶׁר לֹא נְטַעְתֶּם אַתֶּם אֹכְלִים.

14 NOW THEREFORE FEAR HASHEM, AND SERVE HIM IN SINCERITY AND IN TRUTH AND PUT AWAY THE gods WHICH YOUR FATHERS SERVED BEYOND THE EUPHRATES RIVER, AND IN EGYPT, AND SERVE HASHEM.
15 AND IF IT IS EVIL FOR YOU TO SERVE HASHEM, CHOOSE TODAY WHO YOU WILL SERVE. WHETHER THE gods WHICH YOUR FATHERS SERVED THAT WERE BEYOND THE EUPHRATES RIVER, OR THE gods OF THE AMORITES, IN WHOSE LAND YOU LIVE.
BUT AS FOR ME AND MY HOUSE, WE WILL SERVE HASHEM.
יד וְעַתָּה יְראוּ אֶת ה' וְעִבְדוּ אֹתוֹ בְּתָמִים וּבֶאֱמֶת וְהָסִירוּ אֶת אֱלֹהִים אֲשֶׁר עָבְדוּ אֲבוֹתֵיכֶם בְּעֵבֶר הַנָּהָר וּבְמִצְרַיִם וְעִבְדוּ אֶת ה'. **טו** וְאִם רַע בְּעֵינֵיכֶם לַעֲבֹד אֶת ה' בַּחֲרוּ לָכֶם הַיּוֹם אֶת מִי תַעֲבֹדוּן אִם אֶת אֱלֹהִים אֲשֶׁר עָבְדוּ אֲבוֹתֵיכֶם אֲשֶׁר בעבר (מֵעֵבֶר) הַנָּהָר וְאִם אֶת אֱלֹהֵי הָאֱמֹרִי אֲשֶׁר אַתֶּם יֹשְׁבִים בְּאַרְצָם וְאָנֹכִי וּבֵיתִי נַעֲבֹד אֶת ה'. **טז** וַיַּעַן הָעָם וַיֹּאמֶר חָלִילָה לָּנוּ מֵעֲזֹב אֶת ה' לַעֲבֹד אֱלֹהִים אֲחֵרִים.
16 AND THE PEOPLE ANSWERED AND SAID
FAR BE IT FROM US THAT WE SHOULD FORSAKE HASHEM, TO SERVE OTHER gods

יז כִּי ה׳ אֱלֹקֵינוּ הוּא הַמַּעֲלֶה אֹתָנוּ וְאֶת אֲבוֹתֵינוּ מֵאֶרֶץ מִצְרַיִם מִבֵּית עֲבָדִים
וַאֲשֶׁר עָשָׂה לְעֵינֵינוּ אֶת הָאֹתוֹת הַגְּדֹלוֹת הָאֵלֶּה וַיִּשְׁמְרֵנוּ בְּכָל הַדֶּרֶךְ אֲשֶׁר הָלַכְנוּ
בָהּ וּבְכֹל הָעַמִּים אֲשֶׁר עָבַרְנוּ בְּקִרְבָּם. **יח** וַיְגָרֶשׁ ה׳ אֶת כָּל הָעַמִּים וְאֶת הָאֱמֹרִי
יֹשֵׁב הָאָרֶץ מִפָּנֵינוּ גַּם אֲנַחְנוּ נַעֲבֹד אֶת ה׳ כִּי הוּא אֱלֹקֵינוּ.

19 AND YEHOSHUA SAID TO THE PEOPLE,
YOU CANNOT SERVE HASHEM (INSINCERELY); FOR HE IS A HOLY G-D; HE IS A JEALOUS G-D; HE WILL NOT FORGIVE YOUR TRANSGRESSION OR YOUR SINS
20 IF YOU FORSAKE HASHEM, AND SERVE STRANGE gods, HE WILL TURN AND DEAL HARSHLY WITH YOU, AND DESTROY YOU, AFTER HAVING BEEN SO GRACIOUS TO YOU.
21 AND THE PEOPLE SAID TO YEHOSHUA,
NO, WE WILL SERVE HASHEM (SINCERELY).
22 AND YEHOSHUA SAID TO THE PEOPLE,
YOU ARE WITNESSES AGAINST YOURSELVES, THAT YOU BY YOUR OWN ACT HAVE CHOSEN TO SERVE HASHEM.
AND THEY SAID
WE ARE WITNESSES.
יט וַיֹּאמֶר יְהוֹשֻׁעַ אֶל הָעָם לֹא תוּכְלוּ לַעֲבֹד אֶת ה' כִּי
אֱלֹקִים קְדֹשִׁים הוּא אֵל קַנּוֹא הוּא לֹא יִשָּׂא לְפִשְׁעֲכֶם
וּלְחַטֹּאותֵיכֶם. **כ** כִּי תַעַזְבוּ אֶת ה' וַעֲבַדְתֶּם אֱלֹהֵי נֵכָר
וְשָׁב וְהֵרַע לָכֶם וְכִלָּה אֶתְכֶם אַחֲרֵי אֲשֶׁר הֵיטִיב לָכֶם.
כא וַיֹּאמֶר הָעָם אֶל יְהוֹשֻׁעַ לֹא כִּי אֶת ה' נַעֲבֹד. **כב**
וַיֹּאמֶר יְהוֹשֻׁעַ אֶל הָעָם עֵדִים אַתֶּם בָּכֶם כִּי אַתֶּם
בְּחַרְתֶּם לָכֶם אֶת ה' לַעֲבֹד אוֹתוֹ וַיֹּאמְרוּ עֵדִים.

23 NOW THEREFORE PUT AWAY THE ALIEN gods WHICH ARE AMONG YOU, AND DIRECT YOUR HEART TO HASHEM, THE G-D OF YISRAEL.
24 AND THE PEOPLE SAID TO YEHOSHUA,
HASHEM OUR G-D WE WILL SERVE, AND WE WILL LISTEN TO HIS VOICE.
25 YEHOSHUA MADE A COVENANT WITH THE PEOPLE THAT DAY, AND MADE FOR THEM A STATUTE AND AN ORDINANCE IN SHECHEM.
THIS STATUTE AND ORDINANCE IS REFERRING TO TEN ENACTMENTS THAT YEHOSHUA *INSTITUTED*.
1. PEOPLE MAY *PASTURE* THEIR SMALL ANIMALS IN PRIVATELY OWNED FORESTS. IN A FOREST THAT IS *NOT* THICK WITH TREES, ONE MAY NOT PASTURE ANY SIZE ANIMAL WITHOUT THE OWNER'S PERMISSION.
2. ANY PERSON IS PERMITTED TO *COLLECT* NON-VALUABLE WOOD FROM A PRIVATELY OWNED FIELD.
3. ANY PERSON MAY COLLECT GRASS ANYWHERE THAT IS GROWING ON ITS OWN, *EXCEPT* FOR A FIELD OF FENUGREEK THAT WAS PLANTED SPECIFICALLY FOR ANIMAL FEED.
כג וְעַתָּה הָסִירוּ אֶת אֱלֹהֵי הַנֵּכָר אֲשֶׁר בְּקִרְבְּכֶם וְהַטּוּ אֶת לְבַבְכֶם אֶל ה'
אֱלֹקֵי יִשְׂרָאֵל. **כד** וַיֹּאמְרוּ הָעָם אֶל יְהוֹשֻׁעַ אֶת ה' אֱלֹקֵינוּ נַעֲבֹד וּבְקוֹלוֹ
נִשְׁמָע. **כה** וַיִּכְרֹת יְהוֹשֻׁעַ בְּרִית לָעָם בַּיּוֹם הַהוּא וַיָּשֶׂם לוֹ חֹק וּמִשְׁפָּט בִּשְׁכֶם.

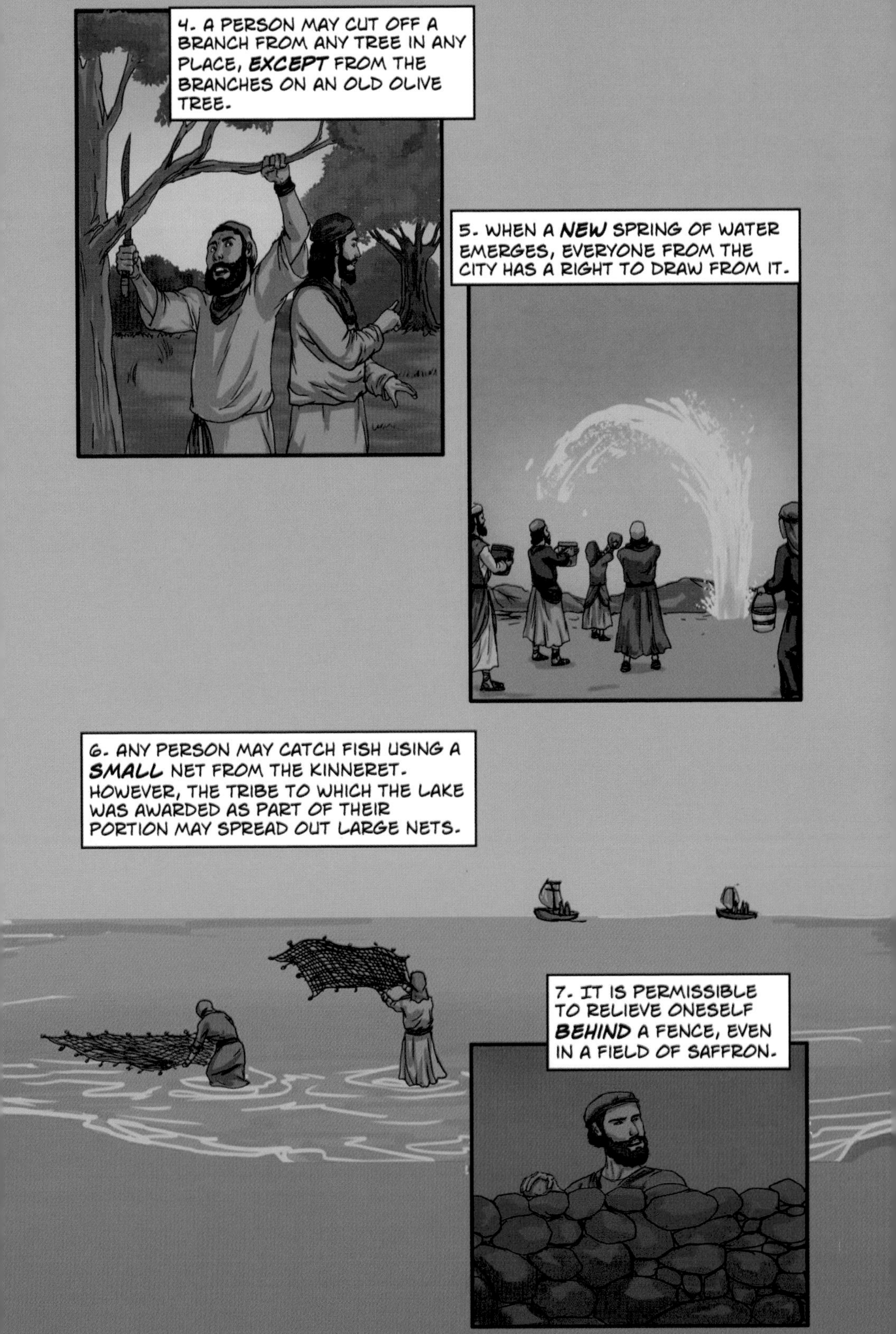
4. A PERSON MAY CUT OFF A BRANCH FROM ANY TREE IN ANY PLACE, EXCEPT FROM THE BRANCHES ON AN OLD OLIVE TREE.
5. WHEN A NEW SPRING OF WATER EMERGES, EVERYONE FROM THE CITY HAS A RIGHT TO DRAW FROM IT.
6. ANY PERSON MAY CATCH FISH USING A SMALL NET FROM THE KINNERET. HOWEVER, THE TRIBE TO WHICH THE LAKE WAS AWARDED AS PART OF THEIR PORTION MAY SPREAD OUT LARGE NETS.
7. IT IS PERMISSIBLE TO RELIEVE ONESELF BEHIND A FENCE, EVEN IN A FIELD OF SAFFRON.

8. IF SOMEONE GETS LOST AMONG THE VINEYARDS HE HAS THE RIGHT TO **CUT** DOWN BRANCHES AND ENTER OR EXIT AN AREA OF THE VINEYARD UNTIL HE FINDS HIS WAY BACK TO THE ROAD.

9. IT IS PERMISSIBLE TO WALK ON PRIVATE LAND ON THE SIDE OF THE ROAD, WHEN THE REGULAR PATHWAYS ARE **MUDDY.**

10. WHEN A CORPSE IS FOUND, AND NO RELATIVES CAN BE TRACED, THE BODY MUST BE **BURIED** IN THE PLACE IT WAS FOUND, EVEN IF IT'S PRIVATE PROPERTY.

26 AND YEHOSHUA WROTE THESE WORDS IN THE BOOK OF THE LAW OF G-D. – –

THERE IS A **DIFFERENCE** OF OPINION AMONG THE SAGES OF WHAT YEHOSHUA WROTE.

ONE SAYS YEHOSHUA WROTE THE **LAST** EIGHT VERSES IN THE TORAH WHILE THE OTHER STATES HE WROTE THE SECTION REGARDING THE CITIES OF **REFUGE.**

כו וַיִּכְתֹּב יְהוֹשֻׁעַ אֶת הַדְּבָרִים הָאֵלֶּה בְּסֵפֶר תּוֹרַת אֱלֹקִים – –

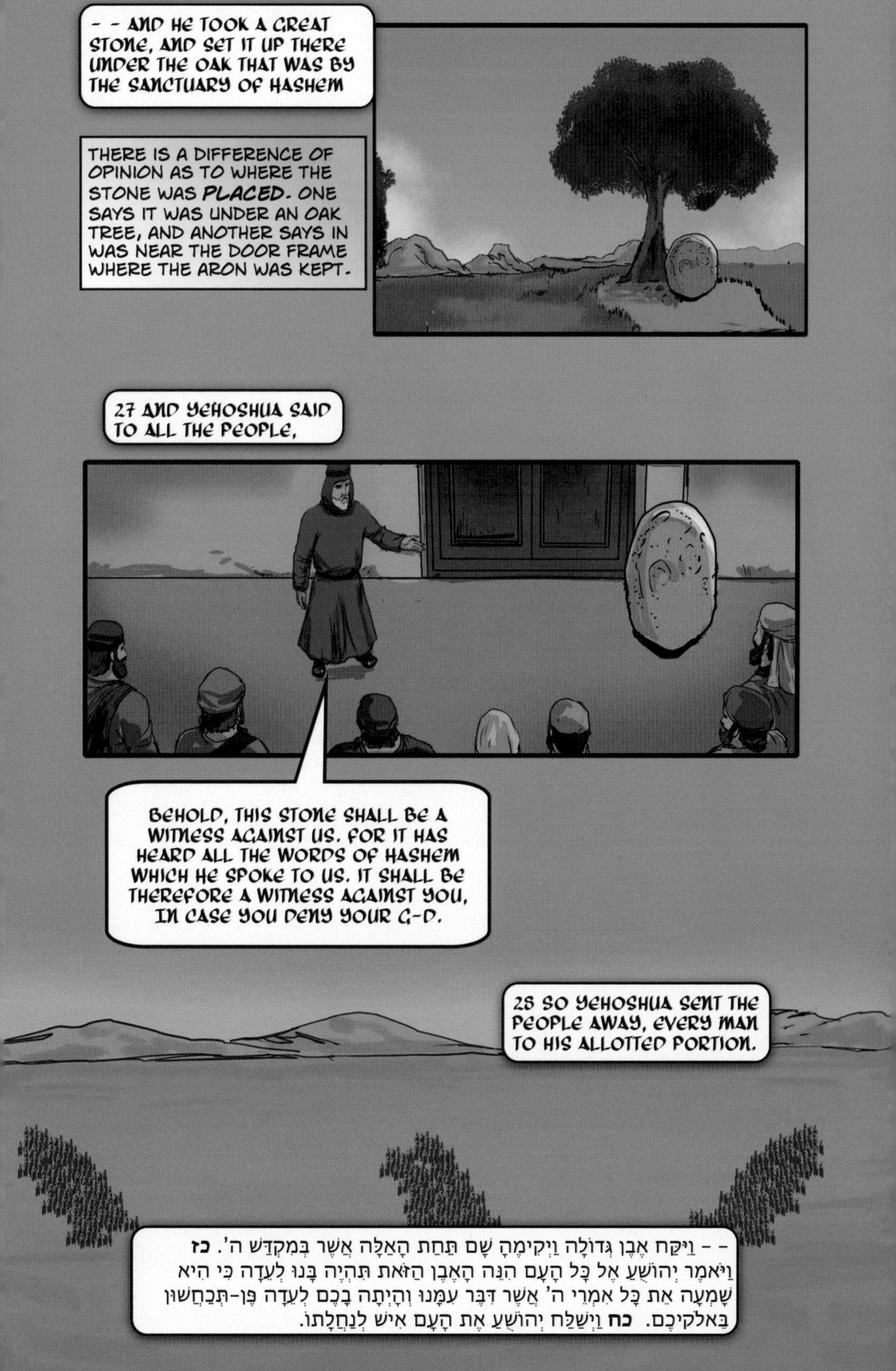
- - AND HE TOOK A GREAT STONE, AND SET IT UP THERE UNDER THE OAK THAT WAS BY THE SANCTUARY OF HASHEM
THERE IS A DIFFERENCE OF OPINION AS TO WHERE THE STONE WAS *PLACED*. ONE SAYS IT WAS UNDER AN OAK TREE, AND ANOTHER SAYS IN WAS NEAR THE DOOR FRAME WHERE THE ARON WAS KEPT.
27 AND YEHOSHUA SAID TO ALL THE PEOPLE,
BEHOLD, THIS STONE SHALL BE A WITNESS AGAINST US. FOR IT HAS HEARD ALL THE WORDS OF HASHEM WHICH HE SPOKE TO US. IT SHALL BE THEREFORE A WITNESS AGAINST YOU, IN CASE YOU DENY YOUR G-D.
28 SO YEHOSHUA SENT THE PEOPLE AWAY, EVERY MAN TO HIS ALLOTTED PORTION.
- - וַיִּקַּח אֶבֶן גְּדוֹלָה וַיְקִימֶהָ שָּׁם תַּחַת הָאַלָּה אֲשֶׁר בְּמִקְדַּשׁ ה'. **כז**
וַיֹּאמֶר יְהוֹשֻׁעַ אֶל כָּל הָעָם הִנֵּה הָאֶבֶן הַזֹּאת תִּהְיֶה בָּנוּ לְעֵדָה כִּי הִיא
שָׁמְעָה אֵת כָּל אִמְרֵי ה' אֲשֶׁר דִּבֶּר עִמָּנוּ וְהָיְתָה בָכֶם לְעֵדָה פֶּן-תְּכַחֲשׁוּן
בֵּאלֹקֵיכֶם. **כח** וַיְשַׁלַּח יְהוֹשֻׁעַ אֶת הָעָם אִישׁ לְנַחֲלָתוֹ.

29 AND IT CAME TO PASS AFTER THESE EVENTS, THAT YEHOSHUA THE SON OF NUN, THE SERVANT OF HASHEM, DIED AT THE AGE OF ONE HUNDRED AND TEN YEARS. 30 AND THEY BURIED HIM ON HIS OWN PROPERTY, AT TIMNATH-SERACH, IN THE HILL-COUNTRY OF EPHRAIM, NORTH OF MOUNT GAASH.
NOT VERY MANY PEOPLE SHOWED UP FOR YEHOSHUA'S EULOGY...
I KNOW, FOR ALL THAT HE DID FOR US. YOU WOULD THINK PEOPLE WOULD AT LEAST SHOW A LITTLE RESPECT...
SO DIFFERENT FROM MOSHE RABBEINU'S EULOGY.
THIS IS THE ONE WHO CAUSED THE SUN TO STAND STILL.
WOE TO THIS ONE WHO PERFORMED SUCH A GREAT FEAT AND DIED.
WHAT IS GOING ON HERE, THE MOUNTAIN IS FLARING UP?
BECAUSE YISRAEL DID NOT GIVE YEHOSHUA A PROPER DIGNIFIED BURIAL, THE MOUNTAIN BEGAN TO ERUPT.
כט וַיְהִי אַחֲרֵי הַדְּבָרִים הָאֵלֶּה וַיָּמָת יְהוֹשֻׁעַ בִּן נוּן עֶבֶד ה' בֶּן מֵאָה וָעֶשֶׂר שָׁנִים.
ל וַיִּקְבְּרוּ אֹתוֹ בִּגְבוּל נַחֲלָתוֹ בְּתִמְנַת סֶרַח אֲשֶׁר בְּהַר אֶפְרָיִם מִצְּפוֹן לְהַר גָּעַשׁ.

31 YISRAEL SERVED HASHEM DURING THE LIFETIME OF YEHOSHUA AND THE LIFETIME OF THE ELDERS WHO LIVED AFTER YEHOSHUA, WHO HAD EXPERIENCED ALL THAT HASHEM HAD DONE FOR YISRAEL.

32 AND THE BONES OF YOSEPH, WHICH THE CHILDREN OF YISRAEL BROUGHT UP OUT OF EGYPT, WERE BURIED AT SHECHEM IN THE PIECE OF GROUND WHICH YAAKOV HAD BOUGHT FOR A HUNDRED COINS FROM THE CHILDREN OF CHAMOR, SHECHEM'S FATHER, AND HAD BECOME AN INHERITANCE OF THE CHILDREN OF YOSEPH.

ELAZAR, THE SON OF AHARON, ***WROTE*** THESE LAST SENTENCES...

YOSEPH WAS BURIED IN EGYPT, IN THE BURIAL PLACE OF KINGS. MOSHE WENT THERE AND ***ANNOUNCED***, "YOSEPH, THE TIME HAS ARRIVED WHICH THE HOLY ONE, BLESSED BE HE, SWORE, 'I WILL DELIVER YOU'. AND THE OATH YOU PLACED ON YISRAEL TO BURY YOU IN THE LAND HAS COME. IF YOU ***SHOW*** YOURSELF, WELL AND GOOD. OTHERWISE, WE ARE FREE FROM YOUR OATH." AT THAT MOMENT, YOSEPH'S TOMB SHOOK AND MOSHE TOOK HIS BONES OUT OF EGYPT TO BE BURIED IN THE LAND OF YISRAEL.

RAV CHAMA SON OF RAV CHANINA SAID: FROM SHECHEM THEY (THE BROTHERS OF YOSEPH) ***STOLE*** HIM, AND TO SHECHEM WE WILL RESTORE WHAT WAS LOST.

33 AND ELAZAR, THE SON OF AHARON DIED; AND THEY BURIED HIM IN THE HILL OF HIS SON PINCHAS, WHICH WAS GIVEN TO HIM IN THE HILLS OF EPHRAIM.

PINCHAS THE SON OF ELAZAR WROTE THIS ***LAST*** SENTENCE...

לא וַיַּעֲבֹד יִשְׂרָאֵל אֶת ה' כֹּל יְמֵי יְהוֹשֻׁעַ וְכֹל יְמֵי הַזְּקֵנִים אֲשֶׁר הֶאֱרִיכוּ יָמִים אַחֲרֵי
יְהוֹשֻׁעַ וַאֲשֶׁר יָדְעוּ אֵת כָּל מַעֲשֵׂה ה' אֲשֶׁר עָשָׂה לְיִשְׂרָאֵל. **לב** וְאֶת עַצְמוֹת יוֹסֵף אֲשֶׁר
הֶעֱלוּ בְנֵי יִשְׂרָאֵל מִמִּצְרַיִם קָבְרוּ בִשְׁכֶם בְּחֶלְקַת הַשָּׂדֶה אֲשֶׁר קָנָה יַעֲקֹב מֵאֵת בְּנֵי חֲמוֹר
אֲבִי שְׁכֶם בְּמֵאָה קְשִׂיטָה וַיִּהְיוּ לִבְנֵי יוֹסֵף לְנַחֲלָה. **לג** וְאֶלְעָזָר בֶּן אַהֲרֹן מֵת וַיִּקְבְּרוּ אֹתוֹ
בְּגִבְעַת פִּינְחָס בְּנוֹ אֲשֶׁר נִתַּן לוֹ בְּהַר אֶפְרָיִם.

YEHOSHUA SOURCES

פרק א

(א) רד"ק, משלי, במדבר רבה כא:טו, ילקוט שמעוני כא:תקמט

(ב) רש"י, אמתחת בנימין, תמורה טז., מעם לועז, אברבנאל ילקוט שמעוני, ספורנו

(ג) רש"י, אברבנאל, ב"ר ו:ט

(ד) מצודת דוד, רש"י, ב"ר ו:ט

(ה) ספרי, אברבנאל, ארטסקרול, אלשיך

(ו) מלבי"ם

(ז) הגר"א, רמב"ם הלכות תלמוד תורה א:ח

(ח) דעת סופרים, רש"י, בית אלוקים ג:לז, מעם לועז, ע"ז יט:, מנחות צט:, ב"ר מט:ב, ש"ר מז:ה, רמב"ם הלכות תלמוד תורה א:ח

(ט) רש"י

(י) רש"י

(יא) רש"י, רד"ק, ילקוט שמעוני

(יב) מעם לועז

(יג) אברבנאל

(יד) ילקוט שמעוני

(טז) אברבנאל, מלבי"ם, אלשיך

(יח) סנהדרין מט., רלב"ג, תנחומא שמיני ב, רמב"ם הלכות מלכים ג:ח

פרק ב

(א) רד"ק, רלב"ג, אלשיך, תרגום יונתן, מעם לועז, בן פורת יוסף, רש"י, ברכות מג., אהבת יונתן, במ"ר טז:א, מלבי"ם רות רבה, ספרי, שיר השירים, מגילה יד:, מנחה קטנה

(ב) מלבי"ם, מעם לועז, לב אהרן

(ג) אהבת יונתן, אברבנאל, רד"ק, מדרש תנחומא

(ד) במדבר רבה טז, מצודת דוד

(ה) רש"י, מלבי"ם, מצודת דוד, בן פורת יוסף

(ו) גביע הכסף

(ז) אלשיך

(ח) אלשיך, כלי יקר

(י) ברכות נד:, חומת אנ"ך

(יא) אברבנאל, מלבי"ם, רש"י, זבחים קטז., סוטה לו. ילקוט שמעוני רמז י, יחזקאל א:א, תוספות לה, סוטה

(יב) מלבי"ם, רד"ק, הגר"א

(יג) מלבי"ם, אברבנאל

(יד) רד"ק, רלב"ג, אהבת יונתן, מצודת דוד

(טו) אברבנאל, רש"י, ילקוט שמעוני שכו, ירמיהו לח:ו פסיקתא רבתי

(טז) רש"י, ילקוט שמעוני

(יח) קהילת יעקב, תורת חכם פ'שלח לך, כלי יקר, מצודת דודת רלב"ג

(יט) רש"י

(כא) אברבנאל

(כב) אלשיך

(כג) אלשיך, רש"י, דעת סופרים, ר' יעקב פידאנקי

(כד) אלשיך

פרק ג

(א) ארטסקרול, חיד"א, מלבי"ם, רלב"ג, אלשיך

(ב) אלשיך, מלבי"ם

(ג) תענית ט., מדרש תנחומא בשלח ג, חיד"א(ד) רש"י, סוטה יג., רלב"ג, רד"ק, מדרש

(ה) רש"י, רד"ק, מטה בנימין

(ו) רש"י, סוטה לג:, מהרש"א

(ז) קהלת רבה א:יב, רד"ק, שמות יד:לא, אלשיך

(ח) רש"י, מלבי"ם

(ט) בראשית רבה, רש"י

(י) רש"י, אלשיך

(יא) פסיקתא דרב כהנא טו, מלבי"ם

(יב) רש"י, אלשיך

(יג) רש"י

(יד) אלשיך

(טו) רש"י

(טז) מדרש

(יז) רש"י, מעם לועז, כלי יקר

פרק ד

(א) רד"ק, רש"י

(ג) אלשיך

(ד) רד"ק

(ו) אלשיך, מלבי"ם

(ז) מעם לועז, מלבי"ם

(ח) מצודת דוד, מעם לועז, סוטה לג.

(ט) רד"ק, רש"י, מעם לועז, מלבי"ם

(י) רש"י, סוטה לד:, רד"ק, מצודת דוד, אברבנאל

(יא) רש"י, סוטה לה.

(יב) אלשיך

(יג) חיד"א, כלי יקר

(יד) מעם לועז

(טו) רד"ק, רש"י

(טז) ר' בחיי

(יז) רש"י, מלבי"ם

(יח) רד"ק, מעם לועז, מצודת דוד, ר' יעקב פידאנקי.

(יט) ילקוט שמעוני, מוסר הנביאים, רד"ק

(כ) מעם לועז, רלב"ג

(כא) אלשיך

(כב) מדרש

(כד) פורת יוסף , העמק הדבר, רש"י, סוטה לו.

פרק ה

(א) מלבי"ם, פורת יוסף, אברבנאל, ילקוט שמעוני

(ב) מעם לועז, חיד"א, אברבנאל, רד"ק, מצודת דוד, בראשית רבה יבמות עא: עב. תוספות

(ג) אברבנאל, יבמות כה:, רש"י, ילקוט שמעוני, במדבר כג:ט, מאירי יבמות עא:, במדבר כג:י, שלחן ערוך יורה דעה רסה:י,ראב"ד על ספרי דברים לג:ח,ט

(ד) רש"י

(ה) תנא דבי אליהו רבה

(ו) חיד"א, רש"י

(ח) קהילת יעקב

(ט) מצודת דוד, רש"י שמות י:י, אברבנאל, רלב"ג

(י) אלשיך

(יא) כלי יקר, ראש השנה יג., קידושין לח., מלבי"ם

YEHOSHUA SOURCES

(יב) רש"י, דעת סופרים, ילקוט שמעוני, מכילתא בא יח
(יג) רש"י, רד"ק, מעם לועז, מלבי"ם, לב אהרן
(יד) רד"ק, מגילה ג., רש"י, אברבנאל
(טו) אברבנאל, שמות רבה ב:ו

פרק ו

(א) אהבת יונתן, תרגום, הלכות תשובה ג:ד, מכתב מאליהו, מצודת דוד, חיד"א, מעם לועז
(ב) רד"ק
(ג) מכתב מ'אליהו
(ד) מלבי"ם, במדבר
(ה) רש"י, מלבי"ם, הרכב דבר, ברכות נד:, מצודת דוד
(ט) אברבנאל
(י) מלבי"ם, קהילת יעקב
(יא) מלבי"ם
(טו) מעם לועז, רש"י, בראשית רבה, רד"ק
(טז) מלבי"ם
(יז) ילקוט שמעוני טו:ו, רד"ק, אברבנאל, ויקרא כז:כח, דברים ז:כו, ישעיהו לד:ב, מלבי"ם
(יח) מלבי"ם, אברבנאל
(יט) רד"ק, מלבי"ם
(כ) אברבנאל, אלשיך, ועי' ברכות פרק הרואה, לב אהרן
(כא) בהעלותך י, ספרי במדבר י:ח
(כג) רד"ק, מדרש רות רבה פ"ב, כלי יקר, במדבר רבה פי"ד, ילקוט שמעוני, אלשיך, רד"ק, רש"י
(כה) פסיקתא דרב כהנא פי"ב, תוספות מגילה יד: רמב"ם הלכות איסורי ביאה יב:א, רד"ק
(כו) מורה נבוכים ג:נ, ערוך לנר, תוספתא סנהדרין יד, מעם לועז, אברבנאל
(כז) מוסר הנביאים ס, ספרי

פרק ז

(א) דעת סופרים, מעם לועז, כלי יקר
(ב) מעם לועז, מלבי"ם
(ג) מעם לועז
(ד) מעם לועז
(ה) בראשית רבה, סנהדרין מד:, רד"ק, מצודת דוד
(ו) אלשיך, מלבי"ם, דעת סופרים
(ז) אברבנאל, רש"י, מרגוליות הים
(ח) מצודת דוד, מעם לועז
(ט) תלמוד ירושלמי תענית ד:ו
(י) רש"י, רד"ק, מלבי"ם, סנהדרין סג., חיד"א, ספר המצות רצ,
(יא) מצודת דוד, אלשיך, סנהדרין מד., מלבי"ם, רד"ק
(יב) דעת סופרים, מלבי"ם
(יד) מצודת דוד, מעם לועז, רש"י, רד"ק
(טו) רש"י, רד"ק
(טז) פרקי דרבי אליעזר לח
(יז) רש"י
(יט) דעת סופרים, רש"י, מלבי"ם, ספר המצות רצ, סנהדרין מג.
(כ) מוסר הנביאים, רש"י, מעם לועז, סנהדרין מג:, רד"ק
(כא) סנהדרין מד:, רד"ק, מלבי"ם, רש"י, מדרש
(כב) רד"ק, רש"י
(כג) במדבר רבה כג:ו, מצודת דוד
(כד) פרקי דרבי אליעזר לב
(כה) סנהדרין מג:, רש"י, רמב"ם הלכות סנהדרין, עמק שאלה קמב
חתם סופר אורח חיים רח

פרק ח

(א) חיד"א, מצודת דוד, אילה שלוחה, לב אהרן
(ב) רש"י, מלבי"ם, אברבנאל, לב אהרן
(י) אברבנאל
(יב) כלי יקר
(יג) רלב"ג, רד"ק, מגילה ג.
(יד) מעם לועז, רש"י, רד"ק
(טז) מלבי"ם, רד"ק
(יז) מעם לועז
(יט) אברבנאל
(כ) מלבי"ם, רד"ק, רש"י
(כב) מלבי"ם
כו) אברבנאל
(כז) כלי יקר, מעם לועז
(כח) פורת יוסף, רד"ק, ילקוט שמעוני
(כט) רד"ק, אברבנאל, רלב"ג, סנהדרין מו.
(ל) רש"י, מלבי"ם, העמק הדבר, אברבנאל, ירושלמי סוטה
(לא) אבן עזרא, רמב"ם מורה נבוכים, רמב"ן, מצודת דוד, ר' סעדיה הגאון
(לב) סוטה לה:
(לג) רד"ק

פרק ט

(א) רמב"ם הלכות מלכים ו:א, ירושלמי שביעית ו:א, מצודת דוד, רלב"ג
(ג) אברבנאל, מצודת דוד, רד"ק, לב אהרן
(ד) רש"י, מדרש תנחומא, אברבנאל
(ה) מעם לועז, קהילת יעקב, ומאמר חז"ל במתא שמאי וכו' בשבת קמ"ה, כלי יקר
(ו) מצודת דוד, כלי יקר, אלשיך
(ז) רש"י, רד"ק
(ח) מצודת דוד, אברבנאל, מעם לועז
(ט) מצודת דוד, רד"ק, מלבי"ם
(י) רד"ק, ילקוט שמעוני
(יא) מצודת דוד
(יד) אלשיך, מלבי"ם, רלב"ג
(טו) אברבנאל, מעם לועז, תרומת הדשן
(טז) פורת יוסף, אברבנאל
(יז) גיטין מו.
(יח) אברבנאל
(יט) אברבנאל, מעם לועז, מפרשים
(כא) דעת סופרים, ר' אביגדור מילר, רד"ק
(כג) מעם לועז, כתובות כט., רבנו תם, יבמות עט.
(כד) מלבי"ם, אברבנאל
(כה) אברבנאל

YEHOSHUA SOURCES

(כז) ר' א רוסנברג

פרק י
(א) מלבי"ם
(ג) מעם לועז
(ד) מלבי"ם, דעת סופרים, אברבנאל
(ו) מעם לועז, רלב"ג
(ח) מלבי"ם
(ט) מעם לועז, קהילת יעקב
(י) ר, יוסף קרא, מעם לועז
(יא) מלבי"ם, מדרש תנחומא וארא, מעם לועז, ברכות פ' הרואה נד, ב ורש"י שם
(יב) אלשיך, בראשית רבה, מצודת דוד, מדרשים, אברבנאל, רש"י
(יג) רש"י, מלבי"ם
(יד) תענית יט:, מעם לועז, מלבי"ם
(כא) רש"י
(כד) מלבי"ם, רלב"ג
(כו) מעם לועז, רמב"ם הלכות סנהדרין והעונשין המסורין טו:ז
(כח) רד"ק
(ל) מעם לועז
(לא) פורת יוסף, כלי יקר
(לז) רד"ק
(לח) מלבי"ם
(לט) מלבי"ם
(מ) רש"י
(מב) דעת סופרים

פרק יא
(א) חיד"א, לב אהרן, מעם לועז, רלב"ג
(ג) דעת סופרים
(ד) מלבי"ם, אברבנאל
(ו) פורת יוסף, מעם לועז
(ח) רש"י
(ט) כלי יקר, רלב"ג, רד"ק, מלבי"ם איוב לו:יט, ילקוט שמעוני דברים כ
(י) כלי יקר
(יג) רש"י, מדרש רבא פא:
(יד) אברבנאל, חיד"א
(טו) מדרש שמואל יח:ד
(יז) רש"י

(יח) במדבר רבה כב:ו, מהרז"ו, רש"י
(כ) רד"ק
(כג) רד"ק

פרק יב
(א)רמב"ם ספר המצוות עשה קפז, זכריה יד:ט, רש"י
(ב) חולין ס:, בראשית לב:כה
(ז) מלבי"ם, דעת סופרים ב"ר נג:י
(ח) רד"ק, מעם לועז, בראשית כא:ח, בראשית כא:כג, ד רש"י, ספרי

פרק יג
(א)אבן עזרא, רלב"ג, רש"י
(ב) רמב"ן
(ג) רש"י, רמב"ן, חולין ס:
(ה) מלכים ה: לב
(ו) רש"י, אברבנאל
(ז) מצודת דוד
(ח) ספורנו
(י) רמב"ן
(יב) נידה סא.
(יג) מצודת דוד
(יד) רמב"ם הלכות שמיטה ויובל יג:י
(טו) מצודת דוד
(יח) דברי הימים א, ו:סג-סד
(יט) ירמיהו מח:יא
(כ) תוספות סוטה יד.
(כא) רמב"ן במדבר כב:ד
(כב) רד"ק, תרגום, מדרש
(כג) מצודת דוד, רד"ק
(כה) במדבר כא : לז
(כח) רש"י
(ל) דעת סופרים
(לא) רד"ק
(לג) מהר"ל

פרק יד
(א) רבינו בחי', מעם לועז יח:ב
(ב) בבא בתרא קכב.
(ד) רש"י, במדבר לה א, ח
(ה) מצודת דוד
(ז) סוטה לה.. רש"י במדבר יג:כב, רד"ק
(ט) סוטה לד:
(יא) מלבי"ם

(יב) מלבי"ם, לב אהרן
(יג) מצודת דוד, אלשיך, רד"ק
(יד) ערובין עג
(טו) בראשית רבה פ' נח, לב אהרן, ילקוט שמעוני, תורת כהנים

פרק טו
(א) מצודת דוד, הגר"א
(ג) הגר"א, זבחים נד:, ארטסקרול
(ד) תרגום יונתן במדבר לד:ה, תרגום ירושלמי, רד"ק, הגר"א, ר' סעדיה הגאון
(ה) מצודת דוד
(ו) רד"ק
(ז) הגר"א, קצבי ארץ, רש"י, מהר"ץ חיות נידה ח:, שמואל ב יז:יז
(ח) עירובין יט. מהרש"א, רד"ק, ישעיהו יז:ה, מצודת דוד
(ט) יומא לא. רש"י, ארטסקרול
(י) הגר"א, מלבי"ם
(יא) תבואת הארץ
(יב) מלבי"ם, מצודת דוד
(יג) דעת סופרים, מלבי"ם, מצודת דוד
(יד) מעם לועז
(טו) רש"י
(טז) ילקוט שמעוני, תוספות תענית ד.
(יז) רש"י, בראשית רבה נח: ב
(יח) רד"ק, מצודת דוד
(יט) באר משה
(כא) רש"י, גיטין ז., מעם לועז
(לב) רש"י
(לה) רש"י
(לו) רש"י
(לז) רד"ק מיכה א: יא
(מה) ארטסקרול
(סג) רד"ק, רש"י, ספרי

פרק טז
(א) מצודת דוד, ירושלמי ברכות ה:א, מלכים ב ב:כא
(ב) תרגום שופטים ד:ה
(ד) מעם לועז
(ה) באר משה
(ו) זבחים קיח:
(ט) רש"י

YEHOSHUA SOURCES

(י) דעת סופרים, מצודת דוד

פרק יז
(א) הגר"א, רש"י במדבר, רד"ק, דברים לג: יז
(ב) מצודת דוד
(ג) במדבר,כו:נב, במדבר,כז:ד רש"י, בבא בתרא קיט, דברים כה:ה -י
(ד) מעם לועז
(ה) רש"י
(ז) בראשית יב:ו ארטסקרול
(ח) רש"י
(יג) רמב"ם
(יד) רמב"ן במדבר כו:נד, רד"ק
(טו) רש"י
(יז) מצודת דוד
(יח) ר אברהם יוסף ראזענבערג

פרק יח
(א) חיד"א, רד"ק, רש"י, הגר"א
(ב) אברבנאל, רש"י, מעם לועז
(ג) מלבי"ם, מעם לועז
(ד) מעם לועז
(ה) רש"י
(ט) מעם לועז
(יג) רש"י
(יד) ארטסקרול
(יט) רש"י
(כ) רש"י
(כח) רד"ק, שמואל ב כא:יד

פרק יט
(א)רמב"ן בראשית מט:ז
(ט) רד"ק, שופטים א :ג,יז
(יא) מלבי"ם
(יג) תבואת הארץ
(טו) רד"ק
(יט) תבואת הארץ
(כב) ר"מ זיידל על סנהדרין צה. ורש"י איוב כח:ח, הגר"א
(לב) מלבי"ם, בראשית מט:כא, רש"י, דברים
(לג):בג ספרי
(לד) ארטסקרול, תבואת הארץ
(לז) משני למלך הלכות רוצח, פיסקי תשובה

(מב) ארטסקרול
(מה) סנהדרין לב:
(נ) רלב"ג, רש"י

פרק כ
(א) מכות י:, רמב"ם הלכות רוצח פרק ו, רש"י מכות יא.
(ב) דעת סופרים, כלי יקר
(ג) תוספות בבא קמא כו.. סנהדרין מה: רש"י
(ד) מעם לועז, מצודת דוד, רד"ק, מכות י.-יא.
(ה) רש"י, רמב"ם, מעם לועז
(ו) מעם לועז, מכות יא.. תרגום יונתן במדבר רבא לה:כה
(ח) רש"י, מכות י.. בראשית לז:כא

פרק כא
(א) רמב"ם הלכות שמיטה ויובל יג:יב-יג, ילקוט שמעוני, נבייאים טובים, בראשית מד, חיד"א, מעם לועז
(ב) אברבנאל מכות יב:, תוספתא ביכורים יא:ד, ראשש ברכות כ.
(ג) סוטה כז: במדבר לה:ד, חיד"א, מלבי"ם, משך חכמה
(ד) מלבי"ם
(יא) רד"ק
(יב) רש"י במדבר יג: כב
(יח) רד"ק
(מ) מלבי"ם
(מא) מלבי"ם
(מב) מלבי"ם
(מג) מלבי"ם, רלב"ג

פרק כב
(א) אלשיך, לב אהרן
(ב) אלשיך
(ג) אלשיך
(ד) מעם לועז
(ה) אברבנאל
(ו) בראשית רבה צח:טו
(ז) ב"ר לה:ג
(ח) ב"ר צח:טו
(ט) בראשית רבה צח, ויפ"ת ונזה"ק

(י) מעם לועז
(יא) מלבי"ם
(יב) אלשיך, כלי יקר
(יג) מצודת דוד
(יד) רד"ק, ילקוט שמעון, אלשיך
(טו) כלי יקר
(טז) מלבי"ם
(יז) מלבי"ם, מדרש, תוספות סוטה יד. מהרש"א
(כ) מהרי קרא
(כב) מדרש שוחר טוב
(כד) רש"י
(כח) רש"י
(כט) מעם לועז
(ל) מעם לועז, כלי יקר
(לא) אלשיך

פרק כג
(ב) במדבר רבה כב:ו
(ג) כלי יקר
(ח) אברבנאל
(יא) אברבנאל

פרק כד
(ב) זהר ג:רצח
(ז) מעם לועז
(י) במדבר בלק כג:י, יב
(יב) אברבנאל
(יג) פורת יוסף, מעם לועז
(יד) אלשיך, תורת משה
(טו) אברבנאל
(יח) מצודת דוד, אלשיך
(יט) אלשיך
(כ) מצודת דוד
(כא) אלשיך
(כב) רש"י, יחזקאל כ:לב
(כה) שיטה מקובצת, בבא קמא פא, רמב"ם הלכות נזיקי ממון
(כו) מכות יא.. מצודת דוד
(כז) תרגום
(כט) במדבר רבה כב:ו
(ל) רד"ק, תוספות סוטה לו:, אור הישר זבחים קטז:
(לא) רש"י
(לב) סוטה יג:, רד"ק
(לג) בבא בתרא